SIX WAR YEARS
1939-1945

By the Same Author

TEN LOST YEARS: 1929-1939

SIX WAR YEARS 1939-1945

Memories of Canadians at Home and Abroad

BARRY BROADFOOT

1974
Doubleday Canada Limited, Toronto, Ontario
Doubleday & Company, Inc., Garden City, New York

I.S.B.N. Number: 0-385-05814-4
Library of Congress Catalog Card Number: 74-3692

Printed in Canada
First Edition

Design: Brant Cowie
Printed and Bound in Canada by The Bryant Press Limited

Pc

*Unless otherwise specified, all photographs
in this book are courtesy of the Public
Archives of Canada.*

Contents

Preface

This is a book about war—about Canadians in the last war. But Six War Years: 1939-45 *falls into the category of no war book that I know. It has not been written by a general, an admiral, an air commodore, any military person. It has not been written by a politician, a statesman, a financier, a war correspondent, a professor or an historian.*

This book has been written by the Canadian people, men and women, who served on the home front and overseas. It has been written by people who spent the war in their own distinct yet typical **roles***: the twelve-year-old girl knitting socks for the Red Cross, her mother assembling bomber wings in the aircraft factory, the thousands of faceless men and women instructing in the bases and camps across Canada through dreary years, the young nurses near the battle lines in Normandy, and the boys and men in the terrible winter battles before Ortona, or fighting waist-deep in water in the hell of the approaches to Antwerp, or tossing about on the North Atlantic during winter gales, or flying Lancasters to targets deep in Germany night after night.*

This book is about and by the men who helped build the Alaska Highway during a vicious winter, and those who manned the explosive tankers on the North Atlantic convoys, and the soldiers always near death in Japanese prison camps.

This book is about and by the housewife, her husband at war, who tended a Victory Garden through summer's heat, and the youngster who took his girl to the school stamp hop—admission two War Saving stamps—and the woman next door whose only son was wounded at Dieppe; and those who waited, in constant fear, for a telegraph boy to bring the most terrible message of all—news of the death of a loved one in battle.

I know that war is grim; I know. But, this is not an unrelievedly grim book; in fact, in many ways it is an exuberant one. The Second World War was the most exciting time of their lives for many Canadians looking back from the '70s. It was certainly not something which many people would want to live through again; but I recall three or four dozen people I interviewed who said, "I wouldn't have missed it for the world."

When I finished Ten Lost Years, 1929-1939, Memories of Canadians Who Survived the Depression, *the pre-publication enthusiasm at every level was so high that it was inevitable there had to be a sequel. And that sequel had to be the Second World War, for so often the Depression stories I got from the people I interviewed all over Canada spilled over into the war years. And, better still from my point of view, the war was even fresher in people's minds than the Depression.*

So, from April, 1973 (long before Ten Lost Years *was published and became a bestseller), for nearly 12 months I used my tape recorder and reporter's notebook as I moved across Canada asking strangers and friends and friends' friends the one main question: "What did you do in the war?" As simple as that.*

The playback this question sparked was truly astonishing; a total outpouring of experience, as you will see. And often I was asked the question: "Why hasn't somebody before this asked me what I did? Why hasn't a book like this been written before?"

I don't know the answer to that, other than to say that the times now seem ready for such books, books of oral history.

In oral history, one never knows when the book is finished. For Ten Lost Years *I recorded about 270,000 words and about 115,000 were used. A great deal of wonderful material could not be used; there simply was no space. In this book, with such a wealth of material—more than a million Canadians in uniform and everyone in Canada involved in some way in the home war effort—I recorded about 340,000 words. Almost all of that was first-class material but, as before, it had to be edited, chopped down, discarded, to about 120,000 words. But that's oral history for you.*

There are things missing in this book. The furor over the firing of General Andrew McNaughton, for example, is barely mentioned, because it apparently had no bearing on people's lives during those days. The grand sweep of campaigns, through Europe and elsewhere, mattered little to the soldier in the slit trench and the woman on the home front. In this book there is almost nothing about great events, the highest level conferences at Yalta and Tehran and Quebec, and the Russian demands for a Second Front in France. To learn about them you must seek out books by the top military men, the politicians, the historians. I make no apologies for this; they write their books and I write mine.

What I am saying is that Canadians did not seem to care about the major events. Although the newspapers and radio were filled with such news, there was always the feeling that the news was so censored, just so much propaganda, that perhaps it was not worth hearing about or reading about.

But the soldier in Italy wondered when spring would come. The housewife hoped packages of Jello would show up on the shelf on her shopping day. The farmer hoped his request for a

German prisoner of war to help with the crop would be okayed. Will we get a Victory Mail letter from Billy when his corvette docks at 'Derry? Will there be gas this weekend for the trip to open up the cottage at the lake? How is Mrs. Jones taking the loss of her husband in the North Atlantic? We must get another next-of-kin parcel off to Joe in Stalag Six prisoner-of-war camp. All these things, and a thousand more.

I am not saying Canadians at home and abroad did not care about the war. Quite the opposite is true. But as the war years moved on, three, four and then five, all these things were considered normal, and everyone adapted to them and carried on as normal a life as possible. Wars are for generals to fight, and we keep things going in the few yards around us that we call our own.

Six years is a long time, and at war's end there was very little in Canada that was as it had been in '39. For one thing, the war lifted Canada right out of the Depression. It produced an enlistment record that was extraordinary—about one person in every eleven in uniform. It produced a record of industrial achievement—of ships and guns and tanks and planes and another 10,000 items of material produced—which was equal, on a percentage basis, to what the United States or Britain or Russia could do.

Canada was the only Allied nation, of that great array, which did not accept American Lend-Lease or any aid after the war; indeed, she gave Britain more than four billion dollars of aid free during the war. Canada led the way in setting up the Commonwealth of Nations as an equal partnership with Britain, an achievement in itself that few realize.

In short, Canada's war effort was massive, heroic and done of her own free will.

But I am not talking about figures, the bottom line of a bill of goods. What I am concerned with at all times is people, and Canadians as citizens of one of the great nations on earth. That is why I write of the individual accomplishments, the disappointments, the triumphs of the spirit and the flesh of these people. As usual, I have respected their anonymity for a variety of reasons; because I promised, because I didn't know my companion's name, but above all because these stories, amazing though they may be, happened to the ordinary, anonymous people you pass on the street every day.

And, as in the writing of Ten Lost Years, there was rarely a day in which I did not experience some new experience, some delight, some rare surprise in meeting you, in your homes, your pubs, your trains, your cafés, offices, streets.

I will always be amazed at your enthusiasms, your resourcefulness, your strengths, your good humour, your pioneering spirit, your natural neighbourliness, your determination to try to do what is right, your ready laughter and your quickness in welcoming a stranger into your own worlds.

All of you, the few I talked to and the millions I did not see, I salute you, and I thank you. This is not my book; it is your book, and I am passing it on.

Barry Broadfoot
Vancouver
June, 1974

A Summary of Canada's War

Sometimes statistics are meaningless, but when you consider Canada's wartime contribution in terms of statistics, then they become powerful. Through them one can realize the massive effort put forward by Canadians during the Second World War.

First, the military effort, because that is really what war is all about. In 1939, Canada's three services had a grand total of about 10,200 men; each service did have a back-up force called a militia or reserve, but these "Saturday night soldiers" were trained only in the rudiments, badly equipped and all but totally neglected. By way of armament, to fight a war in 1939 the Canadian Army could have mustered 29 Bren machine guns, 23 anti-tank rifles and five three-inch mortars. This is not joke time; those are facts.

Then the years rolled by. By May, 1945, the army alone had more than 700,000 men, had fought hard and well in northwest Europe and in Italy, and had been described by other commanders as one of the best armies in the world. It had suffered 23,000 dead.

The Royal Canadian Navy, from a dead slow speed in 1939 with only six old destroyers, had grown into a force with more than 480 vessels, a force at sea and ashore of more than 100,000 men and women who made up the third largest navy in the world. It was a navy of smaller ships—corvettes, frigates, destroyers. Its role was to patrol the North Atlantic convoy channels and fight it out to the very end with the German submarine wolf packs. During the long years when Britain stood alone in Europe, the R.C.N. escorted more than 180,000,000 tons of the supplies that kept the island in the fight. Read that figure over again— 180,000,000 tons.

The Royal Canadian Air Force in 1939 virtually existed in name only, with a holding company of about 4,000 men. By war's end, it had risen to more than 250,000 men, and about 100,000 of them had manned the stations and bases across Canada which turned out 130,000 trained air crew for the Commonwealth Air Training Plan. Four out of every five men flying in Commonwealth squadrons anywhere in the world were trained in Canada, usually by Canadians. There were 48 Canadian bomber and fighter squadrons in England, and as many on Coastal Command in Canada backing up the navy in submarine detection. Twenty-five percent of flight personnel in the R.A.F. was Canadian, an astonishing percentage.

War is waged with money. In 1939 the Canadian government spent a mere $553,063,000 to keep the country going. By 1945, the defence bill alone was more than $19,000,000,000. Not bad for a country with only 11,300,000 people.

In 1943 an English writer made a tour of North America and was astounded to learn that in 1942 Canada had sent to Britain 90,000,000 bushels of wheat, 4,500,000 barrels of flour, 5,249,000 hundredweight of bacon and ham, 7,661,000 pounds of dried eggs, 4,375,000 pounds of eggs in the shell, plus enormous quantities of cheese, canned meats, canned herrings, canned salmon, fish oil and other goods too large and numerous to mention. That was just for the year 1942—with three more years to go. That was the contribution of the overworked farmer, dairyman and fisherman.

On the production front, the totals are staggering. In 1939 Canada had no war industry. By war's end, 1,100,000 men and women—about one-tenth of the total population—working in war plants had turned out 900,000 rifles, 794,000 motor vehicles for military purposes, 244,000 light machine guns, 16,000 aircraft of nearly 80 different types and 486 navy vessels plus 391 cargo vessels and 3,500 craft for various support purposes, all necessary to the war effort. In 1939 probably only a few Canadians had ever seen a tank; but by 1945 the nation had produced 6,500 which, it could be pointed out, equalled 13 months of tank production from Germany, one of the mightiest industrial war machines the world has ever seen. And of course, Canada also produced what the auction ads describe as "other articles far too numerous to mention." Thousands of articles, everything needed to wage modern war.

In addition, the products of the mines kept the Allied war effort going—asbestos, tungsten for armour plate, radium, aluminum for aircraft, coal, manganese, paper (which is as necessary a war material as the great quantities of top-grade steel we produced), plus hundreds of thousands of tons of chemicals and explosives.

These are the hard facts about Canada's war effort. I hope this book will tell you, in the words of Canadians themselves, how this was done, how they worked and how they felt about it.

SIX WAR YEARS
1939-1945

The Best of Times, The Worst of Times

*Getting to Jerusalem ... Pork Chops—a Good Day ...
Fourteen and a Half ... I Was a Zombie ... The Deserter
... The Guy with the Rifle ... A Place to Live ... I Met
Churchill Once ... The Earth Moved ... Red Crosses ...
Dates Whenever They Wanted ... Escape to Belsen ... It
Only Took a Minute ... A Good War ... The Christmas
Tree ... V-E Day ... Daddy, What Did You Do in the
War?*

---

*As you will see, the war meant many different things to many
different people. I believe that their own words express that far
more clearly than I can.*

•◆• *Getting to Jerusalem*

I didn't want to go to war. Why should I join up? Get myself
killed off by some German guy who didn't want to be in the war
either and didn't know me, like I didn't know him, or vice-versa.
You get what I mean.

Except for one thing. I'm Jewish, and while my old man
doesn't want me to go, to join up—like why don't I go to the
University of Toronto, be a doctor, a lawyer, something, but keep
out of the whole business—my mother, she's a battleship that
woman, she wouldn't hear of it. Isser's gonna go when his time
comes, and when he gets to Jerusalem he's going to the Western
Wall and he's going to take out his Psalm Book and he's going to
read the 83rd Psalm.

Mom sort of had the war all twisted up in her mind. She'd
read the headlines about the British Eighth Army fighting near
Cairo and she'd look at a map and holy smokes! That's only two
inches from Jerusalem. Two inches on the map, like maybe 250
miles. One son of hers is gonna pray at the Wall, you bet your life.
So while the old man is against it, there's Mom practically pushing
me out the door on my eighteenth birthday down to the recruiting
station. "Join the army, my boy," she says, "and you'll get there
faster. Look where they were on the front page of the *Star* last
night, not that far from Jerusalem." It doesn't fit her thinking that
the whole idea of the Eighth Army is to get far *away* from Cairo,

over to the west. As far away from Jerusalem as it can. She was one woman with tunnel vision.

I join up. So? A year in Canada, four months in England, then France, Germany and home again. About two and a half years. Home, and my folks meet me at Union Station, brothers, sisters, brothers-in-law and their kids and cousins. A real big Jewish reunion right in the centre of the station. God, but when I think of it!

Mom gets to me first and I get hugs and kisses and everybody is around and finally she says, "Isser, did you use the book?" I ask what book. "The Book of Psalms I gave you on your last leave." Then it hits me. The Western Wall, Jerusalem, the 122nd Psalm, the 83rd Psalm, standing up there with all those old men crying and weeping, the kind of a Jew I just don't like.

I tell her, "Mom, I didn't get to Jerusalem. I didn't get anywhere near it. Our army wasn't going that way. We turned right instead of turning left." Now that was the wrong thing to say, making fun of something like that.

She stops me cold with that look in her eyes, and she's a little woman but solid steel and she says one word. She says, "Schlepper!" Just schlepper. That's what I am. A schlepper.

For Mom I don't fight the war for democracy and Canada. I fight it to go to Jerusalem so she can tell the neighbourhood women, Hadassah, Mrs. Moser down the street and all the rest about her son Isser.

The crazy thing is that later when she'd calmed down I told her I was sorry that my war career hadn't worked out the way she wanted it and she came up with a beautiful line. She said, "Isser, you just didn't try hard enough."

•◄►• *Pork Chops—a Good Day*

On the base I was at, near Canterbury, there wasn't the high rate of A.W.O.L. you got in the army because our crew was mixed with Limeys and we were all fitters and we just had to keep those crates in the air so we worked like hell. I mean really worked. You knew when your leaves were, to the minute; weeks ahead you knew when you'd walk past the guardhouse, down the road to the station and catch the train for London, so there was no excitement there. Letters, the same. Your mother would write once a week. Your girl, three times a week. Your wife, twice a week. That kind of stuff.

No, the big thing was food. This will kill you, but it was true. Food, and even the lousy food we got. It was like this. If you had pork chops for supper on, say, a Wednesday, then that was a good day. If you got bully beef and dehydrated potatoes, then that was a bad day. If on Sunday you got that pressed turkey, that was sort of a so-so day, but if you got real turkey, like once every six months, that was a good day.

We were like a bunch of dumb kids. Food we thought was good, like pork chops, that made the whole 24 hours seem good, no matter if it was blasting down rain outside. But that's the way it was. You were so goddamned cotton-picking glad for small mercies.

•◄►• *Fourteen and a Half*

When I join up I'm fourteen and a half years and when I discharge I am one month under eighteen.

So in France I was a despatch rider going around on my motorcycle and this day I had just picked up a despatch and I was going back and this German gun, an .88, the crew had sneaked it in behind us during the night or maybe she's been hidden there, see, and just as I come along they fire and kill one of our tanks and I get this steel in my chest. Torn all to pieces.

I'm not in one piece when they carried me in and I've lost all this skin—my legs, my chest, my fork—and as I go in they look at me and they're carrying some guy out and my doctor says to another, "Is that one dead?" and he says yes, so he tells them to bring the dead guy back, see. Then they take the skin off of him and slap it on me or how they do it, and with saws and knives and all that wire they fix me up and I spend nine months in hospital and now I'm pretty good. Except in the cold. When it's cold I feel it, and by Jesus I really do. I have to have special underwear. There are 44 inches of silver wire in me, holding my chest together. All inside. The only reason I'm alive today is because of those doctors and because I was seventeen and, by Jesus, I was tough.

•◄►• *I Was a Zombie*

Sure, I was a Zombie. If anybody asks me I'll tell them. I'm not ashamed. If Mackenzie King in all his wisdom felt it was politically expedient to have one law for the French Canadians and another law for the rest of Canada, then that was his problem. I had suffered a double hernia, so of course I could not be sent overseas and I should not have even been in the service. But I was posted as a clerk to Dundurn and, as punishment for standing up for my principles, and every Canadian's principles, I was not discharged until July of 1946.

You'll never know the harassment we underwent. If my name had been LaPointe or Desroches or anything of French extraction, I would have been packed off to some Zombie regiment and made to suffer out the war in the bush. But as my name is old and honourable and very Anglo-Saxon, Carpenter, I was a marked man.

Would you believe I was forced to do basic training four times, and advanced training four times? That I was put in platoons, twenty-five men active service and myself the only Zombie, and they were told, and the n.c.o.'s were told, and the platoon commander was told, that I was fair game?

Shit and slops for four years, and every time I got slapped in the face with a wet fish it strengthened my resolve. Keep it up, chaps, I'd say to myself, I'm ten times the man you are, and if I stayed with a bunch long enough they'd come to respect me. Trouble was, I kept getting moved around like spit on a hot griddle. But I did get to know some fellows quite well and we still write to each other, and you'll admit that's unusual, and when I go to Toronto there's two I meet for a bit of a beer-up.

King had to play politics, with Canada, with people's lives and Canada's honour, and for that I can never forgive him.

•◄►• *The Deserter*

There must have been hundreds of guys like me. Maybe thousands. Ever seen any figures on how many deserters there were in Canada?

I was just eighteen and when I finished training at Shilo [in Manitoba] they called out some names and I was on it, and they told us to get our kits and a sergeant marched us to the main drill hall. I found out from a corporal I knew that we were going to Suffield. Suffield Camp or Camp Suffield was out on the bald bloody prairie near Medicine Hat, and it was where they tested gases, poisonous gases, chemicals, special weapons and all that sort of crap. Blister gas. Get it on you and goodbye skin. We were going to be guinea pigs. They had a lot of German prisoners there and Italians and they used them as camp workers, but good

Canadian soldiers, *we* were going to be the guinea pigs. That's what the corporal said. That's what really tore my ass. That most of all.

After Shilo the next stop on the railroad is Brandon and it's a small city overrun with soldiers and air force, always fighting, raising hell, and when we get there I just hop off the train. It was just like getting off a streetcar at my own stop.

I left my kit and rifle behind a big pile of ties, railroad ties, and I go over the fence and soon I'm downtown and the train pulls out. Next morning I go back and I break down my rifle and stuff it into my kit bag and get out on the highway. There's darn little traffic going south, but an oil tanker picks me up and takes me down the road. After a while he starts to get snoopy. Who was I and where was I going, yakkety-yakkety-yak-yak, so we come to a crossroads and I say this is my place and I walk up and go into the first farm.

I ask for a job and I get it damn quick. That farmer, he doesn't care if I'm Field Marshal Montgomery. He's offering 75 dollars a month and stooking is coming up and the ante then is 100 dollars and this is 1944, June of 1944. About two mornings later I'm sitting in the overalls he gives me and we're listening to the news about the invasion of France, D-day, and I'm just as glad that I'm sitting in his kitchen on a rainy morning and not mucking around on those beaches.

I stayed with him until six months after the war and he never asked any questions and I never gave him no answers and we got along fine and nobody in the district blabbed.

If the Canadian Army wasn't going to treat me like a human being, then to hell with them. To bloody hell with them.

•◀▶• *The Guy with the Rifle*

I don't care how you say it in this book of yours, but remember this. You could have tanks with armour a yard thick and a gun that could shoot a mile and a big bloody flame-thrower to boot and Kittyhawks and Typhoons and Thunderbolts and 1,000-mile-an-hour Spits and bombers dropping factory loads of that god-damned napalm and the artillery, back there in the hills, throwing shells into the Jerry crap cans, and you could have all this in spades—but remember this. It was still always the guy in the infantry, the rifle company, the guy with the rifle, who got the job done. Give him a Bren and he might get it done faster, but it was always the guys like me on the ground, moving up to the Start Line for an attack, it was that guy, me, who finally won the battle. Me.

•◄►• *A Place to Live*

You tried every way you could to get a place to live. Naturally you wanted your wife with you, and if you had kids, what's the point of them living in rotten digs in Winnipeg and you living in rotten digs in Edmonton? Why not all be rotten together?

I was posted to Edmonton. Air force. This is the time of the start of the Alaska Highway and Yanks, for Christ sakes, Yanks everywhere. Mary, my wife, and young Tommy, the first, come out and we live in a hotel and on an air force sergeant's pay. Try it sometime. But we're looking for a house, see. We try everything. Little limericks in the classified ads, real clever stuff. Funny, but not a nibble. I make friends in the Queens beer parlor with a guy in the circulation room at the *Bulletin* so I can get the paper first, and Mary and I rush out there and there's three in line already. This is the way it is. One month goes by. Two months. Another. Hell, it looks like a divorce could be coming up. We love each other but three in a hotel room about 10 by 12. Try it, my friend, just try it.

So we're trying this tip again from my pal in the paper's circulation and we can't afford cabs, so we take the rock-'n-roll trolley out there and, well, the same old story. Third in line. We're coming home, about five o'clock, and I'm desperate. She's desperate. We're both desperate, and I say, "Mary, old girl, when this car stops next, somebody's going to get on and walk up to me and say would we like a suite, big, nice and warm, good for kids, good for parties." I went on like that. Just as a joke.

And so, the next stop—*screech, clunk, clank*—and somebody walks down the aisle. He is a guy I worked with right here in Toronto. A nice guy. He's in the army and he's got this big house in the west end of town and the guy who's in the upstairs suite, he's suddenly posted that day to hell-and-gone, and his wife is going back east and there's this suite. "Harry," he says, "it's yours if you want it."

I think my wife started to cry. I'm not sure, but I know I was damned close to tears.

••◆►• *I Met Churchill Once*

He came down in a big limousine to inspect some of our units, and he got out, the cigar coming first, and then this big baby face and one of those ridiculous uniforms, or clown outfits he wore. This one was a pale yellow cover-all sort of thing.

The Jerries were giving Dover a bit of a pasting and while we were around a couple of shells fell on the town and Winnie would clench that damned cigar in his teeth and shake his fist across the Channel and the photographers would be hopping around taking pictures.

Later in the mess, I got the impression then and there that he was an insatiable publicity seeker, the posing, the cigar, the V-for-Victory sign which came later, I believe, and those outlandish costumes. But we had a short talk and he seemed to know more than the English brass about what Canada was doing in the show. He should have, but what is important, he did know.

•◄◆►• *The Earth Moved*

Ha ha. I remember once when Jerry was blitzing London and I'd picked up this tart on Bayswater Road and we went to Hyde Park. As I recall we had to climb over the fence but anyway, it was a warm spring night and we got down to business and just when I started there was this tremendous bang. Bang, bang.

As you'll remember they had aircraft batteries in the place, and somehow we'd got just about as close to a battery as we could without trying, and then Jerry came over and the batteries opened up and the sky lit up and the ground shook and my God, the hair on the back of my neck stiffened and every time the guns fired the ground heaved. This little tart I was with, she pulled my ear down and said, "Take it easy, luv. Just relax. They're doing the work for us." But I got up and said to hell with it and pulled on my pants and the ack-ack gunners are laughing their heads off at us, right there in front of them, about 25 yards away.

•◄◆►• *Red Crosses*

I was with the South Alberta Regiment in northern France and I took a patrol down a side road in behind a village, and in a farmer's field we came to a German field hospital.

It wasn't a real setup, just canvas shelters and tents where the wounded could lie, maybe until ambulances could come for them. There was no enemy around except two doctors who said they'd decided to stay with the wounded, and all the rest, the orderlies and the truck drivers, they'd taken off. There were a lot of wounded, and a pile of dead, in a long row, out behind.

There had been a lot of air support from the Americans the last two days and the doctors had put out red crosses. Like "Hospital, do not shoot." The sad thing was, the red cross banners were sheets, pegged out on the ground, on the trampled-down wheat, and the red cross was smeared on each sheet in blood. Human blood.

•◄►• *Dates Whenever They Wanted*

It was supposed to be a real class system. You know, the nicest girls went in the air force and the mediocre ones went in the WRENS and the scruff went in the army, that type of thing. That's the way people at home thought of it.

That's not the way it was at all, though. I've seen some pretty awful air force ones, and those navy girls, they were no darlings either. Some of these could drink like you wouldn't believe. This business of air force, navy and then army was so much hogwash and I know. I saw them all.

Girls around a bunch of men, hundreds of men, and dates whenever they wanted, picking and choosing, all the booze—is it any wonder that some of them got pretty tough? Spreading it around, they used to call it, some of them. Hitting the mattress on every date.

And yet some were still incredibly naïve. Two or three girls in our quarters got pregnant, and one girl said she thought it must have been from some chap, apparently a real rotter, who had screwed her. I was making notes, of course, because I had a report to make, and when she said it was three years ago I nearly dropped my pen. Some didn't even know the score, and that was even after the lectures they got.

•◄►• *Escape to Belsen*

I escaped once. Not really an escape, but I broke away from the march at the end of the war. The Germans were marching us west towards the Americans and British, hoping, I guess, to try and negotiate a better settlement or peace by turning over thousands of prisoners. A way of showing good faith, I suppose, if you could follow some kind of Prussian reasoning. The march, by the way, started in Poland and our area was next and we kept picking up prisoners from other camps. Thousands, thousands.

I organized about 30 others to take off. Stupid, I guess, but we did it. Stupid because we were going home anyway, and we weren't heavily guarded and less guarded as we got closer to the Allied front, but we took off and headed north, up to Stettin, blundering around, not knowing where we were going, and as the senior officer I gave orders, and we were wandering into towns and villages, being fed by the Germans.

And then we blundered into Belsen. You know Belsen, the concentration camp. Gas ovens, tens of thousands of Jews killed. I remember being in this farmhouse near Belsen this night and I felt sick to my stomach although I didn't have that much on it, but finally I couldn't stand it any longer and I went outside and vomited. Threw up everywhere, and suddenly it came to me. There was a west wind blowing and it was blowing the stench of dead, of death, from the Belsen concentration camp, and this stink of death, which I well knew, filled the air. It was everywhere.

You must realize, of course, that I did not know what was happening to the Jews. I had been locked up for years. I did not know there *was* a Belsen. It was only later, after the war, when the news began to unfold, about the murder of millions of Jews, that I was able to connect that smell that night and my vomiting, to connect that with the town I had led my gang to, Belsen. The great death camp.

•←→• *It Only Took a Minute*

I don't think we were any better than the Germans, I don't think that for one minute. We did a lot of things too. I've seen them. You couldn't be up to your arse in the thing and not know that what they were doing, we were doing too.

There's one man in this town—and I could point him out to you—who's killed lots of Germans. And he's one of the nicest guys I've ever met. Officer in the Legion. Helps with the kids' soccer league. Good, decent businessman. But I was in the same outfit with him. I know.

This was in Holland. There was a lot of snow on the ground. We were on patrol and we ambushed this bunch of Jerries. Eight of them. Two were Panzer officers, because they wore those black uniforms the captains of German tanks wore. The other guys with them were their crew. We saw them coming around the edge of this little forest, and they just walked in and that was it.

One officer was a young guy and his English was good and he said they had been trying to get back to their lines. I guess they didn't like the snow any more than we did, or the cold. He made a couple of little jokes, one about if they got the firewood then we could light the fire and we'd all stay warm. Another little joke he made was we could roast a pig, and we sort of laughed too. He said they'd passed a Dutch farmyard back a bit and there might be a pig and schnapps. The war was over for him, and I guess he was glad.

So we're standing there and I'm thinking that we'll have to take these prisoners back, so that would be the end of the patrol. And then this lieutenant, he just turned to the guy with the Bren and he said, "Shoot them."

Just like that. Shoot them down. I knew something had been bothering him for a few days and maybe this was when it all came out. But he just said, "Shoot them.'

The officer with the blond hair, the one who was making the jokes, he sort of made a little run forward and put his arms across his chest and he said something and the guy with the Bren just cut loose. He just opened up. He just cut them down every which way, about chest level because he's shooting from the hip. There were two, I think, still flopping like gaffed salmon, and this guy we called Whitey from Cape Breton—we called him Whitey because he was always boasting how good a coalminer he was—he shot those two with a pistol the lieutenant let him carry. That was it.

It probably went into our history, I guess, as a German patrol wiped out. None of us really thought too much about it. They might have done the same to us. But I'll tell you this, a year before, if I'd been there, I'd have been puking up my guts. It only took a minute. Maybe less than that.

One of our guys who understood German said what the lieutenant said just before he was shot down was "Mother."

•◄►• *A Good War*

It browns me off that our kids don't know what went on, and they don't realize they are living today like they do, and their kids will live tomorrow like they will, because of what you and I and my sister and my old man and my mother and yours did in the war. It doesn't matter if you were in Italy or Prince Albert, Saskatchewan.

It was a good war. I'm not talking about a good war from the standpoint of any high moral purpose. If going out and killing millions of Krauts to get Hitler off his goddamned pedestal is a high moral purpose, then I'm all for it.

But it was a good war for Canada too, because it made us a great nation. I mean, hell, it showed us what we could do. We just weren't a bunch of wheat farmers and Nova Scotia fisherman and lumbermen in B.C. We were a nation. A big and tough and strong nation.

And another thing. Listen to this. If you take the terror and the horror and the death and destruction out of it, it was a good war. It was a party. I enjoyed myself. I'll never have so much fun again in my life. I mean it. Ask anybody. It was a good war.

•◄►• *The Christmas Tree*

In our house we had this tradition on Christmas Eve. We'd gather around the fire and the kids would decorate the tree and bring out the presents and neighbours might drop in for a drink. This one year we're sitting there and the talk gets around to Vietnam and one of my youngest boys suddenly said, "What was it like in the war in Italy at Christmas, Dad?"

I must admit I was a bit surprised and then I thought, "Oh, he's young, he doesn't understand," and so I just said, the war went on, the shells kept coming in and men got killed. I was quite surprised at the reaction. Fighting on Christmas Day! They were amazed.

I relieved their minds somewhat by saying there were no actual battles. No advances. Patrols, yes, line-cutting parties, probably, but that winter of 1943 in the Ortona area, both sides just dug in. It was more artillery and mortar with the odd sniper. Christmas was just another day in several months when Jerry had fire superiority over us and he plastered us every day. In fact, I think he let go a few more salvos on Christmas Day than usual, sort of a Christmas present if you like. I told them a lot of men died.

The youngest asked didn't we even have a tree, and I told this story. A sergeant and a couple of officers drove up from headquarters with a tree. A scrawny little thing, but they meant well. But they didn't know bugger-all about our front and they parked their jeep on what passed for a road. We were dug underground, and I should say that there was hardly a house or building remaining because the Germans had systematically levelled every house and cowshed within range. Suddenly there's a howling and the whole earth goes jump, jump, jump and that's unusual. Our post was pretty safe, dug deep. What had happened was this. The German gunners' forward observation post had spotted the jeep and drawn in artillery fire, and let loose and blew the jeep to inch-square pieces with that one salvo.

Our fir tree was still in the jeep, of course, and so it was chopped up like firewood. How we cursed those officers, parking the jeep not 100 feet from where we were dug in.

My Christmas story to the family gave them a different aspect to war, that it wasn't fought by Errol Flynns and John Waynes but by bookkeepers and farmers and guys who owned a service station like their old man. I'd like to think it increased my stature in their eyes.

•◄►• V-E Day

I'll never forget V-E Day. It was the most vivid thing. We were in Victoria. We were just kids, we wore skirts and sweaters and bobby socks. Just kids.

The whole place just went crazy. You wouldn't believe it. We heard about it and everybody in our school cut classes, even the teachers cut classes, and it was just kissing and hugging and screaming, bands and parades and people just going up and down the streets, just absolutely mad. There was no such thing as time or not knowing somebody; you hugged everybody you met and sang. There were sailors and soldiers with bottles of rum and men from the shipyards with cases of beer, and everybody just was drinking everywhere and fellows climbing lampposts and going through the downtown streets singing and laughing.

Nobody was throwing things or anything and the police just stood by and let people have a good time, and they had a band playing "Roll Out the Barrel" and other war songs and this must have gone on for hours but nobody got tired, not that I know of, and people were singing and shouting just as hard as when the first whistles blew until it got dark that night.

My girlfriends and me, we were about thirteen or fourteen, and I don't think we even knew there was a war on except for the blackout curtains and because we didn't have the kinds of clothes we wanted, and some of our older brothers had gone to the war, but we just went crazy as anybody that day and got kind of hysterical and whooped it up just as if we'd won the war ourselves.

•➤• *Daddy, What Did You Do in the War?*

How'd you like to have been a postal clerk in Edmonton and joined the LER's (Loyal Edmonton Regiment) and get a big party and sendoff from the gang and march off to camp and then to war, and get slammed back into the Postal Corps, and go to England and handle letters and parcels, and go to France and handle letters and parcels, and the Netherlands and Germany and still throw those letter bags around, and never get closer to any action than from here to Red Deer. And then come back home, with all the medals, the whole works, and like that kid in the comic strip, have your kid ask you: "Daddy, what did you do in the war?"

Do you tell the kid that all you were was a lousy postie?

Joining Up

*Anything Was Better Than What I'd Been Doing . . . Good
Canadians . . . A Decent Pair of Boots . . . This Hitler
Fellow . . . Straight From the Stable . . . The Day Paris Fell
. . . The Mountie's Boot . . . Jack's Death Did It*

*Patriotism was the reason most of their fathers enlisted in the
1914-18 war. The bonds to Mother England were still strong then,
and the traditions of King and Empire still seemed glorious. In
1939 when Canada declared war on Germany, 10 days after
England, tens of thousands of young Canadians did flock to join
up and fight. Some joined up because they thought it was the thing
to do—and perhaps that is the best definition of patriotism. But of
the men I interviewed, few discussed enlistment in terms we think
of as patriotism.*

*For most of them, joining up was a great opportunity to
be useful again (or for the first time), to get away from the Depression and wear clean clothes and eat three good meals a day.
Some were men running away from their previous lives for a
hundred different personal reasons; but they all eagerly lined up in
the thousands for what was in fact a chance to die.*

*Could they ever have dreamed, these young men of 1939,
that the next six years of their lives would be devoted to war, and
that many of them would be among the 41,000 Canadians who
would die or the many thousands who would return crippled
in body or mind?*

•◄►• *Anything Was Better Than What I'd Been Doing*

Me? I didn't know what the war was about. All those names didn't
mean a thing to me. Oh sure, Hitler. Everybody knows that.
Mussolini too. But Chamberlain, the English leader, he was just
somebody else, and so were the French. Quite honestly, I didn't
know anything and I don't think anybody else did either. Who
read the newspapers anyway?

I joined up because I was making three and a half bucks a
week pumping gas in a station on the main drag of Kelowna and I
was giving two bucks of that to my mother and living like a king
on the rest. Like hell I was! I was twenty, I didn't have a bean, no
hopes, nothing. As they say now, there was no light at the end of

the tunnel for me. *Anything* really was better than what I'd been doing, so I joined up. Went down to Vancouver in a freight car in October and joined up. As simple as that. No patriotism. No saving my country from the Nazi hordes. Just simply, I joined up, the army, and there I stayed until '45.

•◂▸• *Good Canadians*

My father was German and my mother was German but all us kids, the four boys and me, we were all born in Canada. At Redwater, Stoney Lake, through there, just north of Edmonton.

When the war came, two of my brothers were old enough to go and two weren't, but by the end of the war all four were in the war, in the air force and army, and all because my mother forced them in. My father, he didn't say much, but my mother said that all the boys, every one, had to go into the war so that this would prove that we were good Canadians.

•◂▸• *A Decent Pair of Boots*

Without a word of a lie, I think there was some years when we didn't have 20 dollars cash money in a whole winter. We had food, and you could always go out in the bush and get a load of wood, but I can't remember seeing any cash money.

Then the war comes and my brother Steve, he goes into Edmonton and they tell him to come back in two weeks. So in two weeks Steve goes in again and three days later he's back and he's in the army. He's got his uniform on and everything.

It's Mike's turn. My cousin who lives with us. He's got to walk, like Steve did, and it's about 25 miles if there ain't no lift and so he takes Steve's boots. In a few days he's back and says they told him with his bum leg he's out.

So I says it's my turn and I take Steve's boots. You see, there's only the one pair. Steve's boots. Mike and me, we use rubber boots we get from the Goodwill, but you can't go and fight for your country wearing rubber boots and no socks. So I take the boots and walk in and I say I want to join up. I go to the army too, and I don't get no song and dance. They say come on in, and I wind up with the Edmonton Regiment eventually, and it's good.

So I come home with Steve's boots under my arm and Mike says, "Gimme those goddamned boots," and next morning away he goes, and this time he tries the air force. Mike's still got this limp but they take him in the Royal Canadian Air Force and he comes back and he's proud as a peacock and he says he isn't going to have to use this bum leg of his because they're going to put him in an airplane. So the whole damn family is in and we're just about the only ones in the district too. This is Hunky country. I'm one, too, but at least we joined up.

After the war we're sitting around shooting the shit, and we get talking about why we joined up when half the neighbor guys went Zombie, and Steve said he joined so he could get a decent set of clothes. I says, "Boots, for me. I wanted a decent pair of boots. Never had any." Then Steve says, "Yeah, I guess it was boots for me too. That did the trick," and Mike who is half corned pipes up and he says, "Shit, I seen you two guys with those boots and I figured if the army wouldn't give me a pair then the air force would. So I joined the air force."

That's how Steve and Mike and me joined up, and that's a true goddamned story. Like it or lump it.

•◄►• *This Hitler Fellow*

I sure don't want to sound like a dad-blamed hick, but this guy who used to come around, he and I was playing gin rummy one night and he asked me what I thought of this Hitler fellow. I said something like, "What's he done now?" This fellow Jeff looks at me and he says, "Well, what he's done is fighting the whole world." "Canada?" I says, and he says, "Yes, Canada," and so next day I locks the place up and lets the chickens go wild and rides my horse into Regina, and when I get everything straightened around I find myself going to join up in the army.

•◄►• *Straight from the Stable*

I can tell you why a hell of a lot of guys joined the navy and the air force. It was so they wouldn't be called up in the army, wouldn't have to carry a bloody rifle through the mud and the shit. That's why. Wouldn't get shot in the belly. That's what it boils down to.

If that's patriotism, then put it down as patriotism. This business about King and Country was just so much horseshit, anybody can tell you that. It might have been all-Canadian grade-A premium-brand horseshit, but it still came straight from the stable.

•←→• *The Day Paris Fell*

I was prospecting up around Barkerville and the day Paris fell we're sitting around the Jack-O-Clubs Hotel in Wells and the owner is a Frenchman and he's crying in his beer about how terrible it all is, what a shame, and I say to the other fellows, "C'mon, let's join up. We'll show them buggers," and we get some more beer and get in a truck and drive down to Quesnel and by God if we didn't join up, and that's the way I joined up. Well, I guess I didn't show them buggers at all. I never got out of Canada.

•←→• *The Mountie's Boot*

Take a look at this hand. See these three knuckles? Punched right down. You could say there are no knuckles there. You know how I got them?

This is '39, September, and I'm working south of Calgary on a ranch and I want to join up and it's a Vancouver regiment I want to join, naturally. Friends, buddies and all that. So I'm on a C.P. freight with about 20 other guys, and most of us are going back home to enlist.

At Hope we're nearly home, and they jump us. Railway cops and the Mounties, and they come at us from both ends in the yards there. Eight, ten, twelve, and why they're doing this I've never figured out, but I don't get off the car quick enough. I mean this right hand is still on the rung of the ladder and pow! This goddamned boot at the end of this Mountie's leg comes down and bloody near destroys my hand. I fall, of course, flat on my back on the cinders and there's the guy laughing at me, looking down at me and laughing. And me with this hand that looks like a bull-dozer has run over it.

I get into the hospital at Chilliwack and they send me to Vancouver. They arrange a bus ticket with the relief, and it's three or four months before I can pick up anything, even a pen to sign my name on the bloody enlistment sheet.

Yeah, that's the way it was. The cops were on us, against us all the time, even when we were going in to town to join the army and save the world from Mr. Hitler. I got these scars to prove it, and I remember that grinning face too. You bet your life I do.

•←→• *Jack's Death Did It*

I joined up because a guy I knew got killed. It was as simple as that.

His name was Jack. Never mind his last name. I was a friend of both his younger brothers, but Jack would take us hunting, south of Currie Barracks, over into the coyote and jackrabbit country east of there, and we all had 22's and sometimes we'd stay overnight and we made a boat and did some floating down the Bow River and fished, although what we caught I'm not sure.

Anyway, Jack would be about three years older than I was, and four years older than his brother, my friend, Bobbie, and about another two years more than Keith, but we were a kind of team. One for all and all for one, that kind of thing. Jack did everything well. You name it. The high jump, a tall guy who could just go up and up and over. The Western Roll. He had the best stamp collection in the neighbourhood, could ride a bike obstacle course mostly no-handed, used to tell us about the girls he took out.

I guess it is pretty obvious he was my idol. Well, he was to anyone who knew him.

Their house was almost back to back to ours over by Mount Royal. Their kids walked into our house and my young brother and I walked into theirs. If my folks were out, nobody asked me to stay for dinner over there. I just did, and vice-versa.

I remember he was doing a lot of running, cross-country, and leg exercises and stuff like that, and he'd say it was to put him in shape for the army. It was never the air force, not the navy. Nope, the army. All the way. He got hold of a training manual somewhere and he could probably hold, aim and fire an army rifle better than most instructors, and this was while he was driving a truck around town as a delivery boy waiting for his time to come.

Okay, it did—this would be early '42—and he went in and through his training and that would be about six months, and before you know it, well, he was a sergeant. I think he went from private to sergeant, missing corporal on the way, and that was unusual. Next we heard he was chosen for officer training and then he was an officer, one of the 90-day wonders as they called them, but everybody in the neighbourhood knew Jack wasn't going to be any 90-day wonder.

Then D-day came. Invasion. Jack's outfit went in the first or second day and then there was this silence.

I remember this as well as I'm remembering today. I was working at the Ogden Yards and I had dinner and then I strolled over to Jack's house and walked in. They had this big den where all the kids gathered—boys and girls from the neighbourhood. Bobbie and his sister were there, just doing nothing, and then his father walked through and said hello. But there was this awful feeling, but at seventeen you're pretty dumb to the shades of difference in people. Then his mother came in. She was a lovely woman, with just a wonderful face and this little smile. A sweet little kind of shy smile. She talked to me for a few minutes, asking how I was, and about work, my girlfriend, but she wasn't taking in my answers and then Bobbie said, "Jack . . . " and then he started to cry.

His sister Mollie, who was about nine, I guess, said, "My brother's dead. They killed him."

Her mother said, "No, it's just missing . . . he's missing," and her face sort of came apart and she sat down on that old chesterfield. I can see it yet, the world's oldest and beat-up chesterfield, with flowers on it. She looked up at me and said, through tears, "I knew it was going to happen. I was waiting for the telegraph boy even before he came up the driveway. Something just told me he was coming, and I went out to meet him, and I didn't even know he was there until he came up the driveway."

I was seventeen, but what's wrong with crying at seventeen anyway, and I got up and held her arm, and I guess it was the way a football coach would grab his star player, and I said, "I'm sorry. I'm so sorry. I'm terribly sorry."

I remember this very well. I went out onto the street and walked to a little park and I remember climbing over the fence, getting tangled up in some caragana bushes and there was two girls sitting on a bench and I went right by them. They said hello, I remember that. I didn't want them to see me crying.

Across the park I leaned up against a big elm, one of those huge elms, and I cried a bit, and I didn't—well, I don't want to sound dramatic so I didn't curse or say I'd revenge him or I'd get those dirty Germans. Nothing like that. All I knew was that he was missing. But I knew deep down he was dead.

I leaned against that tree for a few minutes and it was getting dusky and then I went home. I didn't tell my parents and next day I didn't tell my boss, but I took off from work at ten o'clock and rode my bike into town and signed up. Not the air force and not the navy. The goddamned army. I was under age by a bit, but I bluffed that and my eyes were rotten, but if you could see lightning and hear thunder you were in, and that's the way I joined up.

It wasn't patriotism. Who the hell dies for King and Country any more? That crap went out in the first world war. And it wasn't to avenge Jack's death, because you and I know that is nonsense. But Jack's death did it. It made the coin flip right. I didn't have to join. I wasn't old enough, bad eyes, underweight and I'd had a hernia, I could have gone on working in the Yards or some war plant, but no, when I heard he'd got it, something snapped inside me and that was it. No monkeying about. I was going, and I did. As simple as *that* [and he snapped his fingers].

Leaving Home – or Staying There

A Sucker ... On Our Way Overseas ... Just Another Soldier ... Stoney's Hand ... Just Like Paul Revere ... Leaving Home

---

More than 700,000 Canadians—soldiers, sailors, airmen, women in the services, nurses, merchant sailors—went overseas in the course of the war. That meant more than 700,000 goodbyes had to be said. Parents, remembering the 1914 war, would fear that they would never see their sons again, and would weep. Wives and children would cling together in a little family huddle at the railroad station as the husband said goodbye, bitterly regretting what he had got himself into.

"Leaving home—and why? To go over there and have some guy who didn't really hate you shooting at your ass," said a Toronto man. "Why? Why did you do it? I don't know."

And of course there were those who were determined not to leave home, men who moved heaven and earth to stay out of the services. Every war has its draft dodgers.

•◄►• *A Sucker*

Can you remember? You're at your graduation and there's the principal standing up there with the carnation in his buttonhole and he's not saying the boys in the class of '42, Kelvin High School, Winnipeg, should rush out and sign up, but he's making all sorts of sounds like "duty" and "responsibility" and "devotion to our cause" and stuff like that. Everything except "take the king's shilling, boys," and telling the girls to pass among us handing out white feathers.

Not all of us were old enough to tear right down to Smith and Portage and sign up for the army, but in six months most of us would be. The army wasn't it anyway. Most fellows would have tried for the navy first, the safe service, and then the air force, even safer as long as you could stay on the ground, but awfully glamorous if you did make air crew.

I went to work, strictly a part-time job doing nothing until I was old enough to enlist. So mid-September comes along and there I am, and in an hour I'm in, but good. If you were infantry, which I was, you went across town to the University of Manitoba where they had a basic training camp.

In my class there were 18 guys, and they'd all got the pep talks—"serve your country," "your country needs you," and all that. But all through the weeks of training out there on the campus, I'd see these guys lounging around with girls on the grass, just enjoying themselves, spending their old man's money—guys who had been my best friends, or so I thought. Hell, I guess they were. Coming in from a 12-mile route march, soaking wet and breaking in new boots and cursing life back to our great-grandfather's time, and here would be a couple of guys I'd grown up with, dressed for tennis, walking across the campus to the courts. I found out later that of those 18, only three joined up. The rest went to college or university. Oh, you can see how this rankles. I'm not sure I'm mad because I'm missing out on the girls, and tennis and living the good life, or if I'm cheesed off because I've been had, that I could have gone to university.

I met this one guy out at the campus once. We stopped to talk and I said, and I remember: "When are you enlisting?" To the point, get it?

He said, "Never. If you don't have to, why do it?" Something like that.

"Ever feel that somebody might call you yellow?" I asked.

"Probably, but anybody who knows me knows I'm not," and he walked away. I had to admit that was true, that he wasn't yellow on the face of it. Then he called back, "Ever feel that somebody might call you a sucker?"

I know it sounds dramatic, maybe corny like out of a bad play, but it happened, and the army never seemed right for me after that. Where it was lousy when I first got into it, it became putrid as I kept going.

You know, three guys out of 18. Three out of 17, I guess, because one guy was practically blind. That's a hell of an average, isn't it? You wonder what patriotism is all about. It still rankles in me. Still, after more than 30 years.

•◄►• *On Our Way Overseas*

There was this fellow from Kenora and his name was Allan. I can't remember whether Allan was his first name or his last name but it didn't matter. What mattered was he was the best damned soldier I've ever seen, and this was before he even got into the fighting.

He was twenty-five or so and had worked for the railroad, and when we were going through Kenora on our way overseas his wife was at the station. How she found out I don't know, but he got word to her somehow. It was only a five-minute stop, I think, and she had their three little girls with her and they all clung close to each other, the five of them, and the rest of us sort of hung back and just looked, and a lot of the fellows weren't feeling too happy. It was what you'd call a sad little scene and a lot different than saying goodbye in the house on the last day and then going back to camp. This was it, going overseas. This was when you got down to the nuts and bolts of it.

The train gave a hoot, you know, some blasts and our officers were yelling at us to climb aboard and we did, and Allan did and he's crying, and suddenly a guy named Johnston climbs out. Now this Johnston is a real bastard. The things I could tell you about him. Nothing meant anything to this guy. Just a thoroughly bad egg. He runs up to Allan's wife and he kneels down and kisses each of the little girls, you know, four, six, eight, and then he kisses Mrs. Allan on the cheek and grabs the train as it starts moving out. And when he comes into the coach, he's crying too.

Never forget it. He'd told us he'd spent his embarkation furlough with a whore somewhere in Winnipeg and I don't doubt for a minute he did, but I have a real strong sneaking suspicion that somewhere he had a nice wife and little kids like Allan had. Funny about guys in the army. You could never tell about them.

•⟷• *Just Another Soldier*

My father had a section and he rented another half and you're darn close to a thousand acres and remember, this was 1940 and that was a good-sized farm then. So I get my call. Dad goes into Brandon and says, "Look, we've got about 600 acres in crop at any one time, and with this boy at home he and I can handle it. It's going to be tough, but we can do it, and look at the crop I can take off." He even said, "You tell me what to plant and I'll do it. Barley. Oats, Wheat. Look at the wheat we could grow, and that's far more valuable than having just another soldier lugging a rifle around some training camp or guarding some C.P.R. rail bridge."

The chairman of the call-up board—he's an old retired gaffer as I remember and he hums and haws, hmmmm, hmmmm, hmmmm—and he asks my dad hasn't he got another son at home? "Sure," says my dad, "and he's sixteen and he's weakly, nose always in a book, and he couldn't sit on a tractor seat on a hot July day for 4 hours, let alone 12 hours. He'll never make a farmer and I don't intend to make him one," the old man says. "He can go to Winnipeg to university. That's what he wants to do."

Well, the old chairman of this board, he hmmms and hmmms some more and says, "Mr. Patterson, we'll consider your case. Thank you."

A week later the letter arrives. No deferment. I have to go, and so I go. And you know what happens to that farm? This is what happens because I'm telling you. The old man's arthritis gets worse and he can't work the farm and the kid is no help, and in '41 he puts in a smaller crop, and by '43 that farm is out of business—and that was a farm which never had a crop failure, not even during the hard years. Always good rains in July and no frost or rust. So they get one soldier, me, and the country loses thousands and thousands and thousands of bushels of food. It just didn't make sense.

When I got home in October, 1945, the farm looked like L'il Abner country and it took me six or eight years to get her back in shape.

•◄►• *Stoney's Hand*

I'm in this mill near Doaktown and there's this big guy Livingstone feeding rough cut into the planing machine, and one day he tells me the army wants him. Now there's nothing new about that. I said, "The army wants everybody, there's a war on, Stoney, don't ya know there's a war on?" Something like that.

Next day I hear a yell and I see Stoney and he's got his right hand stuck into the sawdust under the machine and his face looks mighty damned white and I say, oh oh. I run over and sit him down and then I grab his arm and hold it over his head and I've got my finger on the pressure point on the wrist and I look and he's got two fingers left, a thumb and the pointing finger, the first one, and there ain't much blood because I've got it shut off and the fresh sawdust makes a fine bandage. I yell for the foreman and he shuts down and we get Stoney into the truck and high-tail it for Doaktown, and then we decide it better be Chatham, so we take off for Chatham and they fix him up. There's nothing wrong with him, except he's got two fingers where the rest of us got five.

Sir, about three weeks later Stoney walks into the site and asks for his job. Sure, the boss says, but can you do the work, and Stoney goes over to the planer and hell, it ain't no different, he can work just as good. Three fingers don't matter. I knew what he'd done, and in the back of the truck that night going to town I tell him so. I said, "Stoney, you cut them fingers off, didn't you?"

He laughed and said sure, and it didn't hurt much at all and he wasn't going to be anybody's soldier boy, no sir, and he could still handle a fly rod and go deer hunting, and if it was an extra-special thrill the girls wanted, why, he could give that to them too. He was laughing like hell. A big joke.

Stoney stayed with that crew for about another year and he could do anything with that right hand, anything I could do. That was one way of staying out of the scrap.

•➤• *Just Like Paul Revere*

If a farmer was getting on and he had too much to handle alone, his son would probably get a deferment because food was vital to the country's defence. But if he had two sons, well by Jesus, one would be marching off to war pretty damn soon. Unless, now get this, unless that son was *married.* If he had a wife, he was home free. This is what the government put in about September and I think it was 1940. Don't hold me to it, though.

There was this family down the road with three sons. The youngest, Brucie, is no good, kicked in the head by a horse when a little tyke, and all he can do is help his mother feed the hens. Poor fellow. Robbie, he's twenty-two or so, and so lazy he drives the snow plow every winter for the government and just fishes or chases girls rest of the year. Not the brains God gave a goose. That leaves Tom, my oldest boy's age, about twenty-eight, and a good man in the field. He's the only farmer in the lot, including his old man. So they got to keep Tommy home. But he's the one would go. He wouldn't shoot off his big toe like that Robbie was likely to.

They're sitting around after dinner this Sunday and I guess listening to the news from Brandon, and what should it say but that night, that very night, everybody not married, well, they're going to be called up. Well, Jesus, that means Tom. If Tom ain't hitched by midnight, then that's it. Goodbye farm, the town loses its best hard-ball pitcher and I guess the poor godforsaken country loses the war, without old hero Tom. Mind you, Tom wouldn't have minded going. He wasn't holding back that way, oh no. He just knew that the farm would fall apart if he did go away.

Old man Lauder tells me the story a couple of years later, and he is just busting his gut.

He tells Tom to get in the pickup and get over to Gwendolyn's, six miles east of here. She's the girl Tom has been taking to dances since snakes first laid eggs. Nice, but plain as a mud fence. Then he gets one of Tom's sisters to phone her to tell her to get ready. Just be standing by the gate when Tom comes by. He'll pick her up on the fly, I guess, like a through train grabbing off the mail.

So back they come and I guess it's getting on about nine o'clock now, and in the back piles Robbie and his sister, and they high-tail it down the road to the first town. The object is to get married, you see, and if you think that Gwendolyn is protesting, then you got another think coming.

First town, Shoal Lake, and the manse is dark. The darn-fool preacher is out, over at Isabella eating cake and drinking tea after the service. Its ten-thirty or so now. Over towards Hamiota. The United Church minister there won't marry them, because I guess the old codger knows the game they're playing.

I often wonder, you know, if the roads all over the prairies weren't dangerous that night with the Model-T's and democrats and other vehicles scurrying down the roads to get people married off in time, seeing as how the government seemed to have sneaked that rule in at the last minute.

So time's running out, and Tommy has to get the ring on her finger and I guess Gwendolyn's got it figured out that this is the last chance. I guess, like with the ship sinking, she's still got a chance and she still is going for it.

The way the old man tells it, if they'd had a flat or busted a wheel on a culvert or hit a cow on the road, goodbye marriage. I guess Tom could hear those machine guns already.

They got into this town, forget the name of it, but it might have been Binscarth, and they had to wake up the cop to find out where the United Church preacher lives and he tells them. It's maybe eleven-fifteen then and he's in bed, so's his wife, and they can't understand what the hell it is all about, this rushing around, and Tom yanks out a tenspot and holds it up to the light and says, "You get this business over with in 10 minutes, before midnight, and I'll double this." Well, that was about a month's wages for a sky pilot out in that country, and he grabbed the good book and went at 'er, tearing through the ceremony and filling out the paper, and everybody signed it and there they were, about 10 minutes or so to spare and old Tom there had been saved. Heh!

Wait. You think folks in the neighbourhood thought this was bad? Hell no. A lot of people thought Tom was a smart young fellow, that it was a smart thing to do. If the government was going to be sneaky, then he'd be sneaky too. I guess you could say it was quite a natural thing to do. They'd been screwing us on prices and things since before our fathers could remember, the farmer always got it in the neck, and when somebody came along and give it to them, then that fellow was pretty much of a hero. Tom. Racing around those roads, just like Paul Revere.

•➤• *Leaving Home*

I left for overseas on November 10, 1943. I guess that's one red circle on the old calendar I'll always remember. When you're twenty, well, what the hell. The thing is, you're only twenty and you've got those pilot wings. Manning pool, ground school, the Piper Cubs, advanced training. Hoo hah! Know what I mean. Telling this I feel like that kid again.

Oshawa isn't all that big a town and then it was smaller, and everybody on the street knew little old Jerry's leave was up, going away to serve the king. Fly the big bombers or *zooooooooom* [making a diving motion with his hand] a fighter. I'd been home, what was it, twelve days, fourteen.

I didn't seem to have many friends and it seemed most of the guys I knew in school were in the services anyway, so the last time home was just marking time. Walking around the neighbourhood. That was a pretty big deal in the morning. Downtown in the afternoon. The rink if there was a game at night. I might have a few beers with my father in the Legion.

I'm sort of setting the stage. Quite frankly, I was bored. Nothing to do. Nothing to talk about anyway. Do I talk about war, fighting, and have my mother get up from the table and go to her bedroom? That kind of stuff. They knew I was a pilot, and I knew I had three choices. If I went on coastal patrol it would be a piece of cake, just monotonous. Bomber Command and I had a good chance of going for a Burton. Casualties at that time were pretty fierce. And if I was a fighter pilot, glamourous as all get out, I could expect a good chance of seeing them thar Pearly Gates too. So I didn't talk about it.

The day came. Breakfast was as usual, and Dad stayed home. He worked in a department store. My sister worked at the phone company and she gave me a hug and said, "Look after yourself, Buddy, and write Mom and Dad, please. You know how they are." Then she left.

It was an hour until the taxi came at ten. A condemned man, I know what he goes through. We just sat in the parlour and I guess Mom asked me eight times if I'd like a cup of tea. My gear at the door. Coat on the chair, and hat too. I thought I'd better take a look around and see this place, because maybe it would be the last time. My home, you know. I don't think I was being dramatic or anything like that and certainly not heroic. At twenty? Even at that age you can get pretty realistic.

My mother, she was being brave. A bit trembly and you might say erratic, when she'd start a sentence and trail off and go over and spend a couple of minutes picking a couple of dead leaves off a rubber plant. Straightening a picture. Then asking if I wanted a cup of tea. She was wearing those old slippers from the Boer War and a mauve skirt and a sweater, wool, I think, brown, with a patched hole in the right sleeve. You can see, if I was a painter I could paint that room, that scene, the old mom and dad waiting for their son to go off to war.

My father. My dear father. He'd never missed more than five days off work in his life, I suppose. A real workhorse, loved the company and had a pride in his work, selling men's clothing. The first suit he'd pick off the rack, that would be the right one for the customer. There are men like that. And there he was sitting on the piano bench feeling guilty about missing half a day at the store and yet, here was his only son, first born, that sort of thing, and he had this duty. Stay and see him off. We talked fishing and he went into the back room and got out his notebook and there it all was, on April 19, Buddy had caught three trout, a pound, pound two ounces, a pound six. That passed a bit of time. Fishing data. My one big day. Three fish.

Remember that clock in the movie *High Noon*? Gary Cooper. The big clock going tick-tock tick-tock towards noon when the train with the killers on it would come? Same difference. Our grandfather's clock.

Finally it was ten and I stood up and said, "I gotta go." I put on my gaberdine and picked up my hat and fixed it at the hall mirror. You had to get that right angle. That was important. Off we go, into the wild blue yonder, flying high into the sky. Remember the song? Then the taxi beeped. Twice. I turned and hugged Mom and she had her arms tight around my neck, squeezing as hard as her little body could, and her face was in my shoulder and she said, and I'll remember this, she said, "Goodbye my darling son. Goodbye. Goodbye. Our prayers . . . " And then she gave me the Bible. I knew that Bible, it must have been 40 years old. It was the one she had when she came out to this country as a girl to work as a servant in the house of some mill owner in Stratford. That just about finished me there. Just about finished me.

Do you really want this kind of stuff? Okay.

Then it was Dad's turn. He stuck out his hand and said, "Good luck, son," and that's about what I expected. No nonsense. Just good luck. I grabbed him and hugged him and his eyes were glistening. The old goat. I loved him. I didn't know it until then, but I did. All the shit life had handed out to him, and he'd taken it and come back for more.

I picked up my little bag and said to my mother, "I'll read the guid booook, mither," imitating the Scots way of speech she had. Then I put my foot under the cat's belly and gave a heave. She'd go up in the air about three feet and come down and come over and brush her tail against my leg. She was a Persian and I'd done it a thousand times and I said, "Okay, Mugger, that's the last time you get boosted for a while."

I went out the door and said, "Bye, folks, I love you all to pieces," and got the hell out of there, down the walk, because I wasn't sure how much more I could take.

There was this old Mr. Lake across the street, an old busy-body if there ever was, and there he was, up against his gate and waiting, waving that old cane of his and yelling, "Give the buggers hell, Buddy. Shoot 'em out of the skies," and I had to laugh. I got in and looked back at the house and maybe it was just the skies, grey, November, remember, and I think it would be snowing in an hour or two, and my father and mother at the door, arms around each other as if they were like two old apple trees growing old together, branches wrapped about, and I waved and I could hear a sob. It was me, and I was crying, but it felt as if the tears were coming from everywhere, like out of my eyes and my forehead and my cheeks and as if my whole face was swimming in tears and I was fumbling around for a hankie as we drove away and I re-member the cabbie saying, "Let them come, kid. It'll be over in a minute or two. Christ, I've seen guys ten times as tough as you suddenly start to overflow. Just sit back and let 'em come."

It's funny, you know, sitting here 30 years later, and remembering all this for the first time and being able to remember even that cab driver's words, but I do.

Anyway, end of story. I was glad when the cab turned the corner and the house was out of sight and we drove to the station. It was a damn funny feeling. Yes, I guess you could say I felt airborne. Everything in the past was over. Airborne.

Patriotism on the Home Front

The Major and the Light . . . They Thought We Could Be Brainwashed . . . Suddenly They Were Austrian . . . Victory Gardens . . . A Girl Like Me . . . "If" Day in Winnipeg . . . Treason at the University . . . She Was My Friend

Ugly things and stupid things and funny things happen inside a nation that is at war. Canada, oceans away from any real danger, was no exception. Anyone who was a little unusual was liable to be denounced as a spy by an overzealous neighbour. People avoided, and then quietly dropped, their friends with German names, while the man down the street who decided he was a pacifist and went off under guard to a barbed wire camp was "An Enemy of Canada," although his ancestors were United Empire Loyalists. At home, patriotism reached heights of fervour unknown to the men who did the actual fighting.

Propaganda played a major part in keeping up the patriotic fervour on the home front. As you will see, many Canadians remember the propaganda of those days with a mixture of disbelief and indignation. But then, as a wise man once said, in war the first casualty is truth.

•◄►• *The Major and the Light*

We didn't always have blackouts but we had a lot of test blackouts, ones where the whole town would be blacked out solid from the naval base at Esquimalt, all through Saanich which was the countryside, and Caulfield too. The whole area around Victoria.

The Air Raid Precautions Centre was in the old Belmont Building and the head of it was Major Moody, and when he looked out the windows and got his reports in from all around, he was pretty pleased. Then he figured a personal inspection was in order, so down the stairs we go and goddamn it if there isn't a big round light right outside our door, and it is on. The only light shining in Victoria and vicinity. Jesus, you should have heard that man! He had a hair-trigger temper at the best of times, and now the air was blue.

Somebody suggested finding the master switch but that had been done and this operated on its own switch, and somebody said we should put a round in it, but nobody had a pistol. So finally a sergeant and a couple of ranks dragged out an office table and then got a chair and up goes the major. He's going to handle this thing personally. He always carried this swagger stick and now it finally came into use, and there he is, flailing away with his swagger stick—and the thing won't break, because it is tough glass. So much for swagger sticks. But finally he does break it, and then the bulb inside, and there's glass all over the place, and it was the funniest thing, the head of A.R.P. beating to death the only god-damned light visible in the city of Victoria. The guys were killing themselves laughing—but behind the old boy's back, you can make sure of that.

•➤• *They Thought We Could Be Brainwashed*

It was like in every big city there was one big building full of people turning out propaganda. I used to say to my husband that I wished we could read a happy story about the war, or one where somebody had done something other than knitting ten pairs of socks for the navy in one day, or hadn't found a new way to make rhubarb edible, or whose six sons weren't in the air force.

The newspapers, they were just propaganda sheets. My goodness, on the front pages, war, war, war, and in the insides, how to cook cheaper, how to do Victory gardens, why we should have car pools, buy Victory Bonds and tell your friends they were traitors if they didn't load up on them too, and how to teach the children that all Germans were monsters with poison dripping from their jaws. And the family down the block were Germans, Schmidt, and as fine a family as you'd find, and our kids went to school with half a dozen Italian families and played on the same hockey teams and went to the same birthday parties.

Or remember that story about in the German prisoner-of-war camp down near Lethbridge where the prisoners stopped three canteen workers, girls from the town, from getting raped by a bunch of Canadian soldiers who were drunk and mean. And in this fight the Germans beat up the Canadians and saved the girls. That was one piece of news that wasn't in the newspapers, but everyone sure knew that one. But that wasn't propaganda.

You'd look at the front page and there it was. War in the Pacific, Japs bombing women and children refugees, while all we bombed were military targets. We were the good ones. Now, Pop, I'm saying these things and nobody is going to come around and take me off to the pokey. Not now. *Then*, maybe. That's why so many people said they were Austrian when they were German. But you never read *that* in the papers. Only what the government wanted you to know, what they wanted to tell you. It was a farce.

When Dieppe came along, and I had a son in it, although he didn't get ashore as he was in one of the boats that were in reserve—why, it must have been two weeks before we found out what was happening. That was a kind of propaganda too, no news.

The kind which was the worst was the casualty lists, and if they could have kept them out I guess they would have, but they couldn't. I remember Dickie Johnson was missing in action, a bomber, you know, and we wondered why we hadn't seen his mother, Mrs. Johnson, a widow lady, why we hadn't seen her for days and weeks. And then it came out in the *Herald* and I went over right away. Right next door but one, mind you, and there she was, nearly dead with grief. No, half mad with grief, mess all over the place and her cat dead from something and she didn't care.

There were all these mysterious shortages, and we weren't to ask why. Just do as you were told. Just buy bonds and don't ask for a decent pair of shoes or zippers, and my God, zippers, what a crisis there. *No zippers.* Back to elastic.

You remember those Sunday supplements, they were jammed with war stuff. How to cook cabbage, make cabbage rolls and then drink the cabbage juice. Or carrots. Swiss chard. Spinach. Did they think we didn't know that stuff, like how to make a dollar do the price of ten? You'd think the idiots in their big offices in Toronto and Ottawa didn't know about the Depression we just went through—ten years of nothing.

It was all war, war, and how brave our boys were, and I don't care if they were brave, did we have to have it shoved down our throats year after year? I surely think they sat back on their seats in Ottawa and Toronto and thought we were just a bunch of idiots, from Halifax, Nova Scotia to Vancouver Island, and we could be told anything and believe it. Yes, that's it. We could be *brainwashed.* I don't think it worked. We did what God in our hearts and Holy Mother told us was right, but we'd have done it anyway.

I have a few of those old papers. The one where my son was wounded. I mean the one with his name on the casualty list. When my sister's son was killed on a navy ship. The peace stories, and the D-day landings. I saved those kind of papers as souvenirs and if you want to see just how bad that propaganda was, you should read them.

If there is another war and we survive the first day and if they read this in your book, then maybe those in Ottawa will do something about all the baloney about war and have a few people who can write funny things and make us laugh a bit. Nothing chases the blues like a good laugh.

You're a younger man and perhaps wouldn't understand all that much, but I'll say this. We knew there was a war on. We could read the posters, listen to the radio, and we read the newspapers, and a war isn't ring-around-a-rosy. It is serious, and many people are killed. I think we would have done just as well without all their propaganda if they'd just had the sense God gave a goose. Canadians aren't stupid, you know.

•—•—• *Suddenly They Were Austrian*

Remember the Canadian German Bund, or German Canadian Bund, whatever it was called? In cities like Winnipeg and Toronto they had big parades in the 30's and wore uniforms with armbands with swastikas on them and did Hitler salutes and talked about how much they loved Canada, but how great Hitler and the Fatherland were. They were caught up in the mass hysteria in Germany, the parades and the Sieg Heiling. There must have been 5,000 in Winnipeg alone, and God knows how many in Toronto.

We did nothing about them. Remember? They were against the Commies, as we called them then, the Bolshies, Reds, all that. It was like the enemies of my enemies are my friends, I guess, and that's why the police and the government let all these Germans parade about and kick in the windows of Jewish stores. Well, they'd arrest them if they saw them kicking in the windows, but they could always look the other way. Know what I mean? Oh yes, it went on. Don't you believe it didn't.

Then the war came. Hah! Now they weren't Germans. Oh no, they were Austrian. Viennese. The Polish-occupied part of Germany. Not a bloody one would admit he was German, even with German names 400 years old. Nope, all Austrians. You see, a few had been turfed into internment camps. Not many, but a few.

Here were guys I'd gone to school with, knew their parents who only spoke German in the home, guys who two years ago had been trying to get me to read their damned literature on Strength Through Joy, the German Youth Movement, how great Hitler was and why it was so bloody important that Germany build up a great navy—here are these guys I'd seen marching in their Bund parade just two years ago, here they are looking me straight in the eye and saying they were Austrian.

•←→• *Victory Gardens*

Victory gardens got to be a laugh, but I guess a lot of city people found they had green thumbs they didn't know they had. You remember, the government said grow your own vegetables. This must have been about 1941 and it caught on like the hula-hoop, take-out Chinese food or, oh, any one of those things that catch people. It was a fad, I guess.

Parts of the city, West Edmonton I'm talking about, had dozens and dozens of vacant lots, and soon there were families out there with spades and forks digging away and having a whale of a time. Some people would take one or two lots and others just a plot. The newspapers printed diagrams on how to lay out the garden, and Kiwanis clubs and such gave prizes for the best garden, the biggest pumpkin, the best-looking bowl of radish, things like that, and in a way it was like the city was going back to the old-time country fair like when I was a kid.

A lot of city people once were country people, but they must have forgotten just how much a big city lot would grow— radish, lettuce, beans, corn, peas, potatoes, squash, pumpkins, Swiss chard and another thing they must have forgot was how much work it took. My lands, you'd see people out until dark down on their knees weeding and pulling weeds, and it got so that anybody with half an eye could tell what was going to happen.

That's right. The horn of plenty overflowed all that summer and fall. Tons of potatoes and baskets of green beans and cabbages this big, as big as a milk pail, and you'd be sitting next to somebody on the streetcar in from Jasper Place and you'd ask him if he wanted some free vegetables and he'd laugh. He could give you twice what you gave him.

People used to take baskets of vegetables to work and put them on a desk and people would take their pick. You see, an awful lot of stuff was rationed, so the government decided that if people grew their own, then this would add to their diet; the vegetables would make up for the loss of some things. But what was rationed was sugar and butter and meat and things like that, and you can do very well without those things anyway, as long as you have a little.

And then there was the canning. Can, can, can, said the government. Pickle the stuff, put it in brine. Boil it and put it away. Dry it. Store it in cool temperatures. Make sauce of the pumpkin and squash. Bottle your corn, your peas, your everything. That was fine, except there weren't enough bottles around, and to make more they'd have to take glass materials away from what they called the vital war effort—which probably meant panes of glass in the windows of barracks at army camps. So not every-body could preserve the stuff, and by this time an awful lot of people didn't want to see another cabbage or cob of corn.

It was a good idea, of course, and it worked very well in England, we all know that, but in Canada where our bounty was almost biblical, so vast, it didn't work that way.

•◀▶• *A Girl Like Me*

Nobody could make a living in that part of the country, it was the Depression, you see, and my mother and father had worked them-selves to the bone trying. So about 1938 they applied to go back to Switzerland where an uncle was old, and my family would take over his resort, my mother cooking in the chalet and dad running the resort. Anyway, about 1939 when the application came up they were turned down, and then the war came along and that was that. By the way, my parents were German, but they had been in Canada a long time.

They came and took away my father's 22 rifle he used to pot rabbits, and he had to report to some probation board once a month. I was sixteen by this time and had moved to Calgary and had a job and I was going with a young fellow who was in the navy. One day an R.C.M.P. officer came around and told this young chap I was going with that didn't he know that Elvera—that's me—was German and that her family was under surveillance by the authorities, and did he think it wise to go with a girl like me.

Did you ever hear anything quite so stupid in your life?

•◀▶• *"If" Day in Winnipeg*

It was like kids playing cowboys and Indians, this "If" Day. They had it in Winnipeg in '42. I remember there was snow on the ground. The idea of the "If" part was what if German troops occupied Winnipeg. Then what kind of a life would we lead?

About 3,000 troops took part and about half, I think, were dressed up like Nazi troops, and the rest were in Canadian uniform. I think the German duds came from Hollywood from one of those war movies.

That was one part of the "If." The other part was that this here invasion of Winnipeg would go on until a Victory Bond drive was subscribed. Paid up. V-Bond days were big then. Everybody was supposed to buy, and if he didn't then he was a traitor. I spent any money that would have gone on bonds for booze. I had a bootlegger at Fort Whyte out by the cement plant.

I had one kid in Mulvey School, and that's just off Portage Avenue, you know, the main drag, and these guys dressed like monkeys came into his classroom and tore all the patriotic slogans off the walls, yelling and shaking their fists. Carrying on like monkeys.

Oh, sure, the Canadian troops lost. The Germans were supposed to have a division and armoured vehicles, and they zoomed up and down Portage Avenue for a while and burned some old books from the public library and captured the Manitoba Cabinet and put them somewhere. Can you really imagine people in the middle twentieth century giving a damn about such shenanigans?

I remember there was a picture in the paper showing the German troops giving a hard time to the newspaper seller at Portage and Main. For selling newspapers, I guess. They tore up his papers. They did some looting too, carrying furniture out of a downtown hotel. I mean, what the hell, why carry furniture out of a building into the snow?

It was so dumb a plot that even an idiot wouldn't believe the darn thing, and Winnipeg was laughing about it. Laughing their heads off. How far was Germany? Six thousand miles, I guess. But maybe that didn't have anything to do with it.

I can't remember if they got their war bond money but I guess they did. They always seemed to, even if they had to put the Prime Minister on the radio and get him to cry his eyes out for the people to give.

That was "If" Day. And it was a farce.

•◄►• *Treason at the University*

I think a lot of people will remember this, when *The Manitoban* put out a special literary edition. This would be about the spring, I think of '44, maybe '45. *The Manitoban* was the students' newspaper at the university.

Jack Ludwig, who is one of the big Canadian novelists now, was editor of this special paper and Ken Williamson was editor. Bert Hamilton was president of the student body. Anyway, Bert wrote this poem, an anti-war poem, and it ran down one side of the paper. It was quite a terrific poem, saying that the guns of the war should be turned on Mackenzie King. This is about the time when the Zombies were causing such a political uproar in Canada.

And the *Free Press*, if you remember, went all out against *The Manitoban*, insisted on a complete investigation of the whole university and its structure, made a big issue of these people who were going to university when they should have been fighting the war. And Bert Hamilton was not allowed his degree, and he would have been eligible for a Rhodes Scholarship. He was deprived of his degree until after the war and I think he was given a hard time.

The whole thing caused a terrific uproar. It was as though he had committed treason. Which he hadn't, of course, not in the least, the slightest.

I noticed in the alumni bulletin that he now is a professor somewhere. By the way, he had already enlisted in the navy before that poem was written.

•◄►• *She Was My Friend*

Nobody questioned anything. It was war and everything the government did was right.

Except there was one friend of mine, her family was Communist or something like that, her family used to question the war, how things were done and I used to report them to the R.C.M.P. [*She laughs, nervously.*]

And she was my friend.

This was the way we lived. I can't remember too clearly but I remember picking things up around her home, pamphlets, which I thought were absolutely terrible, and the whole country was going to rack and ruin. I didn't think anything happened. That was the time when we were friends with the Russians. Allies. But I did report them to the R.C.M.P.

It is crazy when you look back on it now. What we did.

Training

*On Horses . . . The Water Tank . . . A Doctor or a Killer?
. . . The Dentist's Teeth . . . Buller Started in on Him . . .
What a Bayonet Can Do . . . Tank Training . . . Right on
the Bull . . . The Mountains*

---

*Everyone in the forces hated training. It was intended, of course,
to instil absolute discipline. Do this, soldier, or do that, sailor, and
don't ask why. But so much of it was, in the military term,
chickenshit. Too much time was spent on parade square drills. Too
much on the art of saluting. Too much on the correctness of
walking-out dress. Too much on how to pack a haversack, stow a
hammock, board an aircraft. Too much bayonet drill. Who would
ever get close enough to a German to stick that thing in his gut?*

*But then came the realization of what it was all about. The
almost automatic action of cleaning the rifle after firing could save
your life because a jammed rifle barrel could mean a blow-up.
Those hours of digging silly slit trenches in the rain paid off when
shells were bursting around you. All those hours and days and
weeks of training, apparently meaningless, all came together. The
soldier, the sailor, the airman in combat had to ignore fear but still
live with it—and it was the housekeeping lessons learned long ago
in some Canadian training camp that helped him live with war.*

*But, oh God, like everyone who went through it, I remem-
ber the frustrations, the chickenshit, the rules and regulations and
the cocky corporals and the overbearing sergeants of those training
camps, they were enough to break a man's spirit. But if they did,
perhaps he was not much of a man.*

•◄►• *On Horses*

After I saw the Panzer divisions in the newsreels slicing up the
Polish Army, in thirty days or something, I knew that was the way
the war was going to be fought. So I joined up with the Hussars.
They called themselves cavalry still, but their designation, you
might call it, was armoured regiment. This was in late '40.

About 30 of us came down to camp and they still have
horses, see, and the sergeant puts us on horses, and away we go
across the country, and only about six of us come back. He said to
me, "You'll do." And the only reason I did was I had the bloody

sense to hang on to the horse and let it do its own work. I didn't know anything about horses.

It didn't take me long to find out that Canada had no tanks and it looked like being a long time until we got some, and with Germany knocking off France just like that and making bigger and better tanks and getting more experience, here we are at Camp Borden still currying and feeding our horses and bouncing our asses off across the country.

•◄►• *The Water Tank*

There were always the terrible frustrations of barrack life. I'll tell you a story.

I won't tell you the camp or my name, but it was a camp on the prairies and for some reason nobody was given any kind of leave for six weeks. It was winter, very cold, and if you were under twenty-one you couldn't go to the wet canteen. The brigadier was a straight-laced old man from New Brunswick and despite the saying, "Old enough to die, old enough to drink," he closed the canteen on the young guys, who made up more than half the camp. I was eighteen. The only rationale I can give for this type of order was that the old bastard sincerely believed he was doing right. No demon beer for his young recruits.

You can imagine a camp on the prairies, in January or February with a whipping wind from the north, and training every day and lying around in our stinking H-huts the rest of the time. Fighting, feuds, arguments and, in retrospect, some homosexuality, although I didn't know what the word meant then.

One Saturday night I snapped. The spring that is inside everybody's head, well, in mine it just went *booooing*. I had one round of live ammunition that I'd sneaked off the rifle butts. Just as a souvenir and nothing more—you could really be in serious trouble if you were caught with live ammunition. Soldiers weren't supposed to have the stuff.

There was a chap named Crandall across the aisle from me and he'd been hauled off to the sick bay the day before with something or other, and I picked up his rifle off his bed hook and shoved the round in and half the guys at my end of the hut were watching me. Nobody moved to stop me and the corporal wasn't in his cubicle, so there it was.

Looking back, I know all I meant to do was go outside and fire the round off and maybe let out a yell and that would be it; but when I got out the first thing I saw was the camp water tower, a huge affair, tens of thousands of gallons, I'd guess. It was bitterly cold and there it was, all white and gleaming in the moonlight, and without another thought I snapped the rifle to my shoulder and drilled my one bullet into it. That was all. I went back into the hut, ran a pull-through through Crandall's rifle, threw the cartridge into the back of the big stove and washed my hands.

Well, in about five minutes there were officers and orderlies and provos running around, but in ever-diminishing circles. There were six huts where the shot could have come from, maybe 3,000 men, and they stomped up and down, looking and sniffing and yelling—you know how it is, and nobody in our section of the hut knows a thing. Not a goddamned thing. Nothing. The Code of the Mafia, so to speak.

It wasn't until daylight that some n.c.o. noticed this stream of water coming from the base of the tank. About the size of my little finger, but it had been going, say, ten hours by that time. Amazing nobody heard it, but I supposed it was congealing on the way down and ice by the time it hit, but there it was, and what a sight! Like a giant man pissing, this great arch of water, and very pretty too, because it was turned shiny by the sun, the morning sun. It took them all day to fix it, and it gave the whole camp a great lift in spirits.

The camp commander started all sorts of investigations, made promises right and left, but nobody squealed on me. I thought I was probably a goner because I'd had a rough fight about a week before with a chap in my platoon named Butler and here was his chance to grab off a few days of leave by turning me in. I think he might have, but I think the rest of the section might have turned on him and killed him, and he had to think of that. Or maybe he was just a better guy than I thought he was.

Okay, I confess. I was the chap who shot the hole in the water tank. There must be a few around who remember that.

•◄►• *A Doctor or a Killer?*

My brother Arnold finished pre-med at University of Manitoba and they said he had to go into the army, but he'd go into an accelerated medical course. So there he is down at Queen's University. During the day he's taking all these speeded-up courses, how to patch up bodies that have been shot at or bombed or banged up, and he writes and says the course is very hard.

He also writes and says that a couple of nights a week and part of Saturday there he is with his bunch, out on the field drilling, marching, taking bayonet practice, all the things he's got to take—because, you see, when he gets out he's going to be an officer, and so he's taking an officer's course and a medical course too.

He used to get so mad. How crazy it is, he would say. All day I'm learning to fix up bodies and at night I'm taking bayonet practice to learn to kill people. What am I, a doctor or a killer? I'm a doctor, he says, and if I'm to be a doctor in war I should be using those hours at night and on Saturday to study medicine and not stick bayonets into dummies that are supposed to be men.

•◄►• *The Dentist's Teeth*

There was the air force, the navy and the army, my choices in that order, but every dentist had the same idea so I wound up in the army, commissioned as a captain.

New Brunswick was the frontier. The vast body of the citizenry, the poor, lived like dogs. What I mean, in my terms, nobody gave a damn about their teeth.

One day in camp this lumberjack fellow needed a dozen fillings, and I was going to freeze. He didn't have much, and what he had was a Christly mess. In goes the needle, and in those days it was like a horse needle, big and long. You could say mean-looking. In goes the needle, in, out, in, out, I was working fast and this fellow was stiff as a board and he's scared witless, his eyes are rolling and sweat coming off him and then the stuff starts to take effect. This was a new experience to this man, and a terrifying one. Finally his lower right jaw is frozen and he feels it, pats it, pokes it, bites down and that did it! He jumps up and yells, "You've ruined me. You're killing my mouth, you white-coat bastard. You're trying to starve me to death." You see, he couldn't feel his own gums, his lips, his chin.

Then he yells, "You Hitler bastard," and smashes me one. Knocks me head over heels, into the equipment tray, busting two teeth—what a mess—and he's heading out the door still yelling.

I knew the major was going to charge him, but I explained that this was a chap out of the bush who'd never been in a dentist's office before.

There were a lot like that. Not as bushy-tailed, but the first time in the office you had to watch your step. Better still, watch your mouth or you could get a mouthful of knuckles. It happened to others too.

There was this guy named Buller. I don't think he actually hated these Bohunk kids off the farm, kids of eighteen and nineteen. I'm not sure what his motives were—maybe he was just one of those guys who liked to entertain others, be a big shot, and these kids were his meatballs. Like the guy with the black face that you threw balls at in the circus to knock him into the water.

This Buller was a big guy, and a few of us tried to stop him tormenting but he was tough and he had this trick. In a fight, instead of hitting you in the face or stomach he'd give you a stiff right to the Adam's Apple. Sort of like a judo chop or a karate chop. I never saw anybody take one of those punches and be able to swallow food decently for several days. That's why we had to let him get away with it. In that outfit they'd just say, "Okay, put on the gloves." Everything was settled man to man, in the centre of the ring of us guys, on the parade square, or inside if it was lousy out. It was always murder. Buller was too tough.

Then a new draft came in, half a dozen guys, and one was just chocolate pudding for Buller. He was Hunkie through and through. Pure. I think he was the only guy I've seen that had no intelligence, actually none showing in his eyes. Mouth half open all the time. He sort of shambled like a bear walking. I wouldn't have trusted him to peel spuds in the cookhouse.

I noticed a funny thing, though. When these recruits were being taught to assemble their webbing and kit, this guy Ewasiuk, some name like that, he put his together like it was a simple puzzle. I knew he'd been around, but it sure didn't show.

Buller started in on him. About the third day. You know, dirty cracks, talking phony Polish to him. Calling him Hunyak, General Hunyak, leader of the Vegreville Army. Vegreville is in Alberta and has a lot of Ukrainians. He'd give him a hip, step in front of him in the mess line-up—all those little things.

This went on for a week and this guy Ewasiuk, his face never changed expression. And then one night, just before lights out, he grabbed Buller by the shoulders and gave him a shove that sent him reeling down the hut and he banged his head against the fire bucket. That was it. There had to be a fight.

But not that night. It was next day after dinner in the drill hall and the officers knew about it and so it was all on the up-and-up. There must have been 2,000 guys there. Everybody in camp. The word had got around. This was to be the fight of the century, Joe Louis against Jack Dempsey and poor Ewasiuk, this dumb Bohunk, was going to die. They'd scrape him off the cement.

After that build-up I guess I don't have to go on. I knew

how it was going to be when I saw them putting the gloves on Ewasiuk. Cool, boy, he was cool. I thought, "I wonder who the hell this Ewasiuk is?" Buller came out swinging and got knocked on his ass right off. I don't mean he went down, but he took a left hook that made him wonder what it was all about. He kept coming, though, and kept getting his block knocked off. Lefts, rights, one into the gut, on and on, and Buller was wandering around looking like he'd lost something. It was brutal, and this Ewasiuk didn't have a mark on him.

It was pretty quiet in there by this time because we were watching a guy getting the shit kicked out of him. And then Ewasiuk moved in once and the referee somehow knew and made a dive for him, but he was too late. Ewasiuk just sort of slipped him, and in about four seconds he broke Buller's nose, chopped him one in the throat, sank a right hand into his belly, which was sticking out like a beached whale and as Buller went down, he chopped him a terrible shot behind the right ear.

I think that finished Buller for the rest of the war. He never came back to our hut. Somebody said he had a busted voice box or something, and had been discharged. You could say it served the son of a bitch right, but it was an awful hard way to learn a lesson.

• ◀▶ • *What a Bayonet Can Do*

I'm sure there were battles where men actually used the bayonet on each other but, sorry, I never heard of one. I can't even imagine it. No thanks.

I know what a bayonet can do, though. We were taking training in Shilo and on this obstacle course there was a fence. Not too high, I'd say, five feet, perhaps. This chap missed or slipped or made a miscalculation, and instead of landing on his feet he fell to his knees and his bayonet went into his belly. For a minute we didn't know what was wrong with him, but when we started looking, yes, he'd punctured himself. It was a tiny hole about the size of a pencil and a bit blue around edges. By the time the ambulance came and got him back to the camp hospital he was dead. I can't remember ever being so shocked, because the guy said he wasn't hurt and wanted to finish the course with us.

The medical orderly at the hospital said the doctor told him the bayonet went in only about an inch and a half, into that soft part of the belly. But he was dead in maybe five minutes. Ten at the most.

·◄►· *Tank Training*

I doubt if any nation in the world, any nation of any importance, was so ill prepared for war as was Canada in 1939, and in that lumping I include the United States.

Let me give you an example. In 1940 we had no tanks. We used personnel carriers as tanks and some small French tanks, worth nothing, but inside of them you at least got the feeling of a tank. We'd practice gunnery and you must remember, the closest thing to a shoot-out in a Western movie is two tanks. In most battles where artillery and troops with anti-tank weapons were not involved, it was tank against tank. Maybe two on one, or troop against troop, squadron against squadron, but still his tank against my tank.

It was like kids in the schoolyards playing cowboys and Indians. You know, bang, bang, I gotcha, you're dead. We fought without tanks and without guns, naturally, but we were getting the feeling, and some of the lads would say they were getting pretty good at hitting the other fellow. You see, these were swirling, constant pseudo-battles. This went on for some time, this dummy practising of moving tanks shooting at each other.

Then we had a new officer, a Canadian who'd been wounded and shipped back, visit us. This was many months later, you see, and he'd been in retreat to Dunkirk and, I understand, the Western Desert and the early stages of the big tank battles there and he watched us practising, going through our simulated paces, and he nearly fell off his vehicle.

First, he told us that the tanks had to keep moving. Move, circle, advance at angles. Yes, we knew that. But he said when you shoot—and as I said, accuracy was the name of the game—you had to stop your tank. Immediately. Fire. Watch for your shell exploding. Correct. Fire again. If you missed once more, then get moving again because there you are, dead in the water, you understand, and in the next few seconds, it is you who will be hit. Your tank becomes the target. Stop, creep up to a hill, poke your snout over, fire.

He was most emphatic that a tank gunner when his tank is moving cannot hit another tank at 300 or 500 yards, less or more, while that other tank is moving. And here, for quite a while, this was what we had been doing. He said it was impossible, and if you did get a hit, it was an incredible shot.

Well, we had an expert, and when the division moved to Italy we could see he was right. Losses were horrendous sometimes, but a lot of it was from artillery, that goddamned .88, the finest weapon of the war. It was mobile, self-propelled, a big cannon of a thing for anti-aircraft or tank warfare, and the Germans knew how to use it.

In months I don't think I ever heard of one of our lads knocking out a Jerry in a straight duel when both were moving. Stop, aim, fire and shove another up the hole and fire again. That's the way it was done, and here, back in Canada in our innocence, we were doing it all the wrong way. I was always thankful that captain came along when he did. After a while if you keep repeating mistakes you can't correct them.

•◀▶• *Right on the Bull*

At this camp I was at in British Columbia there was a battle training school and they taught all sorts of things, but one was long-range firing. With a Bren. Machine gun. It was like this. About four hundred yards away there was this bit of woods and a truck would drive out, and about 100 feet behind it, it would tow a drogue. A drogue, that's a dummy. A dummy anything. A tank, a truck. All it was was cardboard, you understand, and that was the target.

This morning we had a new gunnery officer. He was a young kid out of officer training school, I guess, and I guess he got his signals crossed or didn't know, but when the truck came out from behind the woods he yelled, "Fire!" The machine gunner, this guy named Boyd, well, I guess he was concentrating so hard that he just let go a burst. At the truck. The drogue wasn't even in sight. You couldn't blame Boyd.

Anyway, every fourth bullet was a tracer so they could see how the firing was going, what the trajectory was, that sort of thing, and we watched—and I guess you can say with horror—this burst of maybe twenty, twenty-five bullets, and you could see it was perfect. Right on the bull. There were four guys in that truck, two in front, and two minding the towing gear. You get me?

Well, I'll be damned but we knew those guys were dead before they did. You could watch the tracers go in among them. I was driving the stand-by ambulance because they were using live ammo, and by the time we got down there, only about a few hundred yards, all four guys had breathed their last.

I've always wondered about one thing. If you can see tracers going away from you, can you see them coming *at* you? And if that is the way, then did any of these guys see those tracers coming? I mean, did they know they were going to be killed in the next second?

Remember, this wasn't in France. This was right in Canada — British Columbia.

•◂▸• *The Mountains*

I remember this kid, we called him Red. Orange hair and big splotches of freckles all over his face and big blue eyes. You know the type, and he was a real farm boy. If he was in television today he'd be type-cast as the farmer, the hayseed. Nothing was ever going to change him.

He was from Saskatchewan. We all were, for that matter, and Manitoba, and we were taking final training at Camp Shilo in Manitoba and then it was overseas for the company. But before we went everybody got a 48, a two-day pass, to go home and see the folks, wives or girls. It wasn't much, but by this time, after about five months in the army, you didn't expect much. There was always some idiot of a clerk in the orderly room, some lance jack, to say, "Don't you know there's a war on?" when anybody asked for extra time.

I remember Red. We'd been out this day in the hills, just tramping around and going through the obstacle courses and putting in time until they got our papers ready and we were all sitting on this ridge, just lying around in the snow and bullshitting and there was Red as usual, a little ways away from us and keeping quiet. He never did say much. His last name was Corrigan and he had red hair and he kept to himself, and that's about all I really knew about him. All anybody knew, I guess. I don't want to sound funny about this, but Red was always looking off into the distance as though he saw something the rest of us didn't. The sergeants and the lieutenant liked him because he was a damn good soldier.

I remember we were quiet and Red said, right out of the blue, he said, "I'm going out west to see the mountains." I guess somebody laughed and he turned on him and said, "You know, I've never seen mountains. Dreamed of them, but I've never seen them."

Okay, fine, he was a farm boy from Saskatchewan, maybe from some place around Regina where you can see for miles and he had a right to use his last 48 any way he wanted, but most people would have gone home to see their folks.

I thought later that mountains he had never seen were what Canada meant to him. You know, getting away from that farm, the work, the cold, the hot, getting into the cool of the mountains.

Yes, he got on the C.P.R. and he went to Banff and sat up all the way, train travel being what it was those days, and I think he had six hours there before he had to get on the train and come right back. Somebody asked him what he had done in Banff, and he said he'd just walked around and looked at the mountains and gone up a little road and then a trail and there was a waterfall and he'd looked at it and then he said he'd walked around and looked at the mountains again and then it was time to get on the train.

This was in February of 1944 and when we got to England we were split up into different units, and Allan, a guy from Port Arthur, he said that he and Red and a few others were put in with the Regina Rifles and got into combat in a hurry and Red got killed the second day. They were just walking along this road and Red just went down, just like that. Nobody even heard the shot, the sound. That's the way it was a lot. A sniper just picking out one guy of twenty, just like picking any card, and bang.

When I heard that, I was damn glad Red had seen his mountains, because if he'd got as far as the rest of us he'd have been pretty disappointed in some of those little hills the French call mountains.

Standing on Guard for Thee

Blacking Out Winnipeg ... What Six Good Men Could Have Done ... An Explosive Incident ... Defending the Skies over Halifax ... A German Spy in Halifax? ... Has There Been a Sinking? ... The Whole Coast Was Booby-Trapped ... To Cause a Forest Fire ... Sten Guns Against Battleships

---

In 1939 the combined land, sea and air might of Canada couldn't have defended Prince Edward Island from attack by any small and moderately armed European nation.

The navy consisted of a few ships, all old and tinpotty. The air force was just being whipped into some kind of organization and the magnificent Commonwealth Air Training Program was taking shape. The army was constantly growing, but was woefully ill-equipped. Tanks for training were 1918 French vintage. First World War machine guns and rifles were in use. Many men trained with wooden sticks and called them rifles. Training methods had not been perfected nor modern tactics fully assessed.

However, there was the spirit! That counted for a lot.

After Britain's glorious defeat at Dunkirk, Canada was Britain's main ally, and every available Canadian soldier was sent to England. Canada itself was left virtually undefended.

Coastal guns did appear on both coasts; they were not sufficient to repel invasion, but there they were, manned faithfully throughout the war, a symbol far more than a deterrent.

When a Japanese submarine threw 25 shells at the lighthouse on British Columbia's Estevan Point one Sunday morning—and missed with every one—the whole rather bizarre act was a shot in the arm. Canada had been attacked! But when German U-boats cut down shipping and warships in the Gulf of St. Lawrence and sank four ore boats and a dock only 20 miles from St. John's, Newfoundland, nothing was said. Secrecy, you know, although they couldn't stifle the news of the U-boat sinking of the Caribou, *the ferry between Newfoundland and Canada. Fire bombs, floated across the Pacific on high winds from Japan, landed in B.C., where they were intended to start forest fires. They didn't.*

Despite these isolated incidents, Canada fought her war at long distance. Safely out of range of the Japanese or German bomber bases, and with the German surface fleet contained in Europe, there was little danger. But throughout the struggle, thou-

sands manned the guns, the sighting posts, the radar stations, and carried out practice drills for air raids and evacuations even though they knew that the country was safe from enemy attack.

•◄►• **Blacking Out Winnipeg**

Do you think people really, even today, think about how dopey some of the things were? My old man told me this. In Winnipeg they were having big discussions. Should they order blackouts? Blackouts, for Christ sake, man! The nearest German bomber must have been 7,000 miles to the east and the nearest Japanese bombers must have been 9,000, and here are some of the world's greatest idiots wondering if there should be blackouts. And they're talking about air raid drills—Air Raid Precautions, the old man told me it was—and actually practising it.

•◄►• **What Six Good Men Could Have Done**

You know, right below Lytton on the Fraser River, there's two railway bridges. Right. The C.N. going from this bank to the other. The Canadian Pacific going other way. They sort of criss-cross. They guarded these bridges during the war but it was a farce. A goddamned farce. Half the time the guards were asleep, or down on the river fishing or playing cards, doing anything. I know, I used to fish at Lytton.

How many Germans were put in the can? Damn few. I'll bet there were ten times more poor little, big-eyed conscientious objectors with Bibles in prison camps than Germans. If Hitler had a brain in his head he could've easily had saboteurs landed in Vancouver by submarine. The defences were a joke. Row ashore with suitcases full of dynamite or whatever made the biggest boom. Get on a bus for Kamloops and get off at Siska Lodge. That's where the bridges are. Then sneak down and wire those goddamned bridges and boom, and I mean *boom!* It doesn't take all that much to blow a bridge, especially an old one. Not if you know dynamite. I handled it for years in the Kimberley mine, the Cominco mine, and I know what it can do.

Okay, so look at it this way. Everything for the Pacific war for Canada and all the war stuff made on the coast, it had to travel up the Fraser River by rail. Okay? Then you just pull the plug on that and you've done a lot to screw the war effort. And I say, if you really want to do the job up brown, you'd do the same to the two criss-crossing bridges on the Thompson. Then you'd double-screw them, because they couldn't get crews down from Kamloops or Calgary to help on the Siska Lodge bridges.

It would have been a snap. A goddamned snap. Six good men could have paralyzed half the country. Think of it. Half of Canada with about 100 sticks of the stuff. I worked with the stuff and I know.

•◄►• *An Explosive Incident*

There was this explosives plant outside Winnipeg at a place called Transcona but I didn't know that. I was home on furlough and the way things had been going in the two years I had been away, overseas and such, the British Houses of Parliament could have been there.

When I got home, well, the first thing I did was phone an old girlfriend of mine and yep, she was still around, still able and sure as hell willing, and so I borrowed my dad's car and picked her up and she wanted to go for a drive. Gas rationing being the way it was, I guess even an ordinary car ride was a big deal.

We drive out towards Transcona and she's getting hot and I'm getting horny and suddenly, and it's dark, remember, I see this big lighted gate and without thinking too much I wheel in, boom, right through and not stopping, and I ask her what this place is, and she doesn't know so I just drive a bit more until I come to a big parking lot. There are no cars on it, but it's lighted up.

I pile into the back seat of this old Dodge and she's in on top of me in a second, and away we go, jiggy-jig-jig, and it's going fine.

Then what? I hear smashing glass and I look up and there are about sixteen guys with guns, rifles, uniforms, the whole frigging army and one guy has just bust in the driver's window and they reach in and haul us out. And I mean haul us out. Like we were sacks of flour. Handcuffs, the whole bloody issue.

There's more goddamned bloody bastards yelling questions at me and I don't know what it's all about, but finally we get it sorted out. It seems I'm liable for the firing squad or life behind bars or a good kick in the ass, whichever hurts more, because I'm loose in a war plant. One that makes dynamite or forcite or H.E. [*high explosive*] or something, and there are about sixteen acts of Parliament which prohibit all this.

It takes about half an hour to get the yelling stopped, but they finally let us go, get back in the car and escort us out and blah blah blah blah. At the gate, and this is no lie, the head guard, or night superintendent or something, says, "Don't be too hard on my boys, soldier. I guess they did act like a bunch of kids, but you just provided them with the first bit of activity, real action, they've ever had at this plant." I laughed and said it was okay.

But to this day I can see some little shaver saying, "Grandpa, what did you do in the war?" and the old guy says, "Why, Johnny, I once stopped a soldier from screwing a girl inside a dynamite plant in Winnipeg."

•◄►• *Defending the Skies over Halifax*

I don't think Mark Twain could have written it and Charlie Chaplin played it any funnier than it was in real life when Canada suddenly realized that there was going to be a war and we'd be in it.

There was one case I remember where an anti-aircraft battery, right on the day Germany did the dirty deed, this battery was shifted from Kingston in Ontario to Halifax. Now, that was tactically a sound move. But who was going to attack Halifax when a German bomber's range was something like 300 or 400 return? And it took weeks, I believe, to get the position prepared for the battery.

But do you know what that battery consisted of? That battery was composed of one gun. One pop gun. One little pop gun to drive the Germans from the skies. If you knew what was happening, you didn't know whether to laugh or cry, and it was months before things began to take hold and people started acting like rational human beings.

•◄►• *A German Spy in Halifax?*

Early in the war, about spring of '42, I was based at Shellburne and I was going up to Halifax for the weekend, on leave, and the commanding officer said he had some secret, confidential material that could be delivered only by a commissioned officer to the admiral's secretary in Halifax. He gave me this briefcase all beautifully sealed and with a sticker on it reading *For the Eyes of the Admiral Only* in red letters. Very hush-hush, very secret.

So with the briefcase clutched to my breast I took the bus to Halifax and went to the Nova Scotian Hotel and in those days, as you know, every city was jammed and it was quite the rule to put two complete strangers in the same room. Everybody just expected that, of course, and you were often lucky to get a room at all. It turned out my roommate was a civilian, a big powerful man of about fifty-five or sixty who appeared of Teutonic strain, and when he asked me my name and what I did and I told him, he said, "My name is Albrecht," in the most guttural German-tainted English I think I have heard. But what I liked about him was that very prominently displayed on the dresser was a large bottle of Seagram's V.O., and I hadn't seen that for a long time. It was almost impossible to obtain.

So I sat on one bed and he on the other and he poured me a drink and himself one and we promptly proceeded to demolish the bottle, and in very quick time indeed. It was a very hot afternoon in early June and so I opened the window but I didn't move the briefcase with the secrets, just left it lying on the windowsill. Well, we finished the booze and I figured I better get over to the admiral, and when I looked, the briefcase was gone. Just not there. I ran to the window and looked down five floors to the street—nothing there. I had been to the can once so I thought, maybe the German took it. Maybe he was a spy. But as you can imagine, my brain wasn't working all that well, so I ran downstairs, out the lobby and there was this very formidable older gentleman in a uniform, the doorman, and I asked if he had seen a briefcase. Yes, he informed me, he most certainly had. In fact, it had just missed him by inches. And no, he didn't have it. The manager of the hotel had it, and it was now in the manager's safe.

And do you think I could get it off the manager? I did, oh yes, I did, but it took about fifteen minutes and I practically had to get down on my knees. Then I dashed upstairs again to see this Mr. Albrecht, who I had become rather suspicious of. He had been quite outgoing when we were drinking and he had told me he was a British agent, that he had just returned from Spain where he had bought some material of war in competition with Nazi agents and that he was on a Swiss passport. In fact, he showed me the passport. That much was correct. But the whole thing just didn't ring true. Of course, a bottle of rye on a hot day . . .

Well, when I got to the room there was no Mr. Albrecht. No clothes in the closet where they had been, no shaving equipment in the bathroom, no luggage, nothing. In fact there was no evidence that there had been anybody in that room that day except myself. Except for one thing—the empty bottle of V.O. in the wastebasket.

By this time I was quite convinced. He had told me he had just arrived that morning, and this was only about three o'clock and he had disappeared, bag and baggage, and where did he go? Why did he check in and then just leave?

What the hell was it all about? You see, it was a good story, but it didn't have an end. I never did find out. Was he an English spy? Or a German one? Did he drop the briefcase to an accomplice who couldn't get it because it fell right beside this big fellow of a doorman? How did he know I had the documents? How did he know I would stay at the Nova Scotian? And if he did know, how was it arranged he would get the same room as I did? And, in fact, how in hell did he get a bottle of Seagram's V.O. when even the King of England might have had trouble getting one in Halifax in those days?

That story has troubled me ever since. Baffled me.

•←→• *Has There Been a Sinking?*

This was in '42. I think my cousin said August. The German subs were all around the St. Lawrence River, Cabot Straits, Straits of Belle Isle and they sure used their torpedoes. One day five ships were sunk. I know two American destroyers were sunk one day too.

My cousin is one of those screwy Frenchmen and he says there were spies along the St. Lawrence and they'd tell the Germans by radio that the ships were coming. It makes a bit of sense, doesn't it? Like if you saw a ship loading tanks at Quebec City, wouldn't that be a better ship to sink than one loaded with lumber or apples or something? Or if you saw a ship loaded with troops, wouldn't you want to get that one more than one with just a lot of flour?

This cousin of mine had a cousin, not my cousin, and he said he saw one German submarine come to the surface and the guys go for a swim. Now that's not so crazy. He says the guy swears it was that way. For about an hour. Right there by where the old lighthouse used to be, I think he said.

Anyway, this screwy French cousin, Maurice, says one morning the subs got a ship down by Natashquan. From shore somebody sees it and calls the mayor. He's the boss of the town, you phone the boss. He phones the airport at Mont Joli, like for Christ sakes send a bomber and get that bastard, and Mont Joli, the air force there, they phone or telegraph or radio or something to Ottawa. They say can we? Can they what? For Christ sakes, can they send out this bomber with the bombs? And the mayor tells my cousin that Ottawa phones the police guy at Natashquan. Has there been a sinking? Damn right, I guess the cop says. Just off the wharf, or something like that, but he makes sure they understand. So Ottawa phones Mont Joli and they send out the bomber. Bzzzzzzz, low over the water, up high maybe looking for the shadow of the shape in the water. But there's no sub there now. If he wanted, he could be 40 miles away.

So you want to know how long since the mayor phoned to say the ship had been sunk until Mont Joli sent that bomber over? It took seven hours. You ask anybody who was there at Natashquan. They'll tell you. Seven hours.

•◄►• *The Whole Coast Was Booby-trapped*

The Pacific Coast Militia Rangers. A guerrilla-type thing, local vigilante units along the coast, cooperating with regular types and acting as scouts for the military if the Japanese landed.

At the height of it, there were 18,000 people from the American boundary right up to Alaska and in through there. Right, 18,000 people, all fishermen, loggers, people in mining, in every town, village, city, inlet, fishing camp, logging outfit, mine along the coast and it eventually spread right into the Interior, to the Okanagan and the Cariboo and through there. There were 120 companies, with a captain at the head of each company.

When I came along Tommy Taylor, the head of it, had a small headquarters staff and he was a lieutenant colonel and he wanted a magazine, a training manual and it wasn't to be in all the military jargon. Simple, straightforward language that these men in essential industries—mining, fishing, logging—could understand. I was to put out training stuff in the language of the woods, so loggers and miners and fishermen, although they might have different languages for their trade, would be able to understand each other.

I travelled up and down the coast doing this, and the thing that is not known, and has never been known, was that the whole damned coast was booby-trapped. In mines and logging you had people who knew powder, were familiar with explosives, and every bridge, every logging bridge and trestle, every place where there could have been an ambush, these guys had put their booby traps. And they had radios and had worked out special ways to communicate over long distances, if the Japanese ever did show up.

It was made up of young people exempted from military because they were in essential industry, and of older guys too, but what was important was they knew the woods. The coastal rain forests. They knew how to dress, dry pack, a very practical outfit. What's that special rifle so good for the bush? Yeah, the Winchester 30:30, and the Canadian government bought up every available 30:30 in North America. We also got the first Stens, small machine guns for close infighting, to come out this way and every ninth man was issued one. But the important thing was, these men knew the bush and anybody invading a coastal rain forest would be in real trouble.

They were a guerrilla group, to go into action before the regular army could move in. And up there in some of those really godforsaken places, what was more important than all the regular training in the world was their knowledge of guns, their toughness, and, because this was their country, their local knowledge. They knew every trail, every place of ambush. As time went on, they were also trained in commando tactics and there were ten travelling commando instructors going around all the time.

The character of each company depended on the area. Like in West Vancouver or Victoria, its companies would be for a lot of open fighting, but at Port Alice or anywhere up the coast, like that, ambush and booby-trapping and fighting like Indians—that would be their job. Or like in Pemberton, they had a company mostly of Indians. I would have liked to see those buggers in actions, real bush-wise.

The whole outfit was quite a deal, and I know I shouldn't say I'm sorry they didn't get into action. But I know if they had, they'd have given the Japanese one hell of a scrap.

•◄►• *To Cause a Forest Fire*

Not too many will remember, but the Japanese set off these fire balloons. From Japan. They were about 60 feet in diameter and very light and they had a heating arrangement, a sort of small heater that swung below and got the balloon up high into the jet stream and it didn't take long to cross to our coast. They were made of waxed paper.

They had a sort of piece of metal rod hanging down and on it were metal washers about three inches in diameter and half an inch thick, and when the balloon came down and the metal rod hit a tree branch, some obstruction, then it would tip and some metal in the washers would leak out and react with the metal rod and it would burst into flame and cause a forest fire.

They didn't do much damage but they ranged from northern B.C. to California and we knew of two or three fires where we just couldn't pinpoint the cause. But we weren't positive. They'd certainly cause a fire if they landed right.

Some even got over the mountains, right into Saskatchewan, and the odd one is still being picked up by hunters or prospectors in the bush after all these years.

•◄►• *Sten Guns Against Battleships*

The nearest Japs must have been 3,000 miles away, and here were we, stuck up on Cape St. James. That's as far north as you can go on Vancouver Island, the end of the world. The very end. Give me Siberia any time.

As I recall, we were to stop a Jap attack with a handful of Sten guns. They'd throw a 9-mm. slug about 50 feet and then it would start to tumble. They called it the plumber's dream, and I think it cost about 9 bucks to make one. They were good in house-to-house fighting, but not so hot holding off the battleships of the Japanese Navy.

I remember one sergeant telling us, "Now look. If we are invaded, there is nothing we can do. Not a damn thing. Not a solitary thing. The only thing is to take to the woods and get the hell out of here."

Trains

*Everybody Travelled by Train . . . I Always Got a Bunk
. . . They Saved Our Lives . . . Supermen . . . A Man's Kind
of Woman . . . The Wild Men . . . Following Him Around*

*There was no other way to go. Men with briefcases and bowler
hats and important looks had priority on the few tiny Trans-
Canada planes. There was never enough gas to travel any
distance by car, if you had the tires to carry you there. Buses were
few and far between. But there was the train. During the war
Canada's railroads hauled hundreds of thousands of people back
and forth across the country.*

*There were signs: "Is This Trip Necessary?" In other words,
"Please travel less, folks, because our transportation system is
overloaded." But it was a restless time: a mother and two young
daughters going from Winnipeg to Claresholm to be near the air
force station where Daddy was; the troops, by the tens of thousands, travelling back and forth on 48-hour leaves, 72's, furloughs,
embarkations; the construction workers heading for the Alaska
Highway or a munitions plant at Transcona or a parachute factory
near Windsor. On the move, back and forth, endlessly, a nation on
the move.*

*But each trip was an experience. Every piece of railroad
equipment that could be wired, stuck, nailed or jammed together
was put into use. Soldiers, sailors, airmen, young wives, youths,
old men and women, good people and bad people, sharks and
sharpies, farmers and flunkies, businessmen and housemaids all
travelled together, and there was a spirit of camaraderie, a feeling
of good times. Everybody talked to each other, a bottle would be
passed around cheerfully, card games started and nobody fought,
pushed or cheated to get into the diner—which usually had three
sittings—and the best meal in Canada then was the C.P.R.'s dinner
of roast beef and Yorkshire pudding at $1.50. Or was it $1.25?*

*For many people, those train journeys are their most vivid
memories of the war.*

•◆• Everybody Travelled by Train

I was a "butcher." I sold things on the trains during the war. The
old-timers on the run still used the name "butcher" and, funny,
but I never asked them ever where that name came from.

Canadian National. Winnipeg to Vancouver, back to Winnipeg, and that was a long haul. My boss in Union Station, Winnipeg, when he hired me he said, "You can work your own hours, but just make sure I don't hear any complaints against you."

It worked this way. You sold sandwiches, ham, cheese, egg, soft drinks, pop, soda and coffee you'd get from the dining car. That's the main things you sold, and then there were other things too. Like you sold playing cards. Those prairie runs were long and the guys, the servicemen, were always wanting cards. You sold French safes. Maybe somebody wanted to screw a little CWAC in the men's toilet late at night. I'd keep some on my head, under my round hat. I'd sell a few, but not too many. Whiskey—if you could get hold of whiskey you could sell it and make a lot of money. Candy. Hair pins. Nail files. Writing paper. You stocked up on stamps, but I always sold them for what I paid for them. I think it was some Federal law which said you couldn't make a profit on them, something like that. You sold hankies, and I got some black market silk stockings once and made a fortune. If you wanted, but I didn't, you could buy crooked dice and sell 'em.

What you did was this. You sold everything you thought would sell. Just like a grocery store or a drugstore. Remember, she was wartime then and everything was hard to get. You scrounged and scrunched around, getting what you could, and took everything, because you could damn near sell anything them days.

Everybody travelled by train. No gas, you see, for private cars, and the roads were still pretty lousy for bus travel although people did travel by bus. The trains were jammed. Troops, troops and more troops. Women with kids following their husbands around. I don't know how many million times I've put a baby's bottle in my big coffee urn and warmed it for some mother. I had a little rig I built in so the bottle would sit in straight up. Everybody travelling, going to new jobs, leaving home, Christ, you name it. I've seen people stand up in the aisles in the coach cars between Winnipeg and North Brandon, about three hours. Just no seats, and that train swaying and swaying along on that lousy roadbed. Anyway, this is where I made my money.

I'd be under way, going through, soon as the wheels got rolling and I'd work until eleven at night, and I'd be making my first coffee run about six in the morning. I'd sell out twice on that one. Everyone wanted coffee. You could sell every ham, cheese, jelly sandwich you could carry too. People didn't have all that much money or they didn't want to stand in line waiting for the diner, three sittings three times a day on those trains, and it was murder for the kitchen and the waiters.

Then I'd sell pop, Kik and orange and other stuff, and comics. By God, I nearly forgot the comic books. *Famous Funnies, Brick Bradford,* I think. *Lone Ranger.* Movie books too. *Silver Screen,* ever heard of it? All second hand, I'd buy them all from the Jew second-handers and I'd sell them for 50 cents. Bitch, bitch, that was a high price and the guys would say I was rooking them. I'd say, "Okay, if you feel that way, you keep these in good shape, just like you got 'em off me and I'll buy back from you, twenty cents each." Okay, that was fine. What I was doing to those dumb kids was renting those books to them. I could buy a comic book for two bits and in two weeks, until it was ready to fall apart, I could rent it out for about three bucks. And movie magazines too.

You could count on three days between The Peg and Vancouver, travelling time and my getting ready and cashing-out time, and I'd get about four or five hours' sleep a day. That's all. I worked like a dog, but boy, I was nobody's dog. I was making good money, up to 200 dollars a week, and nobody but me knew how much.

I guess you could say that my job was about the lowest on a train. Even the nigger [the porter] would try and give me lip, and some of these guys working on war jobs, on the big contracts, they'd give me the lip too. Making big money sawing boards and hammering them together. Shit, any twelve-year-old kid can do that. They'd be travelling to another job or something and they'd have these big rolls and I've seen a smart-ass peel off a hundred when all he's buying is a sandwich and an orange. I'd just peel off four twenties and a ten and a five and dump the rest in change in his hand and to hell with him. I know he's got fives and deuces in that roll. I don't care. I could cash a 1,000-dollar bill. I never did.

People would say, kindly, why didn't I go work in a ship-yard, or for Boeings on the coast or somewhere. They could see I was a little too old for the army, so why didn't I get that big money while I could, instead of balancing up and down those swaying cars. I just would say I like to help people.

I could have said I was doing all right and if I'd wanted to, I could have put down cash for the first Cadillac to roll off the assembly line in Detroit when that old war was finished. I never did, though. Just kept my mouth shut on matters like that.

***

•◆• *I Always Got a Bunk*

Here I was, twenty-three, right out of university and I thought I had the best job in the air force. I loved to travel and that's the thing my parents didn't like about it. They didn't think it was right to travel with all those men, a girl like me. Looking back, I have to admit I was pretty green to the world, but I learned.

I'd be on the road 15 or 20 days a month, just carrying documents from Toronto to Winnipeg or Montreal to Moncton, travelling first class. There was always one thing. You see, the railroad would see me as a lieutenant, but they wouldn't catch on that I was female. I don't think they ever did.

During wartime it was nothing for the C.P.R. to double-book you. Two persons to a lower bunk and you took your chances. Triple-booking was common too. Why they did it, I'll never know. They just did, trip after trip after trip, but if you got at the head of the line and were in first, you usually got that bunk. Sometimes you had to stare down some other officer, but chivalry always came through and I always got a bunk.

Sure, I used to get suggestions. Let's share it. A bunk is good enough for two. Let's not waste a good bunk with just one person. I was a little prude, I guess, but I never went for those suggestions. Now, it probably would be different.

I only lost once. To a colonel, and he wasn't backing up an inch. I was only a lieutenant and that was that, in his figuring, and he didn't want any double arrangement either. Under the circumstances—long ride, cold night, hard chairs—I just might have gone for any suggestion, but it wasn't coming. Not from that one.

•◆• *They Saved Our Lives*

It wouldn't be exactly right to say that everything was rosy for anybody. It wasn't for me. Not in Edmonton and this was in 1941. My husband was dead and I worked in a plant making uniforms. The owner may have been making a fortune, but it was all going into the cash drawer. I had a girl sixteen and a boy thirteen and I knew if I could get to Vancouver, where my brother was in war work, I'd be okay.

We had really nothing to sell and after shipping suitcases to Vancouver we had not enough for fares so my daughter said, "Mom, we can hitchhike." This was in late September or October and what a sight we must have made. We got to Banff in car rides, but half a day or so there and I knew we'd have to hitchhike on a train. So we waited until a freight train came through and there was this open door. I boosted my daughter and son up into the car with a couple of sacks we had and then I had to figure how to get up, and I couldn't, and then the train started to move and I couldn't let the kids go and they couldn't jump, so I grabbed on to the ladder at the end of that car.

Did I say it was cold? It was bitter cold, with a bit of snow, and I'm hanging on to the ladder with bare hands, this steel ladder and I can't climb up and I know I have to drop off soon. And then this brakeman is coming along the top of the train and he hears the kids bawling and he runs down to the caboose and yanks a whistle and the train stops. He and another man come running up and they take the kids and me into the caboose where it's warm and feed us. And that journey is a long, long way, and it's cold and snowing most of the way, and we just wouldn't have survived.

At Kamloops the brakeman passed us on to the next brakeman taking over. We got to Vancouver because that brakeman passed us on to another brakeman. Those three or four railroad men saved our lives. Saved our lives, and that's as sure as I'm sitting here with you this afternoon.

•◄►• *Supermen*

We were travelling east, heading overseas, a boiling hot summer day and I can't remember why we weren't in our summer issue, but there we were in our heavy battledress. A wonder some jerk didn't make us wear overcoats. To top it off, there were about 120 or so in one of those 1908 immigrant cars, the kind with the cooking stove at each end, and there were probably seats for 80 or so guys. A real madhouse, and we'd come all that way from Calgary like that. What a scruffy lot.

The train stopped at one of those places on the top of Lake Superior, Marathon or some place like it, and we all got out to breathe some air and scratch.

Now here's what happened. All of a sudden, out of the bush down a trail come this bunch of guys. About 40 of them, I'd say, and every bloody one was a giant, six-foot-two, six-foot-four. You never saw such a bunch. All fair-haired, blue-eyed, thighs like hams and tanned like Charles Atlas, Mr. World, and we thought, "Christ, who *are* these guys?"

We caught on quick because a couple of ginky little Veterans Guards, about sixty, were herding them along. Better still, they were just following. They had rifles, sure, but they probably hadn't fired one at anyone since 1918. We caught on quick because of the guards, but also because of those hats these guys were wearing, the kind German troopers wore. We'd seen them a hundred times in newsreels, you know, and here they were, going down to the lake for a swim. Well, Jesus Christ!

We asked one of the guards who these guys were, and he said they were of the Eighth Army, Rommel's supermen, Hitler's elite, and they'd been captured in North Africa. The desert war was winding up then. Here were these supermen, and I do mean supermen, and they looked at us as if we were common clay. The way we looked I guess we were. A pretty scruffy lot.

Then the whistle tooted and we piled back on, into our sweatbox, and we sat around quiet for a while and then somebody said what we were all thinking. He said, "God, do we have to fight guys like that?" It kept us thinking for a while.

That's not the end of the story, though. In Normandy when we were taking hundreds of prisoners at a crack, just digging them out of culverts and nunneries and old stables, I thought of that bunch of supermen. The men we were herding into compounds weren't the same breed. They never are. Bullets flying around, body lice, no food for a day or two and that cheap brandy everybody was drinking, and the smoke and the stink, our stink and theirs—it takes just about every bit of parade square out of a man. Most of the German boys we picked up were about as scruffy a lot as you could find, and I don't think I saw one superman in all that time. I guess maybe we got them all in North Africa. Just as well anyway. They wouldn't have liked it around Falaise.

•◄►• *A Man's Kind of Woman*

My husband was a government inspector and when they were building all those training stations in the West, and I think I was in every one from Gimli, Manitoba, to Penhold, Alberta, south of Calgary, Jerry would have to be there.

He would leave for a new job, say, a week or two before the old one was finished, and then some time later he'd come back and give his final inspection, and it was always little Jeanie, that's me, to wrap up everything and move on to the next job, and it was usually half the continent away.

It wasn't the travelling, I mean by train, that got me down, but the getting ready to go. Someone would always help me, some lady I'd have met in the district, but I really didn't know too many. I'm not too much the sort of person who gets into neighbourhood things. I still don't, I guess. I'm more a man's kind of woman.

I used to like the long trips because you got to know the fellows on the train. They were all in and around my age, about twenty, in around there, soldiers, sailors, air force fellows and those were the ones I liked best. They were like the kids I went to high school with at St. John's, and we'd have a lot of fun.

In the morning I'd have breakfast in the diner and it was easy to sit at a table with some of the guys. You know, four chairs to a table in the diner and you could start talking and find where they were and go down after breakfast. I used to get a kick if there was an officer across the aisle or something and he'd see me talking like crazy with some cute sailor and he'd look severe, mad, because I wasn't giving him the eye. I didn't like officers.

I always had Craigie with me—he was two then and the guys in the coach cars would be surprised that a little thing like me would have a kid. Craigie's thirty-five now and lives in Vancouver, an engineer. I always had this figure, like my husband used to say, the sand was in all the right places, and you remember skirts were pretty high then and I had a little velvet kind of a thing with white fur trim at the neck and the neck was kind of dished and I never was short down in that department. This friend of mine, a friend of Jerry's really, a guy he did some business with, he got me all the nylons I wanted—he'd send me ten or so pair a month and nylons in those days—gold, solid pure gold.

Craigie? Oh, sometimes I took him with me and sometimes I'd give him to a porter to look after. Those black fellows didn't make hardly any money, you know, and if I gave him 5 dollars at the start he was my slave. Jerry always made sure I had lots of money. Sometimes an old lady would take him and look after him, you know, the grandmother bit. I didn't mind.

I'd be back in the coach all day and we'd have sing-songs and play cards, and at Moose Jaw, for one place, you could run across the street to a hotel and grab as many bottles as they'd give you and then there would be a party. They called it Moose Jaw Green. They meant the beer was green, brewed one day and sold the next. It made you go to the bathroom a lot.

At night when they turned down the lights sometimes I'd stay and cuddle up with some fellow I'd got to like, somebody maybe that reminded me of the fellows back at school. They were just like a bunch of kids. It felt good to be held close and the train going banging along and swaying sort of, and the two of us cuddling up and whispering, but I never let them go very far. They were just kids anyway, no more than my age.

Oh, sometimes, once or twice, we'd sneak back to my sleeper, if it was a guy I really liked and if I was really feeling that way, but I'd always make him get out at about five o'clock in the morning. I had this little wrist watch Jerry gave me which glowed in the dark.

I did that for more than two years, just as long as Jerry was supervising those air force stations, seeing that the contractor was doing the job. It was fun and I met a lot of swell guys. It was a lot of fun.

Most of them knew I had a baby boy and a lot saw my husband when I'd meet him at the station and give him the big embrace, but that didn't matter. I liked them all, those fellows.

A lot of times the guys would ask for my address. They'd want to meet me if they were in the town I was going to be in, or the city, or they wanted to write me, and I always gave them my name. I'd write it out for the sailors on the inside of their cute hats in ink, but of course I never gave out exactly my right name and I never gave them my right address. I didn't think that was right.

•◄►• *The Wild Men*

I can only speak of northern Ontario, of course, because that was where I was; but men would come out of the bush. They'd been working cutting pulp, trapping, a bit of guiding and fishing or just living by their wits, you know, because we were still in the Depression, more or less. This was '40, '41. These were men who lived lonely lives, maybe into a town, Marathon or Dryden, two or three times a year for a big steak, a big drunk and the biggest girl they could find.

So they came out and joined the army. Always the army. I guess they couldn't understand aircraft or boats, but they certainly knew what a rifle was. At the town they'd be signed up and given a travel voucher and meal tickets and it was usually three or four travelling together.

We had a lot of people travelling the trains in those days— Trans-Canada [Airlines] was just a puppy—cabinet ministers, civil servants, high military officers, businessmen, many, many of them, ordinary people going back and forth. And you'll remember the service in those days. Superb. World-famous. Really, I mean it. I doubt if any railroad could compare with it. Those table covers, thick and white, and the rose in the vase, the silver cutlery, and some of it is collectors' stuff now and the service, my God, the service. We could have worked in the world's finest hotels, any time, I assure you, and when you were served by us, by God, you'd been served. Hah! I remember getting a 10 cent tip from the Anglican primate of all Canada. You took things home like that and framed them. T-I-P. Canadians never knew the meaning of the word then.

The freshest food. Lake Superior trout, right out of the water. Winnipeg goldeye. I once saw an English colonel eat four orders for breakfast. The finest beef, freshest vegetables. Coffee, thick cream—ask for anything and if it was possible, you got it. And all this was done, swaying and banging and rattling and bumping over those bloody rails, but the atmosphere could have been in the finest hotel in Monte Carlo.

We also put on a daily sideshow. I'm going back to these woodsmen, the soldiers-to-be with their dining car tickets, like cinema tickets. We'd try and put them in the big table at the back, in the corner where the galley starts. Not out of sight, but maybe out of line of sight, but it didn't always work. They'd sit down at noon and one would reach out with one hand and clean out the celery, the olives, everything, off the appetizer plate, and sometimes you'd hear another fellow say, "Why, you son of a bitch ...." Or one would hold up an olive and say, "For Chris' sake, what's this thing?" We served soup in small cups and they'd drink it and as we'd pass by, they'd hold out the cups for more. *Oliver Twist,* right out of *Oliver Twist.* You could count on filling the bread and bun basket three or four times. We always gave them beef whether they asked for it or not, and this is the truth, I'm telling you the truth, they would clean a plate in five, six, never more than eight sweeps. Some, I'm sure, did not know the use of a fork, or had been in the bush so long they'd forgotten how.

The C.P.R. fed well, but it was not used to these men. No, these were men of a different breed. Call them Canada as effete Europeans imagine us, I guess. Something very much like that. Not monsters, not bullies, but strong men of the bush.

Another thing. We always took the finger bowls off the table before they sat down. I never felt I was confident enough to explain to some fellow out of the bush just what a finger bowl was, and I'm quite sure he wouldn't have believed me.

I'd often have people, and often American tourists in the summer, ask me who these men were, and I'd tell them they were men going to Port Arthur to enlist in the army. The train was the only means of transportation, I'd say, as if to apologize. But often they'd ask, "But who *are* they?" I'd say, simply, that they were trappers, lumberjacks, the like, and they'd lean back and smile and

I knew why. I was telling them, and they were seeing, everything they had read about Canada, the north, the woods, the wild men. I think it probably was the highlight of their whole trip.

This lasted for about two years and then I guess the woods were drained of these men because we never saw many more after 1942 or so.

Yes, it was quite an experince to see a man take a large dinner roll and squeeze it like a steel mill-hammer into a small pellet and pop it into his mouth, or use a spoon to eat a large plate of roast beef, potatoes and string beans. The Yorkshire pudding seemed to baffle them but they ate it anyway, just because it was on the plate.

One thing I should mention. I would be remiss if I didn't. These men were always polite. They actually caused us less trouble than men with ten times their education, wealth and, of course, breeding. They took everything that came along, and smiled.

•◄►• *Following Him Around*

It was this cold night, bitterly cold, and I was on a short run to Brandon. Mixed freight and they'd stuck a couple of passenger cars to deadhead out for the train in on Friday afternoon which would pick up a couple of hundred troops from Shilo going into Winnipeg. Shilo was a big military camp.

It was about then when I came down Higgins and headed over to the depot to check in and I saw this little thing of a girl standing in the station, and I wondered at the time. I didn't know of any trains coming in, going out or what, but there she was with two small kids. One was maybe three and the other was a baby, and she looked no more than eighteen or so, in a thin coat and galoshes and the kids quiet, not crying or anything. I guess I didn't think any more of it.

We're due for the light at eleven and there's a lot of work to do although they've got the train made up okay. That was something in those days. Anyway, I thought nothing more of her and when we get to Portage about one and let a troop train go by, I'm walking along—and I see her sitting at the window of one of those empty passenger coaches. In the dark. It was spooky. Those two cars were not lighted and they had no heat and it must have been 10, 15 below out and there she was. How she ever got the door open I don't know, and I never asked, but I took a yard worker with me and we went in and she talked a bit of half English but mostly Ukrainski, and I sent the other fellow running for the brakeman and he came up and he could talk to her.

Left: Clad in his first set of army long-johns, this soldier signs up, and if he survives, his smile will be twice as wide six years later when he is discharged. In the first two months of the war, more than 58,000 men joined the army.

Below: Any old soldier will tell you this is an early-war picture, noting the civilian auto used as transport, the firing in an open field (at Long Branch, Ontario) and the rifles used—several makes, mostly World War One vintage. He would be right: the picture was taken in November, 1940.

Above: The most unsung of the 750,000-man Canadian Army was the Veterans' Guard, almost exclusively veterans of the First World War who wanted to get into the war but were too old for combat. These troops, on parade in Toronto in 1940, had duties protecting bridges, P.O.W. camps and fortifications, and did a thousand and one "joe jobs."

Below: Perhaps the most frustrated of Canada's 1,040,000 armed forces were the men of the Royal Canadian Artillery, manning coastal defence anti-aircraft guns on both coasts, while the Germans and the Japanese were several thousand miles away.

Above: Thirty-two years ago when a Japanese naval invasion of the West Coast was feared, this gun turret was built in Vancouver harbour. Long since deactivated, it is now a plaything for adventurous boys. Several emplacements were built, but none fired a shot in anger.

Below: Through low but punishing swells H.M.C.S. Santa Maria, *a seine boat of the Fisherman's Reserve, pushes up the inland waters of British Columbia, alert for danger in 1942. Danger never came but the ships, manned by fishermen in their requisitioned small craft, kept the faith.*

Left: After a long flight to German targets, a bomber crashes on landing, blowing up in a pillar of flame. In Bomber Command, 16,000 Canadians died, the vast proportion on operations but many as in this holocaust. But still they flew to the very end.

Toughened by two months of war—although usually a week in battle was enough—Sergeant Ben Landriault of the famed Toronto Scottish pauses for a break "somewhere in Normandy," as official despatches used to put it. Canadians went in on D-day and fought almost continuously until the last Nazi flag was hauled down.

Opposite: The Spitfire. Winner of the Battle of Britain. Small, fast, heavily armoured. And deadly. No other aircraft produced more heroes—and no other machine devised in war became such a hero.

Above: Closing in, and in moments the submarine will be dead. One officer told me he had made 13 trips to Ireland and never so much as "smelled" a German sub. Others had a kill on the first trip. The fortunes of war.

Below: Grisly bags of evidence are carried ashore at a British base by Canadian naval ratings, proof that their ship had sunk a German U-boat. So meticulous were authorities that they demanded evidence—particularly bits of human remains—be shown.

Above: "You kept your eyes peeled on those skies and you never stopped while you were in the box," said an anti-aircraft gunner on a troopship. So from St. John's to Derry, Liverpool, Murmansk, Durban, they stood to their guns and waited.

Below: Firing party ready. Shots blast out in the chilly Icelandic air and more Canadians of the North Atlantic Squadron are laid to rest. Casualties aboard the corvettes, frigates and destroyers on convoy duty over three million square miles of dirty ocean were not all that high, but weather conditions were terrible—described as the worst ever experienced in modern sea war.

Top right: Six Japanese Canadian fishboats are tethered to a government vessel in the Fraser River after being seized in 1942.

Top left: Torn from their coastal homes, separated from their families, Japanese were allowed to work as loggers in B.C. woods for a few dollars. While bitter at losing their hard-won possessions, most accepted the wartime measure stoically.

Below: At large Tashme camp, 110 miles east of Vancouver in the mountains, several thousand Japanese Canadians lived for years behind wire. The Japanese ran the camp themselves, but the huts were flimsy and the winters cold. Most Canadians outside B.C. did not realize the extent of the forced relocation.

The same old story. She said she'd come from Sandy Lake, that's up in the hill and marsh country northwest. The solid Ukraine. She'd married a boy from her district, he'd been pulled in by the army, and now she was following him around 'stead of going home to her folks, or his. She was going to Shilo and she'd seen this train. How she'd slipped up on the platform, past those guards, was something I forgot to ask her. And here she was.

I wanted to call the military police in town and they'd look after her but the brakeman said no, couldn't we take her in the caboose as far as Shilo and just slip in there, stop 10 seconds and let her off. He said her husband would be there. I thought, "At one in the morning?"

Well, we took her into the caboose and warmed some milk for the kiddies and got to Douglas, which was the stop for Shilo, and I could see the lights of the camp shining. It was down a long, long slope about 12 miles away, and every light was winking and in the moonlight you could even see the water tower. But there was nobody on the platform and no truck lights coming up from the camp and you could see nearly every blamed foot of the way. I said we could wait a few minutes, three or four, but no lights. The world was dead except for the platform light.

Ever been to Douglas? In 1943 it was like Siberia. Oh, I'm sure some nice people lived there, but it was your gawd-awful prairie town. Two elevators or so, a general store, a hotel I guess, a bakery, a few houses where old-timers lived and a school, and there'd have to be a couple of garages, but that was it and I think I'm being charitable too. Douglas and all those little towns— Sydney, Melbourne—all Siberia.

The town was wrapped up tighter than the bark on a tree, and nothing coming up from the camp and there she was out on the platform, maybe 20 below now, after one in the morning and no luggage, nothing. Just some baby clothes in one of those carry-alls your wife takes to the Safeway. Christ, how some people live. She'd freeze to death, and she didn't even speak English.

Nothing to do, okay? Damn right there was something to do. I told the brakeman and he got her back into the caboose and away we go to Brandon and everything's fine. The brakeman, this Harry Sekulik, told her to hang on tight, kid, the boys of the C.P.R. will see you through. Something like that. Even the little baby was smiling.

At Brandon, Harry and I took her and the kids to the yard office and, hell, we knew we were breaking half the rules in the book, but there was a bunch of guys there, waiting to go out, just coming in, getting warm, you know, and I told them what happened. Somebody brought out a dollar and soon there were one's popping out from everywhere and yours truly came up with a fiver, which I couldn't afford, and Harry took her downtown and got her fixed up in a hotel. Then he said he phoned the orderly office at the camp and he was a nervy bastard, he gave the whoozit there complete hell, as if it was his fault.

The little Hunyak and her two kiddies couldn't live at the camp, of course, but her husband got a special pass next day. She sent a letter, or her husband did, thanking us, or somehow the yardmaster got the word. She got fixed up in a little apartment in town and I guess that's all.

Not much of a story, not after I've told it and thought it over. But in those days there were so many like that little girl, following their husbands all over hell's half-acre and not knowing what they were doing and not even having the sense to come in out of the rain. I often wondered how they survived, but I guess they all did.

In England

The Canadian First Division were the first troops from abroad to land in England, and unfortunately that first winter there was a bad one. Snow, sleet, hail, rain and freezing temperatures followed each other for months on end; many of the troops were under canvas all that time, while the others were expected to cope with the rigours of English heating.

So living conditions were tough, and the English, while they welcomed the Canadians, were a little cautious about them. They had heard stories about these rough, wild men of the frontier, and armies in a strange land, even allies, usually spell trouble.

But, with time, each side learned about the other. The learning experience was one that nobody who was there will forget. As you can see, everyone had his own story.

•◄►• *"I've Got to Go Home"*

His first name was Roderick. Rod. He taught me something about England I never forgot.

I was from outside of London, the Canadian London, and his parents had a home southeast of London, in Kent probably, and Rod and I were sharing a small apartment in Toronto. The University of Toronto. We were working with new materials in physics and chemicals and we were both post-grad. We hit it off very well. Sailing. Riding. Hiking. We both liked the same type of girl. That sort of thing. This was in '38 and then into '39. It was all great fun.

Then the war came along. I remember going into the apartment and Rod was packing, throwing mounds of things in the corner to be taken away. Tennis shoes, blazers, scarves, and he looked at me and said, "I won't be needing this stuff. I've got to go home. England needs me."

Oh, I know, I could have said things like he was being dramatic, but he was Rod, he was my friend, and while I didn't think his country was in trouble, I knew he felt that way.

So I used some connections of my father's and an uncle and we got him on to just about the next ship out of Montreal and that was that. We wrote a couple of times and then about a year later his sister wrote and said he had been killed. He was a fighter pilot, she said, and you'll remember things were still pretty hot and heavy in the air then.

I joined the air force as soon as I could and landed in England early in 1942. After about a month I put in a trunk call to his family home and explained who I was, expecting an invitation, which came in the mail about a week later. Of course, the house was just as I expected. About 1700. Main house, two wings. One wing filled up with evacuees from London. Great grounds, looking down and away and then up again to the sea, and winter wheat beginning to show and sheep and cows, cattle grazing, and such an air of tranquillity.

Rod's uncle—they called him the Colonel—had been a soldier all his life. The old boy took me on a tour and I guess we walked two hours. At one time he raised a cane and pointed down a slope where sheep lay and he said, "My boy, I have faced guns and spears in many places of the world, but if I have to die in battle, I want to die right here"—he thudded the turf with his cane—"and be buried right here, with this slope before me and the sea beyond, and those sheep there."

I mumbled something like "Yes, sir," and I'll say this. My family came from England a long time ago and I think our highest attainment was some very distant grandfather becoming an alderman in one of the woollen towns, and then we left the United States and came to Canada as Loyalists, and that was a long time ago, a very long time ago, so it really can't be said that I am an Anglophile. But when that old man said that, and pounded his stick into the ground and we both looked down that slope, then I knew what Roderick was talking about. What he meant. What he felt, because I felt that too. That somehow this was my home. England.

•➤• *Like a Son*

I must have had a dozen leaves and I went to London once and that was enough. I never saw so many whores in my life and I saw Westminster Abbey and where the Crown jewels are kept and visited a cousin at Cheam and that was it. Up to Edinburgh another time and the train on to Dingwall, in around Inverness where my mother's people came from, and it was early spring and cold—I thought I was back in Ottawa. Mind, the people were kind but I found a better place to go.

A fellow in my outfit named Philip Williams said to go to Wales and he wrote one of his cousins and said I was coming, could they put me up, and I was a lad from near Smith Falls and knew a bit about farming and I might take a seat on the tractor once in a while. This cousin's name was Davies, and there's a pretty good Welsh name for you.

I went down to London and slept in Victoria Station and took another train, and by the time we stopped at this wee station it was near teatime, and I had the instructions on a piece of paper, and in a mile or so I was there. The house was bright and warm and in the big kitchen there were buns, scones, a chunk of yellow butter big as a curling stone, and a bunch of hog hams and bacon hanging and the farmer's wife sliced me off a big chunk of ham and slapped it into the pan. I hadn't had a piece of meat like that since I'd left home. There was cookies and tarts and jam and tea with thick cream. Mind, this was just tea. We'd have something later too. That much I knew.

The captain had lost a leg at Dunkirk and that's why he was farming again instead of in the war, and we went for a walk around his farm. It was the family farm. Two or three hundred years old, but you never saw a farm like it. Like the green bay tree, a marvel of a farm. I think we walked around every field, and it was about 100 acres, which is a good farm.

At seven we went back for dinner and I thought I could never eat with tea only three hours behind me, but I did. A grand meal. Roast beef. The captain, I remember, said, "Most goes to the war effort, but some stays with us, and that's only fair, wouldn't you say?"

After dinner I brought out my sack and gave them about 20 chocolate bars and two bottles of whiskey—I forget where I bought or got or stole them, but those bottles were hard to come by. We had a few drinks and a few more and a sing-song and I guess we got a little drunk.

Now the thing to remember is this. I had never met these people before and they treated me like a son. They were the finest people in the world.

I stayed for ten more days. I fished and picked rocks off the land and drove the tractor and did hard work and I loved it. And every leave I got, every time I could get 72 hours off, there I'd be, up in the mountains. Catching a few trout for dinner, or helping the farmhands to build fences of rock and meeting all the neighbours and going to church. There was even a girl I would have liked to bring back to Canada with me, but it wasn't to be. Sometimes it doesn't work out—but I know half the county was on my side.

•◄►• *"Who Are Those Chaps?"*

A hell of a lot of funny things went on. There was this old pub at the end of this lane southwest of London and I could get there from Aldershot in about an hour. It was another world. England wasn't at war in that land, just farmers working their fields and women going to the post office, gossiping, talking about grandchildren, I guess, and old old men in the evening going down to the pub, the Red Lion, the Yellow Dog, the Puss 'n Boots, or whatever it was called and sitting in the snug, nursing one or two pints till closing time. You know the kind of place. I'd say it was England at its best.

There was a group of chaps, maybe four or five, who'd come in and sit and drink beer and the villagers and farmers knew them. Knew them quite well, I'd say. They were quiet, might play a game of darts or buy a pint for one of the old men and I had them figured for Poles, but there is quite a Polish population in Hamilton and these fellows were more subdued. I thought maybe they were some kind of soldiers or airmen who'd escaped when France was knocked down, from Alsace-Lorraine, or they might even have been Danish. Danish, Norwegian, but I never saw them in uniform. That puzzled me too. They had every appearance of farmhands, including the smell.

Finally I asked Mr. Mundy, my host, "Who are these chaps I see in here? They sit over there. I've seen them half a dozen times."

He just looked up and smiled and said, "Jerry."

"You mean Germans?"

Mr. Mundy laughed and said, "Quite so, my lad. There's a camp not all that far from here, and these chaps are let out sometimes. They're off a submarine that had to come to the surface down this way. If you think they want to escape to go back the the Fatherland so they can go back on a submarine, then you obviously have never been on a submarine. And these lads have."

This stumped me and I asked if anyone knew, and Mr. Mundy laughed and said everybody, with the possible exception of the War Office.

"They came around in the spring and cleaned up my orchard and they put a new chimney on an old gentleman's cottage after it had been knocked off by a piece of one of their very own planes." They do odd jobs around the district and they get a few shillings for beer and fags," he said.

I mentioned that soon they'd be walking out some of the local girls and he said, "I should expect so, yes, I should expect so."

Then he said, "After all, lad, isn't a German nothing more than an Englishman without a sense of humour?"

I guess he had me stumped right there."

•◄►• *My Last Duchess*

I'll tell you about my duchess. I met her at a party. And how did I get to a party, me with my three stripes?

There was one fellow in our regiment who had three uniforms, all Canadian, a naval lieutenant's uniform, a captain's uniform and an air force officer's uniform. Lord, don't ask me how he got them, except he must have had them made up by a London tailor because he had loot. He'd lend them out to us, the two that he wasn't using. The only deal was, we were on our own. Get caught and we wouldn't rat on him.

So I'm an air force chappie this time and drinking in this bar and I meet a naval chap from Halifax whose uncle was an admiral or something and he said did I want to go to a party? Sure.

And I meet this duchess, of something or other. Beautiful. I was maybe twenty-two and she was about thirty-two, thirty-five, in around there, and the duke is in Washington on some sort of big-shot mission, so here is this sergeant, me, taking her home.

At her flat, she pours me a drink and I say, what the hell, so I say, "Let's go to bed." She says, "Just like that?" I say, "Yes, just like that." She says, "You bloody Canadians," and I say, "Well?" and she says, "Yes." So we went to bed and I stayed with her for two days, all day in bed, breakfast in bed, butler and maid and all the trimmings and even dinner in her suite. And when I left she says will I please come back next leave. I would have, but I could never get hold of that air force uniform again — and it would have been too hairy to go as a naval lieutenant or an army captain."

I remember in school you read about kings and dukes and lords in England and big castles and estates and I guess I just assumed that everyone in England was rich. I went overseas in 1940 and when they gave us a leave in about three months, in early November, I went to visit my aunts and uncles up north.

Good God Jesus Christ. Rich? They were poorer than any Indians on some northern reserve. It was in Manchester and I stood up all the way from Aldershot, to London and then to Manchester, and walked for miles to this street where they lived. They didn't know I was coming. It was going to be a sort of surprise, you know, Canadian cousin comes to visit rich relatives.

The place was a bloody slum. You wouldn't keep your dogs in it. The blackouts were on and when I did find the door they wouldn't let me in. Thought I was a neighbour or something come to rob them. Rob them of what? They had nothing. A cold-water flat and two sacks of coal piled in the kitchen and a loaf of bread, some jam and some tinned milk on the table and the two girls were about sixteen and eighteen and one was pregnant. Some guy sent to Egypt or Malta or somewhere had knocked her higher than a kite. Her nose ran. Both their noses ran, and they asked if I had brought them silk stockings from Canada. They pronounced it Canader. The old man worked on the docks or something and he hadn't bothered to wash the dirt off him, and next morning it was still there. The old lady, my mother's sister, she was worse. Anything like my mother in her was coincidental. More than that. It would have been a bloody goddamned mistake.

In their way, though, they were kind. I shared my ration book with them and they shared what they had with me. I can't say we ate well, but we didn't get skinny and I think on private's pay I was making about 3 pounds a month, 10 bucks, no 15, and we'd go down to the corner and have a few pints at their local and they treated me fairly, I guess.

They never seemed to have any idea about the war. The Confiet, old Bert used to say and you'd think he was still talking about the first world war. All about the Kraut, and the zeps coming over. That was 1918 stuff, zeppelins, and even when they knocked the street about in one raid he was still cursing the bloody zeps. Just an ignorant man, and the two girls were hopeless. Their two boys were in the army. Just the right place for them. Foot-sloggers. Percy got his in Normandy, just like it is expected, I guess, of such an English family. The dogans send one boy into the priesthood and the English send one boy to get his head blown off in some fucking war.

I think I hated them. I think I even hated them then, but before we were sent to France I'll bet I visited them on leave six times. I'd sleep in the flat below with an old widow whose two boys were in the merchant marine, and I'd give her 5 shillings a night for bed and breakfast. I often wondered, now why the hell do I go up to that bloody slum, that crummy local, nothing to see, nothing to do? Ever been to Manchester? Mate, it is the asshole of the world. Why not London and see the sights? The girls.

I finally got it figured out. Whatever these people were, how grubby, how common they were, they were my relatives, my relatives and we were of the same blood, my aunt and my mother, and no matter what they were, they were my people. My kinfolk, you might say. We all had the same grandfather and grandmother and I guess that was it.

We used to have this expression in the army. A guy would say he was fucked and far from home. Well, the army was screwing us all, just like the war was, and these Moores, this family, were giving me a kind of home, dirt and coal in the corner, and knocked-up daughters, and dirty-mouth talk and all. That was it.

•→• *Young Tuck and Old Jason*

There was this little English village and when you walked to it all you saw in the distance were the tops of tall trees and when you came over the top, it was down there. If there had been snow the first time I saw it, I'd have sworn it was a postcard my father's English relatives used to send him when I was a kid. Half a dozen streets winding around and maybe 25 or 30 houses. And there was a pub called The Grey Ox. The pub is gone now, so I'm told.

I was a young Canadian soldier and I didn't know the customs, but this old pub had a huge fireplace with two seats in it where you could get right close to the fire. Two people could sit in it, across from each other. The people in that part of the country call it a snug.

This is a cold night about February and I had been hiking around on the first leave, a 48-hour pass, that I'd got since we landed in England, about Christmas. I wandered into this place, this pub, about the size of your living room, and I guess I was the first Canadian soldier ever seen in that place. I'm sure I was. The owner was polite but that was all, and the locals around weren't putting themselves out for me. I didn't expect them to, but I wouldn't have minded a nod or a smile or a sort of salute with a mug. Oh well, so I took my mug of mild and I wandered over to this snug and I sat down and just looked at the fire, getting warm. Christ, but an English winter can get cold. Give me Sudbury or Thunder Bay anytime. At least you know it's cold.

Then I hear this tapping with a cane and an old man is coming over, a very old man. Very old, and all bent over and this big Russian kind of cap on, and he sits down opposite me and says, "Ev'nin, Tuck," and I nod. What the hell, none of my business. Then the bartender comes over with a pewter flagon or mug or whatever it's called and the old man very carefully takes a poker out of the fire and puts it into the mug. He's mulling it, you see, like you'd do to wine.

Then he says in this high, funny voice, "Innkeeper, I see we've got Tuck back with us," and he waves his stick at me and the owner says, "No, Old Jason, remember Tuck's been dead for six years. This is a young Canadian soldier come to visit us." Well *bang, smack, bang, whack.* That's me taking it on the head and neck and shoulders with the old man's stick. It didn't hurt, but it sure surprised, and I yanked it away from him and came out of this little cave, so to speak, and everybody's watching. I said, "I don't know what I did, but what do I do now?" A young fellow about sixty comes over and says, "Give me that," and he goes over to the old man, who is all quiet now, and says, "Old Jason, there's no reason in what you're doing. The lad meant no harm," and the old man nods and takes the stick. So, what the hell, I go back in and he looks up and says, "Tuck, how're those ewes of yours coming? Need some help come their time?" and I sort of muttered, "Thanks but no. I'll handle them, but thanks for your help."

That was in '40, early 1940, and you know the way things sometimes go, for three years I was never more than 25 or 30 miles from the Ox. I'd visit it every time I could, sometimes two or three times a month. I pretty well made that part of the country my stamping grounds. I liked the people and they got to like me and I'd go to their fair and once I was asked to judge a dress-up contest for the kids and I gave first prize to the boy who dressed up like me. I went to their whist drives, teas. I kind of adopted that village.

It was funny, too, that I was just the only service guy who went there. There was a Yank air base not too far away, those Thunderbolts, the screaming brutes of planes, but they'd never go near it. One told me once on the train that the place gave him and his pals the willies.

But I'm away from my story. For three years or so I was Tuck. I was to Old Jason, and when he wasn't around everybody called me Young Tuck. That was my name. "Young Tuck will now read the lesson," the rector would say. "Young Tuck, we're going haring, want to come?" "Young Tuck, a whiskey for your birthday." That from the landlord.

Old Jason would come in, tapping away, and he'd sit down, and if I was there he'd make some comment, and then another maybe 20 minutes later. Things like, "Well, Tuck, we survived the Somme," or, "The old King is dead." A long pause, then, "Long live the King." I figured he must have been talking about Edward the Seventh. All in the past, forty, fifty, sixty years ago.

This went on for years. The villagers got a real kick out of it.

I don't think he was senile. I don't know what he was. He could look after his cottage and milk a cow and do his garden, and he certainly knew shillings from pence and he was a neat old fellow, very precise in his movements, the times he came and went places. I just don't know.

Then it came invasion time. I didn't know when, nobody knew but Eisenhower and Churchill, maybe. But I went down to the Ox the last time. Borrowed a motorbike like I usually did and I went around buying ale and whiskey and gin for everybody. It got to be quite a party and for once, Old Jason was late.

When he came in, his daughter Grace was with him and she had a cake. A big one, about all she could handle, and it was done up for me. "Good luck, Young Tuck." That's all it said. I damn near broke down, and to show you how senile that old man was, he had done this himself. He had no pipeline into the war office but he knew D-day was coming, and how the hell he knew I was coming so very soon I don't know. Senile, in a pig's eye.

I thought of the many, the dozens of pleasant evenings we'd sat there, he on his side, me on mine and talking maybe 50 words all night until, "Time, gentlemen, please." Yes, I'll admit, it was kind of an emotional time. I felt it. The villagers had been my friends, but this old man was something different.

So I got up and I didn't make a speech but I went over to the old man leaning on his stick and I kissed him on both cheeks and said, "Thanks, Old Jason," and he said, "You'll be going to France, Tuck. Tell them I'll be along soon. And remember, give the Boche the bayonet. Cold steel. That's somethin' the beggars can't stomach."

Then he reached up and pulled my face down and gave me a kiss, on the right cheek and then the left, a soft and dry kiss, and that's where I really came apart. Don't mind saying so. I ran out into the road and jumped on my bike and then I jumped off because it was a cranky starter, and the last anybody saw of me, I guess, is me pushing the B.M.C. down the road and crying my fool head off.

I never went back. I had no chance. I was wounded and shipped to a hospital and then another and then on to a hospital ship and home to Canada and that was it.

•◂▸• *"I Really Felt at Home"*

You never thought that behind you parts of Berlin or Dortmund or the cities of the Ruhr were burning and people dying in the ruins, because you'd be coming in over the Channel and there would be England ahead, hazy, maybe, but old England and every time I'd switch on and tell my crew: "Dead ahead. Home. There she is, boys, England, the greatest little fortress in the history of the world."

The flight engineer was a New Zealander and he'd always say, "I'm right with you, skipper. She's almost as peaceful-looking as at home."

Others would chine in, the tail-end Charlie who was a runt from Toronto and the bomb aimer was an American who'd skipped across the border and joined. Name of Schmidt. He'd go into a pub and introduce himself and say, "My name's Schmidt. I'm a Kraut and I'm fighting for England." He was quite a guy. And two Englishmen, sergeant and flight sergeant, who came from Midland towns and thought us mad, and then this crazy Aussie named McCracken who was Irish and sang to us over the intercom whenever I let him, and was one hell of a mid-upper.

Myself, I was born in a cabin chinked with a mixture of cow manure and sand and lime and they never sent a decent teacher to our school because we were just a bunch of Ukrainian kids out in the bush, in Manitoba, but there I was, at twenty-three, the skipper of a beautiful Lancaster.

Back in Canada, at home, a name like mine, at university, Manitoba, it just cut you out of everything, and that's why I quit after my second year, but in Britain in '42 and '43 I found my name didn't mean a thing. It didn't matter, high or low, big or small, I was a Canadian and a pilot of a bomber, and I was in there with my two bits' worth.

In those days I felt more like an Englishman than a

Canadian. I did. I honestly did. I felt somehow in those days that to be an Englishman was to be a citizen of the world, and I used to feel that Churchill was the number-one citizen of the world.

I really felt at home with the British. I was with them, their backs to the wall and fists up and saying, "Come on, you bastards, see if you can take us." I think most Canadians felt that way too. I think that's why they fought so well, and why they were such good airmen and soldiers and navy and why the English loved them so much. I think so.

•◀▶• *"Pass the Cream"*

Military life brutalizes. After understanding this I could then understand why fellows from good homes, good education, good breeding, good everything, could sink down to the level of the lowest. I mean, the lowest common denominator was the one that was obvious, and anyone who fought against it was considered suspect, a queer, a nut, a Christer, a brain — all these derogatory terms.

I think it was best illustrated in the use of the word "fuck." That wonderful four-letter word which was used as noun, verb, adjective and adverb and anywhere from one to six times in any sentence. I've seen the same thing out of the service too, because it occurs wherever men are isolated together, away from the womb of love in the home, away from women, away from intelligent conversation, away from what I'll call the finer things of life. How many intelligent or meaningful conversations, intelligent conversations with intelligent men, did you have in the army? I don't mean at the officer level. I mean at the barrack-room level? None? Very few? So few you can't remember? Probably.

I think a good example would be to tell you a little story, and I'll bet it has happened to you. When I was in England my wife's cousin and her husband in High Wycombe asked me for a weekend, and the first meal we had was breakfast on this Saturday morning because I'd arrived late the night before. Buffet style. Very English, very nice and something I hadn't seen for a long time. And so we're sitting there and I said, quite casually, "Would you please pass the fucking cream?" Just like that. Not thinking. Just pass the fucking cream. All I could say was, "Sorry, I've been in camp too long," and they, being that special type of English couple which they were, they understood.

The Punchbowl Murder

To my knowledge there never were any Canadians executed in the field, for desertion or cowardice or what-have-you, but to my mind one of the saddest stories was the one they called the Punchbowl Murder. A famous case.

I wept for the poor bugger. This Indian from Northern Saskatchewan. A sniper. They were very good snipers, those fellows. This was in England, in Hampshire, and this Indian was not built for the communal type of life of the army, so he pitched a tent down at the bottom of this huge depression. A very deep depression called the Devil's Punchbowl. Nobody really knew what was down in the bottom of it. Streams. Deer, I guess. Trees, brambles. Giant ferns. You know. And whenever he got a leave or a furlough this Indian would go down there to his tent and live more or less the life he'd lived in the north. Maybe kill a deer, live off the land. Right in the heart of England.

Then he met this girl in a pub, I think it was around Hazelmere, and she was pretty fascinated by this Indian and his life, and on his leave she'd go down there with him and live like a savage too. We'd be off to London and there he'd be down in the Punchbowl with this girl. Well, she two-timed him and he found out so he murdered her.

So they brought him up in front of a jury and sentenced him to death and hanged him. That was all, the end of him.

But there he was, thousands of miles from home, in a situation completely alien to him. His strict Indian code of morals had been violated by this English girl and he was entirely out of his element and he was executed. I always felt very sorry for him. Poor devil.

Good Shooting

My outfit was camped all around this big wheat field in the south of England. This was in August, '40. Around there.

One day this German fighter comes stooging around and he gives us a run, shooting the camp up, and then he came around and did the other side of the field, causing a lot of trouble. So the colonel phones for some help, to a Spitfire base not too far away. Those days, right in the Battle of Britain, every station would be on full alert.

So when the German goes around for another run at us, we're ready. We've only got a couple of old Lewis guns from the first world war, but we're set up and this plane comes *swwooooosh* towards us and this old gun just throws up a hose of bullets, right into his path and he just barely makes it down to the end of his field and goes belly-up in the next field. Well, Christ, we're running down there, yelling and whooping like hell and what do you find? No need to guess.

The German hadn't come back but a Spitfire had come over to have a whack at him, and so there was this nice plane smouldering right there in the field. Not burning, just smoking a bit, and the pilot standing a little away from it. He wasn't hurt, not a scratch, but his plane didn't look too good, and when they carted it away they counted 47 bullet holes in it. Forty-seven right out of that old Lewis. Now, you might say it's not right to shoot down your own planes, but you have to admit it, that was goddamned good shooting.

•◄►• *Terror*

The V-2 made no noise, and that made it a terror weapon. Imagine sitting in your office right here and not knowing that, maybe at 10:09 A.M. or when you're walking back from lunch or at 3:09 in the afternoon, you will be wiped out or maimed by a weapon you never saw, never heard, never knew was coming. That's terror, in my books.

I'm there, Intelligence, during those months. I can see what is happening. So can any Londoner. In the summer of '44 you can hear the explosions. You can see the V-1's and V-2's at night by their flare. Sometimes you'd see fighters chasing their tails off during the day. Some little Cockney secretary you're kind of fond of phones and says she can't be in for work. Why? House destroyed. V-1. Oh, sorry, my dear. Look after your Mum until she gets settled again. Can't. Oh, why? Because she was killed by the bomb. Oh, sorry. And on and on and on. See what I mean?

But the English held out, although I'll tell you this. If it had gone on another few months, London might very well have been destroyed.

•◄►• *An English View of Canadians*

I suspect a lot of us were just a little apprehensive when we heard a Canadian regiment was moving into our area. It was the Princess Patricia's Canadian Light Infantry. This was quite early in the war and quite frankly I was probably somewhat surprised.

These were men from the western plains and I suppose we visualized wild men and trappers, cowboys and lumberjacks, men of the outdoors, rough and tough and strong. Big muscles and roaring laughs and prodigious drinkers and fighters. I suspect we had been reading too many magazines of this sort of thing and confusing American Wild West movies with Canada.

We had a delightful surprise when they did come into the camp and, if I'm not mistaken, this would be some time after the New Year. Oh, there was the odd ruffian but hardly any. In fact, they were perfect gentlemen. One group would visit the local down our street and they couldn't have been kinder. There were no fights, no hooliganism, and I heard more than one villager say it was just as if our own sons had come to stay with us. We got to know many of them and I know a lot of them were killed in the war, you know, but I know that some still correspond with village people, and how many years ago was that? My goodness, about thirty years.

There wasn't one I wouldn't invite to my home for dinner or tea, and they often brought things that had been sent from home in parcels, chocolates and sweets, and they willingly shared them with us. The children of the village loved them. I'm sure there are grown adults now who were children then who remember your Canadian boys very well, for their pleasantness and their generosity.

Gentlemen of the Air Force

Training in Canada ... Like Young Princes ... My Own People ... We'd Just Made Love ... German Traps ... Caught in a Burning Plane ... At Fence Level ... Incident in Samoa ... On Sub Patrol ... Bombing in the East

When the bugles blew there was a rush to join the Royal Canadian Air Force. But alas, it had a permanent peacetime strength of about 4,000 and a few decrepit aircraft worth nothing. Therefore, while some volunteers were enlisted immediately, most had to wait.

The British Commonwealth Air Training Plan had to be set up. Camps and training sites and air stations from Prince Edward Island to Vancouver Island were established. Men by the thousands had to be trained, to train those that followed. Plants had to be established in Canada to make the planes to train the air crews. All in all, it was a truly massive undertaking, perhaps Canada's most outstanding achievement in the Second World War — more than 130,000 air crews trained were English, Australian, New Zealanders, South Africans, but the majority were Canadian.

On active service, the Canadian flyers' contribution was magnificent. A Canadian fighter squadron fought with high honours in the Battle of Britain, and many Canadian air crews were spread throughout the Commonwealth air forces. At war's end about 25 percent of the R.A.F. air crew was composed of Canadians, a fact too few people know. But still, the R.C.A.F. had a strong identity. The Allies knew it was there, and so did the Germans.

•◄►• *Training in Canada*

In the early days of the war the Commonwealth Air Training Plan was just getting started, so there were few places we could train. So our first field after leaving Toronto depot was a very small field called Elmsville, near Huntsville. There was a little air strip there which, in those days, would have been a Trans-Canada Airlines emergency airdrome. We were right in the bush and it was bitterly cold and we set up in tents. When I think of us living in tents in bitter weather and of what they had in later years in the way of luxurious living in the training centres, well, I just wonder.

There were Canadians, English, Norwegians and at that time the Americans weren't in the war yet, so a lot of them were coming up to get in the action. There were about 90 of us at that time. This was at the very beginning, you must remember, and we took our elementary flying on Fairchild Cornells.

Half of us went on to Medicine Hat where they had twins, Ansons, and we went to Moose Jaw where they had Harvards, and that's where the single-engine training really began. Well anyway, time goes on, we got our wings, we went to England, to a squadron, into action to fill in for all the boys who'd been wiped out by the Battle of Britain, and that took only a year from enlistment to North Weald, England.

There were 43 of us graduated, 43 of us went to England. There were only three survivors. I am one of the three lucky guys who lived.

•◄►• *Like Young Princes*

Oh, it was a wonderful life. The English treated us like young princes. One reason, I suppose, was we were all they had. We'd do up to three sweeps a day, although the squadron or wing total probably would be up to five.

We lived in what you'd call a stately home. A lovely place in South England. Everything was just right. We were officers and we got the best, the best of food, the best of housing, expensive linen on the tables, expensive cutlery, flowers on the table every morning and I had a batman. I shared a batman with another chap. A batman! And I was 19.

Nobody thought of dying. We knew it would never happen to us, it just couldn't. Of course, we knew it was happening all the time and we saw it every day we were up, one of our chaps getting it. But we never even thought it would actually happen to us.

•◄►• *My Own People*

The Americans we had in the war with us, we felt they were awfully good types. These were chaps who joined the R.C.A.F., and when the States got into the war, they didn't transfer to the U. S. Air Force.

Our airdrome was near an American base, and I remember sitting in a pub once, and, Jesus, in comes this bunch of Americans, drunk, and those goddamn cigars stuck in their faces. Every guy, a cigar. And loud. Yelling about how they were winning the war. Hell, we knew all they'd been doing was gardening [laying mines] off Le Havre. Real exciting stuff.

So this chap, Sparwood, this American, is sitting with us, and he's got his American identity like they all had, on his uniform, and some drunk major comes reeling over and he says, "Hey, fella, come on and join your own people, over here," and Sparwood looks at him and says, "Sir, I am with my own people."

With that, this fat bastard of a major says, typically drunk, "Oh, we're not good enough for you, eh, is that it?" You know, it was so predictable. God, but it was predictable. Sparwood looked at the rest of us and said, "Jesus, let's get out of here," and we went down to another pub down the road.

•◆• We'd Just Made Love

I was lying on the grass with this girl from the village where I was based. It was May, I remember, and it was one of those great English days, sunny, blue skies. There's no place in the world where you get bluer skies than jolly old England in May. There were flowers around us and we could smell them, and gun pits and barbed wire and all that junk around us, but where we were it was like a little hideaway.

We'd just made love and were on our backs, just looking up at the sky.

I heard this sound coming from the Channel and it's engine sound, and we sit up and look around and here comes a Heinkel. A bomber. That's one thing I could never figure. Jerry used to send these bombers over, just one, and it was certain death. No way he was ever going to get back. I remember the girl grabbed my hand and held on tight.

I wondered why the battery next door hadn't opened up and then I saw. Four Spitfires were above this Heinkel, just swanning about until he got in position, and they must have radioed to leave this one alone. No sense messing up the fields with a lot of flak, shrapnel from the guns. Besides the German was pretty low.

This one Spit just broke off and came down and in behind in an instant, and I could hear his guns banging away. I think I could almost see the bullets. Bits of the German flew off, metal, and then the bomber just dropped its nose and came down. Straight down. Like standing on a haystack and firing an arrow straight into the ground. He didn't have far to go, maybe 2,000 feet, and God, did he ever come down, and then he hit, in the next field and there was a shower of junk, like a big bit of fireworks going off and the ground shook and that was it.

It was as if that Heinkel and the crew had never existed, and all there was to say for it was a piece of English meadow black and burned, about the size of this restaurant. Nothing more.

Somebody could write a poem about that, I guess.

The girl was crying and I asked her why and she said she'd never seen a man die before.

•◄►• *German Traps*

They'd lay traps for us. Ack-ack. About 10,000 feet or so there would be this German aircraft. A kite, maybe a bomber but usually just a reconnaissance type, and it would just be circling around and you'd think, "Oh boy, here's one for the taking." So you'd go in, both of you, and just as you got close the Jerry would dive, power-dive right out of there, and the flak would start flying all over the sky.

You see, they had this air space blocked out and a flock of ack-ack just zeroed in on it, that one area, and when they saw us coming they let fly and the phony reconnaissance plane got out of there and there we were, right in the bloody-awful middle of it all.

I got caught twice in these things and the second time my buddy, a guy from around Paris, Ontario, got shot down, and that was one out of four for the German battery, 25 percent average, which wasn't bad at all. Sort of made the waiting worthwhile, I'd say.

It made us all awfully suspicious of one or two German planes just circling around up there in the blue, not doing anything. Very suspicious.

•◄►• *Caught in a Burning Plane*

Me and a buddy were walking behind an English pub once, going back to our base, and we saw this plane come over heading for an American base just across the valley. Its starboard engine was on fire, flames coming out, smoke streaming away, and we saw it hit. It didn't hit all that bad. It hit near us.

We didn't know if it was aborting a mission and it still had its bombs aboard or if it was coming back from Germany, so we didn't dare go near it. I ran and tried to phone the American bombing base, but I couldn't get through. The line just didn't work.

Fire brigades came from all over because England had a pretty good fire water system set up by that time, but nobody dared go near it because it was on fire and we couldn't find out if it still had its bombload and tanks full of gasoline fuel. The front of it had ploughed into this field and it had buckled up the fuselage so that the crew couldn't get out. We could hear the men inside screaming and pounding, pounding and yelling, and there was nothing anybody could do because of the bombs. They died, five of them.

Then we found out later it was on a training mission.

•◄►• *At Fence Level*

We'd gone in to Paris. It was Bastille Day and we always made a point of going in to Paris and knocking the marshalling yards about, just to let the French know there still was a war on, and we were on their side. Sort of like that. This is your national holiday and we're there, with Forts and Libs and the rest.

We got engaged and when my own fight was over I was all by myself in the middle of bloody France. That was a funny thing. There could be bombers and fighters all over the sky, maybe hundreds of them, and you get in a scrap with some Jerry and when you get him or you both disengage, you look around and there's not a plane in the sky. You're miles from where the action is by then.

So I pushed her right down and headed for home, staying as close to the ground as I could. You always stayed as low as you could when you were alone and far from home. Then I could see the coastline, and once I got over the Channel I knew I'd be okay.

And right ahead I see this bloody barracks and these pillboxes as they started to fire at me, and then I saw there was a parade square there and a whole lot of soldiers, little figures marching up and down, and so I pushed the nose down and pushed everything, and every gun in the plane was blasting right into them and they're scattering about and I didn't see what happened and then I'm over them and gone and I skidded, left rudder, right rudder, even turns, and I'm out of there and I start laughing because I figure I'm a real hero.

But that was a long way to come out, 100 miles out of France at fence level and then that big jackpot of a parade square at the end of it.

•◄►• *Incident in Samoa*

As Air Transport Command we moved out all over and that is why pretty soon after Pearl Harbor, we were sent down to Hamilton Field [north of San Francisco] to ferry 50 planes down to Brisbane and then up to Darwin and then up to Port Moresby. When we landed there, the Japs held one end of the airstrip and the Americans the other, and they were sniping at us as we came in.

They sent Canadians down to do this job because in Air Transport Command we had so much experience and we were both radio operators and navigators. The Americans didn't have the men yet for such a job.

We got all 50 aircraft down there in New Guinea, where they were used to bomb the Japs except one and would you believe me, it was the Flying Whore that I was assigned to. That goddamned aircraft just didn't want to fly.

When we took off from the airport in Samoa, there had just been a terrific downpour and the heat waves were coming up and we weren't getting power, Jesus, because one motor was running wild and then the other would run wild. At the end of the runway we dipped down and we're just skimming along the water and hitting the water and the skipper is jiggling the controls and he gets it up just high enough and angles it so that the port wheel clears this breakwater. But the starboard wheel hits and locks in, useless from then on.

So there we are, flying around for three hours in this goddamned B-26, burning off all the gas we can and figuring out what to do. But the skipper said he'd brought in a fighter on one wheel once and he'd try the same thing. "I'll land on the one wheel and hold the starboard wing up as long as I can and then let her drop off," he says, and that's what he did. Jesus, I didn't even feel that airplane land and that port wheel, you didn't even know it hit the ground and then he somehow just let it all ooze down and for half the length of the runway there was huge sparks, twice the length of this room, from the wing, but nothing happened. We got down, lucky to be alive.

I went into the officer's mess and I drank a bottle and a half of rum without even showing it. A marine captain told me next day. I didn't even know I'd done it.

•◄►• *On Sub Patrol*

We were flying east of Iceland on sub patrol. Those Sunderlands could keep out for, I think, about 18 hours. We'd make tea and have cookies and watch. Ever watched the Atlantic for hours at a time? You think you're going nuts. You get hypnotized. The water looks like mud.

Then, this time, I'm looking down and, by God, there's this sub right below. I know it's a German but what the hell is it doing out here, with about 30 guys on deck, and they're scrambling for the tower. I let out a yell and nobody knows why I'm yelling, but I get that big gun down and tear off a belt. There's tracers every fifth one, I think, and it's like one of those movies where you see troops coming at the camera and just before they meet it, hit it, you see them go off to the left and right, left and right. That's the way it was, yes, just like that, sailors diving left and right into the water, and I'm hammering away at them.

The skipper drops a yellow smoke bomb and we make as tight a circle as we can, but by that time the sub's gone. Those big birds didn't come around easy. All we see are bodies in the water and they're, well, we don't know who they are, but we radio our position and hang around, and in an hour a frigate comes up and fishes them out and yes, they're Germans and each one has got several big holes. Those Browning slugs, you know.

We go home. We're based in Scotland and in the mess that night I ask the skipper why he didn't depth-charge the sub. We knew where it had gone down, and if you could hit within 20 feet you stood a good chance of cracking her plates.

He looked me straight in the eye and he said, and these were his words, "McInnes, I didn't because there wasn't supposed to be any German U-boats where we were, and if there were, they wouldn't have been on the top sunning themselves."

I said, "Then you thought I'd given the goods to one of our subs." He said, "Yes, I honestly thought you had."

•◀▶• *Bombing in the East*

You know, our boys in Europe thought they had a long flight if they had seven or eight hours, but for us fourteen hours was pretty much of a routine flight.

We were flying Liberators, American aircraft, and we would hit Rangoon, Siam, Malaya, Burma, and once we even did a pamphlet raid on Singapore. There was not too much heavy stuff by then. The Japs were pretty well finished, but we used to blow up a few troop concentrations with fragmentation bombs. But the Japanese had pretty well had it.

Gin and lime cordial was the big drink then. We'd fill up our flasks with booze and on the long flights, when we came back we'd be smashed. I think there was a guarantee that either the pilot or the co-pilot would stay reasonably sober to get the thing down.

When you're nineteen, it was still a pretty exciting war.

A Hell of a Way to Run a War

Emergency Rations . . . Church Parade . . . On the Garbage Dump . . . Fighting for Players . . . Such Beautiful Weather . . . Field Detention Camp . . . A Few Men Died . . . Just One Vast Screw-up

I remember one officer, on a night manoeuvre, asking another officer: "How did it go?" And the reply was: "Just another SNAFU." SNAFU, for your information (after a bit of cleaning up) means: "Situation Normal, All Fouled Up."

That phrase sums up the way the people who fought the war saw the military system. And like all soldiers since the beginning of time, they bitched about it. All the bitching came down to one statement: "This is one hell of a way to run a war." Not win a war, just run a war. I don't think anybody, officers or ranks, took the military system all that seriously. They knew nobody really wins in uniform, and that they all play a little game. Just like in civilian life.

•◄►• Emergency Rations

My brother was in the army and somehow he and about eight other fellows wound up on an island somewhere up near Alaska watching for Japanese submarines or something. It was a useless existence because there was nothing they could have done anyway, and their radio never worked and they were never sent parts to fix it.

There was supposed to be a parachute drop every two weeks. But this time there was no air drop, and when the next one was due, nothing happened. The poor kids were getting desperate, but they did some fishing with dynamite and kept going that way.

Finally one morning a plane came over and flew low along the beach. This box tumbled out, and when they got to it they could see that it wasn't food, not even emergency rations. Do you want to guess what was in that box the plane dropped? All right, hold yourself. It was a carton of applications for Canada war bonds, Victory Bonds, which the guys were supposed to fill out and send back.

That's my favorite war story.

I remember my father telling me when I joined up that I was never to discuss politics or religion. They were taboo. All you could do in an argument on those two subjects was wind up with a broken jaw.

I was Protestant. That's what my dog tags said. If you weren't that, then you were R.C. or Jewish, and the Catholics had their own chaplains. I can't remember what the Jews did, because any camp I was in there was never enough of them to warrant a, well, whatever they have.

So after about five church parades—and the damned things were compulsory—about 10 of us decided to refuse to go any more. We were atheists, we told the hut corporal. He told the sergeant and the sergeant told the lieutenant and so on. So we were excused church parade this Sunday, but it wasn't a case of going back and hitting the sack. We were given special duties. Now get this.

Ever oiled down a barrack room? First, you lug in these little barrels of oil off a truck. Then you push all the bunks and all the barracks boxes from one end down to the other, and you gotta find space there, which is another problem. Then you sweep the floor like it's never been swept before. Then you take these bloody big flicky brooms and mops and you start swishing that oil on the floor and spreading it over with the brooms, and when you finish one side of the hut then you move everything back in place, and then move everything from the other side down to this end, and then you sweep some more and then smash on the oil again and then move everything back.

And just to rub it in, do you know what that sonovabitch of a company commander did? Well, when the guys came back from church parade they couldn't use the hut, so the captain ordered up about five big troop trucks, and all the rest of the company got in, and they threw in a whole lot of bread and butter and cheese and oranges and big crocks of tea and milk, and they were all driven down to the beach about 10 miles away for a swim and a picnic.

We finished about three in the afternoon, oil from head to foot, bow to stern, and the corporal in charge of the detail wouldn't even let us smoke, and we only got half an hour for lunch.

Next Sunday when the company lined up for church parade, the sergeant major bellowed out that all those wishing to miss the church parade because of, as he put it, religious dissent, they were to fall out. Not a person moved. Not one man. Last time they had us oiling the hut, and I figured if we tried the atheist stunt again they'd either have us doing the next hut in line or painting the goddamned water tower blazing red.

I learned then, if the army wants you to do something and you don't want to do it, and you're within your rights in not doing it, then for Christ sakes, do what the army says, and fast. No frigging about.

•◄►• *On the Garbage Dump*

I think I'll always remember the waste in some of those camps. You've got to remember everything was rationed on the home front, or was in very short supply, and Canada was sending everything to the military camps or to Britain. Trainloads, shiploads.

Yet you'd go into a camp—and I'm thinking of ones in British Columbia—and the waste! I just don't mean things that the men wouldn't eat at meals, but on the garbage dump. Honey, butter, chicken, boxes of bread. Steaks, roasts, sides of meat. Those 25-pound tins of raspberry jam and strawberry jam from B.C., the sort of things that civilians never saw. Beef, not just chunks of cooked beef, I mean uncooked beef, raw beef and just thrown away. Flour, sugar, all the things that just weren't available in stores and people would give their eye teeth to get.

It was terrible, the waste. At times I just couldn't believe it. In the city I couldn't get half the stuff for my children, and here it was lying in the sun rotting, or they'd pour gasoline over it and throw in a match. Terrible waste, and nobody cared about it. Lots more where that came from, that was their attitude.

•◄►• *Fighting for Players*

One of the scandalous things, I always thought, was the way hockey players were used by a bunch of generals, air vice-marshals and admirals for their own ego trips, building up super teams of the best hockey players for their own districts.

It happened everywhere, in lacrosse and softball and baseball and football, but mostly in hockey where you'd get some town like Nanaimo with a line-up of NHL players on the army team, or some little town in Quebec would have half the good baseball players in Canada. But it was mostly hockey.

Like the Ottawa Commandoes. Anybody who got within reaching distance of Ottawa and was an NHL player was stuck there. It was put together by Tommy Gorman, who was running the show in Ottawa. His first line was Colville, Colville and Shibicky and the rest were all NHL regulars.

It wasn't Canadian policy. No, I don't think so. It was the generals. They were fighting among themselves to get the players, and they had some damn good teams. Damn good.

But the thing exploded in the spring of '44 when Turk Broda [goalkeeper for Toronto Maple Leafs] went into the army, answered his draft call and got caught in the middle on whether he was going to join the army in Toronto or Montreal. The Montreal general won and he took that late train from Toronto to Montreal and after midnight, technically he was a draft dodger from the Toronto district and the Toronto general was so bloody mad at losing him he had him hauled off the train at some place down the line. Of course, this made the papers, the shit hit the fan. There was one hell of an explosion and the whole service hockey setup was scrapped and all these healthy guys were sent overseas.

I knew some of these guys. I remember Johnny Quilty. In the air force in Victoria. Like a lot of them, he was very unhappy about the whole setup. They felt they were being used. He said he had no wish to play hockey in the service and hadn't joined up to play hockey. He'd joined up to fight, and if he came through it, then he'd play hockey after the war. In fact, Quilty was quite bitter about it and felt he was being used by the brass as their plaything and when the Broda thing blew everything up, he and others were glad to go overseas.

•◄►• *Such Beautiful Weather*

This is the way the army worked. If it made ten mistakes a day, only the people directly concerned knew about it, because the whole organization was so vast that it just rolled on anyway. Like the Mississippi, it just kept rolling along.

We were billetted in an olive orchard, at San Vieto Chieta. Just above there in a valley a few miles north of Ortona. Christ, it was cold. It was freezing, still winter. We'd be washing our mess tins out with toilet paper and snow. That's what it was like. We melted snow to soften up our bully beef too. You talk about sunny Italy!

Our encampment was a wallow. A wallow. Up in San Vieto some of our guys were living in warm buildings and cleaning their teeth every morning with vino, but out on the line, we were in mucky, muck, muck mud.

Anyway, this day we're paraded. Covered up to our gudgeons in mud, snow filtering down our necks, shivering from the winds off the sea and wondering what the hell the high command was up to this time.

What it was up to was eminently sensible in a way. High command was in Rome. Rome was sunny. The Mediterranean was blue. The flowers were blooming. The farmers were planting and the girls looked so pretty that somebody in high command said it was time to issue the men in the field their summer kit. The parade, in short, was called to issue one and all with the dicky little shorts and sundry other summer kit which was just fine for Saskatchewan on a hot July day but in San Vieto, *murder*! Snow, wind and mud, and we had to change into summer kit because the high command in Rome said since it was such beautiful weather, the troops must be in summer kit. My God!

•◄►• *Field Detention Camp*

This time in Italy I'm called into the company commander's headquarters and I walk in and I don't salute and he says, "Didn't they teach you to salute in this army, Corporal?" and it had been a bad day and a bad week and I said, something like, "Well, sir, it's just this goddamned war." Something like that. I was just saying I was browned off, everything was SNAFU and well, you know, to hell with it.

He threw me on charge. The old conduct prejudicial, fucking et cetera. The Gothic Line business is coming up soon so he feels he's whacking me with the most he can give me and still get me back in time by giving two weeks' field detention.

Field Detention Camp was rough. It was prison, of course, and I could have gone to the old man and appealed that this was cruel and unusual punishment, but I thought, what the hell. You got thinking like that. What the hell. Like, in F.D.C. at least I won't get hit by a truck. Like that. But let me tell you, once you've been through that, you're going to be a pretty good laddie for the rest of your career. It gave me an idea what they used to do to the guys in the Base Detention Camp. When they came back, half of them were no good for the rifle companies. They had no life, no spirit. Whipped right out of them.

I don't really believe these stories you read today about guards in prisons being sadists and all that—but they sure as hell were in the camp I was in. I often wondered what kind of men they were like once they got out in Civvie Street again, how they treated their wives and kids, and what kind of jobs they got. I often wondered what would happen if I met a certain sergeant face to face downtown when we both were out. I mean, would I have killed him, beaten the shit out of him, spit in his face or just walked on by? Probably just walked on by. No time for crud like that.

•◂▸• *A Few Men Died*

Give me a Saskatchewan winter any time. Winter the way we had it in Italy was a plain old pink-eyed stinking bugger. Rain, rain, rain and we had one officer who was so dumb he wouldn't let us sleep in barns, no, because that's what the Germans would aim for.

Maybe so, but more good men died or were loused up for a long time sleeping in those slit trenches than if Jerry had been lucky to throw a shell into one of the stables or houses. Half our guys couldn't fight. The rain. Cold. Pneumonia, pleurisy, trench-foot, the works. But there I was fit as a fiddle and ready for love.

It's the things you learn on the road, during the '30's. Hay's not the thing, but straw is and there was lots of straw around. Those Italians, I think they ate it. All through that winter every night I'd half fill up my trench with straw. You see, straw is hollow, and she's a damn good insulator, and I'd lay one blanket under and another on top, and then I'd crawl in and pull in some more straw. What I'd do next, I'd pull my groundsheet in around me and I'd have a better sleeping bag than they're turning out today. Let it rain or snow, nothing bothered me.

The officer I drove, he finally asked how I could be up and chipper at five in the morning when I took him back to the staff conference and I told him. He said, "Well, I'll be damned." I said, "The best thing, sir, would be to let the men sleep under cover," and when he found out what the captain had ordered—no sleeping in stables or houses, but out in the rain—he blew his top. It did no good, of course. He complained, but the captain had seniority and pulled rank, too, and we kept on sleeping through rain and blizzard, and a few men died of pneumonia because of that asshole captain. That was the army for you, in a nutshell.

•◂▸• *Just One Vast Screw-up*

When we got to England with the First Division, it was just about Christmas and they put us in old barracks near a place called

Woking. That 1939 winter was one of the worst Britain had had in a long time and the huts had no heating and being Canadians, that's one thing we were used to. We had to scrounge wood and coal, and we weren't very good at that because we were just recruits, so all in all, it was a pretty miserable winter. We were at the Inkerman Barracks.

The lights were still on in London. They were still selling bananas and oranges in the stores and we were having a great time. The air raid shelters were there, but not used yet. There was no sense of pending doom, but a lot of comradeship. The feeling was the British would fight for a few months, put these people down, go back to the usual, you know. Running the world.

At Woking we got our basic training. Sort of training. What we could pick up. They showed us the end of the rifle the bullet came out of and gave us the red patches. You know, the famous Red Patch of the Canadian First Division. I was in the service corps by this time. We didn't get much training, but we were training with the Seventh British Corps and the 51st Highland Division, the infantry, was part of it, and so we just fumbled our way through the winter. I think it was late February, the 51st Highland Div went over to France, and they were wiped out when the Germans took over France.

I want to say this. We didn't know what was happening. We knew the Germans were going like hell but we didn't know anything more. Nobody did, I think. So they bundled us up and took us down to the coast and put us on a ship and we disembarked at Brest. We had all the food supplies, the petrol supplies, all the ammo and it was our job to get it up to the front. So there we were, with the Germans maybe only a hundred miles ahead and the whole of France had collapsed, and we were going on our merry jaunt.

We marshalled in a vineyard and proceeded to get good and gloriously drunk. We got loaded on to a cattle train and were unloaded at a little place called St. Denis, I think about 22 miles outside Paris. A suburb. All our trucks were there. All lined up. Brand new. Ford trucks. About 150 miles on each. Everything for the division was on them, the works. I got a real thrill, because I was given a three-ton truck. And we hung around there for about three days, and nobody knew what was going on, not a thing, but we could see the refugees. I'll say, it was like you're at a football game and when its over everybody just surges for the exits and pushes and shoves and nobody cares about anyone else. French troops, civilians. Old men, women, kids, bicycles, baby carriages, carts pulled by horses or cows, wagons, push carts, all going down the road, tens of thousands of them and they didn't know where they were going except they'd say the Germans were coming. They called them the Boches. But we didn't have any orders. We just sat there. This was the time of Dunkirk.

And then they say to get the hell back to Brest. Get back any way you can. That's when we scattered, every truck for itself. So my partner and I headed back and I think the Germans were only a few miles up ahead and these refugees, it was tough going past them. Thousands, and they didn't know where they were going. Where were they going? Where was there to go? It was lucky there was no strafing by the Germans.

To show you how stupid it was, we'd pass British troops going back towards Brest—but we'd also pass British troops moving up to the front! There was no communication. Nobody was directing us.

All the way down the road if we saw an army vehicle out of gas we'd stop and give them some of ours. We had half a truck load of canned peaches and boxes and boxes of C-rations. We used to call them McGonigal's Stew. But we had no meat. We'd hand out cans of peaches and get wine and bread and cheese for these, and meat. I think it was horsemeat but you fry it up with some onions and it was goddamned good. You could buy anything with a can of peaches.

We followed the road right back to Brest and hung around there a couple of days and still nobody knew what was going on. I remember my buddy and I went in to a little square and bought some wine and bread and we're sitting on the curb and drinking and I said, "Hell, it's a pretty day and look at all the great broads walking around and I like France. I don't want to leave it. Let's stay," and we kind of decide to stay. To hell with going back to England. That's how little we knew about the situation.

But I figure I better send my wife a souvenir and we go into this shop and when my chum is talking to the lady I swipe two pair of silk pants and then I buy a bottle of perfume. When we leave, there's a couple of big British military policemen and they tell us to get the hell down this street to the docks, so we go. There are hundreds, thousands of troops and the ship I get on, it has Indian troops, French, British, R.A.F. pilots and about ten other Canadians. I don't know where the rest of our company has gone.

Getting on the ship, they told us to destroy our equipment. Take what you could carry, that's all. Those wonderful Ford trucks. We were busy for a couple of days just on demolition work. So much equipment you couldn't believe. Firing anti-tank rifles through the engines. Burned them. Burned the supplies. We didn't leave anything. And that's when we got on the boats.

Then they started to bother us. The Germans. They'd come in over the harbour strafing and bombing and every guy on the ship would be firing. Guys with Lewis guns, guys with rifles and even guys firing pistols. Pistols at a dive bomber. We had one anti-aircraft gun mounted kind of shakily on the ship but I didn't see any planes shot down. We missed being hit, but the one next to us got a bomb on the deck and there were about 140-150 casualties.

The ship we were on was pretty big. We had a couple of navy escort things. It wasn't like Dunkirk up the coast, fishing boats, launches, sailboats and that stuff. Troops were still coming down the road, without rifles, packs, or anything, just themselves and wandering around, not knowing what was going on, and they'd get on the boats. Finally somebody must have said we should get the hell out of there and we sailed. Not in a convoy, but by ourselves. We just went. Somebody said go. Landed at Southampton, and that was the end of that jaunt in France.

It was chaos. There was no order that I could see, no regimental discipline, nothing. Just one vast screw-up and it lasted like that for some time, as I remember. Anybody could have conquered England if they could have got ashore. Britain had nothing to defend itself with. All the prime fighting forces were on the other side of the water and when they got back after Dunkirk it was just a great mass of men, no material, no guns, no ammunition, or organization, and no nothing at all.

The Navy—the Senior Service

Fine Sailors from the Prairies ... "Lovely Morning, Sir"
... Short of Lifeboats ... On the Murmansk Run ...
Limping Home ... Everything Was Confused ... Christ-
mas in Londonderry

In 1939 the Royal Canadian Navy was perhaps 2,000 men, six
destroyers that could put up some sort of a scrap, and a few escort
and support craft. It was really kid stuff.

But by war's end, the R.C.N. was third largest among the
Allies, in numbers, right behind the United States and Britain. Its
killing ground was the North Atlantic, one of the world's dirtiest
and meanest oceans, where it hunted the German submarines, the
U-boats which Churchill feared "most of all." But those bouncy
corvettes, those frigates (bigger and more powerful and faster, but
still just as uncomfortable) and those sleek destroyers patrolled
the sea lanes between New York, Boston, Halifax, Montreal,
Quebec and St. John's across the heaving blue-grey North Atlantic
and, assisted by land-based long-range bombers from Newfound-
land and the Old Country, they defeated the German U-boats.

But it wasn't only the North Atlantic. The navy protected
the West Coast against possible Japanese attack and operated in
the Pacific, in the Mediterranean and sailed on the truly horrifying
midwinter convoy escorts to Murmansk in northern Russia. During
the D-day invasion, 109 Canadian warships and landing craft took
part. They saw many strange incidents and, like seamen every-
where, wove them into spellbinding tales of the sea.

•◄►• Fine Sailors from the Prairies

The Canadian farm boys, the lads from the prairies, they were
dedicated sailors, superb sailors. Both officers and men.

They'd come out from the prairies to Vancouver, cross
over to Victoria to H.M.C.S. *Naden,* stick their finger in the water
to see if the water really was salty and then they were ready to
start learning to become truly first-class seamen, officers. I admired them all very much.

What brought them into the navy, not the army? Well,
they were from the prairies, so flat, such sameness, so I guess their
philosophy was, "There's a mountain, climb it; there's the ocean,

sail it." A challenge and a love too. They were first-class, all the way.

•◄►• *"Lovely Morning, Sir"*

We were in St. John's and this old sot of a skipper, Shanghai, a China coaster type, called me in and he said, "We're going it alone," meaning we had orders for Ireland but just ourselves, and then he looked at me, this very young lieutenant, and he said, "And I say, old boy, can you navigate?" and I said, "Oh yes, sir."

My first ship, and there I was, told to navigate this huge ship, in my eyes, across the North Atlantic in winter. Gales. My God! The truth was, I had taken a quick 10-day navigation course some time back, failed it, knew nothing whatsoever about navigation and barely could read a road map, let alone a chart. But I said yes and away we went.

I go below and I dig out my navigation textbook and make some notes and decide on the Great Circle Route, right up within sight of Greenland, and I was young in those days, and I thought, "Oh well, we'll manage somehow," even though I knew that without refueling, it might be touch-and-go whether we'd even make it across under our own power.

But away we went and the weather was terrible, I couldn't take a sight and so it was all dead reckoning, and this morning we get this signal saying, "Submarine reported, position X." Well, position X on the chart was about 300 miles south of where I thought we were, so away we go again, and of course, there is no submarine there and probably never had been, but when we get there I have to set up another course back towards Ireland.

Another three days go by and we get another signal to go to position Y, another submarine, and it's away off in another direction and, when we get there, naturally no submarine, and probably never was one either. So now the charts looks like a pair of spiders had farted on it. And the old man would come up on the bridge and he'd look at the chart and say, "Where are we, old boy?" and I'd stab my finger down on the chart, and he'd say, "Are you sure?" By this time he was wise that I knew nothing about navigation, and that he was alone with 100 men and a ship on a huge, huge ocean.

There wasn't much doubt in my mind that we'd run out of fuel, if we ever did get to land, and the captain was properly worried. So finally the time came when we had to send an E.T.A. [estimated time of arrival] to London and I got to work with my old instruments and my pencil and eraser and we sent, "E.T.A. 0700 hours Wednesday, Londonderry." Now my course lay to pick up Insterhall Light on the extreme northwest coast of Ireland, which we had to find if we weren't hopelessly lost. But by the signals we were picking up from shore from 200 miles out, it looked like we were somewhere off the Outer Hebrides, which was a long, long, long way away from my lighthouse, and that's what everyone on the bridge thought. There was good reason, because we were getting all these cross-bearings. So the old man was even more worried, but he said to me, "You better go and lay your head down. Get some sleep. We'll try and straighten all this out in the morning," and by this time, everybody knew we were lost and we were running out of oil, and so I said to hell with it and got some sleep.

And about six in the morning, the captain sent down a seaman to wake me up and the seaman said, "Compliments of the bridge, sir, and the captain wishes you to know that Insterhall Light is dead ahead."

Christ, I had got it right within a mile. I went up on the bridge, very casual, said good morning, looked at the chart and made some small remark like, "Lovely morning, sir," or something like that. I was king on that ship then. The greatest navigator of all time, the navigator who knew nothing about navigation.

•◀▶• *Short of Lifeboats*

We were on our way home from the North Africa landings, in the old *Warwick Castle*. In '42. We'd just landed American troops in North Africa and we had got into the Bay of Biscay and it was a real bloody storm and most of the guys thought, oh well, we're pretty safe in this kind of weather.

It was ten o'clock in the morning when the first one hit. Three, four minutes after that, the second one ripped through her. The whole forepeak broke off, and she went down. We had about 25, 20 minutes and we closed the watertight doors and there was a hell of a lot lost, trapped, that way, but our job was to try and save the ship. You see, the first torpedo hit near the bow and that's where all the men were trapped, because that's where most of the crew's accommodations were. We had a crew of 208 and 32 of us survived. That was a rough one.

We were in the water for about 90 minutes and then a lifeboat from the ship came along and took us aboard. Then about a couple of days later a destroyer came along and picked us up. Took us to the Clyde.

If all of us had got off it would have been bad, too, because they'd stripped her of a lot of her lifeboats to make way for invasion barges for the Americans. A lot of our guys got into the water all right, but I think they died swallowing diesel fuel or they drowned because they didn't have life jackets—and as I said, we were short of lifeboats and they drowned. It was a damn good thing I had my life jacket on. I couldn't swim.

•⬌• *On the Murmansk Run*

Bravest men I saw in the war were those fellows who were catapulted off in their airplanes on the Murmansk run. You see, the only thing they could do when they'd finished their gas was to land in the sea and hope that a destroyer would come along and pick them up.

They would be catapulted off the deck of the freighters, and of course there was no place to land back. Just in the ocean, and you had no chance. Only a minute or two. Then the freezing water would get you.

Yes, they were hunting subs. Looking for them. It was more subs than planes up there, off the North Cape of Norway. You would get some planes but mostly subs.

These fellows were all volunteers. Who the hell would volunteer for a thing like that? I guess most of them died in the water.

•⬌• *Limping Home*

We were on a Royal Navy strike force, after the *Tirpitz,* which was in a Norwegian fjord. She was the German battleship, you'll recall, a big one but she was damaged, and we were to get her, and sink her forever. The Tenth Cruiser Squadron, Wee MacGregor was her admiral. I was navigating officer of the *Nabob,* the Canadian aircraft carrier on the strike force.

I laid out a course for that night and next day, and I went to my little bunk above the bridge. I remember it was about 5:15 when suddenly there was a whomp! A whomp! Well, I ran to the bridge, and the worst thing I could see was the rest of the strike force leaving us. We were like a lame duck and by this time listing fairly badly to starboard and our speed was dropping, 16 knots, 15, 14.

The stern seemed to be going down, and the flight decks were taking on an angle, so we couldn't fly off our aircraft, we had Avengers and Wildcats. Captain Horatio Nelson Lay picked up the P.A. system and did something I'd been trained *not* to do. He called, "Prepare to abandon ship," and the seamen grabbed the knives off their hips and started cutting the Carley floats loose and the other floating equipment; but unfortunately we're still going through the water at a good rate, and so all this lifesaving equipment is streaming out behind us towards the horizon. A beautiful cold sea, the only way it could be at 74 degrees north, and all our lifesaving equipment was strung way out behind us, and of course, the lesson is, don't use P.A. system until it's warmed up; because all that those men heard was "Abandon ship" and not "Prepare to abandon ship." However, that was just for openers.

I think the worst thing was the discomfiture of seeing the fleet leaving you, which was the proper thing to do, and then *Kempthorne,* a frigate, R.N., which was left behind to assist us in any way, she suddenly blew up. Another torpedo. One moment she's there, and the next, right off our starboard, she's suddenly a mass of steam and sinking. That was only a few minutes after we were hit.

A couple of days later, a few destroyers, *Assiniboine, Algonquin*, came and took off most of our survivors, and a skeleton crew took *Nabob* in to Scapa Flow. I remember the padre wanted to leave on the destroyer and somebody said, "Sir, I think you've got more souls here to take care of than anywhere else," and he stayed.

And eventually we got back 1,400 miles or so to Scapa Flow at one or two knots. I think two knots. Do you know how slow that is? You probably walk at four knots.

Oh yes, and every day there was the threat of torpedo attack. Every day. We still had our Asdic going, and when we picked up a strong signal that there was a sub near, one skulking about, we'd fly off one of these Avengers. Our pilots, for some reason, were New Zealanders. And they had to go off by catapult, thrown into the air, so to speak. We never did get rid of the list. Our draft aft was 46 feet and our draft forward was six feet. Think of that. Tilt your hand and see just what that deck was. The Germans knew we had these special new homing torpedoes, so they stayed pretty well away from us. Probably they figured why waste a torpedo on the ship, it was going down anyhow. I think, however, if they had really pressed home an attack they could have got us. Think of the condition the old girl was in.

The pilots would crash the Avengers on the deck when

they returned, and we'd push them over the side, dump them into the water. This was the only way they could do it, landing on a side of a hill, and if you've ever landed on an aircraft carrier and tried to pick up that arrester hook, it's the smallest postage stamp you've ever seen.

So by keeping that kind of surveillance on the subs with these torpedoes they left us alone. When we steamed in to Scapa Flow the whole naval base was out looking at us and saying, "Those things aren't supposed to stay afloat. What's keeping that one up?" It wasn't supposed to stay afloat, but the old *Nabob* did.

We found 23 bodies down in the wardroom bar where they'd been getting the rum rations when we were hit. By the time we got her pumped out, it was about six weeks past and they were all so bloated you never saw anything like it. The undertaker wouldn't bring out those bodies, and we had to. What an experience!

•➤• *Everything Was Confused*

At that time, we thought we were being badly led. Our senior officers were what we called boffins, old fellows of 35 years or so who wanted to see the war out, but we were all fired up, up and at 'em. So I went to the flotilla leader and I told him, or requested permission to operate my gunboat independently. A stupid thing to do, but there it was. He said fine, do so.

And so two of us went north on this operation and we spotted a trawler near the mainland. It was a moonlit night and it was a silhouette, a big one, what we called a prime target. About a mile from this target, our sister ship veers off into the dark, to starboard. The skipper didn't even fire a torpedo. He just said to me on the R/T [radio telephone] that he was going to do a reconnaissance. I said, "Fuck them," and so, as I veered off to port, I am now operating independently.

Then we lost the trawler. She just disappeared towards some coastal port. But these two other ships came into view. Well! They were our adversaries, E-boats, so we said, "Whack-o!" and we did this closing bit and they couldn't see us and we got right in on them, and when we let go it was absolutely devastating. Zap! Both started on fire immediately, men staggering all over the deck, and all of this took only about 15 minutes and they were both finished. Completely finished.

Then all of a sudden from the direction of this port was another ship closing fast on us. We couldn't identify it, but we saw it on our radar so my First gets up with the 1039 signal lamp and he gives the letter "R"—you see, that's the challenge we have between us in our flotilla. No answer again and it's closing fast. No response. All of a sudden, this boat comes charging into the scene and there is a great burst of fire from it, every gun they've got, and our only reply to it is, "Oh oh, the Germans," and we fire at this intruder. In a minute or two this third boat was on fire and we kept pounding it in. And all of a sudden, through the battle smoke, we saw the hull of this intruder and, *oooohh, aaaaah,* it was our sister ship, which had sheered off some time ago to go on some reconnaissance or other and left us alone.

By this time the German shore batteries had opened up, after all this time, and we just couldn't sit around there, so we signalled that we'd move off and then slip back and pick up survivors. We sat out in the dark for a while and then we came back. We came back and picked them up, and there weren't too many left, and I forget how many were wounded, but it was the most awful night.

As we reconstructed, the skipper of the first boat must have felt that he had to expend a little ammunition, so he could say he was there. So, to justify himself he charged in, and in the glare of the burning targets he did not see the signal challenge, the letter "R" and he did not know that we were there, that we had done the dirty work. And we, of course, were sure that he was a German ship coming to help his own ships, and so everything was confused. Completely. And, I guess, that's what comes from acting independently.

•⟶• *Christmas in Londonderry*

A group of us, destroyers, frigates, corvettes were in Londonderry the day before Christmas, 1943, and we hoped to have Christmas ashore like ordinary folk. But the people in the shore establishment didn't want to be bothered with a lot of ships in port and a lot of drunken Canadian sailors wandering their fair streets, causing trouble and so on, and so the commodore ashore decided that he'd clear us out. We'd have exercises at sea over Christmas and then we'd come back after having two or three days out there in a howling gale. And of course those ashore—and it was the Americans who were running the port in those days—they would have a nice quiet Christmas dinner without the Canadians roaring around.

So we're easing down the river day before Christmas and the old man, a very decent sort, he's just fuming from the orders, so he calls the chief engineer up and he says, "A bottle for you if you can find anything wrong with the engines," and the engineer says, "With a little provocation, sir, I think I can," and the captain says, "Fine, put a spanner in the works, and if it's bad enough to keep us here for Christmas it's worth a bottle of scotch whiskey for you." So, sure enough, in a few minutes Smitty comes back and he says, "Something wrong with the condenser, sir," and the old man says, "Oh, dammit, have to put back to port. Send a signal requesting permission," which I did and, of course, they couldn't refuse.

So we went back and lay alongside about ten in the morning and at eleven we had Up Spirits and the captain was feeling in a good mood, and we hadn't used up our quota of rum coming over because the weather was so bad nobody could handle the stuff, so we had gallons of it left over. Gash rum, it was called. So, the captain orders a double tot for everyone and then another tot and this is very highly overproofed rum and the upshot of it all is that the whole crew got stinking drunk before noon.

Assured by Smitty that we'd be in for at least 24 hours, and happy about the success of his stratagem, the skipper then ordered that the rest of the gash rum be distributed. His Christmas present to the crew! Then the officers ordered, as their Christmas present to the men, cases and cases of Whitbread's ale, and all that was drunk too. It was meant for the next day, Christmas, but you know sailors.

The day before Christmas, hell, no discipline, let them all sleep it off. Some went ashore to get drunker and some staggered to their bunks and there we were, alongside the dock, and the American mechanics and engineers came aboard and by 4 P.M., they reported to the duty watch that the repairs to Smitty's starboard condenser were completed, and we got a signal from the American commander. Prepare to rejoin the group for exercises. Those Americans just didn't want Canadians around.

So, sure enough, at five o'clock the pilot came aboard. Drunk. So we had a drunken pilot and a drunken crew. Some could work a bit, but a great many were completely incapacitated. The captain was on his feet, though. I went aft to take over the quarterdeck party because the officer usually there had passed out. I was unfamiliar with that procedure and it was six o'clock by this time and blacker than Paddy's arse, so orders come to let go for'ard and let go lines aft and they let go the forward lines, but aft, the hawsers had tightened on the bit, frozen, so we swing on a tangent and we just cannot let go aft and we're drifting out on an axis and swinging around and gaining speed. I'm going to make the rest of the story mercifully short.

By the time I get one of my drunken party running to find an axe and he comes back and I hack through the hawser, we've gained so much speed that they can't arrest the ship and right alongside are three landing craft. Everyone knew the invasion was coming and there were landing craft hidden in harbours all over the British Isles. These were American ones, big ones, for troops and vehicles, and we hit the first one a fearful whack, crumpling it up, and it began to go *glub-glub-glub* and before it went down, with our weight still behind it, it smashed into the second in line and down it went, and before it went down, *glub-glub-glub,* it hit the third and it also sank. Oh, I don't know. Maybe a million and a half dollars' worth of shipping. Maybe less. But on the bottom.

And by this time we were under way heading down the river with a drunken pilot and the captain yelling into the darkness, "I don't give a damn about your goddamned boats," and away we went and, to this day, you know, I don't think there was ever any explanation or inquiry or investigation into how those three landing craft were sunk on Christmas Eve.

"Out with the Japs"

*My Best Friend . . . "Out with the Japs" . . . Thievery . . .
High-powered Binoculars . . . The Little Jars . . . A Chance
to Prove Their Patriotism . . . In Hastings Park . . . A Useless Existence . . . "Missionaries Gave Us Goals" . . . Self-
government at Tashme . . . For Their Submarines . . . It
Was the Propaganda Talking . . . The Signing . . . Tashme
Today . . . The End Result Was Good*

*It would seem that old memories never die but stay hidden, fester-
ing. While researching this book I found several people who were
still convinced that the Japanese Canadians on the West Coast
during the war committed half a hundred different crimes against
the nation.*

*On the other hand, most of the people I interviewed felt
that the 1942 expulsion of the Japanese from their city homes,
their market gardens, their fishing villages was a shameful thing—
probably the most shameful of all Canadian acts during the war. It
is an act that is rarely mentioned, beyond a sentence or a para-
graph, in Canadian schoolbooks, and most Canadians are only
dimly aware it ever occurred. In fact, even during the expulsion,
great numbers of Canadians in eastern Canada remained unaware
that 26,000 law-abiding citizens were torn from their homes and
put into prison camps in the B.C. mountains, while a few were
dumped almost willy-nilly in small prairie towns or in Toronto
with only the clothes they wore and the few possessions they
could carry.*

*So our very own concentration camps were set up, created
by patriotism mixed with fear. The fear was, of course, that if the
Japanese Navy and Army invaded B.C., every Japanese Canadian
would leap to aid the conquerors. But there was never a proven
case of treason or spying by any Japanese Canadian during six
years of war.*

*The expulsion, which was encouraged by West Coast busi-
nessmen, farmers, and fishing interests, had a happy ending. The
Japanese ghettos were broken up. The Japanese lost much of the
sense of being a people unto themselves and became Canadians-at-
large, in every part of the country, industrious, respected, making
a strong contribution to Canadian life.*

It seems that the scars of bitterness have healed among the Japanese Canadians; the scar remaining is still open on the pages of our history books, and in some of the stories I have included here. It is an ugly chapter of our country's story.

My Best Friend

There was a Japanese girl I went to school with. In my class. You might call her my best friend, we did a lot of things together; yes, we were good friends. But the fact that her family was dispossessed, that they lost all they had, house and everything, when she and her family were scooped up, like almost in the night, that didn't really bother us at all.

We never said anything about it—never questioned it at all. I never thought there was anything wrong about taking those thousands of people away and sticking them in camps in the bush. No. No. Not at all. We just accepted it.

It shows you what propaganda can do to you. The Japanese were our enemies—not our Japanese Canadians, but Japanese over the seas, in Japan—so our Japanese friends were bad.

The point is, if authority did it, then it was right. It was a very disciplined time.

"Out with the Japs"

One thing about the whole evacuation, it wasn't just war. It was part economic. They used the war as an excuse.

For example, the other fishermen were more than happy to see the Japanese go, and so were the politicians. Whoever cried out, "Out with the Japs," they got the vote. And so there was no holding back, saying the Japanese were good fishermen and we got to keep them here because fish is food and we need food for the war effort. There was none of that. Get them out of here. And of course it was the white fishermen who got our boats, our gear, our houses.

In the Fraser Valley I would say the majority of the other farmers were more than pleased to see the Japanese go, so they could pick up their farms afterwards. This is what happened. This is something that is not said very often.

•◄►• *High-powered Binoculars*

I was one of seven federal employees engaged in the R.C.M.P. barracks and also up at Hastings Park when the Japanese evacuation was going on, and every one of those 12,000 files went through my hands. And I don't think that some of you people who didn't live through those war years in Vancouver realize just what was going on. If you had seen some of the files on these people you would have realized we had to be very cautious.

Well, for instance, up the coast, some of the dear old daddies were retired Japanese admirals. I can't disclose what was in the files. Some had high-powered binoculars. Now, don't ridicule me, please, and we did sight a submarine off Vancouver Island. In fact, I typed the first report on the sighting.

I admit, there still are some very influential people in Vancouver in charge of this evacuation who made their rake-off on the forced sale of Japanese fishboats and their lands and businesses. Now we didn't go along with that. And we could see that some Japanese were being deferred, didn't have to go to the camps. They were paying the brass, sitting up in their big offices getting a rake-off, to get deferred.

I can't tell you what was in those files. They were all classified, secret. We were at war.

•◄►• *Thievery*

When they threw the Japanese out of the coast they had these so-called auctions of their property and they were a farce. First, those who were running the show, they and their friends got all the best stuff. They'd go into a house and one would say, "I'll take that," and it would be one of these beautiful old clocks encased in glass, the kind they call 400-day clocks, and the other fellow would say he'd put it down for 5 dollars, and that was the way it was done. Thievery, that's all it was. Some of the most beautiful furniture, all hand carved and the finest wood, going for almost nothing.

And then when these fellows had taken what they wanted, they'd have a so-called auction of what was left, the stuff in the houses, in the boat sheds, everything. A cent on the dollar, five cents, never more than ten cents.

There are a lot of wealthy men in this province who should be thoroughly ashamed of what they did. It was little more than thievery to these lovely people. I knew a lot of Japanese very well and they were charming people, such lovely people, and there they were yanked out of their homes and herded off into the back country like a bunch of cattle, on the orders of a bunch of lousy politicians. I am ashamed of my whole generation for what they did, thoroughly ashamed.

•◄►• *The Little Jars*

They moved the Japanese out, and Steveston, which was like their capital, their city, was like a ghost town because most of the stores and houses and that were Japanese.

There was this building, their Buddhist Temple, and my husband was a carpenter and he worked around it so he sort of kept his eye on it, you know, but soon people started going in. White people, you know. All around the walls were small shelves, and out of curiosity the whites who came out to the temple for a look-see would look in the little jars, the containers around the walls on these shelves, and they started to take them. They disappeared pretty fast after that, when people started taking things out of the temple.

You know, there was something in them, but they didn't know what it was. Black and powdery, that's what it was like. And then somebody said that material in them was the ashes of the Japanese ancestors, their fathers and grandparents, and that the temple was a holy place.

So one by one, the white people started to bring them back, and before long, the word had got all around. And soon all the little urns were back in place and a couple of the whites saw to it that the front and back doors had real good locks to protect the place from then on.

•◄►• *A Chance to Prove Their Patriotism*

When the Japanese were in Hastings Park before they were all dispersed, the young fellows would come up to me and ask if I could arrange it so they could join the army. In labor battalions, anything, but just give them a chance to prove their patriotism. I used to be out at Hastings Park nearly every day and these young men would come, pleading for a chance to join the army.

I tried. I went to the authorities—I can't remember who it was then—but it was impossible. I tried but I couldn't get anywhere. Turned down. Flatly. They weren't allowed. No hearing. Just out to the camps in the bush—and those young fellows would have been good soldiers.

The Americans did the smart thing. They called for volunteers among the Nisei and got thousands, and that brigade went to Italy and became the most decorated in the American army. Most decorated and took the most casualties, too.

•◄►• *In Hastings Park*

They put all us Japanese in Hastings Park [in Vancouver, 1942], in the cattle barns, and they whitewashed the walls and put up kind of partitions, and each family would have one of these tiny cubicles. Like little stalls. We were there for about three and a half months. It was mainly a place to lie down and sleep.

There was nothing to do. We used to walk around and get up on a high spot and watch the horse races, and sometimes we'd go to another place and watch the golfers on the golf course they had.

We worked in the kitchens too. Fifteen cents an hour for three hours a day, and my job was to stand at the end and put two slices of bread and a pat of butter on each plate. We washed dishes too. Just to get a little spending money.

You couldn't go out of the fenced-in area unless you had some special purpose and then the Mounties would give you permission. Going to a doctor would be a special reason. The Mounties on the whole were very good, although there was the odd one who tried to get cocky. I remember once one of our people had done some small misdeed and the Mounties came to get him, and he knew judo and he threw three Mounties all over the place. All over the place. They never did anything to him. They wouldn't come near him again.

There was a little hole in the fence by Renfrew Street and there was this tiny grocery store there and the kids would go down there and the old woman who ran the store, she'd always be on the lookout. When she saw the kids she'd come across the street and ask what did they want. Then she'd go back and bring it. Chocolate bars, soap, all the things we couldn't buy in the camp because there was no store.

Then they finally sent us into the interior.

•◄►• *A Useless Existence*

When we first went to Tashme, that first winter of '42 was a bad one, and because we had six children we were eventually able to get a house by ourselves. But when I say a house I don't mean a house, but a place about the size of this living room. About 12 feet by 15 or 16 feet. Little bigger than a garage for eight people.

That first winter the snow was deep and the firewood was cut green. I still recall we had to put the chunks of wood in the oven to dry them out so we could burn them. There was only room for wooden bunk beds and I remember I could wake up in the morning and scratch out my initials on the heavy frost on the inside of the boards. The bunk was against the wall.

By the second winter, after the first winter's experience, there was always a fight to try and get the cardboard boxes that the supplies came in—corrugated cardboard boxes. We'd nail them on the walls. This was insulation and everybody wanted it. They were hard to come by.

There was some farming, but not too much. They grew some potatoes and cabbage but there were very few working on the farm. The men were out cutting wood for winter, and then they finally got a little sawmill to cut some lumber.

There was nothing to do, not for three years. It was a useless existence—an until-the-war-ends type of thing. We tried to make it as comfortable as possible for everybody. There was a little store, a butcher shop, a bakery which sold only bread, no pastry or anything fancy. So you got the basics. If you worked in the mill or on the roads, the pay was 15 cents under eighteen and two bits over, and you could buy wieners or hamburger in the butcher shop but that's all. But if you were eighteen and over and single, then you were sent to the road camps in the mountains.

•◄►• *"Missionaries Gave Us Goals"*

The Anglicans were in just about every camp. The Catholics too. In staff alone the United Church must have had about 15 people in the camps. Helping out, but not only helping out in school and programs for the old and young, but going to bat for us. At the camp I was in, the minister and the missionaries did so much—like coming to Vancouver and getting things like diapers if someone was going to have a baby when we couldn't buy them, and also picking things up for us, things that we had stored with friends, going to these homes and bringing us things like clothes and books—the stuff that we had to leave behind when they took us away. There were a lot of little things like this that missionaries did for us. Just unaccountable.

Unfortunately, our Buddhist priests were not in the same

position as the white missionaries. They were locked in the camp with us, you see. The authorities considered the Buddhist priest an enemy, he couldn't come out to the coast. If it wasn't for the white ministers and missionaries, the hardships would have been twice as bad.

Another thing, I think the church, through these missionaries, was able to help many young people to set their goals higher. In the camp I was in, we had our high school in a barn. We went in at 3:30, after the younger classes had been dismissed. The class I was in had about 30. I would say all or most of them are doing well now, and well over half went on to university. Because these missionaries gave them higher goals to attain.

If I had lived in Steveston or Powell Street when I was going to school, I don't think I would have gone on to university, and I don't think any of the others with me would have either. High school would be it.

I'm not trying to push the Christian gospel down anyone's throat, but giving us goals, something to really work for, that was the most important thing I know.

•◄►• *Self-government at Tashme*

In the Tashme camp there was a kind of self-government. It was called a council and there would be one person from each of the streets, First Street to Twelfth, and one from the two places where the old people were. That made twelve. They made a few regulations.

One was, they wouldn't let us have a cemetery or let us out of the camp to bury our dead in one, so up against the mountain there, they had this crematorium. Whether you wanted it or not, whether it was against what you stood for, everybody had to be cremated. It was the job of the council members to look after the crematorium. You weren't picked. It was in rotation. You knew when your time would come, you and the person of the council next in line with you.

When a person died, you and the other person would go to the crematorium and keep the fire burning. It wasn't far from the other buildings, near the mountain, and you'd keep the fire going all night and then the next morning the family of the dead person would come and collect the ashes.

•◀▶• *For Their Submarines*

I realize most Japanese were indiscriminately picked up and shipped out, but did you know they had refueling stations on the west coast of Vancouver Island?

In Sydney Inlet, for instance. It was a well-known fact among us fishermen over there. The oil was for their submarines. No, not their warships, submarines. Jap fishermen on this coast had cached it there before the war began.

This is definitely sure because I was one of the guys that helped to destroy it.

•◀▶• *It Was the Propaganda Talking*

If you keep hammering and hammering away, it begins to stick to you. In the papers, magazines, on the radio day in and day out, the propaganda. The terrible tortures the Japanese soldiers did on our boys, or on the other side of the world, the Germans bombing London night after night, killing all those children and babies in their beds.

In the war I went back home to visit my mother in Edmonton and she had three little old wooden houses out on the St. Albert Trail, just shacks, and she had rented one to a family of Japs who were thrown out of Vancouver. They were right next to Mother's house, and when I looked out the window and saw two little Jap kids playing there I said, "For God's sakes, Mother, what have you got in your house?" I was very indignant. There was this bitterness, although I'd never really known any Japs in Vancouver. But it was the training, all the propaganda talking. It had worked on me.

Next day she took me over and introduced me to the woman, a little woman my age, about thirty, and I froze. I froze right up. I couldn't help myself. I did. Mother saw it and so did the woman, and Mother was mad at me because she thought just the world of that family, how good they were to her and how wonderful the children were. They became like her second family.

But I couldn't help myself. It was the propaganda. Part of it is in all of us, this suspicion for people who aren't like us, and that is what the propaganda works on. Every day you lose a little bit more of yourself and become a little bit more of what they want you to be. And now I know that what they wanted us to be was not very nice at all. Not very nice at all.

•◄►• *The Signing*

I was sixteen when they had what we called The Signing. This was at the end of the war, the war was just over and they didn't want the Japanese to go back to the coast, to their vegetable farms and their fishing and their businesses in the cities because they didn't exist any more. These had all been taken away from them and sold very cheaply to white people.

I didn't sign. They wanted us to go back to Japan, or if you didn't sign, then they would send you to the prairies or Ontario. My father and my mother, they didn't want to start all over again. They were born in Japan, yeah, and even if it was tough in Japan they'd rather go back there. My father was so discouraged and he was old now and didn't want to start all over. My brother, my sister and myself, we didn't see what purpose it would serve leaving Canada, because we were Canadians. We hadn't been born in Japan. We were Canadians. We wanted to finish our education in Canada. He couldn't see leaving the three older ones in Canada and taking the younger children back to Japan, so they didn't go. About 4,000 Japanese did go back to Japan, and they had a terrible time. My wife's two sisters went and they tell us sometimes how bad it was. The Americans were there and there was no food and the cities were destroyed. They finally came back in two years.

So when I wouldn't sign they sent me to Ottawa, and through missionaries I went to a home there to continue my education. I worked among them and they were good people. I took correspondence high school there because I had taken correspondence at Tashme and they figured it would be best if I just continued on correspondence.

No, I didn't find any bitterness against the Japanese in Ottawa. The people treated me very well. Surprising, they didn't even know the Japanese had been evacuated. It seemed that all the things that were going on here in B.C. and were in the papers here never appeared in the papers in Ottawa. They didn't even know that the Japanese had been evacuated and put into camps in the interior. This all came as a surprise. Even among government officials, civil servants I should say, they didn't know, and of course the people I met and the kids I got to know, they had never heard of it.

•◄►• *Tashme Today*

If you drive out on the Hope Princeton Highway about 100 miles from Vancouver, about 10 miles from Hope, on your right there's this big farm, a ranch with a huge barn. It's a summer resort in summer with cabins and a ski resort in winter, up in the mountains. Happy Valley or Wonder Valley, I think it's called now, but that was the Tashme Camp where about two or three thousand of our people from the coast spent the war. Tashme was the biggest Japanese concentration camp in Canada.

My youngest daughter Tabby, she's thirteen now and loves to ski. She'd ski every day if she could and one weekend last year she mentioned that her gang of kids from the school were going to this Wonder Valley for the day. I knew what it was, of course, so I told her to take a very good look and I didn't say why. She didn't ask either.

When she came home she said that while they were waiting for the bus driver to come and take them home she talked to the man who ran the skidoo school and he took her around. She said he gave her a guided tour and told her that the place was where the Japanese Canadians were kept during the war. She knew about that time because we'd told the kids, but I'm sure they didn't believe it. She said there was only one little cabin still standing and she said just where it was, over the creek against the hill. I knew that place and I told her that had been the morgue when we were there and that her grandmother had been put in there when she died in 1943. That kind of shook her. You know, she'd seen a building and I'd said what it was for and her grandmother had been in it. That sort of brought it home.

Still, next day I guess she forgot all about it. But I think she will remember more about it later, and I'm sort of grateful to that man who had the skidoo school who took the time to show her a bit of it. He knew she was Japanese and he was showing Tabby a bit of her heritage. I thought that was darn nice of him.

•━►• *The End Result Was Good*

Yes, I would say the method they used I'm still against. I'm sure they could have done it in a better democratic and Christian way for a democratic and Christian country. Even the United States did not just turn around and sell all the Japanese property. They returned it to them. But, here, they sold it all, and I still say it was very unfair, say to my father, to have his life's work sold for a few hundred dollars.

To a person like myself and generally speaking, Nisei, I think the end result was good. It meant that we spread across Canada and it meant the end of Japanese towns like Steveston. In Vancouver you'll find a few stores on Powell Street, but it is not the Japanese town it used to be. The biggest Japanese population now is in Toronto.

I would say the Japanese people—in relation to other Orientals, Chinese—have more opportunities today, for anything we care to go into, and I would say we are more accepted because we don't have Japanese towns. We are not in ghettos. Now it is highly unusual if you find two or three Japanese living on the same street. They're spread around. So in that way I have to say I'm thankful that such a thing happened.

Before the war there was no future for a Nisei. Even if you graduated from university you went fishing with your father or on his garden farm or in a sawmill. No company would ever hire us. The only professional who ever made use of his education was a doctor. I mean an engineer I knew was working in a sawmill and there was another man who graduated from university with a science degree and the only job he could get was going around to all these little Japanese corner stores and selling them one-cent candy and chocolate bars. A candy salesman! You don't need a university degree to do that.

The opportunities today for ... well, the door is wide open.

So I say, to the second and third generation the end results were good. I still oppose the method of doing it. I could see their point of wartime hysteria for one thing, plus they said it was for our own protection and safety. If there ever had been an invasion of Japanese it would have been pretty hard for the Japanese, like my parents who were born in Japan, to ignore them completely. But there was not one case of sabotage the whole time.

But on the other hand we should be honest too. Our parents came to this country to make some money, and after a while they could go back to Japan and buy some land, a business, and most of the Japanese here came from the poorest parts of Japan, where farming was very bad, where fishing was very bad. Canada was a land of opportunity. And, well, once they had children and the children began to be educated here, then they weren't nearly as Japanese as they thought. The children would be saying, "No, this is our country. We don't want to go back to Japan." And some of them did go back to Japan and take their kids and put them in high school in Japan, or they sent the kids to Japan, but an awful lot of those kids came back. You see, they considered themselves Canadians. It was then that the parents started putting their roots down. They realized they were Canadians and not Japanese. They were actually putting their roots down after their own children had done it.

Kids

A Kid of Twelve...The Graf Spee *Incident..."Eat Dirt, Nazi!" ... The* Athenia *... Mad Keen to Join Up ... Everything Was Propaganda ... English Evacuees ... I Thought Somebody Had Died ... Flirting ... High School Armies ... Farm Help Was So Scarce ... Helping the War Effort*

What was the war like for a kid in Canada? I found this an unusually difficult chapter to research because so few people remember much. A woman of 40, which would make her just under ten in 1942, would think and say, "Well, rationing I guess," or, "Daddy couldn't get enough gas for our car," or, "My brother went away and was killed in his bomber in Holland," and would remember little more. One man remembers peeping out of his Toronto bedroom window during an air raid practice and hearing the air raid warden sternly telling him to "put out that light." This convinced him that the German bombers must be getting close, and he waited fearfully for the sounds of bomb explosions.

But usually such memories were brief and fleeting. They knew that Hitler was a bad man, and they helped collect rubber and metal and wire and silver paper and chicken fat because somebody had told them that it would help defeat Hitler. But mostly they were too busy being kids to notice, or remember, many details about the war.

•◄►• *A Kid of Twelve*

Mind you, I only heard this story, but it seems there was a kid of twelve joined one of the Maritime regiments, Nova Scotia or New Brunswick, and he was in the army two years and even made it to Italy as an infantryman and was in battle before his parents got a line on where he was and the army kicked him out.

You could meet guys who said they'd seen the kid, although they didn't know he was only thirteen or fourteen. But all I ever heard was talk of him, I never saw him. He must have been full size and pretty mature to get by, and apparently the story was true.

It might make a book in itself, just talking to the kid. How he made out and all that.

The Graf Spee *Incident*

Rationing, shortages, they didn't mean anything to us. I didn't have any brothers or cousins who were overseas and Dad was in essential work, so I don't think the war touched our family at all. A city like Guelph in those days was a very insulated place anyway.

But I do remember the *Graf Spee* incident. That was high drama, enormously exciting. During it and after, for days, the papers were full of it. At that time it was just one hell of a victory. As a battle it wasn't much, because all the Germans lost was one small battleship, but in terms of what a victory meant to Britain, after a long string of misadventures, it was very important. Hearts of oak, the navy's here, Britain rules the waves, and all that stuff.

I was about nine then, and I don't think there is another single incident during the whole war that I can remember. That was the war for me—the kids running up and down the main streets selling newspapers telling about the great victory in a place we had never heard of. Uruguay, down in South America.

"Eat Dirt, Nazi!"

It was funny. No, it wasn't funny in a funny-funny way because it just so happened to be the worst time of my life, in all of 47 years.

I lived in this German community south of Winnipeg. The town we shopped in was called Steinbach. German, Mennonite, but we were far enough away that we went to an ordinary municipal school. I guess there might have been 40 to 45 kids in that school, a good size for a farm school. I remember, there must have been about 30 of us German, Mennonite kids, and 10 of the English. I say English but I mean Scotch, too, and a couple of Dutch kids.

The war came along. I didn't know who Hitler was. My parents never talked about him. We had no radio and I never saw a newspaper, and that went for everybody, really, I guess. We were just kids in grades one to nine. So I didn't know what a Nazi was, who Hitler was.

Then the war—and those 10 English kids made our life hell. To them, we were all Nazis. To them, we had spies hidden in the barns and we fed them at night. Every time we got up in class to do a lesson, they would go "Sieg Heil!" The German Nazi salute. In the schoolyard some of them would get a few of us younger kids and push us around. I remember one bigger kid would push our faces into the ground and yell, "Eat dirt, Nazi!

Sieg Heil!" It all sounds so very dumb now, but believe it, it was terrifying then. And for some reason, I never told my parents, and I don't think the other kids did either.

I don't know why. Maybe we thought we really were Nazis, and we knew by then that Nazis were very bad people. That may have been why. Anyway, after about six months they stopped. Got tired of it, I guess.

It was only years later, long after the war, that I was shopping in Women's Shoes in Eaton's and there is this woman next to me, and she says she knows me and then I recognize her. She's one of these English kids who had pushed all us German kids around. We get talking and she says would I like to have a muffin and coffee in the cafeteria, so away we go. And after a while she says she's always felt bad about that time. The time the English kids pushed all those German kids around and made them eat grass and dirt. She remembered. She sure did.

Then she said it wasn't them, the kids. She said it was the teacher. I remember the teacher, a tall, strong woman with grey hair; we were all afraid of her. My new friend from the old days said it was the teacher, a Miss Campbell, who had got the English kids together the first day of school and told them how to do it. To make life miserable for us, to say, "Heil Hitler," and to have a bunch of them pick on just one or two of us at a time. Divide and conquer, you know. It works.

We laughed about it and after, I was thinking and I thought, you know, she must have been right because half a dozen or so English kids—and they were mostly under twelve— couldn't come up with stuff like that on their own. So maybe those kids, the English ones, didn't really know what they were doing. It was just this woman teacher's hatred for us, because she was English or, I guess, Scotch, that raised all the hell in that school that first year of the war.

•◄►• *The* Athenia

I remember it was a Sunday morning and the paper phoned and said they were putting out an extra. The Germans had sunk a liner, the *Athenia,* off Ireland. It was big news then because the war had only been on two or three days.

My big brother drove me down to the *Tribune* and I got 75 papers and we drove down Portage to where the Furby Theatre is and I got out and started down Furby yelling "Extra, Extra, Germans Sink British Liner." Something like that. I was selling like crazy, people coming home from church or in their yards bought, and my brother just cruised along behind me in the car.

I ran up to a yard where a guy was weeding or something and he grabbed the paper and read the headlines and the start of the story, and he said, "Good. I hope all the bastards drown. Women and children too."

I was so shocked I stood there, and then I ran back and told my brother, who was a big, husky guy. He worked for the C.P., in the roundhouse, and he was tough. He just walked up to the gate and opened it and the guy saw him and started heading for the front steps, and my brother caught him and swung him around and he gave him a right to the jaw so hard you could hear it. He bounced the guy right on his ass, right on the sidewalk and he wouldn't get up until my brother left the yard. Hit him like this, right smack on the jaw and bounced the guy right on his ass.

That's one day I remember.

•◆►• *Mad Keen to Join Up*

We had Industrial Arts rooms in those days, for boys only, of course—fellows who weren't equipped to take the academic courses. These fellows weren't stupid. Slow learners, maybe, or just didn't have the aptitude. Oh, in the long and the short of it they didn't give a damn about the academics of school and were happiest and best employed working with their hands. I was in one of these classes at our school, and in one way I was an exception because I was small. The rest of the guys, mainly, were big. For sixteen, they were damn big, man-size, but not fast enough to play on the football team really. But they were all big boys—200 pounds, in there.

They were all mad keen to join up. Anything, but the army seemed the best bet because with low academic qualifications, well, the army seemed the best bet. Hardly a day would go by but the instructor, a Mr. Leitch, I think, would call the roll and Ralph would be away or John or Pete or Nick or Jack. You know. This school was very big on truancy, or the wiping out of truancy, and if anybody was away they had to bring a note. In grade ten, sixteen-year-olds, had to bring a note. Christ!

Any time a guy was absent, nine times out of ten he was down at some recruiting desk in town trying to sneak his way in, and he'd always get the boot. But these guys kept trying, even to using false identification, and only one or two made it. So the ones who didn't would have to ask the recruiting sergeant, the officer in charge or somebody for a note to the school principal's attendance monitor. You know, a note that would read: "Dear Sir, please excuse Ralph Marks for missing classes on Tuesday, February 16, because he was attempting to join the Canadian Army. Yours truly."

Now, I ask you, how goddamned stupid can you get? A kid hell bent to join some outfit and go overseas and get himself shot at, and when he doesn't make it he's got to get a note to say why he's been absent, just like some little kid in grade four. It was crazy.

•◆• *Everything Was Propaganda*

For kids the war didn't mean anything. It was just excitement. A lot of us hoped the war wouldn't hurry up and end so we could become old enough and join up. That was my circle of friends. Nobody thought about getting wounded, killed, anything like that. We thought of the excitement of travelling, going overseas, seeing London and Paris.

I guess we were all terribly patriotic, sewing bandages and Red Cross classes and all that. Of course, we were steeped in propaganda up to here. They seemed to direct an awful lot of it at the kids, but I'm sure it worked both ways. Movie propaganda for the adults would work on the kids. It seems now that every second Hollywood movie and English movie was about the war, and that was propaganda. I remember *In Which We Serve* now. That's about all. Maybe, you know, propaganda only stays with you while it's needed. Comic books. The movies. The radio. Oh my God, the radio. Can't you still hear the voice of Lorne Green on the nine o'clock news? The Voice of Doom, they called him. Walk down any city street on a summer's night at nine o'clock and you could pick up his voice from house to house. "The Russians are advancing on the Eastern Front." "Fifteen more German subs sunk." That sort of stuff.

Everything was propaganda. *Everything.* Joe Louis went into the American army and that was propaganda. The plane of that famous band leader [Glen Miller] crashes into the English Channel and that was used as propaganda. If they could have used the weather as propaganda against the Nazis they would have.

In the movies, the bright and shiny young soldier got the beautiful girl, every time, when in fact, the thirty-five-year-old businessman with his million bucks would have. In real life, that is.

We never questioned anything. No matter how stupid. All anybody would have to say is, "Don't cha know there's a war on?" and that finished it.

In school, teachers became propagandists. Maybe they took lessons, or read from pamphlets or books, but they stuffed us up to our little gullets too. Red Cross. Saving tinfoil. Bringing 25 cents a week to fill up our war bond books. Writing childish letters to men in Europe, on battleships, telling them about our big jobs on the home front. It was all so silly, those letters. Okay, at least we learned to knit.

Maybe I'm not telling this right. I'll try another way. There was this family across the street and down a bit. Name was Miller—wonderful people. In fact, one of my older brothers might have married Cathie Miller if he hadn't gone off to war. Somebody told my mother that Miller was actually a German name, Mueller. She told us not to play with the Miller kids. So I asked her why. She said Miller was actually Mueller and they were German and she had read, oh God, she'd read one of those absolutely ridiculous war stories the papers used to print about some German families who had secret rooms in their houses, and powerful radios, and were sending all sort of secrets back to Germany.

Now the point is, my mother, otherwise, you could call a sane woman. Not intelligent, maybe, but quick and no-nonsense.

That was propaganda for you.

◦━▶◦ *English Evacuees*

Have you got anything on the refugees? I mean the English refugees who came to Canada? I think they liked to call them evacuees. All children, of course. All children.

I met a few of these children because we set up a little summer camp for them later on. English through and through, mostly, even to wearing their public school grey shorts, blazers and little caps to our Montreal schools, which made them objects of much fun and ridicule to our little Canadian roughnecks. It was a learning process on both sides.

They were mostly good children, and what is so well brought up as a well-brought-up English child? But it was there, of course. We were Canadians and they were in an alien land. One lad who still lives in Canada told me years later that the first two years he had to fight for his life every day after school. They called him "Limey" and other terms. "Vaccy" was another, I think. He'd had had boxing lessons in his English school, so I think he came off all right. It was probably worse for the boys than the girls. After all, girls everywhere have dolls and arrange little tea parties and play hopscotch. With a boy it was different. He said the first two years were not unlike as if he had been dumped into some Hottentot village in Africa.

Somewhere there is a figure about how many came, how many shiploads and how many stayed, and if the truth were known, your next-door neighbour could quite well have been an English evacuee and you wouldn't know it. No, I don't think you would. Children assimilate very quickly.

Many of the boys joined the forces, Canada's, when they reached seventeen or eighteen and I think quite a few of them stayed over here. Settled down—university, marriage—became Canadians.

•◆• *I Thought Somebody Had Died*

It's easy for me to remember the blackest moment of the war in my house. That day I'd gone to a Boy Scout camp for the day somewhere north of Toronto. There was this log bridge, one log over this small ravine, and I slipped off the log but I caught myself and didn't fall, and I was busting to tell my parents about my great experience. I remember just a-bursting into that old house and my mother met me and shushed me. Quiet, be quiet. I remember I thought somebody had died, maybe my grandfather or Aunt Marion. My mother just said my dad wasn't feeling well and be quiet.

I remember going into the living room and it was kind of dark and Dad was sitting in his big easy chair. It always smelled of his Picobac pipe tobacco. There was a bottle sitting on the table beside him and it was nearly empty and he had this big glass in his hand. It was his Christmas whiskey, I knew that. The bottle his boss at the printing plant gave him every Christmas Eve and he always saved for special occasions. It had to be special. One year he didn't use it at all.

It was the first and last time I saw my father drunk.

He looked up and saw me and I remember him saying, "Gordie, turn that thing off, will you?" and he waved to our big radio and I did, and he said, "Come over here, laddie." I went over and he put his hand on my shoulder and tears were coming down his cheeks, rolling down, and he said, "They're gone. Both gone. Gone, just like that, and all those good men." He looked at me and I didn't know what he was talking about, and then he gave me a little shake and said, "Go and see your mother, Gordie, she'll give you a bite of supper."

I went into the kitchen and out on the porch and mother said my dad was so upset because the Japanese had sunk the *Wales* and the *Repulse*. That afternoon. The bulletin had come over about noon. I was only eleven but I knew what that meant. The *Prince of Wales* was a heavy cruiser and the *Repulse* a mighty battleship, and that was all we, I mean Britain, had in the Far East. But you just didn't knock out a battleship with a few lousy little planes. These things didn't happen.

I remember reading later that nothing shocked Mr. Churchill so much, nothing in all those tough and hard years, as the sinking of those two ships. I guess it finally brought home to him just the position we were in.

I know it did to my dad. He wasn't any great thinker, he was a compositor in a print shop, but he had been in the Royal Navy in the first world war and he knew. You're darn right he knew. That's why he got drunk, and believe me he got good and drunk. Right in his own living room.

•◄►• *Flirting*

Our girls' camp, the usual kind of summer camp, was on the other side of the lake and although we weren't supposed to, at night, before it got dark, we'd row in our rowboats across this lake. There'd be three or four girls in each boat and we'd stop about 20 feet from the shore and talk to the German prisoners. A lot of them were young boys, maybe twenty or so, and we were all about sixteen or seventeen, and things went along okay because some of them talked English and quite a few girls spoke German. They spoke it at home. I spoke Hungarian with my parents; even that helped me because a couple of the Germans were Hungarians, and we'd have quite a conversation. In fact, you could easily say we did quite a lot of flirting.

Nothing ever came of it, of course. It was only in the summer, in the camp season about six weeks, and they were still prisoners, although they didn't seem like it lots of times. It was often as though they were just like boys from the towns, but more polite.

◄►• *High School Armies*

Remember the high school battalions? I guess you'd call 'em that. Let's see, they'd start out about grade nine and teach marching. Drill. Then, when you went up to grade ten in the high school, the drills became more complicated and they taught you firing. They had the 303 model, but it was drilled for the 22.

It was all a waste of time. Nobody took it seriously. I mean, how could you? I know we didn't. And when we joined the army we had to forget it all, start from scratch anyhow.

The drill instructors were our teachers. The manual teacher in our school was the commander, whatever you wanted to call him. I think there was one sergeant, one real soldier, for every two or three schools, and it was up to him to make the wheels turn.

The guys who were on the football team were the n.c.o.'s and officers. Biggest is best, I guess. It was hard to take these guys seriously when you knew they were just football players, but if they thought of themselves as heroes, then good for them.

We had a uniform? Sure. Know what it was? A hat. A cap, a blue one, and the sergeants and student officers had the same kind of hat but different colouring. A white band for sergeant, red for lieutenant, that sort of thing.

You might wonder why they had us doing it, an hour a day three days a week, marching back and forth in the school football field. I think it was the same as when they asked housewives to roll bandages when they had machines that could roll bandages 10,000 times faster than all the housewives you ever know, or saving every little bit of tinfoil and metal and junk, no matter how rusted it was. They never used that stuff either. Well, they had us out marching around the field because it was the government's policy to get everybody *involved,* everybody doing something, marching, picking up Wrigley's gum wrappers, being an air raid warden in some tiny prairie town that the enemy wouldn't bother wasting a bomb on.

We didn't know this at the time. We were brainwashed as much as any German or Japanese, and we didn't even know it.

◄►• *Farm Help Was So Scarce*

You were never marked absent if you were away from school. Not in our area, around Lethbridge. This would be in harvest season, mostly, but it could apply in any season, actually, because farm help was so scarce. If Irene wasn't there it was just assumed she was up on the tractor helping her dad, or if Anne wasn't there it meant I was working in the sugar beets.

Becoming fourteen years old then was as big a deal as becoming twenty-one today because during the war they'd give driving licences to fourteen-year-olds, and that meant you could drive the farm truck or go to town for your father to pick up grease or belting. If the trip was necessary, as they used to say, it was okay. I can remember going down the highway in our old car with only my eyes showing above the windshield, zooming along, and if you didn't look carefully, you'd think the car was going along without a driver.

•◂▸• *Helping the War Effort*

The rubber rings off sealer jars—they even wanted us to save them. Tin cans. I can remember flattening them and putting them in sacks, and a truck would come around and pick them up. Lead. Oh yes, lead. They wanted every kid to melt down his lead soldiers or at least turn them in, and for a kid of ten or twelve to give his lead soldiers to the war effort—that was a sacrifice.

That's what they called it, "Helping the War Effort!" In capital letters and an exclamation point. It was as well known as "Zap the Jap" or "Loose Lips Sink Ships."

There was a certain day once a month or twice a month when everybody brought in their finds to the schoolyard. Oh, it was such a big deal. On Saturdays we'd go out in the country on our bikes and look for old cars, old abandoned trucks, machinery, and if you found a vehicle with a battery in it, that was a double find, because a battery had a lot of lead plates in it. It wasn't too long before the whole countryside was cleared up. They'd even take old steam engines and cultivators that were just about rusted into pieces.

And, oh yes, the elastic in women's underclothes, men's clothes. When the garment wore out they asked you to take out **the elastic and throw that on the pile. Even worn-out elastic! You** wonder, you know. Was it all necessary, or was it some bureaucrat or deep thinker in Ottawa trying to justify his existence? At that point, you began to suspect it was all just a game with some people back in Ottawa—but, you know, everybody turned over this worn-out elastic with a straight face.

In those days, you—well, we all did what we were told. I see that now.

Boredom—Then Dieppe

We Were Overtrained . . . Too Long in England . . . Not Fit for Pigs . . . Bloody Chaos . . . Mountbatten's Promised Leave . . . "Like All Hell Had Split Open" . . . Unholy Mess . . . Jubilant Canadians . . . Surrender at Nightfall . . . A Hidden Reason for Dieppe

The Canadians were the first Allied troops in England. And after they got there, they waited, for years. Tens of thousands of men, on virtual garrison duty in England and Scotland, waiting for action, eager for it and, because they were soldiers, frustrated by not getting into the thick of it. There was talk of a division going to North Africa when that campaign began, and a good thing it would have been; but only some officers went to get battle experience.

And so they trained, and they retrained and retrained some more, and took courses here, there and everywhere in new weapons, new techniques, new everything, and became more and more restless. Absenteeism went up and morale went down and one soldier wrote, "There's nothing good about this war. Just like the Dirty Thirties."

Back home, the Canadian people were beginning to wonder, and began to talk. What's wrong with our armies? They fought magnificently in the last war, can't they fight now? What is the matter? Questions were asked in Parliament. The Prime Minister urged that the divisions, or some of them, see action. And finally they did. On August 19, 1942 at Dieppe.

I think it best that some of the survivors speak for themselves on Dieppe. They remember it well; they will never forget.

•◄►• We Were Overtrained

Let me say, from personal observation, that our divisions in the U.K. were disintegrating in '42. They were overtrained to the point where any new training on new weapons, new tactics, meant nothing to them, and they were overtrained to the point where the basic skills of a soldier had almost gone out the window. There were regiments which could have been blown apart by one incident. By that I mean revolt. Revolt is a nasty word, but things were tight there.

"An unmitigated disaster!" the pessimists said. "Important lessons were learned," the war planners maintained. Whatever, Dieppe on August 19, 1942, saw about 3,500 of the attack force of 5,000 Canadians killed, wounded or taken prisoner in the assault on the small French city. To this day, some Dieppe veterans will swear the Germans knew of the raid. Anyway, they were ready. These Canadian troops march through the city towards three years of P.O.W. camps.

Above: Remnants of Canadian forces
return to the south coast of England
after Dieppe, thankful to be alive and
bringing back some German prisoners.
The debacle of Dieppe, to quote an
historian, produced "bitter, violent and
ill-informed discussion in Parliament
and outside it." The controversy, among
old soldiers, still continues.

Left: At portside, England, a wounded
officer from Dieppe is interrogated by an
intelligence officer. "How could it have
happened?" he is probably saying. The
P.O.W. toll of about 1,500 was higher
than the toll in northwest Europe in 11
months—and Dieppe lasted 8 hours.

Top right: Who or what did it? A malicious gunner or a stray shell, German or Canadian? An observation post? Who knows? But the beautiful dome of this church in Italy is a ruin, a casualty of war fought by men on both sides indifferent to the beauties of the human soul and intellect.

Top left: Home bombed. Husband gone. Living in the streets. How can one possibly live? By begging, of course, and families like this one in Naples in late 1943 had good pickings off the Canadian and American troops.

Above: In the service, even in wartime, tradition is everything and the men must be served Christmas dinner by their officers. It is not a mess back home with linen and cutlery but a smashed church in San Vito, Italy, with mess tins and mugs, but what the hell! Nobody seems to be complaining. Would you?

Little acts of heroism, often forgotten the next day. At Ortona—probably the worst killing ground in all Italy—men of the Loyal Edmonton Regiment dig out Corporal Roy Boyd, who was buried for three days in rubble in late December, 1943.

In mountainous Italy, mules were often the only means of heavy transport to the firing line. At dusk, troop reinforcements and mules laden with food and ammunition would move up into the steep hills and mountains. At dawn they would come down, bearing the wounded, bearing the dead.

Below left: Wherever men gather, they acquire pets. It is a fact of life. Lieutenant "Torchy" Morrison of the Saskatoon Light Infantry holds "Vino," a perfectly reasonable name because the officer and his camouflaged truck are in Italy.

Below right: Amid the wreckage of war, a Canadian soldier finds a few quiet moments in the library of an Italian villa to read a few lines.

Above left: Very military—but also very brave because his first ribbon is the Military Cross—is Captain P. L. Cadegan, just one of the many thousands of Canadians who fought across Sicily and then up the long boot of Italy.

Above right: "O Solo Mio"? No, probably "Roll Out the Barrel," the Canadians' song. This soldier in an Italian village has found an accordian and is giving it a whirl.

Above: Month after month, until it seemed they would never end, Canadian troops practised assault landings on the south coast of England, but every "invasion" sharpened them more for the great assault on the Normandy coast on June 6, 1944—D-day.

Right: Finally! The order came, the troops moved to the ports and embarked on the landing boats for the cross-Channel trip. These men of the Royal Canadian Artillery get final briefings on targets from their captain, A. Mendel-sohn.

Opposite: At dawn's first light the infantry landing craft stream like swift beetles towards the pebbly beaches of Normandy and the enemy—part of the greatest invasion force ever assembled and landed. Within six hours the Canadians had taken their primary objectives.

Above: Canadian casualties were lighter than expected, but still many men and machines were lost, victims of German fire from the cliffs, mines, underwater traps, tricky seas and other conditions which produced the acronym SNAFU—Situation Normal, All Fouled Up.

Below left: There were those who didn't make it. Padre R. Seaborn gives absolution to a dying soldier at Caen in Normandy.

Below right: Dead, and some mother grieves in Germany. A youth, lying beside a picture of the dictator Hitler and two others of soldiers—possibly his brothers.

A lot of these men had been in uniform since early in the war. The First Division since September and October, '39. That's a long time to bash about the parade square in a foreign land, a very long time. The war came, not only to the men but to us officers, to have very little relevance. There was no way of relating to it, and I can tell you this; there was a great feeling of depression over the whole army. It was a hair-trigger situation.

The army actually got to thinking, "Well, I guess we're not good enough to fight," and the actual truth was, they were probably the best troops among all the Allies. The Canadian always has been a first-class fighting man. No, when they finally got into battle they were superb. Any officer will tell you that. But we should have had a division in the field before 1943.

Another thing, of course, was the reaction in Canada. No nation wants to see its young men die, but there was this feeling in Canada of frustration. The air force was doing a magnificent job. The navy on both coasts, on the North Atlantic, why, heavens, man, they were virtually winning the war there against the German wolf packs. And the army? What about the army? A nation, despite its air force or its navy, just naturally thinks about its army in time of war, and where was the Canadian Army? Under tents on Salisbury Plain, on manoeuvres again, for the tenth time. The feeling was, of course, what's wrong? Can't they fight? Won't they fight?

It was a distressing situation, almost a shameful one. And, of course, when you lifted the rug there were the politicians. Mackenzie King and his little gang wanted a Canadian Army to fight as a Canadian Army, under Canadian leadership. Well and good, a very worthwhile and definite thrust towards a clear-cut national policy. I applaud it, to a degree, from this distance and 20 years later. But in those days, it just was not possible. But Mr. King was adamant and the War Office was just as adamant. And so we had that situation.

•◄►• *Too Long in England*

You could build up morale in training but the thing was, could you make it last?

You build up a regiment to strength, just as we did in 1940, and you feel you have a good bunch, but once this is the outfit you're going with, then you have to keep morale up. It was tough. It was high crossing Canada, even on the troopships in that convoy, but then it slumped off badly in England, where we were for far too long. Even Dieppe, and God forgive me, was some kind of a relief.

In England things were bad. Very bad. We had a very high rate of A.W.O.L. and there were strikes. Not men refusing orders but refusing to do anything. Half the time in any one company half the men were guarding the other half who were on some kind of charge, and a month later it was just the opposite. The housing was unbelievable and the food was worse. The weather—but you'll just have to imagine what an English winter was like in Bell tents pegged out in soggy ground, and every few days the tents would pull out and collapse. There was a lot of hepatitis, although I'm not sure we knew what it was called then. There was pleurisy, arthritis in some of the older men and of course, plenty of V.D. The clap.

These were some of the bad things, and we tried to keep things rolling along by sending men on courses, courses and more courses, but what they needed was action. They had to get in there and find out what it was all about, and the War Office seemed to have some crazy idea that action was what Canadians didn't need. Our generals used to plead with Whitehall for some assignment. Iceland. Greenland. Go to Russia to help Zhukov and his armies. Well, I'm not sure about Russia but somewhere, anywhere.

When we got into action, in Sicily, you could see the men perk up. Oh yes, we were taking casualties and some quite heavy ones, but it was different now. The men knew they were men and not just some puppets in some big war game being played in Britain. That was the worst part, England.

•◄►• *Not Fit for Pigs*

Our regiment was the Seaforths, a pretty tough bunch, let me say that, and after being confined to camp for months, no passes, nothing, and I think the officers were stealing our packages from home, things were hair-trigger. Very, very dicey.

Anyway, things in this camp were real on edge. The food, you couldn't eat the stuff. Mutton, and you got about four or so ounces a day, and that counted the bone and fat too, and dehydrated potatoes. Ever had mutton—mutton that's maybe been frozen for a year anyway—and dehydrated potatoes and a gummy kind of pudding if you were lucky? I mean, day after day, after week after month?

We didn't have any food, see, so everything had to go in one mess tin. You kept the other, the fit-in half for coffee, with salt petre in it to keep us from raping the vicar's wife—not that she mightn't have liked it. So you'd go down the line, and this was what got to a lot of guys. *Slop,* in would go your ration of meat. No seconds. Just *plop.* Then on top, your potatoes. Dehydrated potatoes are mushy like guck. Then if you wanted gravy, in on top, and on days when there was pudding, in on top again. God, but it was a dog's breakfast.

Then you were supposed to eat this mess. I've seen guys just look at it and get up and dump it in the garbage cans.

One time the mess officers and these guys come along— swagger sticks under their arm, sharp as tacks, that sort of thing— and one says, "Everything all right, men?" It wasn't that we were in a rotten situation and that the food was worse than rotten; it was this fresh-faced little prig who'd probably come right out of university, right to officers' school, right into the King's uniform, this little bastard having the nerve to say anything like that. You could just see the bomb go up, in about five seconds when it sunk in to the guys.

One guy—I forget his name but he was killed in Italy, near Ortona—he jumped up and he yelled, "You call this shit food? This shit!" and he dumped the mess tin about half an inch from this lieutenant's polished brown boot and he looked him right in the eye and he yelled, "My father wouldn't even feed his pigs shit like this," and he got out of that tent and left. The officer did nothing, the sergeant did nothing, the orderly's bum boy couldn't do anything, so they all walked out through the tent and all the guys were laughing at them.

Nothing came of it. The guy wasn't charged, wasn't trans- ferred, wasn't put on coal detail, four and four sentry walk or nothing. I guess they figured if they touched him the whole outfit would go up in smoke.

•◂►• *Bloody Chaos*

Dieppe. Yes. My first operations flight. Nervous as hell. Didn't have a clue. We'd been well briefed, yes. We knew what was going on, but what the briefing was about and what actually happened, well, that's a different matter.

You see little from the air. You're flying fast. Particularly when you're young and nervous and on your first op, you don't really see a bloody thing. There were hundreds of planes all over the bloody place. There were ships everywhere you looked. There was smoke coming from everywhere. Planes going this way and that way, and half the time you were chasing your own fellows. You see somebody down below you so you go down for a bounce, to see if it's Jerry, and often it wasn't. It would be one of your own fellows.

Our wing that day flew five times. That's both squadrons. I think we got nine or ten enemy that day and I think we lost about five.

It was chaos. Bloody chaos. Nobody could tell what anybody was doing. That's all I can remember about it. Just bloody chaos.

•◄►• *Mountbatten's Promised Leave*

I had a very violent leave just prior to Dieppe, and as a result I was absent without leave for 24 hours. I was put under escort of another n.c.o. and I went to London for the briefing for this commando raid, and I was told—and a matter of fact it was Lord Louis Mountbatten—he took a very personal interest in these special raids—who said, "Well, one of two things can happen to you. You can be put on charge or you can go on this raid, and when you come back you'll receive a long leave." Naturally I said I'd go on the raid. After all, that was what I was in London for. That was in 1942.

And I got caught, and I spent the next three years in the bucket.

In 1947 or 1948 Mountbatten came to Toronto to open the Canadian National Exhibition or something, and they brought him up to the Press Club on Yonge Street and took him into the special room for V.I.P.'s and we were all introduced. When I got to him he shook hands and said, "I recall promising you a leave a few years ago." The man hadn't forgotten my face or the circumstances, from 1942 to 1947. Five years.

•◄►• *"Like All Hell Had Split Open"*

She was rough, boy, she was sure rough. When we come in, there was that sand there and those sort of cliffs up there, and it was like all hell had split open, the racket, my God, boy, the racket, the shells and the holy uproar.

When we hit the beach I said, "Okay, McNeill, this is what you left the mines for," and the first five or six guys who jumped out, they just laid down flat in the water and then I jumped, and it was about up to my waist, you see, up to here, and I hollered at them, "C'mon, you buggers, you don't have to swim, she's only up to my waist," and, well it was a couple of seconds before I realized they'd been hit, and the buggers was dead. I can't remember what I thought. Maybe I said to myself, "Tough shit," or something that way.

See this hand? Looks okay, doesn't it? Well, that's a phony hand. All in through here, these bones, they're all made up. They did this in a hospital near London. You never see me pick up anything with this hand, do you? Reason is, I can't. It's like a dead hand.

When I was coming up towards the beach suddenly something yanks me around and throws me down. I'm telling you, boy, I didn't know what was happening, but all of a sudden, there's me lying in the water and a buddy from Glace Bay, my home town, behind me and he grabs me by the scruff of the neck and says to get going. Well, I ain't going nowhere. I look at my hand and it looks like a chicken that's been hit smack by a truck and I said, "Barney, my boy, you've been hit," and then I feel this pain in my left shoulder and I can just look down, and damn if there ain't another hole there. I mean I can see the blood starting to come, and I thought, and I remember, "Christ, twice in one day." That was kind of funny coming from me, because I'm not usually a comical sort of fellow, and not when I'm in a war—even less so, you might say.

Everything got kind of hazy then, but one of my buddies said the crew of our landing boat waded out and dragged back a bunch of us who was wounded. They was brave buggers. Another fellow said he seen me lying there about an hour after we started; he seen me when they was taking him back to boats. That poor bugger, MacDonald, from Halifax, he lost a leg or an arm. Forget which.

I don't remember nothing until we got back to England. In fact, you know, it was even after that. I guess they give me morphine or something like that. Everything was so damned mixed up from then on that I don't remember much, but I remember this nursing sister in this hospital they put me in, and one day she's talking about this here Dieppe raid and she says we were such a lot of brave men and I says, "Sister, we're not brave. We was just a lot of damn fools."

•◄►• *An Unholy Mess*

As far as I can remember, nobody told us much about what we were supposed to do when we got ashore at Dieppe. Follow our officers, I guess that was the general idea. I know I didn't have much of a clue.

I don't remember much, anyway. Getting out of the landing craft, and there were my buddies falling right and left. They have funny beaches in France, not sand, but all kind of pebbles, and I remember slipping and sliding and saying, "Shit!" and there was bullets and mortar and machine guns and artillery and everything they had flying at us and I couldn't even see where it was coming from.

That's when I got hit, I figure. That's where an awful lot of lads were hit, and next thing I'm all messed up in field dressings and I'm on a boat. Or a raft, I'm not sure. Anyway, it is a lot quieter now and we're going out to this big ship, and next thing I remember there is just one hell of a lot of guys in this big room in this ship. Somebody said there was about 200 or more, and I remember asking him and he said 200 or more still alive. You see, the living and the dead were together. The dead had just died. Otherwise they'd have been left behind.

You can hear the engines start and the ship start and on the way back to England we're getting knocked around a lot, bouncing around maybe four times, three times, and guys are falling off the tables they're lying on, and Christ, it's an unholy mess.

I'm coming around by this time. I mean I know what side is up, even though I'm shot up, and I can't understand this bouncing around. It doesn't make sense that a battleship or a hospital ship should bounce around like a jackrabbit. Up and sideways, whoops, up and down hard. Kind of like a goddamned rowboat. It was bombs falling.

Okay, so we get home and I find out later that it wasn't a hospital ship or a cruiser. It was a frigging destroyer, some old piece of tin whose sides are about an eighth of an inch thick. One near-miss and I guess that would have been it, wounded and all.

And our flagship, our naval bombardment, was this old tin can which couldn't sink a rowboat on a pond if its very life depended on it. I often wondered, was there something much more tricky about Dieppe than we know? Hell, I don't mean about the Germans. They were just doing their job, killing off the enemy, the invader. I mean with Churchill and that idiot Lord Montgomery and the other brass who said that raid had to go. One of the grandest screw-ups of the war.

I was at Dieppe. The big raid, they called it. I remember my sister sent me a clipping from some paper, a headline, and it was the day they released the news and it said that Canadian troops were jubilant about the success of their invasion of France.

Now that is pure and unadulterated bullshit. We got the shit kicked out of us. My sister, who lived in London, the Ontario London, kept sort of a war scrapbook for me and my brother for when we got home. We were in the Western Ontario Regiment, you see. So I can read this thing when I get home. Bullshit. Propaganda.

It was about 10 hours of unadulterated hell, from the moment the Germans saw us coming in our dinky little boats until we got off. We were trying to scale cliffs like the bloody Royal York Hotel and the Germans had us criss-crossed six ways from Sunday and it was, well, I guess you could call it a massacre. It sure wasn't any victory, or even a saw-off. It was a German victory all the way. Maybe if we'd have had gunnery support from the Royal Navy before hitting the beaches, maybe that would be different, but in the end it would not have made one sweet continental damn. We were just ducks in a shooting gallery. Look at the casualties. Worse per unit, I think, than any time else in the war. Whole companies wiped out and captured just like that—*zoooop!*

In fact, the casualties were so bad they dribbled them out to the newspapers a hundred or two hundred at a time, and it was weeks before they said how many wounded, killed in action, died of wounds, missing, and, of course, captured. The Germans filled up a prison camp with our guys after that one.

But I'll tell you one thing, and I think most people don't know this. Dieppe had one effect. It taught them swollen-assed generals something. There was a clipping in my sister's book and it was Canadian Press and it was only about three or four inches long and she said it had been way back inside the paper, and it said that Dieppe had been valuable because it showed that in future landings should be on a larger scale. You see, the stink was starting to come up and people in Canada were saying, you know, "What the hell?" Anybody could see by this time it had been a slaughter.

Some genius in the British War Office likely said, "I say, old chap, how do we know the Germans are actually there? Might have a raid, you know. A jolly big one. See if they are there, what they've got. Right?" And Churchill or somebody probably said, "Jolly good thinking, Blithering-Hot, and we'll send the Canadians. See if the beggars are as good as they say they are."

Well, we *were* good, but even King Kong and all his friends from the jungle and John Wayne couldn't have done anything there. It was like telling you to go up to the post office over on Front Street and start hitting one of those big pillars with your fist and keep hitting until you knock it down. All you get is blood and broken bones.

◦◂▸◦ *Surrender at Nightfall*

At this one point, and I'll never forget, about thirty of us got separated from the main force. We got into a copse of trees but there was nothing we actually could do to break out, not with German units all around. We just didn't have the weight or the strength.

Every once in a while the enemy would spray the woods with machine gun fire, just to let us know they were around and would come and get us when they wanted to do so. Probably when the main battle had cleared away, one way or the other.

I nearly got court-martialled there. Our senior officer came crawling over to me and said he was going to surrender at nightfall. I said he'd better talk to Smith and pointed to where he was, across a tiny clearing by the road, and this officer scurries across on his belly to discuss the situation with this officer and, of course, the fellow was dead. I knew he was dead. He'd been dead for quite a while. My senior officer comes scurrying back and bullets are kicking around and he says, "Jack, if I ever get out of this alive I'm going to see you get a court-martial for that." It was just a grisly joke to me.

I decide I'm not going to hang around and surrender and I've always been a maverick so I decide to take off alone. For a while I'd been looking at a French farmhouse across the road and I could look in a window in the back and see a girl combing her hair. A pretty girl, and this intrigued me—a girl, any girl combing her hair in a house and there is a goddamned battle all around her, all those shells flying around. I thought if I could get into that house I might be safe, or be able to hide for a few hours. It was worth a try, and I made a dash and made it across this road. So now I'm beside a hedgerow and sneaking along—and when I move, I hear something moving along the other side. When I stop, it stops. Move, it moves. Stop, it stops. I think it's an animal.

Slowly I stand up, look over the top of the hedge and as I rise up, up rises a fully armed German soldier, and there I am looking down the barrel of a mean-looking pistol.

That ended the war for me. Right there.

Dieppe? I think it was a shambles. But in retrospect I think it had its merits, too.

I was involved with the I-section [intelligence] at that time, and I've always maintained that it was bad planning from our point of view, but the raid went on for two reasons. One, this raid was done to pacify the Russians and also to show the world, but especially the Canadian people, that their troops were at the ready and eager for battle. That's number one.

But the aspect to which I was privy—and I've never seen anything written about this—was that on the 19th of August, the day of the Dieppe raid, the largest convoy up to that time to leave England would pass the mouth of the Channel. It was a 200-ship convoy to North Africa, loaded with troops and equipment to do the final roll-up of General Rommel's forces in Africa. Now, one thing is significant here. The Dieppe raid was to have been in mid-July. It had been scheduled for that time. There seemed no other reason to change the date to August, the day of the sailing.

So, in my opinion, the Dieppe raid had the effect of occupying the attention of the German Navy, the German Air Force, and obviously the land force. It stopped them from interfering with the passage of that convoy until it was out of those dangerous waters and to comparative safety.

So if you want to call Dieppe a sacrifice, then it was a sacrifice. But in retrospect, it was a worthwhile sacrifice in terms of helping to protect that huge convoy which was heading for the the last battles of North Africa.

Women in Uniform

The Best Way to Get to Her Fiancé . . . Insults on the Ottawa Streets . . . Shirley . . . "Your Jacket, Miss" . . . In the Field Hospital . . . Two Singing Wrens . . . Stowaways . . . Treated Like a Lady . . . She Was Toronto, She Was Home

Their entrance requirements were basically the same as those for men—in stature, health, intelligence, schooling—but perhaps a closer look was taken at background with regard to morals. Remember, this was in the '40s and a woman's place, basically, was in the home. Men, after all, ran the country, the army, navy, and air force.

But these girls and women did everything men did, with all the obvious exceptions. They did not serve on ships, although there is a case of two stowaways aboard an R.C.N. ship at Halifax. They did not fly planes, but they helped guide back to base the men who did. They did not go into combat with the infantry, the artillery, the tankers, the engineers—but they worked behind the lines and nursed dying men in the field hospitals. All in all, despite the jeers about "officers' groundsheets," they changed public opinion about a woman's place in society.

•◄►• The Best Way to Get to Her Fiancé

Why did I join the air force? Because the man I was engaged to was in it and overseas and I, dumb that I was, thought it would be the best way to get over to him.

Oh, I got to England all right. I surely did. But by that time he'd married. No letter, nothing. He'd just married. The daughter of a duchess or something. I'm pretty sure I wasn't the first one it happened to. Not on your life.

•◄►• Insults on the Ottawa Streets

I have actually walked down streets in Ottawa when I was training at Rockcliffe and had girls shout insults at me, foul things.

They didn't like us because there was a shortage of men, off to war, you know, not around, and they thought that the W.D.'s [Women's Division, R.C.A.F.] had the men that they figured they should have. I guess they thought every W.D. had 20 men to choose from on the station. It wasn't like that, but that's what they thought, yelling these names at us.

Of course, if they had wanted to, they could have enlisted too, but I guess that was just a bit too much. But it wasn't much fun to go into Ottawa to have a lot of insults thrown at you when the government office girls came out at 5 P.M. There was nothing you could do about it either.

•◄►• *Shirley*

There was this gal, she was from Newfoundland and she was the first Newfoundlander I ever saw, and she probably was twenty-five but she looked forty-five, you know, all rough-skinned, red face— as if she'd been standing in the wind and rain and snow for a hundred years, but she had this fantastic figure. Just unbelievable. What I mean is, only her face looked forty-five.

She was a CWAC, the women's army corps and she was a driver, and she was in the mess hall this morning where I was doing kitchen fatigue. Yeah, I'd been a naughty boy, yeah. It was boiled ham for lunch and there was this big bowl, a helluva big bowl full of mustard, the liquid, drippy kind of mustard.

She's poking around waiting for the orderly officer she was driving to make his inspection and she's dipping her finger in the mustard and licking her finger and looking at me and saying, "Mmmmmmm, just like liquid shit," and the orderly officer and the mess sergeant come up and the sergeant tells her, "For Christ sakes, stop that." Now a mess sergeant is like a king. He can order the colonel out of his kitchen. I mean, he's king of the goddamned castle. Right?

Shirley, this girl's name was Shirley and she had the nickname Punchboard Shirley, she just takes up this huge bowl of mustard, and *I* could hardly lift it, and just as as you please, she dumps it over the sergeant, from stem to stern, head to foot, and she says, "Here, sarge, try some liquid shit."

You know what happened? Nothing. Like spitting at Christ and nothing happens. Because then she says to everybody, "I've slept with everybody in this bloody hole from the brigadier down to the gate officer, and if they want to throw charges at me, just let them go ahead and try. And watch the world split open."

She would've too. She'd have demanded a court martial, refused to take the major's punishment, and let the whole thing spill out. And it wouldn't have only been about the girls screwing the officers, but about everything, every damned thing. The thefts, well, about everything.

Within 24 hours every guy in camp, all 10,000 or so, knew about it, and I kind of think our officers took it a little easier on us from then on. Old red tabs [the brigadier] I know he wasn't as cocky as before.

I often wonder what happened to that gal. For a Newfie she was pretty smart. Punchboard Shirley. Are you out there somewhere, dear?

•◄►• *"Your Jacket, Miss"*

On that crossing to England our captain was an old fuss-pot and he wasn't going to have a lot of hanky-panky between Red Cross and service girls and the officers and civilians he was carrying, but we darn well meant to. And so did the men.

He had guards everywhere. You couldn't go out on deck unescorted after six o'clock but there was some sneaking out. You couldn't even go out to the rail for a smoke. Of course, smoking was taboo. And we had lifeboat drill twice a day, including one at night and then, a couple might have a chance to sneak off, but hardly.

But worst of all, the captain made us wear our life jackets at all times, except sleeping and at meals. A walk around the deck, wear them, and if you didn't, there was a guard saying, "Your jacket, miss," and instead of carrying it, you'd have to put these two great big pillows on, one fore and one aft, as they say.

These things stuck way out, and when you're a big-bosomed girl like I was, well, then it became downright ridiculous. We even had to wear them in the lounge, at night, drinking and dancing. Even colonels, because the captain is master of his vessel. So there's one man you're getting fond of, and Glenn Miller is on the record player and you could dance oh so dreamily, oh so close and what! He's got his big pillow in front of him and I've got my big pillow and believe me, never the twain shall meet.

It wasn't all that funny to a couple of the girls because they had real romances going on that two weeks in that ship, but *c'est la guerre*, I guess.

◆ *In the Field Hospital*

This was in Normandy, in the first Canadian Field Hospital set up. The casualties just came in batches. A lot of it was mortar and rifle wounds, and most would be brought in on stretchers. I was a Red Cross Corps worker so my job wasn't actually in surgery or a real nurse's job in the field, but we had to do all we could to help.

There were so many casualties that as soon as one spot was empty or 10 or 20 spaces, there were others to fill them. That's why we tried to get them out by air or by ship from the coast within two days so they could be taken to England for special treatment.

Some men were cheery, asking for a cigarette, joking. Some were in shock through loss of blood and just torn-up bodies, and some would just want to touch you. Touch the hand of a Canadian girl, and some of these were the ones who were dying. You got to know. They had this look about them, a whiteness, a look in their eyes. Some would die while you sat beside them. One did once, a young boy from Ontario, and he died as I was reading the last letter he got from his mother. He'd asked me to do it. He let out this kind of sigh and his head fell down a bit and then lifted up a bit and then fell down again and I knew he was gone. He had a lot of steel in his chest. I suppose he never had much of a chance.

It was a time when you could work twelve hours a day and another four if you wanted to, and you'd crawl into the tent just dead. The bombing didn't bother us. The shelling. Sometimes it sounded like thunder rolling across the lake, just like at home at the cottage, hour after hour, and it got to be part of you. If it was on, you didn't actually hear it, but when it stopped you did. And air raids, but it was us against them and we'd see the Spitfires and the American planes go dashing over.

But mostly it was work. The usual things to keep them happy. We'd pass out tea with lots of sugar, and papers if we had any, *The Maple Leaf* as I remember. Most or all of them spent less than 48 hours with us so we never got to know them too well and, besides, not too many of them felt like talking. The first night you'd hear them talking to each other, sort of a low muttering, and I often wondered what they would be talking about.

Then there were times when we'd help the nurses and the doctors. Say 25 men would come in almost at once. I nearly fainted the first time I cut off a uniform and saw a terrible wound. Just terrible. I hope he lived. Those doctors, those English nurses, everybody was just super-marvellous, through all that carnage. That's what it was. Carnage. What a waste.

I remember seeing a flash [a shoulder patch] on one jacket lying across the foot of the bed and I knew that flash because it was the regiment which came from my home town. I mean, about four or five small cities and towns had furnished men for it and I had to look at the face and he was unconscious and it was Billy C———and I nearly dropped what I was carrying. I'd gone on skating parties with him, hayrides. I think I had a crush on him once. I don't think I ever knew what war and battle was until then . . . "

•◄►• *Two Singing Wrens*

I was on gate duty at Halifax and you could look down the road to one of the officers' messes, and I saw these two Wrens come out and their arms were around each other's shoulders. They were coming to me and singing "North Atlantic Squadron," just like two ratings in Plymouth, arm and arm like good buddies. Looped, of course. Maybe one big glass of that West Indian rum the boys used to bring back. It'll kill anybody.

So these two little girls are coming along and they start drifting apart, like they are still joined at the shoulders where their arms are around each other, but further down one pair of legs is drifting out to port and other pair to starboard, and what do you know, they're way out like this, almost like the letter "v" upside down. Damnedest thing, but they're still navigating. Then the starboard side develops a 30-degree list at the knees and boom, down they go, still singing "Away, away, with fife and drum" and lying in the road.

I call out the guard and we run down the road to where they are and we grab arms and legs and lug them up the guardhouse and by this time, out like a light. I tell them to put them in the cots at the back and I throw a blanket over each one. And they come to, just like they were twins, right at the same time, and boy, they are a sorry little pair of Wrens. No singing then, I'll tell you. Not even much chirping.

•◄►• *Stowaways*

We all wanted to get over, the war was getting over, we could see that, and there we were stuck in that old Halifax. God, what a Godforsaken dungeon!

Two girls stowed away. One, Helen Marchand, I think, hopped up on a destroyer and the guys hid her away. Somebody said later she had to come out about four days later when she started a monthly. God! She'd gone aboard without a thing, not even a hankie. She made it. What happened to her? Well, I just can't say. She was a kookie kid from somewhere around Ottawa.

Marie, another kid from our floor [of the barracks] hopped on a freighter. The crew took her, got her up the gangplank. Maybe they dressed her as a sailor, I don't know. I often wondered if she had to work her way across to England. You know what I mean, don't you? She was that kind anyway. On her back half her life.

God, to hear me talking like this, you'd think I was up to my eyeballs in the whole thing. The fact was, and God help me, I was a virgin all the way. We all talked so much and did so little. We got a postcard from her later, from a town called Bristol, I think. She was going to stay over there, in England. The rest of us just sat and rotted in Halifax.

•━► • *Treated Like a Lady*

There used to be a saying, "I'd rather have a Dutch whore than a Canadian nurse." You see in Amsterdam or Rotterdam or wherever you were, when you went on leave the nurses or the Red Cross girls, or any others who were in the war for fun, why, they wanted all the things they got at home. Like a corsage. Where the hell do you get a corsage in Amsterdam? Some of those little blue flowers they used to sell on the streets, but that's all. And you'd have to look like you were going on parade. A few drinks in a quiet spot, that's another! Every place filled with other soldiers, and every officer trying to filch away your filly while you went to the can. Then a good dinner, and that would take a soldier's pay for a month, and then, maybe then, and only then, screwing for two.

At the Kras, the Krasnapolski, the only hotel in town. She wanted to be treated like a lady, although she damn well knew what she was was a whore, a whore in lady's uniform.

Give me a Dutch whore. A Belgese. French. There was no fooling around with them. You made up your mind fast and you got your money's worth, and a hell of a lot more if you threw a couple of packs of smokes into the kitty. Then you got the Royal American Show, and she didn't care if you had mud on your boots and your underwear was dirty.

•◆• *She Was Toronto, She Was Home*

It's funny the things you remember, but I can remember one weekend clearly. This one just stays and stays in my mind and I can still be driving down the highway or mowing the lawn and suddenly there it is. It is just a weekend I spent with a CWAC in London. She was a girl I'd known at Collegiate in Toronto. I can't say I ever knew her well in high school or that I got to know her much better that weekend, but it is the one single memory I remember.

It was April 1944. I'd been on those big raids to Berlin and poor godforsaken Hamburg, which had been hit about three times by every single plane in Bomber Command. And then I get a 72-hour pass and I'm off to London.

I get in to Victoria Station about eleven in the morning and I slope off to my usual hotel in Ecclestone Square, and the old granny who ran it was glad to see me. A quid for the weekend, and she used to laugh and say, "I close my eyes and I sleep sound after pub closing, Canada," meaning, of course, what we did after that, she didn't care about. With girls, I mean. Women. London was full of them.

I wandered around. Along the Embankment. Into the Tate. Over to Trafalgar Square, to that madhouse of thousands of troops, sailors, airmen, girls, young and old. Into the National Gallery. Up to Piccadilly. Finding a pub open and having two or three pints and a bun. Just another airman on leave in a big town and not knowing anyone. God, but it is a lonely feeling, and I just wasn't one to make friends with some Yank or Aussie or hunt up some Canadian in a bar and make conversation.

And then I saw her. In Trafalgar Square, just standing on the steps there by the lions and I remember yelling, "Smitty!" and she spotted my arm waving and then my face, and she ran down the steps and into my arms. I can remember it now. Here was Smitty in London, a girl I'd gone to school with in Toronto, gone to Centre Island with on a picnic once, and with the class on a picnic up the Don Valley once. You know. She was in the army, a CWAC, and on leave. I can see her now. She wasn't a good-looking girl, but she did have an interesting face, lots of freckles and what you'd call a sardonic smile. I remember at school she had this dry wit. That's the only way I can describe it. She was tall, almost as tall as I was, and what you might call skinny. She wasn't pretty, but how many beautiful girls did you see in the service? Not many. But she had something.

And she was more. She was Toronto, she was home. She was talk, and she was a friend and she was fun and she knew the people I knew and, above all, she was home and I needed a good dash of home right then. We became lovers immediately. Nothing was said. I didn't ask her if she had a date that night with the King of England. We were just lovers, and if I wanted to pay her a quid I'd buy her whiskey or dinner and not hand it over, as you did and have the tart stuff it in her handbag and pat you on the cheek and say, "Ta, ta, luv. Till we meet again." She wasn't a whore, she was a girl from Toronto and we'd met in London among six million people. We'd found each other.

There was something about England, London, that spring. Everybody knew the invasion was coming and it was kind of like a time, I suppose, when England knew the Spanish Armada was coming and everybody was excited.

We went to pubs, we went to dinner and we strolled through Green Park and looked at the children with their nannies and then we went down to Ecclestone Park and I boosted her over the fence. The park is locked, you know. It's for residents of the area. I think there was a vegetable garden in part of it, but we walked under the trees and then we went home, up three flights of narrow stairs, into that bedroom and we made love. I mean we really made love. This just wasn't a screw. And next morning old granny brought us our breakfast in bed, the lovable old sot.

Saturday we did the same, walked around, went to a picture show. *Mrs. Miniver.* Greer Garson. Britain at war. What a phony. You could hear the people muttering all around, making rude remarks about Greer Garson's clothes. Nobody dressed like that in Britain any more. We went out to Kew and then down into the East End to one of those singing pubs and we went back and made love, and then went out and spent an evening in a local, drinking beer and playing darts, and then we made love again and next morning too. You see, I can remember it all.

That afternoon she put me on the five o'clock train for my station in Kent and I kissed her out of the compartment window just like you used to see in old war movies, and that's the last I saw of her. We wrote a bit, saying we'd see each other back in Canada because the invasion was coming up fast by then, but we never did.

It was my fault, I guess. She didn't blame me, in her letters. It was just, I felt, that in those three days we had done everything we would have wanted to do for the rest of our lives or, anyway, for the rest of the war. And so it was enough. I felt that way, and she did too, I think. It was our own private and special wartime marriage.

Italy

*We Became Soldiers . . . Italy—the First Battle Trophy
. . . A Crash Course in Weapons . . . Peasants . . . The
Private and the Countess . . . The Guy in Peasant Clothes
. . . The Front . . . Twin Brothers . . . Two Days Without
Water . . . "Start Digging!" . . . Screaming, Screaming*

---

*In 1943 the Second Division landed in Sicily, and there, under a
blazing sun, the Canadian Army was blooded. For the next 20
months, 20 terribly long months, the Canadians fought their way
up that infamous Italian boot. Along the way they learned how
tough an opponent the German fighting man could be. And along
the way, too, hardened by combat, they became real soldiers,
tougher than they thought they could ever be.*

*There were set battles, massed artillery barrages, co-
ordinated attacks of thousands of men, against towns, cities,
ridges, river crossings, mountains and fortified lines — all manned
by some of Hitler's finest troops, who could pick their spots to
stand and fight. There was always one more hill beyond the next
to take, one more village beyond to isolate, capture and destroy.*

*Italy may be sunny and warm in story and in song, but few
Canadians who fought there remember the land with affection.
They remember the poverty, the dead and the dying, the suffering
of a country crunched by war.*

•◄►• *We Became Soldiers*

Sicily? We didn't know where we were going. Then about three
days out of Greenoch we joined up with the armada and we knew
we were in for something big. I remember I got a shock when the
officer told us we were heading for the South Seas. That to me
meant Tahiti or Fiji or someplace, but he meant the Mediterranean. Not a joke. The dumb bastard was just confused.

After we cleared out the Italians it was quiet for a couple
of days and then, then it was the Germans. Tough. Very tough.
And hot. Hotter than hell. And those mountains, and those
bloody Sicilians. Ever seen a Sicilian peasant? They're something
all by themselves.

Sicily was where we met the Germans, beat them, and
became soldiers. Before that we weren't soldiers.

•◄►• *Italy—the First Battle Trophy*

You might not believe it, but I captured the first battle flag when the allies stormed Fortress Europe. Italy. We went ashore and there was this city, Reggio di Calabria, and in the headquarters of the Italian Army there was this flagpole and on it were two flags, the Italian flag and the Nazi flag. Of course, the Italians had just taken off when the first few shots were fired and there were no Germans around.

No, I didn't have to cut it down. Just loosened the knot and down it came, and a chap who was with me took the Nazi flag. There was nothing to it, really. I know, years of preparation —and that's the way it's done, loosening a bit of rope for the first battle trophy.

I carried it for a while, a big one about ten feet across and seven feet deep, you might say, and then I bundled it up and sent it back to Moose Jaw.

•◄►• *A Crash Course in Weapons*

The Fifth Division took quite a pounding in the first couple of months of '44. This was in Italy. I don't think many who were there will ever forget Ortona. The weather was incredible, just like I've read the mud and the rain and snow and chill of the trench warfare of France was in the first world war.

Our casualties were high. First, the division had never been in combat and secondly, the regiments were facing rough and tough and trained Germans. We were pushing them back, but so bloody slowly, that they could pick and choose their ground. They had the choice of any number of defensive positions in that terrain, and we had none. Besides, the sickness count from the weather was very high. Somewhere over 1,500, I believe.

But I saw reinforcements who could not handle a rifle. They knew what it was, but to aim it and kill the enemy at 400 yards away—impossible. They had only the barest working knowledge of the Bren [*the standard Canadian medium machine gun*] and the anti-tank weapons, well, I doubt they had ever seen them.

The only thing to do was assign to each new man an older man in a platoon, one who was still on his feet after the pounding, and try and give him a crash course in weapons. This they did, and the division later became the best or one of the best in Italy, by anybody's reckoning and judgement, but that is only because the Canadian soldier is damn good, a bloody fine fighting man. When he knows the score he is a first-rate soldier, a man any officer could be proud of. They were tough as nails and could handle anything. Just a matter of getting their feet wet.

The Germans thought so too. You could read it in the records captured after the war, their records said so. If Canadians were opposite them they walked very carefully, let me tell you.

But those new men coming up and hardly knowing a pull-through from a round, well, I'll tell you. It made us think . . .

•◄►• *Peasants*

This happened more than once, when we'd come into a new valley or some place after some fighting, and take over a villa, the big houses of the rich, the land owners. Like the colliery owners back home. They'd cleared out, you see, when the fighting came along, but they still had their workers. Paisans. Peasants. Very poor people, ignorant people, but kind.

We'd go into a villa or whatever and usually we'd head for the cellar because it was safer—and you know what we'd find, and more than once? The peasants, hiding. Hiding down there in the dark, old men, women, children, and more often than not they were hungry, and I'll tell you this, hanging from the ceiling were smoked hams, sides of beef, dried vegetables, all manner of food, cheeses on shelves, lots of cheeses and that rough flour they have. Food all around them and they were afraid to touch it because, so they would tell us, when the soldiers went away—and they meant us—then the landowner would come back, and if anything was gone then you could be sure there'd be proper merry old hell to pay. Why the Germans didn't clean out these cellars I don't know, but there was the food, hanging around like a store.

We'd do something about that. Winner takes all, we'd tell them, and we'd pass around hams and cheese and that hard bread and soon everybody was peasants from Italy and peasants from Cape Breton, and we were all filling our faces. Somebody would fire a shot through one of the wine casks, Christ, but some were six or eight feet high, and we'd fill up buckets and pails with the stuff, and we'd break up some of his lordship's furniture, the stuff the Pope gave his family 600 years ago, and we'd have a fire and eat and drink and sing and have a great old time, just like a harvesting dance down home. A bit of kissing went on but nothing you could put your hand to, this being Italy and Italians being a different kind of people that way. But singing and sure, some dancing, and lots of good landlord's furniture going up in smoke.

We never wanted to leave those people to face the count or baron or whatever the Christ he was, to take the blame for the mess, so next morning one of the boys would write out something like: "The food and drink and firewood were consumed by the Cape Breton Regiment of Canada. Please send bill to the Government of Canada, Ottawa" and we'd sign it with the name of General Burns who was running the show at that time.

•◄►• *The Private and the Countess*

You should title this one: The Private and the Countess. Or do they have countesses in Italy? I never knew her name. I can't tell you the soldier's name either. He lives in southern Ontario, is married and is a lawyer, and a pretty smart one. I know he was a pretty smart solider. Let's say he was one of the smartest private soldiers in the whole blamed Canadian Army. He could have had stripes or a commission any time he wanted, but he just didn't.

He had a nice Anglo-Saxon name, a nice Anglo-Saxon face and I guess the rest of him was Anglo-Saxon too. He was in the press section and he snagged a jeep out of the pool. A lot of officers would take the rotor off their jeeps to immobilize them, but Casanova had a couple of spares, and as Rome was only 20 miles away from Anagni, where we were recovering from an awful pounding, lots of dead, away he went with this jeep.

You know Rome? Well, there are districts the average tourist will never see in 50 years. You're walking down some alley and there's a door and you walk on by, but inside there's a courtyard and flowers and a pool and trees and stone benches and maybe a few statutes a thousand years old and often a house maybe 400 years old. I don't know how he fell into this kind of a setup, but our Casanova finds such a place, and he isn't even looking.

And in the house is the contessa, with her maids and her gardener and her butter and fruit and wines and brandies, and if there was a war on, she obviously didn't care. She must have had a potful, but you didn't see it. She really was a pretty grand lady, about thirty-five, and knew how to live in proper style.

Hell, how did anybody know what she did when the Germans were there? Maybe she shacked up with the German commandant of Rome, but she was all the way for our Canadian private. The only colour he had was the Red Patch, the division patch, but she obviously liked him. So Casanova somehow got himself transferred and he stayed in Rome for six months.

He took me to her villa once. I think he drove around, twisting up and down streets for twenty minutes. I couldn't find the place after that if I tried, and all I know is that the sun goes down in the west and that gave me a clue on which side of town the house was on but inside, in those walls, you never heard a thing. No bambinos yelling or screaming so it wasn't near a busy residential area. And, you know, she treated that guy like a king. Like a prince. She taught him Italiano, she bought him the finest clothes, and I'll bet she was hell on wheels in bed. She bought him a ring, or at least she gave him a ring, which was big as a pigeon's egg. What a setup! Working about three, four hours a day for the army and the rest at home.

It had to end, you know. Oh, I suggested once that he just bug out. He might have passed for an Italian nobleman anyway, just that look he had. But he said no, they were going to cut his orders before long, and it had been a good run at the good life but he'd be glad to get back. And that's exactly what happened.

Later I asked him what had happened and he said nothing, really. He'd given her the jeep and when he was posted out, to France, I think, they just kissed and said goodbye. I asked him did he ever get a letter from her, or did he ever send one to her, and he said no. He said once it was done, it was over, and it had been good while it lasted. "It was just one of those things that happen in a war," he said.

I felt like saying, "Baloney." Nothing like that ever happened to me.

•◄►• *The Guy in Peasant Clothes*

In Italy near Ortona one morning we're dug in waiting for something to happen, and I see this guy coming towards us and he's waving one of those passes that Italians are supposed to have to get up through our lines. Italian partisans. You know, the underground. I should have said this guy is wearing farmer's clothes. Peasant clothes.

The guy I'm nearest, a real tough nut named Blackie from Fort William or the back woods, he hollers at him in Italiano and the guy just keeps coming, so Blackie ups and blasts. The guy falls back and he's dead, and I yell at Blackie why did he have to go and kill him.

Blackie says, "He was no paisano. That was a Jerry, and I got him smack in the radiator cap," meaning dead centre.

The lieutenant runs up and he's mad as hell, and a couple of us drag the guy in and strip him down—and sure as hell, he's got enough grenades hidden to wipe us out, and papers on him. S.S. Corps. Panzer Division or something like that. No ordinary foot soldier was this one.

Blackie didn't trust a single guy coming in to surrender, and I asked him how he knew, why he plugged the guy, and he said, "Kid, around here, the paisano is a slob. All hunched over, worked like a dog all his life. I know, my parents come from this country. That guy I finished off, he walked like he was marching on a parade ground. He couldn't've been Italiano."

•◄►• *The Front*

Most civilians get the impression that The Front is a stabilized place and shells are zipping through the air and all hell is busting loose. Actually, well, when you were in an area which would be called The Front, the only time you knew you were actually at The Front was because it was too damn quiet. No activity. No trucks going back and forth with rations and shells. No jeeps. No artillery action. Nothing. There was an almost eerie stillness and you had that feeling in your gut that you'd gone about as far as you ought to go, Jack. In other words, there was no company out here. Where was everybody? So you back up.

An example. Up near Siena in Italy there was this First Division infantry regiment and over to their left was this ack-ack battery in a field and I was up there one day when I saw a water truck go by. Two guys in the truck, and I don't know where they thought they were going, but when they passed the battery we could see one guy waving, and then at the crossroad they took the wrong turn. Instead of left, they went right and we sat there with our glasses on them and watched them drive into Cavello, which was still in German hands, and we watched them drive into the square, get out, look around and then half a dozen Germans popped out of a building and the war was over for those two guys in the truck.

The point is, it was a sunny day, a nice day, and there they are and they're tootling along with their load of water and suddenly they're through our lines and through no-man's-land and into German territory, and until those Germans popped out with their rifles, those two guys had no inkling they were at The Front. Hell, all they were doing was delivering water.

While I was in a rest area in Italy, volunteers were requested for the 48th Highlanders and I volunteered for that. I joined the 48th and while moving out of the lines once I got concussed and got ruptured eardrums. So there I was in the 15th Canadian General Hospital. I had also contracted malaria and yellow jaundice while I was being evacuated from the lines and I was very sick for a long time, believe it.

One day my brother Jim, who's with the Irish Regiment of Canada, comes in to see me. He's my twin brother, you see, and we laughed and cried and were so happy to see each other and we made arrangements to get passes to go to Rome together. I got a seven-day pass and Jim had fourteen days, and in Rome we spent all our money and were A.W.O.L. for a few days, so we finally decided to go back to our units. We went and had a shower and got talking more about going back, and Jim said he figured his luck had run out. He said the last two men, the Number Two's with him on the Bren gun, had been killed, and he was pretty shook up when he talked about it.

So I told him that I had had a pretty good rest while in hospital and was being repatriated, so I would take his place in the lines and he could take my place and go home.

So we traded pay books and battle dress and he went to Grelino to be shipped back to England, where I was supposed to go, you see, and I went up the lines to his unit, which was the Irish.

It took me eight days to get the 500 miles where his unit was. I knew a few boys in the Irish and I had been with them before. When I got there I had more trouble with my ears and I had to go to the M.O., and when I was there he wanted to check the wounds that I had gotten in Normandy. I had to tell him I didn't have any wound in my hand. The doctor was quite mad and I got stripped for a complete medical and that convinced them I wasn't the guy my papers said I was, and he gave me a blast and sent me to the C.O. The C.O. put me under arrest and I was charged with being A.W.O.L., desertion and forgery.

Now in the meantime my brother had been locked up as he had been sent to the dentist back at the hospital where he had to report, as me, and the dentist fitted a partial plate they had made for me and of course it wouldn't fit in his mouth. He didn't need any partial plate. So he had to tell them he wasn't the guy they thought he was, that he wasn't me. So he had the same charges as I did. They threatened to throw the book against both of us.

However, things did get straightened away and they eventually dropped all the charges against us. My C.O. said he had read about such things like this, but never dreamt it would happen to him. He said the incident would be down in the history of the Irish Regiment.

•◄►• *Two Days Without Water*

We were on top of this little hill and our ammunition and supplies came up on mules led by Moroccans at night and as we were three miles from jeephead, our one meal a day was liable to be pretty lukewarm by the time it got to us. Also, we had to scrounge our own water — we got it from a well down in the ravine below us.

This well was in no-man's-land, so the peasants used it and we did and so did the Germans. It was funny, but it worked. But then one day we realized the well no longer was neutral. Jerry had taken it the night before, so we were in a pretty pickle.

The next night there was a big fight and we couldn't get down, and the mules didn't come up, and have you ever seen men two days without water? I was sergeant—we had no officers, all killed—so I announced to the guys I was going down to get water. This was in broad daylight. We just had to have water. Searing hot, and we had to have water.

So I took two jerry cans and the Tommy gun and started down. And the further I went, the more I started to get scared, and then I had a bright idea, maybe the first bright idea I'd ever had. The Italians were still using the well, so why wouldn't I dress up as an Italian woman? You know, old and bent, gnarled, black dress, long, black veil. So I crawled over to a house that had hell pounded out of it and sure enough, I found some clothes. Fitted right to a tee.

The last 20 feet were the hardest, but I got there. Fill'er up. And then suddenly it hit me. Italian peasant women carry their water on their heads. Seeing me strolling along carrying two cans, *bzzzzzt*, the end of me. You see, the Germans were all around. I couldn't see them but they knew I was there.

So I kind of kicked one jerry can aside and pick up the other and put it on my head, and I don't have one of those doughnuts the women have to protect their heads so I was going through the tortures of the damned. But there I was, going up the steep path, one hand on hip, mincing along like an Italian tart and the other hand keeping this can from falling off, and when I got to the other line, ours, our guys yelled, "Jeez, our guy's got it!"

Cheering and yells and whoopees. Then we rationed out the water and that night we got the well back. Nobody really said anything much about me getting the water, but I think that incident tells you a lot about Canadians. I think it does.

•◀▶• *"Start Digging!"*

We got the hell hammered out of us in front of Coriano. We lost three sergeants out of the five, our officers, some men who were veterans and knew the score, and at Hill 109 we got pounded there again. So they had turned the ack-ack boys into infantry. Just like that. Four years on the guns and now they're infantry. That's the way we did things then because of the man shortage, the crisis. The crisis, by the way, that Canadians at home did not know about.

They took sergeants and corporals from all the infantry units and sent them in with these guys, mainly the ack-ack guys, who had never had a shot fired at them and said, "You're going into the lines," and somebody called them the Slaughterhouse Battalion and that name stuck because it was going to be a slaughter.

Our first battle, at the Usso I think, we were at the crossroads and in a mop-up position and I told these crazy bastards, "Start digging," because we were due to get harassing fire in a few minutes. And I started to dig, as hard and fast and deep as I could. These other guys were just kind of scraping the dirt away. A couple wandered over to a farmyard and brought back a couple of chickens and started plucking them. Some just sat around and smoked.

Whiss-ss-s-sss-ss-sss, plop, in behind us about 100 yards.

I remember one of these new guys looked up and he said, "Shit, they can't even shoot." I said, "Dig a little harder." Well, the next bunch came right in on us, right around, and I had my trench deep by this time and I made a dive for it and you know what? I was the sixth man in. I was the one who landed almost above ground with my ass sticking up. Those replacements dived in from all angles, right into my slit trench. All ahead of me.

I'll tell you this. From that point on, when I said, "Start digging," those bastards dug, and when I said, "Dig harder," they worked like you never saw any man work before. About two days later—and it is amazing how fast a man learns—one guy says to me: "Sarge, you don't have to tell us to dig any more. You just pick up your own shovel and we'll pick up ours."

I'm telling you this story for two reasons. One, to show you how goddamned rough it was over there, when they had to take untrained men and put them in as infantry in the roughest fight of them all because of one man's stubbornness or politicalness [Mackenzie King] and, two, just how fast a guy would learn the arts of war, the techniques of survival. In just a few days. Sometimes in just a few hours.

•◄►• Screaming, Screaming

I'll tell you a story and this is all you ever need to know about war. We were at Ortona and there were places where their lines and ours were fairly close together. Ortona is in Italy, over towards the Adriatic side. There was some terrible fighting there.

We'd send out patrols, they'd send out patrols. At night. If we got a chance, we'd grab a couple of them if we met, ambush, and they'd try the same. Or we'd try and knock a few over, and so would they. Or, and this happened, almost by gentlemen's agreement, we'd pass by. Like ships passing in the night. Nobody wanted to kill that night.

One night we had two patrols out and we knew they did, and about two in the morning we hear this terrible screaming. It's a guy screaming. On and on. I'm sure you could hear it for miles. Up and down, high and low, screaming, screaming. I can hear it now. Our lieutenant is with us and he says, "The poor bugger's taken some in the belly."

Now, I'm telling you this. It went on for two hours and it seemed like ten. You see, we thought he'd die. Not often did they last that long. But this one wouldn't die.

Finally a guy says he's going out there. He's an Indian, and I think he was from around Cochrane, near Calgary, or maybe his name is Cochrane. An Indian—he gets killed about a month later. Anyway, the lieutenant doesn't say anything and so this Indian slips out and Jeezus! it is one dark night and I ask the lieutenant if we should ask for a couple of flares, just to help him, and he says no.

In about fifteen minutes, all of a sudden the screaming stops. Just like that. Like shutting off a tap. A light switch. In about five minutes this Cochrane comes back and he says, "Damn it to hell. What a shitty way to earn a living."

The sergeant after a while asks who it was out there, and Cochrane says he doesn't know. Well, was it one of our guys? Cochrane says he doesn't know. Was it a German? He says how the hell should he know.

Then—and you might not think there are some very moving moments in a war in the mud and wet and shit—but Cochrane says, "All I know was that there was a dying soldier out there and I just put my hand on his forehead and said a little prayer and then I put the knife right into his throat. I was just helping a poor soldier along the way."

Men at Home

They Took My Land Away . . . Pure Hell for a Guy Not in Uniform . . . "A Photo of Your Dead Son, Please" . . . Zoot Sooters — Wolf Pack of Sheep . . . Running the Farm . . . Frozen . . . Riders of Doom.

While life overseas was hell for many servicemen, the civilian at home was not always on easy street. Wherever he went, the young, apparently fit civilian was never free from being aware of the unspoken question: "Why isn't he in uniform?"

Nobody passed out white feathers for cowardice as they did in England in the first world war, but many men were conscious of the stares. The little button in their lapel signifying they had been rejected as medically unfit didn't help that much.

A man who was an inspector in an aircraft assembly plant said, "It was the worst three years I will ever spend. I knew nobody could do the job like I could, and that my job was absolutely vital. But I always found myself apologizing to everyone for not being overseas. I thought maybe I should have some pamphlets printed and pass them out at parties or on the streetcar saying I was too important to the defence plant to be in uniform."

But men were needed to operate the vast war defence machine while the rest of the country was kept going as in peacetime. And while there were slackers, men with "pull" who managed to get and keep a nice, soft job, many other men, in factories and on the farms, worked harder during the war than at any other time in their lives for little money and less thanks.

•◄►• *They Took My Land Away*

They took my land away. Two hundred acres in one parcel, and south of that piece, they took another 67 acres, and there was nothing in it to do with the courts. They just came and said that within 30 days or 45 days or something my land would be, as they put it, vested with the Crown, which meant that they had expropriated it.

And for what? Well, manoeuvres would be the best way to put it. They wanted to make their battle training areas bigger, and when I went to my lawyer, he went to Ottawa, which is not all that far away, and they said I could have my land back within three years after the war.

The price was poor but it wasn't the best land. But seeing as there was a war on, we got off it because we had to, anyway, and we went to Niagara Falls and London and worked in war plants there and well, to make a long story short, do you know what heavy tanks and other war machinery will do to land? It's called compacting. It presses the soil down so hard that it is like concrete. Mind you, it *looks* the same, but try and plant something on it and get a decent crop. It won't drain and it won't grow and it will hardly grow forage, and getting 18 dollars an acre, which I think is what I got for land which had been in my family for more than a hundred years, well, I just think those fellows in Ottawa had a pretty high-handed way of doing things during the war.

Not that I was against the war. Certainly not. Two of my boys were in it, my brother's boy was killed in a bomber, so we paid our share. But they also ruined my land.

•◄►• *Pure Hell for a Guy Not in Uniform*

Don't let anyone ever tell you it was all blue sky and sunshine for a guy not in uniform in those years. Sometimes it was pure hell.

Fellows who had tried to enlist and had been turned down, they got this little pin they could wear, and if people knew what it meant, then they were okay. I was a deferment, vital to the war effort. A classification like that meant I had no pin, and to a lot it looked like I was just running away from the whole thing.

Well, like hell I was. I was a master mechanic and stationary engineer and I worked in this little factory just outside Hamilton, and the family who owned it had wangled a job making parts for bearings for Liberty ships. If the government had given the contract to somebody bigger they'd have been better off, but as it was, we were vital to the war effort.

I was 29 and just ripe for a uniform, but there I was, keeping that damned plant going, running back and forth between the machine shop and the boiler room like an Olympic champion. Eighteen hours in a day and ten on Sunday was nothing, keeping that plant going. Every time I'd tell the boss to shove it—he was a canny old Scots bugger—he'd give me a raise and run off to the procurement board and get my deferment renewed. I couldn't have joined the army even if I'd wanted to.

That didn't help me, though. Look at me now. Well, back in 1943 I was still six-foot-one, and I was a good 195 pounds and none of it fat, but because I could make an engine part on a lathe out of scrap iron I'd find in the back of the shop, I was essential. And I took shit for it. Ask my wife.

We couldn't go to a dance. We'd be bumped on the floor by army and navy types. The air force wasn't too bad. But you'd hear all sorts of cracks like, "Maybe he's got a wooden leg," or, "Is that silver plate in his head where they pour the sawdust in?" and, "I guess his old man's got money," and on and on. Christ, if there were a thousand insults, I heard them all. We finally stopped going to dances. The wife just couldn't take it any more. She used to cry about it.

You got it on the streets, remarks you heard as you walked by, and I remember once on a streetcar I was sitting at the back and I felt something tapping the bottom of my foot and there was a paratrooper kicking me, and when I looked at him he gave me the up-yours sign. Sure, I could have got up and whaled him one, but he had two buddies with him and if you don't think that's what they were waiting for me to do, then you're wrong. You had to watch yourself.

There were thousands of us, I guess. Maybe we should have formed our own organization. A Mafia thing or something. For me, I just developed a hard shell. It got so I was immune, or I'm telling you now I was. I wasn't really. You kind of got the feeling of what it must be like to be a Negro in Georgia.

My father-in-law, who knew what I was doing at the foundry, he would hear these insults and he'd get madder than anyone. Once we were fishing near Guelph in that little river and some soldiers were down the bank with some girls drinking beer and playing around, and soon we heard a few remarks come up our way. Harry, my father-in-law, that scored him out and he went down and told them a thing or two, what I was doing, and I can still remember one of the girls laughing and saying, "Ah, fuck off, willya. We know exactly what he is."

It all ended pretty well when the war ended. A few of my friends when they got back from overseas would make the odd remark, joking, in a nonjoking kind of way, but that ended pretty soon too. But I can tell you now, right now, that I know I was more valuable in that plant patching up that equipment than if I'd killed five Germans a day.

●◄►● *"A Photo of Your Dead Son, Please"*

My first job at the Winnipeg *Tribune* was picking up pictures of casualties. I don't suppose there were jobs like it in Canada at that time. A job description written by a personnel manager would be a strange document to read. Remember, I was only seventeen. A very tender age.

I'd come on duty at four and about six-thirty I'd call a Moore's cab and I'd have a list of the casualties for the next day's paper. Every casualty had a firm release date—not to be released until such and such a date. It was stupid, really, because whether the person had been killed, wounded or was missing in action, his parents, next of kin had got the word, the telegram, the visit by the chaplain or officer about a month before.

That made my job easier. I mean I didn't have to go into a house cold, to say that Jim or John was dead. No, my job was to phone ahead and ask if they had a picture we could run and could I come out and get it. The answer, invariably, was yes. But if there was no phone—and many people didn't have phones—you just went out and knocked on the door. That could be a little rough.

I can see it all again, a thousand scenes. Say it was the north end of the city. Foreign, Jewish, Polish, strongly Ukrainian. You'd knock on the door of a small frame house, maybe with geraniums in the window boxes and heavy lace curtains in the windows. You'd be asked to come in. The mother was usually big, often a matriarchal type, strong and big-breasted. Big Momma type. The old man was often a stereotype too, work-worn, beaten-down, and his English might be poor or he might not speak English. In some of these households one person, usually the woman, would speak to the visitor and when business came up, they'd switch over to Ukrainian or Polish or whatever.

So there I'd be on the chesterfield. Would I like some coffee? Some cake? Even if I said no, I got it anyway. You couldn't refuse.

Out would come the photo album. Plenty of pictures, from baby to little boy to Boy Scout and on up. A picture of him in uniform, often air force at that time, because heavy army losses hadn't started to come in from Italy yet and D-day was far off. I can see them still. Uniform a bit large, but they meant it that way because they always said you'd fill out on service food. Hell, they just meant you would continue your natural process of growing up—service food had nothing to do with it. Stiff at attention, usually. Always very self-conscious. This type of photo would the on-demand type. Mother demanding it be taken, his first in uniform, and she's proud.

There were others. Usually taken at graduation from gunnery school or when he finished pilot training. Head and shoulders, eight by eleven inches, and tinted. Christ, I always thought that a tinted photo made a guy look like he was in his coffin, made up with cosmetics and embalmed. They used to turn my stomach.

But this kind of photo, and I'm not trying to put these people down, this was the kind they wanted me to take. It looks so natural, they'd say. Often I'd have to pick out the one, and then the whole damned family would argue. Often in Yiddish or Ukrainian.

Sometimes the women would break down. Oh yes, many times I've had a woman just go to pieces, and if she was alone in the house I'd run next door and bring back a neighbour.

Or I'd have to sit and listen while they told me about the boy's life, and show me his report cards, his Y.M.C.A. swimming certificate, his Cub or Scout badges, things like that. I'd listen until hell froze over because I knew I was doing some good. They were talking, and accepting the inevitability of death.

But some didn't. No, some didn't. I'd hate to recall the number of times I've been asked, about a son killed in a bomber crash, wasn't it possible that the government had made a mistake? What was the sense of bullshitting these poor people? I could have, and walked out the door and left them to another month's torture, thinking that Nick or Mike or Steve was still alive. Sure, I could have done that. But no, I'd look at them straight and say something like the government doesn't make mistakes like this. I'm sorry, ma'am, but that's the way it is.

Or if he was missing. Then I could be a soothing balm. Yes, sure, often airmen came back. They'd parachute and be picked up by a friendly farmer or something. But I wasn't telling them much. They knew that. A hundred friends and neighbours and relatives had already told them the missing sometimes return. In fact, the newspapers used to give every one quite a play.

But there was one situation I never learned to cope with. Take a family with no phone. You drive up in the taxi and knock on the door. It's usually just after supper and a kid comes to the door, one of the brothers or sisters. I say I'd like to see your mother, or father. Usually the mother. The kid would yell and the old lady would come down the hall and see me and you'd see that look on her face. Just a flash. I'd say I was from the Winnipeg *Tribune* and I was calling about her son. Well!

Sometimes they'd shriek. Once one fell right into my arms. A Polish household can get pretty excited. And then it would take a few minutes to tell them I was just from the paper and wanted a picture of their son, the flyer, and I wasn't there to tell them that he was alive and well and coming home the next day.

You know, what I'm telling you is straight goods. Somebody could make a movie out of that period of my newspaper career, the butting into people's lives to get a lousy photograph so some layout editor could dress up an inside page with art on the casualty list. When you look at it that way, it was a pretty crummy job, I guess.

When you look at it the other way, I was doing good. I always felt I was doing good. You see, the name in the casualty list, the picture, the caption, killed over Europe, wounded or missing in Sicily, it brought the whole thing out into the open. There was no hiding any more from the inevitability of war, and no pretending that war doesn't mean death, but only means heroes and homecoming parades and medals and pretty girls.

I look at it that way now. Then I didn't. I won't say I was callow, unfeeling, because I wasn't. I listened, I put my hand on their shoulders when they wept again, wept for maybe the last time, and I ate their cake and drank their coffee and looked at the album and said what a good-looking guy he was, and for a while then, I was their friend.

And you've got to remember, I was only seventeen.

•◄►• *Zoot Sooters — a Wolf Pack of Sheep*

I was a zoot sooter. That's not spelled s-u-i-t-e-r but s-o-o-t-e-r, and it was a wartime fad that I've never seen crop up since, or not to my knowledge.

Young fellows, sixteen, seventeen, eighteen, but older ones too—they—we dressed in these outlandish clothes. I'd really need a picture to show you to get the point across, but if you can imagine a pair of trousers that had a 28-inch circumference at the knees and dropped down to 12 inches at the ankle, so you had small zippers on the inside which you unzipped so you could get into them. And then the jacket had shoulders as wide as one of these football players in shoulder pads today, and a cherry-coloured or lime-green shirt and a big floppy bow tie and one of those hats, wide-brimmed, very wide-brimmed like that gangster-looking character wears in the L'il Abner comic strip. The shoes, as I remember, were yellow and pointed. We wore a chain, thinner than a bicycle chain, from our belt and it looped down almost to the ground and then up again to the belt. Jesus Christ, when I think of it!

We were a wolf pack. We even had names like those gangs in New York. The whole idea came up from the States. I remember, we were against soldiers, people in uniform, but I don't think it was because we were against the war or anything like that. They were just somebody to beat up on. I remember we caught two air force guys waiting for a bus late one night and we beat them up. Stupid, but that is what we did. Beat up on guys in uniform. It could have been a fellow I went to school with. Why? Christ, I don't know.

We went together as a gang—about 10, 12, and at night. A gang had to have a headquarters and we chose a café on Danforth. It was more of a diner affair and a Greek guy ran it, from about 6 A.M. to catch the early shift on to late at night. We took over his place at night. He'd beg us to go, that we were ruining his business, and that was for sure. People just stopped coming in. This Andrapopoulos or whatever it was, he'd beg us to let him close, but we'd laugh in his face and make him serve us coffee and we'd flip quarters and play the jukebox until about 1 A.M. When I look back at it, what a bunch of purebred louses we were.

Anyway, until this one night. Nobody's in this diner but us and about midnight a car pulls up and three guys get out and come in. Now this is exactly the way it happened. They're big guys and I spotted them right off as detectives. They are big men, and you know how a real big man is when he's also fast and tough. You know, they have a confidence in themselves. They're like topflight athletes, they just move right. So they come in, and one puts one hand on the counter and vaults right over and stands by the door, the opening into the Greek's kitchen. He just stands there. The second guy, just as big, he stands by the door to the street, right in front of it. You get the picture. And the third, well, the third comes at us slowly and we don't realize it until later but we're being herded back into a corner, just like a lot of god-damned sheep. About 10 of us, against one of him. Or three of them if you like. But what I mean, they've got us. No guns, no billy club or that thing they use, a leather sack filled with lead buckshot, none of that. Just this one guy.

He gives us a lecture and believe me, I'm shit-scared. I am. I admit it. I am scared. He says he knows all our names, and where we live, and we've been bothering this poor restaurant guy who is trying to make a living and he's very upset and so is his wife. Christ, it's just like a television movie. Then he says quietly that if one of us so much as goes into this place again he's going to beat the shit out of all of us. Personally. And he would too. And he says if there is one rock thrown through a window of this place, he'll see each of us and *watch out!*

Then he points to a guy, a kid named Boysie, and he says, "Out," and Boysie goes forward and as he sort of cringes past, this big cop reaches out and knuckles him on the side of the head. Knuckle? That's where you take two fingers and you flick them at a guy's head and it's not going to kill you but it sure hurts, and when he does this to Boysie he also flips up his hat and Boysie's hat goes spinning. He does this to every one of us, knuckle and we lose our hat, and I think what a goddamned bunch of yellow-bellied sapsuckers we are. Aren't we the greatest.

And the cop at the door, every one of us goes out gets more of the same, a boot in the arse unless we can double shift past the guy and avoid it. I tried that and caught his boot on the thigh bone and had a blue mark for two weeks.

I was the second last out, as I remember. I guess I thought the dick would get tired of knocking us about, but he didn't. Everybody got it and when I got out on the street the guys were all across the street. It was like watching somebody get hanged. You know, a public execution.

We could see the old Greek shake hands with the cops, these big, big bastards and he's about five-foot-two, and they come out and they start across the street towards us, all three together, and one cop yells, "Scram, assholes!" I'll never forget that. We started to walk fast and then somebody started running and there we are, running like they were right behind us.

When I got home I took off that silly uniform and I never wore it again. I guess there was a good enough reason for it because I was going to join the army anyway, but I was so goddamned ashamed of myself that I never wore it again. Just ashamed. And I bet I saved up two months in my job to get the money to buy it.

•←→• *Running the Farm*

Oh, I just stayed on the home place and worked. Worked like hell, my own half-section, my brother's half and my father's section, and two sections without help and machinery falling apart—that was hard work in those days.

From '41 on, we got good years and I put in everything I could. Wheat, and then barley for the pigs. We had an awful lot of pigs in those days, mostly for the British market, and my wife was milking 16 Jerseys too, with only the help of a hired girl from town.

The only real help, believe it or not, was the German prisoners, the **P.O.W.'s**. They gave me two and they were farm lads. Some fellows around got city fellows, fellows who had been bookkeepers and like that in Germany before the war, but I got two real farmers and we could make the fur fly. They were good and they knew how to work. I'll never forget those two. Good fellows.

The worst was along about the summer of '43 and we had a real hefty crop. A real dandy. They sent me three fellows from the army. The Canadian Army. These three guys were useless. Oh sure, they knew enough about farming, but they just didn't give a hoot. As long as they weren't in the army they didn't care where they were.

I worked that way for four years, from the time my brother Alf took off one day to Chippewa in Winnipeg and came back three days later in a sailor suit. That's when the old man went in to see our local magistrate or into Winnipeg or some place and came back with a paper, the deferment. That's the way it had to be. Two sections and me running the whole show and all these government boards always on your back. Grow more wheat, grow more barley to keep more pigs, and more milk for powdered milk and cheese and the whole list, and on one hand they're working you to death and on the other, they're raising taxes, and I think it was 10 percent they wanted out of you for war bonds. And try as you did, it was like pulling teeth trying to get tractor parts, let alone a new tractor.

I worked from five in the morning, all morning dead flat as all get out until noon, and I'd lie down after dinner and listen to the grain prices from the Winnipeg Stock Exchange, the grain prices, and then out again doing some damn-fool thing like harvesting or seeding or cultivating or just mending fence until suppertime. Then suppertime and read the mail that came in from town, and maybe look over the *Prairie Farmer* and go to bed about eight at night. I think in those years I only took off Christmas and Dominion Day. July 1.

I don't get much thanks either, not on your life. And that was a lot of responsibility for a kid. I was only twenty-three when it was over, when my brother Alf comes back from the war and thinks he is going to take over the farm. He says, after all, isn't he the oldest boy, and isn't that the way it's always done in our family?

My old man is going to agree with him, but my wife steps in and she gives it to him, both barrels, right between the eyes. She says since I was nineteen I was running this farm while he was sitting on his backside teaching radio training to recruits down in Nova Scotia or New Brunswick. She told him, look at your brother, me, and she says that I looked like I was thirty-five. I remember going across to the mirror over the sink by the pump and, by God, I did. I looked like an old man, and I was only twenty-three.

There was no way Alf was going to run that farm anyway. He stuck around for a month, going into town in the pickup every night, sitting in the beer parlor with his cronies and coming home drunk every night. One night he hit a cow on the hill down from the cemetery. Finally my wife told me what I had to do, so I took Alf aside and offered him a fair price for his half-section and he jumped at it. I think that was what he was waiting for anyway. The war just knocked all the farming out of him, or sitting on his fanny teaching *dit-dad-dad-dit* on the Morse Code sure did. He left, went to Toronto where he had friends, and never did come back.

•◄►• *Frozen*

There were four flour mills in Medicine Hat and I worked for Maple Leaf. We were all frozen. Any mill that had export orders, well, you were stuck. That meant you couldn't enlist, and you couldn't take any kind of a holiday unless someone would agree to replace you. I'm not sure if we even got days off. We were on what is known as a G.B. contract, Great Britain, milling wheat for overseas.

It was a rotten system. Working in a mill at 52 or 55 cents an hour, and somebody across the road working in a body shop or in a lumber yard getting 80 or 90 cents an hour and able to leave when they wanted. But you could see what would happen to a shift at a mill if three or four fellows just took off. That would shut her right down. Practically.

What if you did take a day off? They'd warn you and give you a 10-day suspension, and if you did it again, another 10-day suspension and the third time, why you'd go into an internment camp. Just like a German P.O.W. Impeding the war effort. That was very serious. I tried it once but that's all. One 10-day suspension was enough, especially when you're making only 50 cents an hour with a wife and kid and your rent was 26 dollars a month. Not much now, but then you could starve. So I never did that again. I wanted to join up and see some of the world but no way, no siree—once in the flour mill and you were stuck there, frozen, making four bits an hour and guys all around you in town making up to a buck an hour. It wasn't fair but that's the way it was.

I think we started at four o'clock and most, or many, of our telegrams would be killed in action, wounded or missing in action. As I remember, there were a lot of missing-in-action because this was in the fairly early part of the war and most of the guys getting it were in bombers, fighters, the R.C.A.F. and the R.A.F. There never were many navy and not many soldiers at that time either, but that's what I gathered from the newspapers and not from the telegrams.

We'd get our sheaf, you see. The telegrams had to be delivered at night, because there would usually be a man home, somebody to be home. Maybe out of thirty telegrams, five might be casualties. Sometimes as many as eight or ten, and that was pretty high.

Sometimes if we weren't sure, we could sneak open the edge of the slicked-down envelope and if we saw it was a casualty telegram, then we'd go next door and get a woman there to come with us. Not to bolster up our courage. This was old hat with us, but when a woman just finds out her husband has been shot down and killed, she shouldn't be left alone.

I always remember those telegrams. They'd start out something like this: "The Department of National Defence regret . . ." That's all we needed to know. Zoom, next door and get a neighbour. I always wondered, why shouldn't it be the word "regrets" instead of "regret"? Isn't "regrets" better grammar? I guess we were such a callous bunch of young buggers we didn't really think we were smashing some woman's life to bits. Interested only because a word didn't sound right.

If neighbours saw a telegraph boy going up to a house they'd usually know. Not all that many people had phones then, the Depression being what it was, but there were two mails a day and one on Saturday. Sometimes you'd be in a house and before you'd left there would be a couple of neighbour women or neighbours heading for the house. This would be in the slums, the poorer districts, where people looked after each other better. Not in the richer districts, the poorer ones.

I always hung around a couple of minutes, just to see if they were all right. I'd always ask if there was something I could do. A few times I made tea for women or I'd run to the nearest phone and call the husband or the daughter or something. I think it must have been the telegraph company that said not to leave them alone.

Jesus Christ! When I think of it, what a rotten way to do things. Sending a young punk of a kid on a bike riding down a street so everybody can see him and everybody wondering, "Is he stopping here?" Or, "Where will he stop?" But you got to remember, later on there were thousands and thousands and thousands of those things delivered. My own mother got one, when I got caught. She said it wasn't so bad. I said, "What do you mean it wasn't so bad?" She said she didn't mean it that way, but by that time—and this was in August of '44—the sight of the telegraph boy was a pretty common sight with his black bag and his sheaf of yellow telegrams. After all, the Carpenter kid and the Melnyk kid and the Hudson kid, all within a stone's throw, they'd all got it by then, and they were just around the block.

Remember when Lorne Green, *Bonanza*, was on the nine o'clock news and he was called the Voice of Doom? That big voice and giving us the war news, every night, and a lot of it was doom. Well, I guess us kids, sixteen or seventeen, kids on our Raleighs and CCM's, were the riders of doom, although I never thought about it that way. But I'll bet you a lot of women and men still around who got those telegrams thought of us that way.

I guess I was taking part in just about the toughest part of a non-war and didn't even know about it. Yes, I guess so. Riders of Doom.

The Convoy Must Go On

The Corvette . . . One Day on a Corvette . . . A Floating Pigpen . . . Fighting Glider Bombs . . . A Suspicious Sonar Reading . . . A Precious Atlantic Cargo . . . The U-boat and the Cat

Whether they assembled in Halifax or New York or Boston, to get to Britain, the Allies' fortress in Europe, every convoy passed close to Newfoundland and then on out into the North Atlantic, escorted by the Navy.

And out there the submarines lurked, long, slim, dark shapes loaded with torpedoes, each with a warhead deadly enough to blow any ship to Kingdom Come. A general cargo freighter could go down in minutes. A tanker carrying oil, the very life-blood of war, to embattled England or Russia, could explode in one great roar of flame and smoke. And the convoy would steam on, at the pace of its slowest ship, while any ship that was crippled would be left to the mercy of the lurking sub when the escorting navy vessels were over the horizon.

It was the worst kind of war, fought on a battleground of the enemy's choice, and from late 1939 until late 1943 the enemy was winning. Losses were horrendous, so high that they were never announced, but convoys leaving Halifax or St. John's with up to 20 or 30 ships arrived at Londonderry in Northern Ireland with half that number.

Then why did they continue to sail that North Atlantic route? Supplying Britain with men and guns and planes and material and foodstuff was as important as any task in the war, and there was simply no other route. It was the North Atlantic or nothing. And many hundreds of Canadian sailors—navy and merchant marine—died in those bitter waters to keep that supply route open.

•◂▸• The Corvette

The corvette was built on the lines of a whale catcher, of British design, and originally they carried a crew of about 70 in very, very primitive conditions. But they kept piling more and more special and sophisticated electronic equipment onto them so the crew grew up over 90 and nearly 100. So there were about 100 men living in conditions that would have handled about 50 men with a certain amount of comfort.

Ask any man who served on corvettes, on convoys, and you'll get an earful. Ask anyone who survived North Atlantic gales in one of them and they'll tell you it was a special kind of hell. And they rolled incredibly. Sometimes they would roll approximately 45 degrees and I recall on one occasion, these corvettes had what was known as the dome, an asdic dome for submarine detection, welded on to the keel of the ship, and we were rolling terribly and another of the ships in our group, a frigate, sent us a signal saying, "Oh, what a lovely dome you have." Now, I know this is incredible, terribly hard to believe but we were rolling so much that they could see our bottom, and we could see the dome of other ships. Imagine what it was like living under those conditions.

The corvette had its faults: too slow, the subs could out-run them, and there was a fueling problem, but they were grand little ships. They'd go out when larger ships might come to grief. A lot of good men sailed in them and they did a lot of good work, and while everybody had a part in winning the war, sometimes I think the little corvettes did more than their share, especially in those days when the Atlantic was just swarming with German subs and the convoys had to get through, and if they hadn't, Britain might not have pulled through. It was the corvettes of the Canadian Navy, I like to think, which had a lot to do with getting those convoys through.

•←→• *One Day on a Corvette*

Life on a corvette was pretty grim. One crossing, 'Derry to St. John's, the weather was terrible and everyone was at the end of their endurance. Just going through the motions, just hanging on hoping to survive, and I mean just *hoping* to survive. None of us thought we would make it.

The convoy was slowed down but this fool of a skipper insisted on rushing around in all directions at once, and as a consequence we took a terrible beating from the sea. We lost all of the port wing of our bridge, but nobody was standing on it at the time. All the lifeboats, all the life rafts and we had an ammunition locker up by the foc'sle, called a ready-use locker and it was welded right into the ship. It was part of the deck, and one wave just ripped it clear away as if it was cardboard—lifted right off the deck and away it went.

The seas were so heavy that the depth charges broke loose on the afterdeck. Well, one broke loose and then it knocked down others and there we had maybe 20 or 30 rolling around, each weighing several hundred pounds and filled with high explosive. So there they were rolling around in the waist of the ship, and there was a chance that one would explode at any moment and there would go the ship. I was in my bunk and I heard these things thundering around.

Now, mind you, this is in seas you wouldn't believe. I just can't describe them. There was every fear that the ship itself would go down, let alone being blown to Kingdom Come by depth charges.

I went to the bridge and there's the old man and he says, "Lieutenant, your depth charges are loose. Secure them." *My* depth charges! *Mine!* My depth charges sloshing and banging around and with every sea that came in, there was six feet of water down there too.

Anyway, half a dozen of us went down there and how we secured those big barrels was rather ingenious, I thought. We got some planks and stood them up against the bulwarks and the ship was rolling, almost rolling over, and we'd get one of these barrels to the foot of the planks inside the waist. When the ship was this way, we'd steady the depth charge at the foot of the plank and when she rolled the other way next time, the barrel would roll down the planks, over the side and to the bottom. And we did it with every depth charge, and that was some achievement, believe me.

But what I didn't say was that while all this was going on, an even greater sea hit us, larger than all the rest, and picked me up—and I'm not kidding—and took me up, over the side, into the ocean. And, somehow, there was a cross-wave coming just then and that wave grabbed me and deposited me back on the ship, and as I went by I grabbed on to the rack which held the depth charges and held on, skinning my hand badly. But the rare part of it was, hanging on my coattails was Petty Officer Snow. We'd both gone over together but I didn't know it, and when I came back, he'd grabbed my slicker and got the ride back to civilization with me.

And that, my friend, is one day in the life of a corvette in the North Atlantic.

•←→• *A Floating Pigpen*

Just about the only thing I can remember, apart from how god-damned cold it was on the North Atlantic, and Christ, when I think how those corvettes used to get thrown about, the main thing I can remember is the stink. B.O. Remember the magazine ads?

There'd be about 30 men in our quarters. Once we picked up 12 guys in a lifeboat and most of them came in with us. You could say it was crowded, a room hardly big enough to swing a small cat by the tail. Hammocks everywhere, messing table in the centre, and guys off watch sleeping, guys playing cards, writing letters, just staring at nothing, and half the time the whole god-damned Atlantic was trying to get in at us. That's a mess deck for you. If you opened the portholes any time but a nice summer day you'd freeze, and you couldn't open them at night. Blackouts. God! Just so you wouldn't get fished, torpedoed.

Say, 15 or 20 days across, Halifax to Londonderry—20 days if you had a few old tubbers doing 8 knots—and the smell just got worse and worse. No showers, you see. The navy rule, no showers on ships at sea. Not even for officers and P.O's. You could shave, but some never did and some kids were so young they never had to. Oh, I tell you, it was a grand life, great to be a sailor. The ship was a floating pigpen of stink. You couldn't get away from it. The butter tasted of it. The cooks used to bake bread every night and the bread smelled of feet and armpits. There must be something about eggs. They'd pick up the smell. Everything did, and that goes for meat too.

And you know, you couldn't do anything about it. You just had to wait until we hit Ireland or got into St. John's or Halifax and had a quick shower before hitting the jetty. And then I'd go straight to a hotel, get a room and a bottle from the clerk and lie down in that bath water up to here and stay there until the jug was maybe gone and I was white as a lily. I used to do that every trip. Even if we only had shore time up to twenty-three hundred hours [11.00 P.M.], I'd waste at least half of it in the tub getting soaked. Both ways. Soaking the muck off and getting soaked on rum.

There was one thing that always puzzled me. We're sitting in the Queen's Hotel one night, this A.B. and me and I started talking about the stink and he looked at me funny and then he said, "What're you talking about, Marty? I never smell a thing. Smells okay to me." I just couldn't figure that one out.

•←→• *Fighting Glider Bombs*

We were taking convoys down to Gib, North Africa, and the Germans started giving us a helluva lot of trouble with glider bombs. The Focke-Wulfs would stay off, out of range of our anti-aircraft guns, and they'd let go these glider bombs. Say from 3,000 feet up. Well, there's a whole ocean of ships down below him and the pilot would just pick a target, like these remote-controlled toys you see on the kids' television, and he'd guide it and boom, bang!

These glider bombs were new and they were causing an awful lot of trouble. Nobody knew what to do with them, and they were sinking and damaging a lot of ships, killing a lot of good men. It was just about impossible to hit this aerial-borne bomb; it was only about 20 feet long.

We knew we were in deep trouble, so our skipper sent this information up to the Admiralty, London, Western Approaches, and the Admiralty worked one day and two nights in a row with their scientists, British scientists, and the signal came back. When this aerial bombardment with torpedoes starts, everybody who has one plug in their electric razors. Now not too many officers had electric razors on these ships but some did, and that was enough. It broke up the Focke-Wulfs' frequencies and it did the trick. They couldn't control their glider bombs, so they were of no use, so they quit. They didn't bother us any more after that.

•←→• *A Suspicious Sonar Reading*

A lot of the wives and families of seamen on the frigates and minesweepers lived in Halifax, and that's another reason why that place was such a hellhole during the war. Too crowded. Living in slums, and some are still there.

These ships would be out on patrol, coming in with a convoy, all the jobs the Canadians did in the North Atlantic, one hell of a big job, but life was pretty drab and when they got a few days off to stay with their families, the food ashore was maybe worse than aboard.

They had this deal. Call it a gimmick. Say 20, 30, 40 miles out, the skipper would order a depth charge thrown out. Not a pattern, but just one. Maybe two. When they went off, the ship would circle back and stop engines and they'd put a couple of life-boats over. It would go in the log as a suspicious sonar reading, or because the ship was stopped, the log might read lifeboat drill or clearing the decks or something. Some skippers probably never did a damn thing to the log, figuring what the hell, who's checking anyway.

If they were lucky, dozens, maybe hundreds of fish would come up. Some would be torn up, naturally. After all, a depth charge that can rip the plates off a sub can do a hell of a mess of damage to some Atlantic cod. But most were concussed, knocked out, and the boys filled the boats with these fine, fat specimens of the sea, and my wife said you used to see them coming ashore, each with a sack of maybe 60 or 70 pounds of fresh fat Atlantic cod and the whole apartment house or neighbourhood block would have a good feast for a couple of days.

•◄►• *A Precious Atlantic Cargo*

It was on the *Duchess of Richmond*. We called her the *Drunken Duchess*, she rolled around so much. We were coming back, November, 1940, from Liverpool to Quebec City and we had such precious cargo. There was about 600 officers and other men of the Royal Air Force coming to Canada, Moose Jaw, to teach in the air schools and about a hundred civilians with priorities, gold bullion and armaments and other things, I don't know what.

We left Liverpool in a convoy, freighters mostly, at 9 knots on November 1, 1940, and we stayed with that convoy for two days and then the *Duchess of Richmond* left the convoy. The convoy could only go about 9 knots and the *Duchess of Richmond* about 18 knots.

About 36 hours later the *Admiral Scheer*, the battleship, began to trail us. We knew it was there but we couldn't see it. At night we were blacked out and the old *Duchess of Richmond* got her speed up to 22 knots and she was just about shaking herself apart, but we just had to keep going as fast as we could. That precious cargo, it would have been a disaster if those 600 air force men had been sunk. In November, nobody would have lasted more than a few minutes in the Atlantic, you see.

Then the next night when we were out on deck, suddenly we saw gunfire on the horizon and it was a big fight. Then we saw a ship was on fire and then the flames went out, and we talked to the first officer and he said that a freighter had been sent to intercept the German hunter and they were having a battle. Of course, it was not a battle, really. The freighter didn't have any of the kind of armament that the German warship had, and it was sunk quickly. We could see the battle only a few miles away and we didn't realize until then how close the German ship had come up to us in the night. It had almost caught us.

A lot of the men in the freighter were killed, and 16 or 17 were in lifeboats or in the water, but there was no way the captain of the *Duchess of Richmond* could go in and save them. With such a precious cargo of trained men and executives and gold, he just had to get away as fast as he could. And it was the sacrifice of the freighter which saved our ship.

When we got to Quebec City it was all in the newspapers and then we learned that the freighter was an armed freighter called the *Jervis Bay* and that the men who had sailed in her were being treated as heroes. If she hadn't been there that German would have blown the *Duchess of Richmond* to smithereens. That would have been a terrible disaster, all those highly trained men killed.

•◄►• *The U-boat and the Cat*

My uncle told me this one. About '43 the old bugger was second mate on an old tub. I think they formed in Norfolk or Boston, went up to Halifax, picked up more off St. John's, and away they went, off to the Old Country. Thirty ships maybe. Anyway, a typical wartime convoy.

About four days out, the steering broke down and a navy corvette came tooling over and it was my uncle's watch, I guess, and he signalled something like, "Not to worry, chaps. You go on and we'll follow." That was his kind of humour, actually, because no convoy is going to hang back for one old rustbucket. Leave the bloody thing behind, let it catch up if it can, and good luck. That sort of thing, you understand.

So there they are, and the convoy plodding at its usual 8 knots out of sight, and like "The Rime of the Ancient Mariner," "alone, alone, all all alone on a wide wide ocean." Something like that. Anyway, they get to work and in about 10 or 12 or 14 hours they get the trouble fixed. A bearing, something like that, and they're all set to go chasing after this convoy which is about 100 miles away when rearing up, abeam, is this U-boat.

The hatch opens and ratings come spilling out and break out the deck gun, and you don't have to be an old salt to know that there you are, and 100 yards away from you is a German. So this uncle says, "We're looking down the ruddy barrel of about a four-incher and if we send a signal then we're all dead, right then and there." I should say at this point that some of the R.N.'s light cruisers had six-inchers, so you can see, a big U-boat was a formidable adversary on the surface.

So my uncle and the skipper just stand on the bridge and an astonishing thing happens. A rubber boat comes floating across, so it is obvious they're going to scuttle us. Probably returning from a long patrol, find a tub a sitting duck, so why waste a torpedo. Why waste half a dozen shells. But the sublieutenant comes over the side with some German marines, and by this time my uncle and the rest are goggle-eyed because on the deck of the sub is a man who is obviously the captain. Well, he's in skipper's rig, and he's got a big white cat in his arms. Even at 100 yards you can see it's a big white cat.

The officer is very polite, and what he wants is milk for his cat. Oh yes, very politely he said condensed milk would do. You see, it is the skipper's cat and it must have milk.

The cook rustles up several cans of Carnation and they're put into a bag and dropped into the rubber raft and the officer salutes and hops over and away they go. That's fine, and the captain gives the order to stand to lifeboat stations. I guess he figures they're going to get it—and there *is* one shell. It goes over screaming a foot from the bridge, right over their heads. And then there's whistling on the sub, everybody disappears down the conning tower and in a minute you could never tell if there had been a sub there. Either they'd spared the ship, or that was their last shell, or they'd got a signal from somewhere to get the lead out. Well, that's all that story is about.

Except, they catch up to the convoy, because where the convoy had to zig and zag all the way, they just made a beeline on the nearest course for Ireland, and in about two days they're back in formation, all tickety-boo. Shipshape, Bristol fashion, all hands happy they're alive. That's a great feeling, you know. A great feeling.

Far from Home

Men in war are not angels. They never have been and never will be, especially when thousands of miles separate them from home. In short, it is man's nature to seek feminine companionship, where he can, when he can, and by whatever means he can. It is just a fact of life.

Things done in wartime by men and women should not be marked down in a big book for posterity. Wartime is when no rules apply.

•◄►• *So Easy to Fall in Love*

It was London in 1944, the spring of that year, I remember most. We were going to open a Second Front. Everyone knew that and that a lot of men were going to die.

There was still the blackout, of course, and you'd meet a girl, a civilian or a girl in uniform—and they were around in the thousands—and you'd take her from the club or pub you'd been in and just walk around in the warm London night and everywhere you went, through blocks of rubble or slums in the Strand, there seemed to be the smell of flowers.

There was the feeling that these were the last nights men and women would love, and there never was any of the by-play or persuading that usually went on. People were for love, so to speak. It was so easy to fall in love. I guess it was always like that; when men go off to die their women are beside them until the end.

I won't describe the scenes or the sounds of Hyde Park or Green Park at dusk and after dark. They just can't be described. You can just imagine, a vast battlefield of sex. I had a hotel because I was billetted out from headquarters, so whoever I was with, we had a safe refuge and usually a bottle of wine.

My God, but it was easy to fall in love in those two months before D-day. So easy, and London after dark is the perfect city for lovers. I'll always remember dear old London town that way.

•◄►• *From Mount Royal High to This*

I went overseas as a sergeant air gunner but I was still a kid of twenty from Calgary and what I knew about the world you could put in your hip pocket. I'm not kidding. Green as grass.

At this station I met this girl, an English girl who worked as a sort of welcoming hostess in this rest house for troops near the rail station. Darts, cards, tea and cookies. No booze. That kind of thing. She and I hit it off like that. You know, bang! Uncanny. Or crazy, maybe. Elaine was twenty-three. You could say she picked me up because I wouldn't know how.

In about two weeks she said we should go away together for a few days as we both had a bit of leave. I was scared, and why not? From Mount Royal High to this. We went down to London in a truck going that way and got on a train going to Kent, near Canterbury, and into a big inn that had been some sort of mansion. You know, a hall as big as a hangar, and bedrooms 20 by 20.

The first night went pretty darn good, even though it was my first time at it. A lot of giggling and that sort of thing, but we had a load of fun. Next morning there's this knock at the door and the door opens and in comes this little maid in a yellow and white uniform, as cute as a bug's ear, and she puts down this tray and on it are a couple of small cookies, like digestive cookies, and a big pot of hot tea, and she says, "Breakfast is at eight o'clock, sir," and goes out and all I can do is fall back on the bed and yell, "Wow! What a country!"

•◄►• *The Girl I Was Going to Marry*

Donald was my sister's second boy and I guess you'd have to call him the all-Canadian boy or something like that. Good at studies, very good at studies and in his sports and popular with the boys and later the girls, like when he was in high school. You'd call him very popular and very handsome and very much assured and again, every inch the leader. Soccer and basketball captain and debating captain. I'm sure you've known boys like that, the kind people would say of to my sister, "You'll never have to worry about

Don. He'll go places. There's only one way to go for him and that's up." I'm sure you've heard people say that.

His girlfriend was the same. It's not chance that brings a boy like Don and a girl like Shirley together. There are forces moving which make it inevitable. Both tall, good-looking, except Shirley was downright beautiful. Blonde and slim and a smile. Both school leaders and both tops in their classes and they were the kind that when parties were formed—skating parties or hiking, swimming, going down to the cottage for a weekend—they were formed around Don and Shirley. It wouldn't have been a party if they weren't there. I've seen it often because I lived with my sister. I'm widowed so I saw Don in every light. Just a beautiful young man.

They were sweethearts through high school and she took home economics at varsity and Don began the liberal arts course. I know because I financed him the first year because my sister and her husband, well, things weren't going too well for them. He had had a couple of setbacks.

This was in 1943 and the pressure was on Don, mostly by his former schoolmates. They were coming up to military age and the others thought they should all join up together. I guess they were thinking of a Three Musketeers kind of thing. Anyway, Don joined the air force and he trained as a navigator in western Canada at several places, I believe, and then he went overseas, leaving Shirley behind. She got a job in an office, did Red Cross work like the rest of us and just waited for the end of the war, for her man to come home and to marry and then their life would begin.

It didn't work out that way. You're going to ask if he was killed. Not a scratch that I know of, but around a month or two from the end of the war in Europe Shirley came over one Sunday and I could see something was worrying her. She wasn't a girl to worry so I knew when something was. After dodging around the bushes for a bit she blurted out that Don wasn't writing as much as he had. I knew it used to be every day and she did the same, and here she was sitting on the verandah with me saying it was a week, two weeks, between letters now. The poor girl said his letters were different, but after all she was hardly twenty yet, and how could she know about these things. I told her not to worry, but believe me, I was worried. My sister and her husband had great things planned for Don, and Shirley was part and parcel of it all, and it was the same on the other side.

I told her not to worry and that everybody was under a strain, but as soon as she left I got on that little typewriter of mine and I filled up one of those V-Mail letters, and down to the post office I trotted. I told Don—and I think I could talk to him this way where his parents couldn't—I told him to tell me pronto what was up. Just like that.

I honestly think that was what he needed. Not Shirley's letters full of everyday events of our little city and the I Love You's and the S.W.A.K. [sealed with a kiss] on the flap of the letter, or his mother's solicitations to be a good boy and always wear dry socks. He wanted it from the horse's mouth and that was me, Auntie Joan. I think that very night he sat down and he wrote three Victory letters to us—one to Shirley, one to his parents and one to me. Mine was short and thanked me. I never saw Shirley's, and the one to his parents said he had met a girl. He said she worked in the orderly office or somewhere on the air station he was on. He said he loved her and he was going to marry her and bring her home with him. That was it. He said she was Scottish, came from a good family and he'd visited them in Kilmarnock, that her name was Margaret and he was sorry, terribly sorry, but that is how it was and how it had to be—and he knew there was nothing he could do to make the hurt to his parents and Shirley any less, but he would do what he could.

I remember one thing. He said he'd move with Margaret to another city if it was too difficult for them to accept her. He didn't mean if they drove him away and her away, but just if it was too much of a strain, having Margaret around, when everybody had put so much faith in him and his marriage to Shirley. The marriage that never was, I mean. It was very touching.

Donald came home before the summer was out and started back to school, the University of Toronto, because he was still going to be a lawyer. Margaret came in October and she was a cute little thing, just about up to his shoulder, shy at first but wanting to be friends, and she had this delightful little burr of a Scots accent. We took to one another right off the bat, and finally Donald's father did too, although it took my sister much longer. But because they were living in Toronto we didn't see them all that much. Some weekends, holidays, Christmas.

About two years later Don was driving me up to Toronto one Sunday night. I had a doctor's appointment and Margaret was in the back with the baby, their first, a little girl; they both had fallen asleep and as we were humming along, Don suddenly said, "If it has bothered the family, I want to say this, and you can tell them whatever way you want if you think you should, because I haven't got around to saying it. That's the funny thing, nothing has ever been said. When I went overseas I loved Shirley. I loved her with all my heart, every part of me loved her. But then, after a while her face began to fade. She'd send a picture of herself and you folks at the lake and it wouldn't be her. I'd have to say to myself that she was my girl. Shirley was the girl I was going to marry."

He was quiet for a while and I wished to heaven I had one of those things [my tape recorder] and then he said, "We were flying a lot. It wasn't particularly dangerous, but bad enough. A few fellows never made it back, but it was mostly tiring. Exhausting. Day after day. I met this girl. I was going to Scotland on the first leave I'd had in months, I guess, and there we were all jammed into one of those English railway compartments, and I got talking with this girl. She'd come from the same station and yet I'd never laid eyes on her before.

"I liked her, she was cute, fun, liked lots of funny things I liked, and we stayed together that leave, about five days. Yes, I mean as man and wife, but that didn't mean anything in England then. Not then. Everybody was with everybody else.

"That's how it started. We came back to the station and I told her I'd meet her at the women's quarters' gate the next night if we were wiped out by weather and we were and, of course, she knew it, so next night she was there at eight o'clock and we walked into the village. Oh, half a mile, and we talked but it was just about nothing—little things.

"We got into the pub and I told her to take a corner table and I went to the bar, got my bitters and her gin and water, ugh! and when I got to the table I saw her in the light, the first time since I'd left her and there she was and her face was upturned and she had a little smile, and it hit me just as if I'd been hit by a professional boxer. I knew I was in love with this girl. Not a little bit in love, not infatuated but a great big lot of being in love. And that was it. Right there. That was it right there and you'd better believe it."

And then a little voice came up from the back of the car and it startled me and I knew it startled Don for he gave a little jump, and Margaret said, "And I loved you, I'm sure, when I first saw you squeezing into that compartment on the train. That was when I knew."

That's what I mean, about the fates of war. Don't you see? Donald needed someone, and if Shirley had been there just then, in that one week, then Donald and Shirley would have been married and everybody would have been happy and they'd have lived a long and happy life. But it didn't work that way. Shirley was across the ocean in North America and Margaret was there when Donald needed someone. And that's about all there was to it. A little story about wartime and people needing each other.

•◆►• *"Hi, Canuck, Looking for a Date?"*

I came right off the farm at Weyburn and into uniform and they kept us so busy, there wasn't much time for leaves or that, and then to England, and I remember my father telling me I had to see Trafalgar Square and Piccadilly Circus. He'd seen them once on a trip way before the war when he helped take a boatload of cattle to England.

Well, I come up on the train and I walk over from Victoria Station and I'm seeing all the sights I'd read about, and then there's Trafalgar Square and it's like the pictures and then I go on to Piccadilly and it's kind of disappointing. Nothing to see, really. And then I notice the girls. This is about three or so in the afternoon. Like the poet said, big ones, short ones, fat ones, tall ones. Every kind, and as you kept walking they got thicker. Some were real honeys, too, and they were saying things like, "Hi, Canuck, looking for a date?" and "I'll give you a good time." Others would just say, "A pound for a bound," or, "I've got a girlfriend too," and things like that. Hell, I couldn't take it all in, and there was one street you walked up out of the Piccadilly—I remember it was called Shaftsbury, because I got to know it better after, and you had to walk in the gutter or in the street because of the girls. Young ones and old ones, good-looking ones and some dreary old bags. There were hundreds and hundreds of them, and you had any pick you wanted. I'm not kidding.

By this time, of course, I'd figured it out, that even a farm boy from Sask-atch-e-wan could have his pick for a pound. It gave me a hell of a feeling, and that is no lie. A hell of a feeling. It still does, I guess. Maybe there's still too much Saskatchewan in me still.

By the time the Americans came in full force, yelling their damn-fool heads off, there were more than ever before and the price had gone up to 5 pounds if you went to a room with them. That was 20 bucks, about, and only the Yanks could skin it. If you did it standing up, in a doorway or against a wall, that was 2 quid. Like I say, the Americans ruined it all to hell.

I remember London in the war because of the whores. Thousands of them. All lovey-dovey and duckie-wuckie and darling before—and once it was over, they'd just walk away as if you didn't exist. They made an awful lot of money—just for doing what comes naturally, as the song says.

•◄►• *A Second Family*

There was this one guy, real quiet, he never said anything, always nice and pleasant and would lend you a pound. That sort of thing.

You know what? That guy, this guy from Toronto, he met this woman who'd been married to this lieutenant colonel just for a few days and then the silly bugger goes off to Africa and promptly gets himself killed, so she's got all his dough, you see. It's old money, going back to William the Conqueror or something, and there is this house in Bucks and the lodge in Scotland and the place here and there and the London house. St. John's Wood. Veddy veddy. So he moves in with her, playing house, and then she has a kid and it's his, of course, and then there's another bun in the oven and it's his again and he's happy as a clam—and the guy already has a wife and family back in Toronto, or near there.

What a life he's got, and when he gets transferred to headquarters in London, well, that's the jackpot right there. Mind you, he doesn't tell anybody about all this. I just happen to find out. But I'm sure keeping an eye on the situation because the war has got to be over in a few months, and what's going to happen? See what I mean?

Well, nothing happens. The war ends, he goes back to Toronto, she goes her own way with two kiddies. Of course she's loaded, so money is no trouble, and I guess they part friendly. A smile and goodbye, dear, and take care, won't you. That sort of thing. He goes back to his first family, and as far as I know that was the end of it. That's a war story in itself, wouldn't you say? The quiet ones. Not the loudmouths but the quiet ones, they're the ones you watch.

•◄►• *The Admiral's Wife*

We were out of Dorking, on the road to Leatherhead and we had our outfit set up there on a huge estate. And lo and behold, in one day comes a car flying the goddamned staff flag and it's a major general of a certain Canadian division whose name shall not be mentioned, and what has he got? Well, what do you think? He's got a lovely dose of clap.

And we tried to pry it out of him, where had he got it. Those were regulations. Anybody reported in with a dose, we had to find out who the woman was. They had to use the Army Act against him to get the information, and he finally said he had got it from a bloody admiral's wife.

•━▸• *She Was Sure I'd Like Him*

I was training at Barrie and she came up with a busload of kids from Toronto. A dance. That's the way it started, and I saw her about eight times, like eight weekends before I was shipped overseas. Up to Peterborough, a little town outside it, to meet her parents. Farmers. She came down to Stratford to meet my family. That sort of thing. Quite typical, I guess. We fell in love, got engaged, and so on. Pretty typical wartime, I'd say. Not hot and heavy stuff, though. It just didn't seem right to us, and you've got to remember we were pretty young—like I was twenty and she was nineteen.

So in England and in Italy I lived for her letters, and if a ship went down with some on, you accepted that as part of the whole deal. Same with her. Sometimes I'd get four or five or six at once. She wrote every day and she'd always mark them—301, 302, 303—so you'd open the right one first. Those letters meant everything. Home, Ontario, fishing, tobogganing, baseball, and the school bus and my first job and friends and the street I lived on, but mostly it meant her. Our future—and yet I never did find out from the letters what she looked for in the future. Did she want to live in a small town or on a farm near my home town or in the city, and what did she want me to be? A ditch digger or a doctor?

Anyway, her letters were a link with sanity. It meant so much to all of us because there we were, so far from home. In Italy, winter of '44, it was just rain and snow and mud. Misery. I've seen guys get a letter from their girl and go right into the can and masturbate—you could tell by the looks on their faces when they came out—and they would then lie down on their bunk or wherever and open that letter and read it, and if you watched that guy, he'd read that letter five times, ten times, even twenty. Sure, twenty. Yes, I've seen a guy read a letter five times a day until the next mail came in, maybe five days later.

But she's in Toronto—and by the way her name was Gloria, a pretty name—and having fun, everybody seems to be having one long party, and she tells about trips up to the camps to entertain the soldiers, and how pretty Canada is, and here I'm stuck in a valley in Italy looking up at mountains where the Germans are and they're not coming down to get us and we're sure as hell not going to try to move against them until spring, whenever that is. You get the picture?

I guess I should have known it was coming. After all, eight weekends together and no marriage and damn little sex, if you want to call it that, and she's there and I'm here, so to speak, and two people who really didn't know each other too well—well, I should have figured it out. My mother dropped a hint or two in her letters but I didn't think of them. She was still my Gloria. My postwar future. My gal.

The letters from her got shorter, and I guess mine did, and then I got one and I felt funny about it as I walked back to our dugout. I don't know why. Just that feeling. A hunch soldiers get.

Yep, it was a Dear John. I think that was an American expression. I don't think we used it much, at all, but the gist is that the girl has met another guy back in Canada and she loves him but she'll always love you too—but she can't even remember what your face looks like even when she's looking at your picture, and she can't remember you at all. And so although she cried for six days and six nights she's going to marry the other fellow and she hopes you will wish them luck. Oh yeah, the guy is usually a major in the medical corps or owns a large factory which is vital to the war effort and has a high exemption, and that's why he isn't in uniform. That's just sort of a summary, not what mine said.

Mine said she was ashamed but she hadn't been completely honest with me and should have told me months ago, but there was this guy, some bozo she'd met at a dance at Orillia, and he was a sergeant and she loved him and was going to marry him. First, what the hell is a training sergeant doing at a dance for recruits at a basic training camp and why did she write all those letters over the past months? I was a big boy and I could take it. I'd at least have gone out and got me a popolana and screwed the ass off her long before this. A popolana? Oh, that's one of those girls brought up in the slums of Rome, they're usually only part whore and the rest just grubby, grasping kids about sixteen or so. A lot of the guys liked them. Cheap and eager as hell. Anyway . . . .

The thing that blew my stack, and isn't this a goddamned woman for you, she said that when I came back, which might be never, but she hoped I would meet her sergeant and that I'd like him. In fact, she said she was sure I'd like him. What a load of bullshit!

I was stunned. I mean it. Really taken out. I knew it had happened, but in a letter? No chance to argue. Christ! But then, who wants to argue? The thing is done. I felt like nothing, just washed out, a million miles from my home in a country covered with snow. Just one hell of a long way from home.

I did four things. No, five. First, I re-read the letter to make sure I wasn't dreaming, and then I tore it up. That was number one. Then I tore up all her pictures and took all her letters and made a bonfire outside with them and the goddamned wind blew half of them right up to Foggia. Then I got mad and I swore I'd never write her another letter, not even a have-a-good-time one. Then I got madder and I punched one of those little stunted oak trees that cover half the hills of that part of Italy and sprained my hand. That was number four. Then I went into town and into a blind pig and got drunk and that's number five. There was another. After I got drunk I went down to a house off the town square and I got a girl and I got laid.

Then I went back to the site next morning and the sun was shining and the snow was melting and I felt a hell of a lot better. I knew there wasn't much more of the war to go and I'd make it, and I felt better for that and I felt better at being free again. You see, maybe I was up tight about it all too, going back to marry a girl I didn't really even know. I can't say that for sure, but it sort of looks that way.

If she walked through that door now I could get up and walk over and say, "Hi, Gloria, long time no see," or something like that and ask her over for a drink and if her husband was with her, I'd ask him over too.

What the hell, it was 25 years ago. No, closer to 30. It happened a thousand times, ten thousand times.

•➤• *She Was Two Years Old*

When the ship got into Halifax they took the Truro boys up by bus and dropped them off along the way at crossroads and towns and the like, and at Truro my wife was waiting with my mother and some others, and there was this reunion.

My leg was still tender from the shrapnel cuts and my wife took me to a hotel. She was not letting me go back into that nuthouse my mother ran, all those kids, and in our room at the hotel she just told me plain as she could. She said she'd had a baby, a girl, and she was two years old now and the father was a pilot, an air force boy she'd met at a dance and he was gone and she'd never seen him since, she said, and the baby was darling but if I wanted to walk out there, we'd just say goodbye, and that she still loved me.

We didn't do much talking. We went to bed, and next morning went to my mother's place and I saw the little girl and she was a darling and I hugged her and my mother, there she was crying and smoke was coming up from her big apron because she was up against the old cook stove, and then everyone was laughing and crying and hugging and we had a big party, for the cousins and the neighbours and some of the boys who'd come back. That was all.

I'm sitting in the Legion about five years later and this fellow in the Highlanders with me, but he's from quite far away, by New Waterford, he's pretty drunk and he starts crying and I said, you big ninny, what the hell's got your wind up? He tells me, and it's my story all over again. All over again, and he'd walked out on his wife. You know, when he came back.

I said when you were in Scotland, all the time you were in the old country, how many women did you screw? You yourself. Just you, man. What about those old whores in Piccadilly who'd do it for 15 shillings, eh? And overseas? How many of those foreign girls? I bet you even fucked a few frauleins too, I'll bet.

The poor sock said he had, he'd had a go at many a girl, and I said then he had not much right to sit there blubbering, and his poor wife trying to bring up a wee one. Be a man, I said.

I got a letter about a month later and it was from him. He'd quit the boat, gone right down and cleaned out his locker. He'd gone home and he was with his wife and the wee girl was starting school and everything was hunky-dory, he said. He said thanks.

Laughing All the Way to the Bank

*A Good War for the Businessman ... Housing in Ottawa
... Spare Parts ... This '34 Pontiac ... Treated Like
Slaves ... A Lesson in Free Enterprise ... Names Off
Gravestones ... Rustling*

---

*Little has been written about the profiteering that went on in
Canada during the war. A few convictions of blatant offenders are
documented in the old files of the Wartime Prices and Trade
Board, but they give only a hint of how well some people did out
of the war and the unusual conditions that went with it.*

*Of course, there seems to be an unwritten law that if you
impose restrictions on people, they consider it their God-given
right to side-step them, skirt around them, dodge them or find
loopholes. So evading the rationing quotas or hoarding shortages
was just part of the game. Most people did it, in one form or
another. Beating the authorities was very much a game, and it was
usually small stuff.*

*But others—the contractor on a "cost-plus" arrangement
to build an army camp, or the landlord who divided a dark basement into six cubicles at 30 dollars each, or the factory owner
who paid his workers less than the minimum wage—they did very
well indeed out of the war.*

•◄►• *A Good War for the Businessman*

For a businessman the war years were a good thing. If you had
money, you could buy cheaply. If you had a shop, a factory, a
farm, an orchard, you could make money.

God, but there was a lot of money to be made, and it was
made. In large quantities, and that was just during the war. After,
the same story. The same damned story. Who had the money?
Who had been socking it away and when the new goods came on
the market, the stoves and the new Chevs and the stuff starting to
come in from other countries, who had the money? The businessman.

What about the guy who owns a factory, say clothing, and
he's got 500 workers working for him? The farmer with 1,500
acres in crop? Well, you can name anybody you want. The Depression, it kicked a lot of guys ahead, got them running, and when

the war came along, they were running full out and they never stopped running. They're probably in the marble orchard now but I'll bet you that their sons and sons-in-law are still running, laughing their heads off all the way to the bank.

•◄►• *Housing in Ottawa*

We literally had to scrounge for accommodation and I can tell you that our home in Winnipeg was far better than 90 percent of the houses we ever saw in Ottawa, and yet we had to scrounge. In basements. A basement would be cut up into four suites you could only charitably call cubicles, with one toilet, one washtub, for four families or four couples. The tops of old wrecks of houses would be divided in two and that would bring in 120 dollars a month, 60 dollars each side, which was a lot of money in those days.

No pets. No parties after 11 P.M. No replacing 40-watt bulbs with 100-watt bulbs. No children in some places. No laws protecting the renter. Rent ceilings, all right, but if the tenant didn't pay what was asked, regardless of the ceiling, he just didn't stand a look-in. And other things, on and on. No heat until mid-November and after late April. Half a mile to the streetcar, maybe. And there was never any doubt in some of those landladies' minds that the woman of every couple was a slut just waiting for her husband to go overseas and the husband some kind of a whoremaster.

Oh, it was all very lovely. I don't think we just had plain bad luck in a succession of houses we lived in. I think there's the usual attitude: We are our own tight little island. We don't want outsiders. But they are helping in some way to win the war, so we must put up with them. So while we're here, let's skin them of every single dollar they make. That was one attitude for you, and not a very nice one.

•◄►• *Spare Parts*

I had this garage and two pumps in East Toronto and this was early in the war, 1940, and I had a cousin who was on vacation from the University of Toronto. I gave this truck to him and all the money I could scrape up, and I sent him around that summer, all through the little towns around. He was to buy auto parts, anything he could buy reasonable, things like carburetors, springs, wheels with tires on them, steering wheels and transmissions, head-lights, just about anything that would come off without a cutting torch.

I was gambling that soon production of cars would stop across the border. I couldn't see how the Americans could stay out of the war.

That kid came back in about a week when the money had run out. He had most of the truck filled, and by God it looked like the back room of an auto supply house. There was everything. I'd told him to visit small garages wherever he came to them, and see what he could buy, make up any old excuse why he needed so many parts. But he was smarter than me and he headed down the concession lines, down the back roads. Every time he came to a farm he'd stop, and this way he was getting all he wanted and at a price probably a third of what some garage guy would want. He said it was like taking candy away from a baby. The sight of that cash just made the farmers forget everything.

Naturally I had to rummage around for more money, and my wife's uncle lent me a bundle, and I think by the end of summer I was in hock about $4,000 to him but I had a warehouse full of good parts, everything. The university kid asked for a helper and I got a high school kid who worked my pumps to go with him and they really cleaned up, and they were taking old tractors apart, too, by this time.

Then the Americans went into the war and stopped making cars and they put a wartime price ceiling on cars, and cars and trucks started breaking down and farmers were selling the junk in their yards for scrap for the war effort, and the supply of auto parts just dwindled away. That left me sitting pretty. There I was, and the word got around and over the next three years or so, just about into '45, the word was that I could supply almost any part.

They came to me as far away as Parry Sound, down way the other side of Hamilton, up north—you talk about your war profiteers, the ones who made uniforms for the troops in the factories or got a contract for radio parts or bomb fuses and all that—they made millions, but I can't say I did too bad. All those years I had a big smile on my face. No, I won't tell you what I made, but it was plenty. You buy a part for 2 bucks in 1940 and by '44, some salesman on the road is glad to pay me 20 bucks for it. Just shoving the money at me.

Quite a deal, let me tell you. Free enterprise. I'd got the right idea first and followed through on it and then when the time came to cash in, why, I just let 'er rip.

•◄►• *This '34 Pontiac*

My cousin had this '34 Pontiac and there was this Wartime Prices Board and they set a top price on that. On everything. Sell higher and you were breaking the law. This cousin was going overseas and so he agrees that I can have his car. The price was 350 dollars, that's all he wanted. A real honest guy, and the car was in good shape, had good rubber and, fellow, that was the most important thing of all. You could fix an engine but you couldn't make a new tire.

A year later, in June of 1944, I got my call-up. I'm playing softball on the school grounds one Saturday, a few days later, and I tell a guy I know named Dougie that I got my call-up and he asks what I'm doing with my car. I says I'll sell it. How much? Without thinking I say, "Six hundred and fifty bucks." He gets up and goes across the street to his house and comes back in ten minutes and says he's got a buyer. In another ten minutes a guy, the friend of this Dougie, comes around and we take the car out and spin it around the block a few times and he says okay, you got a deal. Six hundred and fifty bucks. He gives me six 100-dollar bills and the rest in 10's and we go down to the garage on Jasper Avenue and pick up one of those forms, and he fills in 325 bucks as the buying price, and I sign my name and that's it.

Six hundred and fifty bucks for a car I buy for 350, and I'll bet you $10 that when that Pontiac was bought in '34 or '35, I forget which, it didn't cost more than $500.

I never thought I'd see it, but I did. A crazy time, lots of money and nowhere to spend it—and everybody laughing his head off at all the government regulations.

•◄►• *Treated Like Slaves*

I worked in this factory near Montreal, making parts for radios. We'd make some parts and then they were shipped to Toronto, and with other parts the radios for the bombers and fighter planes were put together.

There were two shifts, graveyard and day, and there were no lunch breaks and no smoking periods and no time allowed to go to the washroom and you know yourself, a woman, a girl, has to go to the washroom at least once an eight-hour shift. When you ate, you ate at your bench. You went to the washroom just before you went on shift and then prayed. I got so I wouldn't drink any water or tea for a few hours before I went on shift, and that worked okay on graveyard, but it was no fun, I can tell you, on the day shift.

So a girl named Margaret Clare and another named Yvette Langois, and me, I was the self-appointed chairman, you might say, we complained. But not to the foreman or the boss. The foreman was French-Irish, and can you think of a worse combination, and the boss, the owner, of course, was one of those little Montreal Jews living up in Outremont. On our day off we went downtown to the government board, the war resources board or whatever it was called, and we complained. We had a list of grievances this long, as long as my arm.

Well, things started to pop. Within a week we had inspectors coming out of the woodwork. Poking here and there, asking questions, and the boss, walking around and saying, "Goyls, one of you has done me a dirty trick. Look how I treat you and this is what I get," and I'd think, Christ almighty, he's answered his own question. He treats us like slaves and so he's going to get it himself.

There was a report. My name was on it, so was Margaret's. Yvette had quit by this time. So we were fired. Not bang, but the first mistake, so long, goyls, if you was men, you'd be Judas.

We didn't care, we just walked across the street and got better jobs.

But that report showed 132 infractions. Yep, 132. Everything from no lunch breaks to extremely dangerous fire hazards, like fire doors sealed up. That kind of thing. And you know what happened? Well, you know, this was wartime. *Nothing* happened. The girls could now go to the can, once an eight-hour shift. But only once, and for five minutes. Okay, five minutes can be enough. But nothing else was ever done. The government might have pounded its fist on old Levi's desk and said such and such must be done, but he'd say, and one of the girls says this is what he said, "Okay, if this and this and this and this must be done, two things, you want me to go out of business, okay, I'll go out of business, or you want your components. I go out of business, no radios for bombers." So that was it, in a nutshell. Nothing happened. He had the government right where he wanted them.

Things like that happened all the time. And if you complained, even asking for time to go to the toilet, somebody would say, "For God's sakes, woman, there's a war on, don't ya know."

•◄►• *A Lesson in Free Enterprise*

My brother and me had a freight run southeast of Edmonton, the little towns. It being wartime we could've made a good go of it if we'd had the gas, but there was railroads, too, and the government said the C.N. could do the job we were doing, and so that was that. They wouldn't give us enough gas ration books to make a living.

We had a big Mercury with bald tires and a small pickup, and she carried quite a load, and we practically had to sell our souls but we got some tires for the Merc. But we didn't have no gas coupons.

The way I tell it—and my brother tells it a little different because he says it was him but he was too drunk to know—we got into this poker game in the Yale Hotel, blackjack, and there was a couple of faces I didn't know, you see, but I got to talking about having a business but nowheres to go because of the gas rationing, and I let it go at that. I wasn't sobbing or anything, just that they'd put the kibosh on me.

The game broke up about 3 A.M. and one of these guys I didn't know asked me in the hall where I was living and I said upstairs in the hotel, and he wanted the room number. I thought he might want to sleep on the floor and, what the hell, hotel rooms were hard to get and he looked like a decent fellow, so I told him.

Upshot of the matter was, oh, about half an hour later there's a knock, and I let this fellow in, and his friend with him, and they've got a suitcase. He puts it on the bed and opens it and there it is, full, crammed to the top with gasoline ration books! I guess you could say my eyes bugged out, and my brother who was drunk let out a warwhoop like he'd found the lost goldmine.

They *were* gold, as good as gold, and as I live and breathe here right now, I couldn't tell if they were forged or not. Counterfeited, I mean. The fellow said they'd just come in from Quebec where you could buy ration books for gas, sugar, meat, anything you wanted, and cigarettes too.

Upshot was, I made a deal, and it was that I'd give those two fellows a quarter of my gross take, every week, every month, and they'd give me the books I wanted, and the harder I worked, the more everybody made. It was sure a lesson in free enterprise, I can tell you that. These two guys came through every three months on what they called a circuit, Winnipeg, Saskatoon, the home town, then down to Calgary, back to Regina. And all by train. They didn't trust being on the roads with that stuff. I played it fair and square with them all down the line and it worked out fine. They knew I was on the level and we got to be quite good friends.

•◄►• *Names Off Gravestones*

When everybody had to sign up for the national security cards my uncle went out to the cemeteries at Riley and Tofield and he got about ten names off gravestones, with the birth dates. He used these to get the cards which were good for rationing. He took the names so that the person would never be called up. A man born in 1900 wouldn't be called up because then he'd be forty-one or forty-two and too old for military service. This way he was safe and he put down their occupations as farmhand and a General Delivery box address, and this went on for about three years because the postmaster was in cahoots with him. When any letters came for these guys, he'd put them aside and he'd make out the phony ration books too. Things like that. Half the town knew it.

You could only have done it once. That was when the government was doing millions of these cards. When they started doing them one by one, so to speak, then you could get tripped up.

My uncle did get tripped up when the postmaster dropped dead from his heart and the guy from the next town was sent over to handle the wicket two days a week for a month. Then it was too late. He wouldn't take a bribe, and he reported my uncle to the cops. I think my uncle's first mistake was offering the guy a bribe. He should have offered him a third or half of his coupons.

I think he got six months.

•◄►• *Rustling*

Hell, there always was meat. The goddamned army at Currie Barracks threw out enough every day to feed half the town, anyway. That's the main reason there wasn't enough. All over, I mean.

I had a garage and my customers would come in and they'd be bitching about not having enough gas, wanting to go antelope hunting or fishing or something, and then they'd start in on no tires. All rationed, you see. One guy used to do more bitching than anyone and I said, "Okay, Art, if you're ready to pay for meat you'll get it. Just be ready, cash on the barrelhead." He said, "Somebody's old grey mare?" I said, "Somebody's nice fat steer."

I just said my cousin has a small ranch over by Black Diamond and if he kept quiet, my cousin was in the beef business without ration points and that stuff. Don't tell anybody. I made that clear.

Getting Jeff to work with me was tricky because he'd done

time in Lethbridge [the provincial jail] but he had this '36 pickup, a Ford, and he did come from near Black Diamond and the ranchers over that way were starting to build up again, bunches of 25, 50, maybe 100 cattle. I drove over there one Sunday and he said he'd kind of been thinking along the same lines and we'd try it. He knew a place. We'd need the right kind of night, dark as a hundred feet down a well and with a wind blowing. That way we'd be able to see the cattle a bit but people going by on the road couldn't see us, and the wind would fling the sound of the shot away.

The first time, we bunched about 20 good steers into a corner of the fence and I dropped two with the .22, long rifle shells, and we had this boards-and-pulley arrangement and we skidded the damn things up into the truck. It was no end of trouble, and Jeff said we'd have to find an easier way.

I had high boards on the trucks so we just looked like a farm truck, and we didn't bleed them, though we should've, and we drove right into town and butchered them just like you do a deer. Right in the back of my garage. The blood went down the drain, and the rest we put in canvas sacks and buried next night in a gravel pit out near Bowness.

Selling it was no trouble, but it was trouble enough. We did it for about a month. Guess we rustled maybe 20 steers in that time and I had about 15 or 20 customers for the stuff, my regular garage customers. That was okay. We charged a little less than store prices, they had to pick it up, and nobody was the wiser. Jeff and me we split, of course.

Then one day this fellow drives in and he hangs around talking and then he says he's Mr. So-and-so from over on the North Hill and I say, yeah, sure, and he goes on and on and finally he comes out and says, "Hear you got meat for sale." Not a question, like, he just says it. I make a big fuss about it, saying he's got the wrong person, that he wants a butcher store. He says no, a friend tells him I'm selling good range beef. Well, shit.

Here's a guy from the North Hill, from across town, he says, and he could be a Mountie, a guy from the Agriculture Department or just what he says he was, a friend of one of my customers, but that's getting too close. I never stole another beef. Not one, not even for our own family. That learned me my lesson.

Then I read in the paper that two brothers from High River, south of there, they get caught and it's the prison farm for them. And I figure, that guy snooping around was a Mountie and I was next on the list, only I wasn't. Close call, mister, too close for comfort.

Dead and Wounded

The Pain Came Later . . . "Would Someone Come Here, Please?" . . . The Lord Taketh Away . . . Getting a Blighty . . . In Order of Rank . . . "You, You Get the Shovels . . . Dead Men—What the Hell . . . His Leg Would Be Okay . . . Just One Crack . . . At Dockside, Halifax

---

A man who had been a tank officer told me that when he was wounded it felt as if someone had pressed a burning cigarette against his shoulder. He thought that strange, out there on the battlefield, and he looked and saw his jacket growing red with blood. He was a bit disappointed, he said. He'd thought that being hit would be something big, something dramatic. The pain, the agony, came later.

But the men I talked to didn't want to talk about their wounds, and I understand why. Usually all they would say was, "Oh, I got a scratch," or, "I was in the way of a chunk that flew by."

The section of this chapter that deals with death and the disposal of dead bodies may offend some readers. I hope it will, because it certainly offends me. But that, finally, is what war is all about, and we are wrong to ignore it.

•◄►• The Pain Came Later

You could get hit and not know it, not until things quieted down and somebody would say, "Hey, mate, you're bleeding," and you'd look, and that would usually be a flesh wound. That was nothing, really, just a nick.

In Italy I got hit just walking through a vineyard coming up with the platoon's mail one morning. The Germans had moved up one of their Moaning Minnies during the night and it was a gun with six revolving barrels and it could throw an awful lot of stuff around. I got a bit of the first salvo or blast or whatever you want to call it. It was in the shoulder and it felt like somebody had hit me a hell of a crack on the side. Not that it actually hurt in any one place, but just one hard slug on the side and I was down. I can't remember pain. Not then. That came later.

But there I am lying in the dirt and the mail pouch is away over there and my jacket is ripped half off me, and I said to myself, "Hell, is this what it's like?" I mean, there's none of this war movie crap of a guy sort of reeling around and gasping and reaching out and then taking a long time to fall. No, just *whap* and you're down. My mind was clear as a bell, but the rest of me wouldn't work, and because I was just a runner and bringing back the mail I didn't have battle kit on so I didn't have my field dressing. That's a sort of pad with disinfectant on it, and if you're alone you can slap it over the wound and hold it there and holler for the first-aid guy and hope he comes—which seemed like he never did.

There's another load of these Moaning Minnies going over, deeper, and things were going to get hot, and a fellow comes running back and he's been on sentry go, I'd guess, and I yell at him and ask him for his wound pad. He sort of zigzags over to me and looks at me and he says it looks like I'll make it and he might get it next so he's not giving his pad to anybody. And he runs on past me.

You get kind of philosophical at times, like the army stopped you thinking years ago, so I didn't scream or curse at that guy. I thought, well, I guess I'd've done the same thing. He sees me and I'm talking clear enough and he can't see any blood, and so why should he give up something that might save his life two minutes later?

I start back myself and I even pick up the mail pouch but it's too heavy and I have to let it go. I finally get to our positions or to where the first-aid man is, and that's when I go into shock. Then after the terrible pain hits, and I'm screaming and I get put into an ambulance for a ride way back south to some godforsaken little town where the hospital is, and the only thing I can remember is the sergeant yelling in my face, he's yelling about the mail, where's the mail, what did I do with it. I can't even say anything by this time, and then we go away.

I heard later it took them most of that day to find that sack of mail, and the guys were risking their necks under that bombardment which would walk up and down, the shells would land forward and then move back and then up again. Damned dangerous, naturally. But there they were, out in the vineyard on the hill trying to find it. Finally they did, and I'll bet they were cursing me all the time.

•←→• "Would Someone Come Here, Please?"

They had this field station on the edge of Ortona—the Krauts were defending the stinking town like it was Jerusalem—and they were bringing the wounded guys into this big marble kind of room in this big old house and putting them down. The doctors were working inside in another room with a table and generator and that, and every once in a while, say every hour, one doctor would come out and look at the new guys they'd brought in.

He'd look closely, and if they were dead by then he'd just point and the stretcher guys would haul them out. But there were quite a few, more than just three or four , who were just fearfully smashed up, that the doctor would look at and he'd know the guy was going to last another hour or something like that. He'd point to them, too, and they would be loaded and taken out into the dark and laid down beside the dead to die.

A few were very badly messed up, you know, guts spilled out and everything showing, but they could talk and they knew what was happening. One guy, I heard him say, "Would someone come here, please?" While all this was happening, this fucking hopelessness of the whole thing, the word "please" sounded so strange. He wanted me to give a message to his wife, and I wrote it down and gave it to the chaplain and, of course, the fellow died in a little while.

No, sorry, I won't tell you what he said. It was nothing important, just something he must have said to her before they went to sleep every night, but no, I wouldn't like her to read it.

•←→• The Lord Taketh Away

There was this farmer from one of those towns in Alberta where they have different religions. You know what I mean, they're just this side of being nutty, screwy. Why he joined us Seaforths, I don't know.

He carried this big Bible, bigger than a Gideon anyway, and he read that. All I ever saw him read, I'm sure of it. He had a million expressions. You know, like "the Lord giveth and the Lord taketh away." I mean, when something came up he could reach into his mind and come up with something from that Bible. I've never read it, but it must be some book.

We didn't talk about the war, what it was all about. Hell, we didn't know then. It was still girls and cars and what big shots we were, but Leo, that was his first name, he talked about death all the time. He'd say things like "If the Saviour wants me, then I am his willing servant," and, "I hope I will be the first to hear the silvery trumpet calling us all to a better life." Things like that. Crap. After a while it got so spooky we'd tell him to dummy up and stay that way, but he didn't. Always stuff about how he was in the army and if God wanted him, then he'd be there, first in line. One guy said old Leo had a death wish and this was one way out. Die and be a hero at the same time. Maybe. Maybe.

We go ashore in Sicily, in the south, and it's a laugh. Those Italians don't want to fight, and the Germans don't show up to make it rough for us for five or six days. Anyway, there's just a bit of light machine-gun fire and then the Italians are happy as all get-out to quit. For them the war's over, happy days are here again. For us, compared to what we went through later, Sicily was just more training.

Anyway, old Leo was our one casualty. If I wanted to b.s. you, I could say he was saved from a bullet through the heart by the bullet hitting that Bible he carried in his tunic, but I wouldn't do that. He heard the silvery trumpet all right. Got a burst right in the head, neck and shoulders. Dead before he hit the ground, and that was the only accurate shooting I saw from the Italians that whole day. Gabriel sure must have been blowing on his old trumpet that day.

•◄►• *Getting a Blighty*

My old man took me down to the station. It was 15 miles from Red Deer and he bitched all the way about spending good gas. Didn't seem to matter that I was away overseas and likely to get my goddamn ass shot off. I was an air gunner and their win-lose average wasn't all that good.

We get to the station and the train for Calgary isn't in for 15 minutes and there's no sense the old man and me standing around talking. We hadn't talked for the last ten years anyway. He knew his way of running the farm and I knew the best way, and that would cause trouble among the saints. So I said he'd best take off and he said he had a lot of work to do anyway so he might as well. Then the old bastard stuck out his hand and said, "Try and get your Blighty as soon as you can. A nice clean one. Then marry your nurse. They're the best kind."

You know, that was the first advice he'd ever given me without yelling and the first time he'd ever shown anything like a sense of humour. A Blighty? Oh, that's a first world war expression. It means a wound which will send you back to hospital in England but won't cripple you. He took off then. We didn't shake again, but I felt better. The train came along and I got on and went away.

Four months later I was in a Lancaster over Dortmund and a German flak exploded and blew the ass-end out of the ship and I got about six Blighties, shoulder, arm, leg, ass, yes, the ass, and both legs and that sent me to hospital for quite a while. The arm and leg were broken and they had to put pins in the arm, but it was enough to keep me out of the war. It was my fourth trip into Germany, so I was lucky.

No, I didn't marry no nurse. They were reserved for officers. I was a sergeant.

•─◆─• *In Order of Rank*

We'd taken a pretty heavy knocking about and about 20 or so got it all in a bunch. They were in this ditch and about four or five big ones came in, and I guess you could say they never knew what hit them. There wasn't one left alive.

When we'd cleared up the area next morning the captain tells me to take some men and bury them, and the procedure was to scoop out a ditch if you had a bulldozer handy, or dig one yourself. So we have to dig one because there's no blade around, and then we take what they've got in their pockets and put them in bags, mark the bags, and tie their dogtags to them. Some guys might take boots, too, because they could sell them on leave. No, it was all right. Why bury good boots?

We get the job done about mid-afternoon, all shovelled over and marked well and marked on the map, too, and then the captain comes over and he says, where's major so-and-so? I just pointed to the mound of dirt and I said, "He's in there somewhere. With the rest." Hell, what else would you say?

And so that captain chews out my ass, he'll do this to me and that to me, and don't I know that they should have been buried according to rank, the major at the head of the line, then the couple of lieutenants, and down the line to the last poor dead private. Well, shit. I blew up. I said first, the major didn't care, his wife if he had one wouldn't care, and the privates he was killed with, they couldn't have cared a shit, so what's the uproar. And finally, I told him that this was just temporary anyway. When the right time came, the graves people would come along, dig 'em all up, what was left of 'em, and take them to the official cemetery and put them all where they belonged, and if the major deserved to be at the head of the line, then that's where he'd go.

The fool was still upset but he saw the sense of what I was saying. Then, me, big mouth, my next remark was the one that caused all the trouble. I said the army could lose battle after battle, but when it came to burying the dead in order of rank, they never made a mistake. That crack cost me my corporal's hooks.

•◄►• *"You, You Get Shovels"*

I didn't like doing burials, helping the padre. It was a volunteer job, like, "You, you, get shovels. The padre, you'll find him over by that shed." That would be the sergeant talking.

Sometimes you'd find three or four guys laid there and you dug the grave, in some stupid Italian farmer's yard and they were put in. The padre did all three. I mean, he would bury R.C.'s, Protestants and Jews. Or you'd just go and find them, that is if the battle had moved on. Somebody would have marked them, mostly with a rifle stuck in the ground or a gas cape hanging on a stick. We usually buried them in their gas capes. We'd go through their pockets for the personal things, wrap them up in something, put them in their helmet, something like that. Or in their pack. We never carried much.

Dig the hole. Not deep, because they were gonna be dug up later. What we'd do, I'd put the shovel under the knees and the other guy would put the shovel under the shoulders and we'd sort of just easy, up she goes, and into the hole. Then the padre would say a few words. The right words, of course. Like in any burial. Usually there'd be nobody around.

I remember one chaplain we had once who carried four grenades in the shoulder bag he carried his prayerbooks in. To him, burying was just a business. He thought of himself mostly as a soldier.

•◄►• *Dead Men—What the Hell*

The first time I saw one of our boys go down I thought he'd tripped. This is Normandy, on the beachhead, and there's shit flying loose and goosy and I think this guy has tripped. Of course, he's dead.

All the training in the world isn't going to help all that much when the Germans are over there and we're here, and those things are bullets coming at you. Nothing matters until you get into action and then, wow, you learn fast, and then faster, and then faster again. There is absolutely no substitute for action, and nothing in the world will bring reality home quicker than to see three or four guys draped across some fence all shot up, or a burned tank with a guy hanging out of it and he's burned like a pig caught in a burning grease pit. The first smell of that and, boy, it was a lesson about what war was all about.

And when it happened again and again, then shit, you never thought about it. If you see a hundred dead Jerries, or some of our dead, from the battalion, or maybe from some Yank outfit, you don't go into a big flap. Nothing like that seems to matter any more.

And then you come home, discharged, and a year later you see a dead dog on the boulevard, hit by a car, and you're all sympathies. But over there, dead dogs, dead horses, dead men, what the hell.

•◄►• *His Leg Would Be Okay*

A guy named O'Connell lost a leg when we were training, on Salisbury Plain near Lark Hill. Artillery. I'm not sure what went wrong, but something did and they took his leg off. I think he was run over by a wheel. His leg off, about here, just below the knee. He was a big bastard, a good runner and jumper, loved to hunt and fish and stand at the bar in those wee English pubs and drink until you felt he couldn't take another pint.

I went to see him in the ward. They had this ward in the hospital for guys with cut-off limbs, and my friend wasn't having none of the therapy and workouts. He told me his leg would be okay. Hell, you could look and see it wasn't there, and he could do the same thing, *it just wasn't there,* but there was this thing. Get it? His brain wouldn't accept the fact his leg wasn't there. It had been so used to it for 30 years, you might say. He'd be sitting on the side of the bed and acting out some hunting story, after bear or moose up in the Mirimachi watershed or something, and you could see he didn't think he had only one leg.

So one day he's telling this story and he says something like, "And I'm behind this tree and the bugger comes out, with a rack of horns like this, and I've got him in my sights . . ." and then he stands up. Don't ask me how a guy can stand up on one leg, but he does—and then he topples over. Jesus, he went down like that moose he was going to shoot. And a nurse comes running and he just lies there, and he's sobbing. Ever hear a big man cry? He cries, sobs just like a little boy.

He must have lain there for five minutes, and then he stops and drags himself up on to his bed and he looks at me and he says, "Stan, I guess my left leg is gone after all."

That was the first time he accepted what had happened to him. When he fell. All the rest of the time he had been fooling himself in his mind, and his mind had been fooling him too. That's the way it is with some guys. A doctor told me so.

•⟶• *Just One Crack*

It's funny how men get it. I'm thinking of one guy in particular. Sonny Boyd. We joined roughly the same day, I guess, and wound up at Fort Osborne Barracks the same time and got into the same platoon, same company, of course, and went overseas together. We spent about 18 months crapping around England and we went drinking together, taking leaves together. I had relatives in Ayrshire and we'd go there and hike around and he was always puttering into some farmer's yard and talking. Always the farmer—his dad had a farm east of Saskatoon.

We go through France together and then Germany and we're with that bunch that went north into Holland. Remember that operation? A real shitty one. The thing is, neither of us so much as got a scratch. Not a splinter.

We're in this old Dutch town about noon this day just resting and lying around and eating some cheese the Dutch had brought out to us, and we gave them some smokes. That made us their friends for life. Then this kid comes running down and he says there's some Germans up this street. They weren't taking pot shots or we would have heard them, but the kid said they were there, so the lieutenant gets a dozen of us together and up we go after them. We figure it's just a prisoner deal. Go up and they'll come out when they see who it is.

The street kind of slopes up just a little and we're working our way along both sides. Just then there's a shot, and I look over and the lieutenant is lying in the middle of the street. It's only about 15 feet wide and he's sort of fallen away from the wall, like this, and he's in the middle. He looks like he's had it, but you never can tell, and I tell Sonny we'll get the sniper and I was unhorsing a couple of grenades and that would do the trick.

Then there's another shot and I see the lieutenant's hat go sort of jumpy. It makes a movement, a little jump and I know that means one right through the lid. If he wasn't dead before, he sure as hell was now. He's got that funny look, sort of the way you can tell if a dog is dead if it's been hit by a car. All loose.

Sonny's right in front of me and he says he'd better get the lieutenant, and I tell him not to be crazy, the guy was dead as a doornail. But Sonny says, no, he'd better drag him out of the way. Now there's that sniper, or snipers, looking down that long steel of a marksman's rifle, and the next guy that moves into the street is dead, and I remember saying, "Don't be a damn fool. The guy's gone for a shit."

But no, Sonny darts out, about the six feet to where the guy is, and crack. That's all there was to it. Just one crack and he goes down. Guys don't die like they do in John Wayne pictures. If they're hit, they just drop, and Sonny did. Flop. Well, you can't think about things like that. You save your crying for later, and we dug out that sniper and there only was one. Somebody shot him, I don't know who.

We made sure of the other houses anyway, and then I went back to Sonny, and the hole was right through his helmet and it must have blown his brain apart. That was the end of a good friend.

I rolled over the officer, a guy from Moose Jaw as I remember, and he was twice dead. There was the brain shot, same as Sonny's, through the tin lid but the first was smack through the old heart, I knew he'd got it somewhere that finished him, and Sonny did, too, but there he went risking his life for a corpse anyway.

You could go through a war and get a million bullets fired at you, and you know if you play it easy you're going to get home and then, goddamn it, you do something really stupid. It was like all the lessons he had learned over the months just went out of his head. And the thing was, that officer didn't mean a goddamned thing to us. We didn't even like him.

•◄►• *At Dockside, Halifax*

We used to meet the troop ships. That's what they had us girls doing. If we hadn't been so terribly young it would have been awfully sad, I guess, because a lot of guys came off in baskets. No arms or legs, that sort of thing.

They'd wait until all the other troops, the ones okay, had gone off to trains and buses. Then they'd bring the amputees off, the basket ones.

I never got overseas because I was too young, but if it was to see human suffering, then I didn't have to go overseas. Right there at dockside, Halifax.

Lots of them, and they just disappeared, and to this day I've often wondered just where they took those guys, where they went, what did they do? Did they see their families? Did their wives want to see them? I've wondered, is there a big building somewhere, some hospital where all those young fellows were put, and now have grown into old men?

Buddies

When I interviewed men who had been in the service three or more
years and had seen action, at the end I often asked them what,
above all, did they remember most vividly about the war. Not
once did they reply with the memory of an event in a great land
battle or in a fighter action. Every time, after considerable
thought, they would answer: "Oh, the guys I was in with," or,
"The fellows in my squadron, what a hell of a bunch," or, "There
were these guys on this one ship and we stuck together."

What they remember now with the most affection is the
camaraderie, the strange mix of friendship and, I guess, fear and
love and necessity that holds men from different backgrounds
together through periods of great hardship, risk, adversity, and
carries over into the good times of war, the happy days, the
drunks, the parties. They remember the guys they enlisted with,
trained with, drank with and fought with. As you will see, it soon
reached the stage that they were fighting the war for their buddies.
Only a very few said they carried on these friendships after the
war. The odd letter, perhaps, but very few visits, few long beer-
drinking sessions, and except for special occasions reunions seem
to be a thing of the past.

One more thing. They didn't remember their buddies as
dead in a field, in some bomber's wreckage. They still remember
them as alive and laughing, their pals.

•◄►• To Protect Your Buddies

My name is Andrew Blake and I'm Scots so I'm supposed to be
canny. You know, smart, a good thinker. Well, maybe I am, but it
took me darn near a whole war to figure what I was fighting for.

It was the other guys. Your outfit, the guys in your company, but especially your platoon. When they'd tell you to move
ahead because some shithead at the rear five miles back said so,
you did it, but not because of that brigadier. Not for respect of
the uniform, like they said every time we saluted an officer we
were paying respect to King and Country.

You did things to protect your buddies. Like the song says, the long and the short and the tall. You'd start sorting them out in depot in Toronto and be with them for three or so years, good times on leave and bad times, and when there might be 15 left out of 30 or more, you got an awful strong feeling about those 15 guys. They were more than your comrades, because they were your brothers.

You did things because you knew you had to to protect each other. Him for me and me for him, and that's the way the system worked. It had to. Nothing else was worth a damn, not officers or anything. Just you 10 to 15 guys who were left and the others who had come along later.

That's what I figured. If that fell apart, the brotherhood of battle as some guy said, then the battalion and the regiment and the corps and the division and the brigade and the war and the country went for a Burton. That's the way I finally figured it out, and other guys have said the same bloody thing.

•◄►• *Mutt and Jeff*

I saw it happen several times. Two men would strike up a friend-ship and get close. Going into Rome on leave or going back to the village for a wine piss-up and talking how they might set up a business, a trucking company or maybe a fishing lodge or some-thing, when they got home again.

I remember two guys especially and we called them Mutt and Jeff for the usual reason. One six-foot-two and the other five-and-four or something. They'd even got to the point when Mutt was writing to Jeff's sister and vice-versa, and to hear them talk, they were practically brothers-in-law.

I sent Mutt out on a patrol and the patrol came back and he wasn't with them and that meant three things—dead, wounded up there, or the Jerries had picked him off as a prisoner. Next night I sent out another patrol and I told them to look around where the first patrol had been, and they found Mutt. He was dead, of course. The next night I sent up the first patrol again and they took a mule with them, one of them Algerian mules, and they brought Mutt down.

Jeff had been back at the division hospital getting a pretty bad boil lanced and dressed and he didn't know anything of the Mutt business, so as his officer I felt it best to tell him myself. Hell, they were practically relatives to hear them talk.

I told him the only way. I said, "Mutt got it two nights ago up the hill." He looked at me and he said, "Aw shit." I said, "Mortar, it looked like," and he said, "Shit." Then he turned away, and as he did he said, "Thanks, lieutenant."

I'm just telling this to show that in battle it is never a good idea to make firm friendships. But when men do, they have an inner defence inside that makes them appear almost indifferent to what they know could happen to any one of them at any time. It was best that way. Believe me.

•◄►• *Our War—Up to 400 Yards in Front of Us*

We were mopping up, there wasn't much serious fighting. Hell, it wasn't actually what you'd call fighting at all. Some of the heaviest fighting was between our own guys, seeing who would get a Luger or a magnetic watch off some German officer who'd brought his boys in to surrender.

You see, we didn't have radios and we didn't care what was happening down to the south. A soldier's life is his platoon, his few buddies, meals, liquor if he could get it, and mail. A soldier is a very simple human being. A machine. They made us that way, weeks and months and sometimes years of training.

There was a strong sense of feeling about your platoon. I guess they were our family, each other's family. You protected your buddies, these guys you'd fought a thousand miles with, but what happened to your buddies once the *Ile de France* hit Halifax. Gone, never to be seen again—but by the Lord living Moses, they were your buddies then. You protected each other.

What I mean is this. The war, with generals looking at big maps somewhere 20 miles in the rear, that wasn't our war. Our war was only up to 400 yards in front of us, and from that farmhouse over there to that canal over there. We didn't give a shit what else was going on. Tell us what to do, no matter how stupid, and we'd do it. The thing was, let the generals play their games, we'd win the thing for them and then let us go home, and don't bother us with a lot of details. We don't want to hear or know what everyone else is doing. It doesn't matter.

•◄►• *The Best Soldier I Ever Knew*

You could never tell about the guys you were with. Some you would think would make perfect soldiers and others you'd wonder how they passed the medical and, of course, in between were the great mass of soldiers, just like you and me.

Some were gung-ho, you know, hell bent for leather and ready to eat the Germans alive. Always cleaning their rifles and talking big, and they were the ones the officers liked the best. In my experience, a lot of these jerks ended up peeling spuds in the officers' mess or driving a truck.

The best soldier I ever knew was a little guy and, hell, he must have been 35. At least. He had six kids, yeah, six. He'd been a clerk for Bell Telephone or some outfit like that, and what he was doing in uniform I could never figure out. He was a poor soldier in training. Kept his eyes shut tight firing his .303 and couldn't finish any obstacle course. Hell, he was just hopeless. But overseas, he was the best soldier I ever saw. He'd do anything. He was about five-foot-two inches but he was the biggest guy in our outfit. Fearless and a leader, going around, you know, cracking jokes, helping guys who were overloaded with ammo, volunteering for everything, night patrols, all the shit. He was also the sloppiest bugger you ever saw, and when we'd get a new officer you could see the look of disgust on his old kisser. Then, in a couple of days, you'd see the change—to respect and then admiration.

Funny, but Taylor never got any hooks, not even corporal's stripes. I guess it was because he always looked like Sad Sack [a cartoon character who was notoriously dumb and sloppy]. But he didn't care, he didn't mind. Just kept on doing his job and getting us through.

I'm glad to say he came home with us in one piece and I hope he is living to a happy and wealthy old age.

•◄►• *A Good Friend*

I'm not sure whether the government will deny this, but many a cell door swung open during the war to let out a convict to join the services. Never the navy or air force. No, always the army.

I imagine every company had three or four ex-convicts, men released, and I don't know if anybody cared. I think only the orderly room would know. There was only one guy I knew who had got out of Dorchester. There was this Parker fountain pen on my bed, an enlistment present from my boss at the store, and I saw this guy take it. I waited half an hour for him to bring it back, and then I followed him into the washroom and beat the hell out of him. After that, we got to be good friends and he told me he'd been in the pen for theft, breaking and entering and assault, all in one night. The first time he'd gone haywire, and the magistrate in Moncton gave him years for it.

When the army thing came up, he grabbed it. He was a good guy. Not all that bright, but a good friend, and altogether not a bad chap.

•◂▸• *"God Bless M for Momsie"*

I don't think any of us actually ever got over the loss of a pal on squadron when his plane went down, but it was a thing that we never talked about much.

After a mission and after debriefing and breakfast—and, I remember, flight crews always got real bacon and fresh eggs on our station—if one of our boys had gone down there, we'd meet. There was no note passed around, no word of mouth saying the older fellows will meet in so-and-so's room for a bit. But on our squadron there were four or five old-timers, second time around on operations or that kind of thing, and they'd gradually drift into one chap's room in the hut. There would be the guys, and someone would haul out a bottle of whiskey and we'd sit around, stand around and pour ourselves drinks. And about the second or third drink, somebody would make a remark, oh, I don't know what, just something. A toast, you could call it. A toast to the dead pilot. It might be quite cynical like, "Well, I guess we'll see his D.F.C. turn up in the mail tomorrow," or, "Who wants to take a 72 [hour-leave] to go up to London to comfort his girlfriend?" Maybe something like that.

We never made any big fuss about it. No, it was usually some remark, a lift of the glasses, and bottoms up. Somebody might say, "God bless M for Momsie," or whatever his plane was, and that was it.

You learned to keep emotion at a very low level.

•◂▸• *Farm Boys*

This was in Holland. There must be something about Canadian farmers and animals because they couldn't stand the sound of cows trapped between the lines. The bawling. These kids would crawl out in daylight, within range of the German guns and milk those cows. Lying on their bellies. That's right. Milk those cows to relieve the pressure of the milk on their bags. I didn't understand it.

I remember one kid. I asked him why he was risking his neck crawling out every day and he said, "Boy, if you don't know enough to know what's going on in that cow's mind, then you don't have the right to ask such a foolish goddamned question."

So one night this friend Arne and a guy named Zwicker, and I guess you could call us all city guys, well, we think cows are meat and we want meat. So before first light we go in this field and we kill this cow. No sweat. It didn't bring anything down on us. A shot bounces around, the Germans don't know just where it is. By the time we'd butchered it—crudely, I might say—it's daylight, and we've got to get back. We each take a quarter and I look around through the glasses and it looks quiet and by the time they open up, we'll be long gone. Despite what they say, it's tough to hit a moving man, even a jogger.

So I'm standing there with all this wet beef on me and I get this funny feeling, and I yell, "Let's go!" and I broke into a dead gallop and two seconds later, right where I'd been, a mortar drops in. They seen us, all right. Well, there's a lot of superstition in the lines and the other guys figure, this guy, meaning me, is lucky so we'll stick with him, and away they went too, across that field behind me and we get back, stuff spraying around us but we get back. With all that cow meat, 300 pounds of it.

And you know what those farm boys did? Hungry as they were, sick and tired as we all were of rations, these farm boys beat the shit out of us for going out and killing one of their cows. The cows were going to die anyway, but no, goddamn you city guys, you killed one of our cows. Now how do you like that one?

•◄►• *He Walked His Own Way*

We had this bugger with us, his name was Thomas, very English in name but Christ, the bugger was Indian through and through, and he just loved war. He came from somewhere in Manitoba so I guess he was Cree, but he was a big Cree and had a brush cut and blue eyes but he was all Indian. If somebody somewhere wanted to fill him in, and this Thomas figured he could lick him, then he'd just walk away, and he had that stride, heel and toe, that tall and lean Indians have. But if somebody wanted to fill him in, and Thomas figured it would be a battle, then it was on, hammer and tong, muscle and teeth, boots and fists and only one guy would come out of it, and I never saw our Indian lose. He just loved to fight.

All through Italy, there he'd be. We'd be digging in for the night, ducking around looking for a big stone wall, and he'd get permission for a patrol. There was no damn sense sending out a regular patrol, six or eight guys or so. Just send out Thomas and he'd slip away and in 10 feet he'd just have disappeared and he might be out all night. And just before dawn, you'd be on sentry go, and he'd scare the shit out of you because there's nobody there and suddenly there he is. If the officer wanted a prisoner, he'd usually have one all trussed up, or a *paisano,* or he'd have the gen. written down in a little note pad, so many guns, artillery, where the Germans were. Their fortifications, the pillbox in the orchard, all that stuff. This Thomas just loved it, and by God, the bugger was good at it.

One nice day we're moving along, and there's a bridge and the engineers have posted it for mines, so the platoon goes around it and down a bank and we ford the river just knee high, and that's where Thomas got his. Fifteen guys go through, stepping along and no problem and then *boom* and there's this smoke and dust and I remember the sergeant saying, "Goddamn it all to hell, they got our Injun." He's standing off to one side, and he knows who's going through, he's waving them so he knows it is Thomas—and he's got no head, and his body is still moving ahead a bit, about two steps, as he's falling.

It sort of took the stuffing out of us for that day. That night we're hanging around the basement of this house and somebody says that 15 guys go through and then Thomas is next and he's blown to ratshit and how come? The sergeant says he used to watch Thomas, and he never did go where the rest of the patrol went. He walked his own way, and once too often.

The Alaska Highway

Who Built the Alaska Highway? . . . The Whitehorse Post Office . . . They Were Miserable . . . "The Americans Will Never Miss It" . . . The Generous Americans . . . The Yankee Boys and Their Gold . . . It Was Hard to Figure You Were in Canada . . . Edmonton Was Jammed with GI's . . . All Friendly Games . . . Fuelling the Alaska Highway . . . Like a Battlefield

---

Inside Canada, probably the most lasting legacy of the war is the Alaska Highway. Few projects of the past 50 years became an instant legend the way the Highway did. Today, most Canadians have heard of the way the Americans took over half the western sub-Arctic, of the vast outpourings of men and equipment (equipment which was left to rot) and of the high salaries which upset the economy of the north, although in those days half of Canada didn't know what was going on in their own back yard anyway.

Once started, there was no stopping it. The Alaska Highway opened up northern British Columbia on the eastern border and the Yukon, and gave Alaska Road access to the south. Tens of thousands of Canadians live in the north today because of The Road. It was an astonishing project.

•◆• Who Built the Alaska Highway?

I would like to say this, and this is an over-all fact about the Alaska Highway and I'd like to make this very clear. It has always been an irritation to me to see misrepresentations, for many, many years, of the over-all highway story. The point is this. The Alaska Highway as we know it today was not built by the vaunted United States Army.

That's balderdash. A pioneer trail was pushed through by engineer regiments of the U. S. Army, certainly, but the road was not built by the United States Army. As a permanent road. And the hoopla which was generated at that time by the public relations types in the American Army had it that the road was built in ten months. And there was an opening ceremony at Soldiers' Summit celebrating this great event. That is so much nonsense. All that was was a rough sort of trail, a two-lane road of sorts that would have been unusable in spring and summer.

I know. I was there.

Only then, after that ceremony, did the real construction begin, get under way on the road, and it took two years to build it. The widening, the grading, the gravelling, the culverts, everything. As a matter of fact, that was all done by American and Canadian contracting firms, employing large numbers of Canadians. Each firm would be given a section to work on, and the highway, when it was finished to handle military supplies and traffic, well, by then the threat of a Japanese invasion of Alaska had died forever, about two years before.

More than 80 contractors and subcontractors did the job and they were ridden herd on by the United States Public Roads Administration and under the over-all supervision, yes, of the U. S. Army. But the U. S. Army did not build the Alaska Highway. Very few people know this today.

•◄►• The Whitehorse Post Office

They didn't give us any notice. Not Ottawa or the railroad or anybody. Suddenly, trains started to roll into town and within three days we had 10,000 American construction troops in Whitehorse and remember, Whitehorse had only about 350 people in winter and maybe 700 in summer, what with the boats and shipyards and freighting and tourists opening up. My God, what a mess!

I worked in the post office, a dinky building. Just me and the postmaster, and two weeks after the Americans came he had a stroke, so I ran out on the street and grabbed off two local women and I hired them. No authorization—not even enough money—but I hired them.

Naturally we had no cancellation machine and from maybe 20 letters a day we were shooting out thousands. It was all stamping by hand. I'd hand-stamp for 12 hours a day, and one Saturday I stamped for 17 hours. Callouses. Dead arms. If you want to know what hard work is, it's not pick and shovel. It's stamping envelopes for 10,000 men, 12 hours a day.

Everybody, of course, wanted to write home. Here they were in the Arctic, or so they thought. I very soon ran out of one-cent and two- and three- and four-cent stamps and then I started selling every stamp. Fifty-cent stamps, a dollar, and when I'd sold everything in the post office, I just sent them out without stamps. Cancelled, of course, but no stamps.

By this time the word is down to Vancouver and two

inspectors come up to Whitehorse to see what the hell is going on. One guy wires back to Vancouver, saying what it's like and he's told to stay there and give a hand. You know how long that poor fellow was up there? Two years. It was two years before he got out of there. Maybe they forgot about him, but it was two years he was there and he meant to stay a day or two. My God, what a time!

•◄►• *They Were Miserable*

The Southern boys reacted very unfavorably to the Yukon when they were working on the Alaska Highway, especially the black troops in the labor battalions. Cotton-pickers before they joined up or were conscripted, small farm boys, boys from the slums of the big cities. They were nothing, just labor battalions.

In those days they were segregated and they did all the rough work. Some drove trucks and machines, tractors, but they also did an awful lot of pure backbreaking bull labor, axe work and pick and shovel. And they hated it.

At the beginning they were poorly housed, they just had tents. And it was cold. You'd see them standing around huge fires they'd made of lumber. Lumber to be used for construction, buildings, cribbing, bridge timbers. They burned anything, it didn't matter. They were poorly clothed. They didn't have Arctic type clothing or decent boots. They had no recreation. There was nothing for them to do. They were segregated in a land of nowhere and they were miserable.

Then they'd run trucks off the road. Jeeps, machinery, everything. The coloured drivers would put them into deep ditches and over ravines, and you could drive along for miles and see equipment busted up everywhere, it was often said that the Negro troops had the idea that the more equipment they could break up, the quicker they could get home. And so there was wrecked equipment of every type, from jeeps to bulldozers, scattered all the way from hell to breakfast. All the way, the length of that highway.

•◄►• *"The Americans Will Never Miss It"*

When the American Army came to Whitehorse to build the Alaska Highway nobody was prepared. We weren't prepared for them, and they didn't know the slightest thing about the Yukon.

But they sure came. Thousands of men, and to get them there they were running about 15 trains a day up from Skagway, and the Whitepass and Yukon Railway is, as you know, narrow-gauge, so they went all through Colorado and Idaho and Arizona to these old mining railways and grabbed off their rolling stock. But the old railway was beginning to sink into the ground, and so was Whitehorse.

They had men and trucks and bulldozers and tents and buildings everywhere, but everywhere just wasn't anywhere near enough. You know where the federal government is now? Well, in 1942 that was a softball park and it had a couple of buildings. They filled the buildings up with food, and then they just piled the boxes and barrels of food up, outside, like they were lines of goods in a Safeway, only much higher and much thicker. On the ground, all over the park, filling it up.

And of course, at night everybody swiped stuff. It wasn't guarded. Take what you could carry. I said to myself, "Why the hell not?" So this night I'm walking by and I yanked off a big box and Christ, but it's heavy. I'm a big fellow but this box was almost too much for me, but I finally get it home about two blocks to where I live and in the light I open it up. You know what? Two hundred cans of tinned bacon. The very best quality. Two hundred pounds of bacon. Boy, if I had to steal anything I sure picked the right thing, even if it nearly killed me.

We used to say, the Americans will never miss it. And they didn't. Never would. They spoiled easily as much as they used. The wastage on that job, well, you wouldn't believe it. So what was 200 pounds of bacon? It sure helped me out that winter. Civilians just couldn't get the stuff.

•◄►• *The Generous Americans*

There always was a lot of talk about the Americans coming up and building the road and taking over the whole north country. Well yes, I know, they did a lot of things wrong, but instead of calling them Ugly Americans I call them the Generous Americans.

Some would raise hell as much as they could in town whenever they could, but a lot were just young fellows, soldiers, and I can remember how a lot of them helped other people out, playing sort of Santa Claus.

We'd just come through a Depression and it was still hard times up in that country, very hard times for a lot, and there were old people or young couples with a few kids stuck on tiny farms at the end of six miles of bush trail and they were just scraping along as poorly in 1942 as they had five years before. Forty dollars looked like all the money there was in the world.

On a Sunday some of these young soldiers from around Fort St. John would get a truck and you'd see them heading down the roads visiting, and what they had in that truck! My! Of course it was all stolen, or borrowed and forgotten to be returned, the way armies work—but they'd load up with hams and cases of peaches and pears and blankets from the army hospital and boots and socks and plates and cups and bowls. Why, it seemed that everything that wasn't nailed down at Fort St. John or Charlie Lake or one of the line camps, there it was in the truck and these young boys from Oklahoma and Texas and California, there they'd be tearing down the roads just giving stuff away like a herd of Santa Clauses.

•◄►• *The Yankee Boys and Their Gold*

In a way it was like another gold rush, or as if somebody had come along in an airplane and dropped money all over us. Thousands of these goddamned Yankees coming into the country to build the road, and hardly anybody in that country had a pot to piss in or a window to throw it out of in those days, because any good times the war did to Canada never did get up to us, and all of a sudden, there are the Yankee boys and their gold.

I guess for ten years I'd never made more than 200 to 500 dollars a year, bacon, beans, shells and a couple of new dogs every fall, and then I got me a job. First, I'm to go up every creek and spot for beaver dams and if I find any, then the American soldiers come up and blow them out. Hell, I don't tell them a goddamned beaver will build a dam all over again the next night. I figure they're not going to take their highway away, not with all them Japs up in Alaska coming our way, but I just don't tell them that you don't smash the dams, you gotta kill the beaver. In that country these hundreds of creeks run thisaway and they cross this new Alaska Highway and so they don't want flooding. They'll get flooding anyway, every goddamned spring, but I don't tell them that either. I don't tell them nothin'.

They think I'm a real character of a woodsman, me with my squaw, and I just let them go along thinking I am, and all the while I'm making maybe about 75 dollars a month, I think, and here I'm ordering officers and everybody around, do this, do that, and there are all these nigger fellows they got working as soldiers and my God, I just gotta look at them fellows and they're running around doing anything I ask.

Kind of a shame, though, bringing them niggers into that country, because down in Alabama where they come from, they didn't know cold and I don't even think the Russkies could beat us for cold like we got around Fort Nelson, in that part of the country.

And mosquitoes. You'd think those Yanks would know about skeeters, but their home-grown kind down South were just little fellows. Up that way, we grew them big, with two engines and pontoons. Even I got to admit they were bad that year when we built the highway. They damn near killed them colored boys. Well, if the truth were known, that year they damn near killed me too. Somebody said they must be part of the Jap invasion.

The money was good and the beaver kept building dams and I kept finding them. Well, hell, you know this. When a beaver decides where he's gonna put his dam, that's where he puts it. Blow it out, he comes back. Beaver nature, I guess. So it wasn't no going back and making a big discovery. The dam was always there.

Goddamn but those Yanks were dumb. Nice guys, mostly, but dumb. Course, everything was new to them. At night they'd hear a noise in the bush and think it was a grizzly. It might be a skunk out looking for its dinner. I mean the niggers. They didn't know anything. They'd sit around and one would say something, a mumble, and the rest would laugh. You never knew what they said. Like it was they had their own language. Nice guys though. A couple came back here to settle, but they lasted about two months and then went home. It's a tough life up here. You gotta be tough.

•◄►• *It Was Hard to Figure You Were in Canada*

I'll put it this way. Might as well be square with you. They let me out of Headingly [a prison near Winnipeg] and drove a few of us down to the recruiting station on Portage Avenue. We were supposed to join the army and when we were delivered there the M.P.'s drove away. I didn't skip out, like a couple. In fact, I wanted to join the army.

The medical tossed me out. One thing, I was blind as a bat, and a guy had bust a knee with a bar, a two-by-four in a hobo jungle near Kamloops, so I was a mess. I mean if the army didn't want you, the navy and the air force sure wouldn't.

A guy I knew in the rattler had told me that if I went up north I could get a job on the Alaska Highway which the

American Army was building. This road was to get armies and supplies up to Alaska. He gave me a guy's name to phone, some superintendent of a company doing a lot of work.

And so I dial for long distance and get through to this tool push in Fort St. John, the guy who can hire, and I say I'm just out of the army because of medical reasons. Now, that's not too much of a lie. I'd tried to get in, hadn't I?

He says what can you do, and I says I can drive cat. I says I am good at grading and can fill right even to the top of the survey sticks for miles. That pleases him, and he says how do I know you're on the level? I said phone Tiny Deacon, or Eaton, I forget his name now, and he wouldn't know Tiny is in the can, but he says if he had recommended me, that's okay with him. When can I come?

I say I'm broke but if he wires me 100 dollars to the C.P. Telegraph at Portage and Main next morning, then I'm on my way soon as I can catch a train. He says okay and the money, she's sure waiting for me, and it's a $150. There's another telegram from the American super and it says, "Cat skinners got to eat too, but get here sober." I guess he wants to get on the right side of a real hot-shot cat operator right off the bat. Of course, it's advance on wages but what the hell, I found myself liking the way he did things.

I get to Edmonton and then I take an old scrap-iron thing called a train away up north and then a bus and I get into Fort St. John. It may have been a quiet little place once and it probably is a nice place now but sweet living Christ! Then it was a nuthouse. First of all, it was hard to figure you were in Canada. The Union Jack flying by the post office, I guess, and Mounties, but that was about it. Americans was everywhere. G.I.'s everywhere you looked. You wondered who was out fighting the war with all these guys here, and hundreds of trucks, and they was moving stuff up the road day and night and building this big goddamned airport and hospitals and barracks, and there was mud and shit and corruption everywhere.

Then there was the construction men. They'd brought them in from all over, Venezuela, California, you name it, and one guy said to me that wouldn't it be funny if they built this road to Alaska and then the Japs came a-roaring down that old road and through Canada and right into the U.S.A. Another guy said the place reminded him of Oklahoma in the oil boom. Some oil boom.

There was fighting and knifings and murders; I heard about them, and soldiers fighting each other and white soldiers kicking black soldiers off the sidewalks, wooden sidewalks almost pounded into the mud. The Negro fellows were the work battalions and I thought they were like slaves. Everybody kicked them around, and it was the first time I'd seen more than two black fellows together at once, and over by the railyards there was a camp of thousands of them. All going north.

Kids fourteen and fifteen were working for the Americans in the commissaries, not doing much more than setting tables and washing dishes, and they were making more than their fathers who worked in the bank or a store or something, and kids were making 100 dollars a month and maybe more. Girls too. There was jobs for everybody. And whores, I can't remember if there were houses, whorehouses, or if you just hoisted one up on a stack of lumber beside the road and went at it.

There was mud too. Don't let me forget that goddamned mud. This is a kind of northern mud that would win the title of king in a competition of sticky, gooey mud. Jesus Christ, I'd forgot all these years about the mud.

Money didn't mean a fucking thing to them Americans. Spend it, and then spend some more. You never saw such waste. A piece of grading equipment, it breaks a heavy-duty coil spring or something, so haul it off the road, like when they were building the airport, and let it rust. Thousands of dollars of stuff. No, millions. Everything from draglines to jeeps. You'd have thought the equipment-makers was running the show and not the army.

She was sure a going concern, but even at that there were some people, the folks who had been there, who somehow managed to carry on like nothing had happened. I met a few of them just wandering around because, you see, I hadn't showed up for that job. I meant to but I didn't. One thing, I couldn't drive a goddamned bulldozer. [He roars with laughter.]

There was a dance hall called Blue Heaven and I used to go there and bum a few dollars. That wasn't hard because there was so much money around and I'd tell new guys in town where the bootleggers were. There was one who charged twenty bucks for a mickey and he'd ask the guys to please, for Christ sakes, bring back the bottle as he was so short. Made it himself. You had to stand in line for meals and time meant nothing, like you'd get sausages and mashed potatoes for breakfast and bacon and eggs for supper. Just depended what they had, what came in on the trucks.

Would you believe there was only one barber in that town when I was there, and he'd give you a number and say come back at five o'clock on Wednesday, and that would be four days away. Things like that.

I got to know a lot of the American boys and they were

fine lads and I'd sleep in their barracks a lot of times or hitch a ride out to Charlie Lake where they were set up. That's where I got into trouble. It was just a matter of time, of course, and even if I'm seventy-six, I guess it would only be a matter of time now too, if things were the same.

This master sergeant in the big mess hall got so he was looking for someone to shove grub out the back door to, and as I was eating on the army and playing a bit of poker in the washrooms with the G.I.'s, he lit on me. He and me, we'd go into business and I'd truck grub into the Fort or down to Dawson Creek, and sell it there. Selling it was no problem. This worked okay, just fine, and we split.

One night I go snooping around the big base at Charlie Lake and I find this truck and I get in under the canvas and start messing around and it's half full of hospital stuff, like sheets and towels and pillowcases and bottles and those things you crap in in bed and blankets—and the rest of the thing is filled with cases of Johnny Walker. Well, I know if I can get that whiskey into town, and she's only a few miles out, then I can sure get rid of it, and the towels and blankets. If I can't find a buyer quick I'll run her into a ravine.

Next night I sneak in, and you don't need a key for them American trucks, just a toggle switch, and I switch her on and head out and I've got this G.I. hat on and a pair of cover-alls I'd swiped out of the barracks, and hell-bent for town I go. Five miles, ten miles, I forget, but I'm nearly there and *swooooosh, rooooooar, blink, blink,* and they're on me, and not for stealing. For speeding. Raising too much dust on that fucking road.

The dust is killing everybody, humans, cows, sheep and trees and I don't know they're going to crack down. I don't read that little paper they put out, so here I'm going along at 50 when it should have been 30 or so and boom, and I got no papers and I got a load of stolen goods behind me including about 7,000 dollars' worth of booze for the Yankee officers' mess and so I get five years. In Prince Albert, and when I get out the war is over. That's all.

•◄►• *Edmonton Was Jammed with GI's*

You couldn't go anywhere in Edmonton, downtown, it was just jammed with G.I.'s. On every street corner, every restaurant, the shows, just everywhere, they just had nothing to do. Our church organized a kind of basketball league because we knew Americans liked to play basketball, but that didn't work because they wanted girls.

I don't know why there weren't many Canadian soldiers and airmen, I guess the camps were further away, but all these G.I.'s building the Alaska Highway, thousands of them, they came to Edmonton because that was the only city to go to. Edmonton was like a hick town in those days and I don't think they had much fun.

And you'd walk down the street, 15 and 16, and there would be 10 or 20 American soldiers on every street corner, every square foot. Now when the girls walk down the street they don't know what it is to hear a wolf whistle like we did. It was fun. Some girls where I worked, they had a date every single solitary night with some G.I. You could take your pick, your choice, any one, just like going into a supermarket and choosing apples or oranges.

They were nice guys, mostly. They were far from home and the ones from the South, you know Mississippi, Florida, they suffered from the Edmonton cold. They were young and a lot like the boys we'd gone to school with ourselves. It was fun. We all had a lot of fun. I think our mothers used to be horrified, but I don't know anybody who got hurt by it all.

•◄►• *All Friendly Games*

Sure, I can remember. I was there, and I'm not that old yet. It was when we was building the Alaska Highway. Every tough guy and crook and asshole and bum in North America showed up there.

There was this town called Dawson Creek. It's still there and bigger now, but back in '42 it wasn't much. Just a bunch of merchants rooking the farmers, I guess you'd call it, but then it was sort of the unloading place for the Alaska Highway. Depot, storage, motor pool, whatever. Call it what you like.

Then there was this road north, just used by farmers and guys going into the bush, and then there's this big Jesusly river. Yeah, the Peace River, and I forget who had the ferry, but it was an old rickety thing, farm carts and trucks and the likes, and when the Yanks started driving their ten-tonners onto the thing it was like me stepping on a cigar box in a river. But she held up and she kept working until they got this bridge going. I guess the Americans took over the ferry because they took over the whole country, but even they couldn't make it go faster or carry more loads, but I think they added another one that summer. Anyway, the back-up, cars, trucks, everything, was way up the hill and out of sight. Those Yankees, they sure love to gamble. Bet some of them what kind of a colour the next house is around the bend and they'll bet. They made good money, of course. I had this friend in Winnipeg called Blackie and I sends him a letter and I said that if he wanted to make his fortune without hitting no Klondike, here it was. Bring your loaded dice, your shaved dice, your sure-fire darlings and we'll get going, and pretty soon he come up and we met and that's where it all started.

We had a system and it was this. I'd walk ahead and come up to one of these crap games of the drivers and soldiers and construction stiffs and they was strung out about every 300 yards, on the backtrail of the ferry, just waiting you see, and I'd walk up and watch for a bit and then somebody is sure to pass the dice to you. I mean it was all friendly games. Then Blackie would come up and he'd sort of hunker down near me and after a couple of turns I'd just sort of naturally pass the dice to him, as though I didn't know him.

Then Old Blackie would switch the dice and away he'd go. Make five or six or seven passes and take in a few hundred bucks and then switch, back, and maybe he'd make another pass, maybe not, and he'd be out. Next time he'd switch to his losing dice and that would throw them guys off the scent, and next time, switch, and bang, another couple hundred. It didn't matter if I won or lost. Just call me the stooge. Just to get Blackie into the game. Then Blackie would stand up and . . . no, I would pull out, saying I was cleaned and was saving five bucks for pie and coffee, and next round Blackie would pull out and say he had to get back to his truck. Something like that, and you see, because the line was always there but because it was always moving a bit because of the ferry taking new loads, nobody ever spotted our tricks. Not once. Those southern fellows, those Yankees, they didn't like to lose. But if you've gambled, you'll know a guy can get lucky once in a while, even if you're just walking down the road.

For every 3 dollars we made I'd get one and Blackie would get the rest, 2 dollars. That summer and fall, I guess it was, I made more than 20,000 dollars and Blackie, I know, made more than really 40,000 dollars because I know he was cheating me right and left, but I wasn't like the guy in the nursery rhyme, I wasn't gonna kill no golden goose, which was Blackie.

•◄►• *Fuelling the Alaska Highway*

Canol, the pipeline project, was an adjunct of the Alaska Highway, designed to help fuel the Alaska Highway and its airfields, the airfields along its route.

It was conceived in the spring of 1942, the same time the Alaska Highway was conceived, and behind it originally was Stefansson, the great Arctic explorer. It was his idea but he was dismayed when the U. S. Army did what he said was the right thing in the wrong way. He wanted the oil pipeline laid from Norman Wells to Fairbanks in Alaska and the army decided to go across the Mackenzie-Yukon Divide to Whitehorse where the refinery would be built. That distressed him.

I was hired by Steve Bechtel [president of the Bechtel Corporation, one of the builders of the pipeline] as a northern specialist and after about a year I was taken over by the U. S. Army Corps of Engineers, on both projects to serve as northern specialist and also as historian.

I made two films, 28 minutes of the Alaska Highway and 58 minutes of the Canol Project, and it took two years, in summer and winter, and often 35 below with my 16-mm. Bell and Howell and I wrote my own scripts, edited and cut the film and narrated everything and this took two years. And then, because both projects were coming under a lot of fire in the States—like were they necessary because the Japanese threat had long passed—these two films, two years' work, were taken by the U. S. Army and put into a vault, where they are to this day. History, living history, and it's in a vault. Why? Because the Truman Committee was investigating graft and corruption in armed service contracts and the Alaska Highway and Canol was coming under a lot of criticism. So, two of the greatest stories in North America during the war, they're not being told. Why, there are kids in the Yukon who never knew there was a Canol Project. But I managed to get a copy each of those films and I kept them and I gave them to the Yukon Archives, so everything is not lost.

The Canol Project did fuel the Alaska Highway and its airplanes, and it's been widely criticized, but one thing to remember, in the light of today's problems, the Canol Project was the granddaddy of all large construction projects to take oil and move it in the Arctic and sub-Arctic. It was done by trial and error, and some dreadful mistakes were made, but it was an extraordinary project.

Norman Wells Field was never a big oil field, and additional wells were built, but it never was that big. One of the major criticisms was that the pipe size was too small, only four inches in diameter to Johnson's Crossing and then six inches. It was a 580-mile pipeline, but it had other lines going out to other places in the north which made it more than 1,600 miles long. If you travel by air over the Whitepass and Yukon Railway you can see the original pipeline still there. Products from Skagway still being used. Right along the track. You see, it was such a high-gravity crude that none of the line had to be buried and it would flow in temperatures up to 70 degrees below zero. The actual maximum was only 4,000 barrels per day, to the Whitehorse refinery. It should have been much bigger. The pipe size limited the thru-put. It could have had 20,000 barrels a day and that would have been sufficient, and as it was, only 4,000 barrels a day went through and the initial planning, to make it only three and four inches in diameter, was criticized by the Truman Committee.

They could have used 20,000 barrels a day there. Do you know at that time there were thousands of airplanes being flown to Russia, fighter planes and bombers, Air Cobras, little nasty, snarly fighters, and the American ferry pilots didn't like them. They were afraid of them, they cracked up a lot of them. They were glad to hand them over to the Russians at Fairbanks, and the Russians used them on the Eastern Front. There also were light bombers, B-24's. It lingers in my mind that the figure was 50,000, the number of planes the Russians got from the Americans on that Northwest Staging Route and so you can see, with the demand of thousands of aircraft and thousands of trucks and thousands of soldiers and sailors, the demand for oil was very great. Yes, they could easily have used 20,000 barrels a day.

All of the gasoline and products that could flow through the Canol system, all of that fuel was needed, and all of it was used.

The Canol Project cost, and it sounds ridiculous in terms of today's dollars, billions and billions, but it cost officially $134,000,000 and that was severely criticized in those days. And what can you build for that amount today? Nothing.

Mistakes? Same as the Alaska Highway. Ignorance, mostly. The American engineers knew nothing about Arctic conditions, permafrost. Of course, there wasn't even the word "permafrost" in '43. So up came jillions of construction men from the south who had no idea of what they were up against, so they'd say, "We'll clear out all these trees and put a road here and lay the pipe there and that will do it," and they didn't ask questions. They knew it all. But the job got done, in spite of it all.

The same on the Alaska Highway. The U. S. Army pushed a trail in between places where trails did not already exist and that was the first road. But it took another two years, more than 80 civilian outfits to make it a real, all-weather and usable road.

It was a great project, the Canol Project, and that road we built opened up an awful lot of the Yukon as we know it today. And yet you have to be an old-timer to remember that there ever was such a project. The young people certainly don't. The newcomers don't. But Canol, for all its faults, was the granddaddy of the movement of crude oil from one place to another in the Arctic.

•◄►• *Like a Battlefield*

My Uncle Dave was one of these guys who could do anything, make anything, fix anything and find anything, and if gas was a problem to everybody else just after the war, not to him. He had gasoline and he said he could get more anywhere along the line.

He took my cousin, Don McDonald, who'd just come back from the air force and they left to take a look at Alaska. It was October and things went good and they slept along the way in sleeping bags and he told me later that somewhere north or south of Watson Lake they pulled off on this side road because it was a hot weather fall and the dust was something fierce and it would hang in the air for hours. So they drive down this side road a mile or two and camp and they can't see anything because it's dark. But next morning that old Dave Flynn said his eyes just popped.

It was like a battlefield, he said. Bulldozers and trucks and every kind of vehicle you ever saw, just parked around, the tracks all worn down by rain and snow and trees growing everywhere, around axles, into the engines of station wagons and jeeps, and everything looked like the end of a big tank battle. He thinks there must have been several hundred vehicles, bulldozers, some of it good, some of it bad, but if it was bad Uncle Dave could make it good, he was that kind of a guy. Give him a busted 2-dollar watch and he'd soon have it going.

Now you know what this stuff was, don't you? U. S. Army. All U. S. Army. Do a job on that Alaskan Highway and get the hell on to the next project and they'd leave this stuff behind. Abandon it and then condemn it. Take a sledge to the instrument panel, or a pick-axe and just hammer up the carburetor and then go at the tires with an axe. Truck after truck, cat after cat. Uncle Dave figured even with this gawd-awful damage he could come back and salvage half the stuff. There must have been a couple of million bucks' worth of the stuff, off the road, and unless you

228   *Six War Years*

were flying low and looking for it in a plane, you'd never find it. It was part of the country now because a lot of it, most of it, I guess, had been there since '42 and '43.

That's the way the Americans did things. Just overwhelm. If you need six bulldozers, ship in 12, because six might break down.

He went to Whitehorse or back to Edmonton, I forget, anyway, where the U. S. Army still had an office, and offered to buy the stuff, get it going, sell it. My gawd, man, half the farmers and contractors and loggers in that country were crying for equipment. Just dying for it. Remember, this was '45.

Nope, said the Yanks, that stuff is condemned and that's where it is gonna stay until it falls apart. It sure was a crazy situation.

D-day and After

Ferry Trips Across the Channel . . . D-day Memories . . .
Approaching the Beach . . . Welcome to the War . . . The
.88 . . . Horses in the War . . . On the Road to Falaise . . .
Everything Was Long-range . . . The Flame Thrower . . .
Seven Tanks in Six Weeks . . . German Officers . . . It Was
Him or Me . . . **The Maple Leaf**

For four years, men and tanks and guns and supplies and
ammunition and trucks were piled onto the island of Britain until
it was jokingly claimed that if the anti-bomber barrage balloons
were cut free, the island would sink beneath the great weight of
war supplies.

Then D-day came, and early on June 6, 1944, certainly the
greatest assemblage of ships in the history of the world ferried the
greatest seaborne invasion force of all time to storm Hitler's For-
tress Europe. More than 100 Canadian naval ships and landing
craft took part in the invasion, as well as Canadian troop ships.
The Third Division, unleashed for action after so many months of
training and manoeuvres in England, was among the first units
ashore in Normandy, and by July 23 the First Canadian Army—
long a dream of the militarists and nationalists overseas and at
home—was functioning as a unit with support from British and
Polish troops. Meanwhile, the Royal Canadian Air Force was
flying thousands of sorties and bombing runs on German posi-
tions, as were the many thousands of Canadians in the R.A.F.

The major test of the Canadians came early, at Caen and
Falaise Gap, where, in some of the bloodiest fighting of the war,
many fine German infantry and armoured units were destroyed.
After D-day the Canadians then moved north to open up the
Channel ports.

The men who speak to you in this chapter were there; this
is their view of one of the great military events of all time.

•◄►• *Ferry Trips Across the Channel*

Our time was coming. Late spring of '44. Manoeuvres, practices,
beach landings, all hands on board and everyone knowing what
they had to do and able to do it in their sleep. I was nineteen and I
had never been more than 20 miles from my father's place in
Ontario and now I was on a ship and the invasion was coming.

Yes, we knew about it. That was something nobody could keep quiet. Everybody knew.

There was so much going on, for me at least, it was very confusing, very exciting, not knowing for sure all that much about anything. That first night when we took on the load of troops those soldiers seemed to be a little quieter and more serious-looking. With the countless landing craft and larger ships loading all around, everywhere you looked, this just had to be it.

As I look back to those three days, before D-day, the Day and the day after, D Plus One, I'm not even sure now that I can remember any exact sequence of events. It just seems like a jumbled, confusing bad dream. There I was, so alone, a kid thousands of miles from home and I had to take part in the biggest invasion ever attempted in history. Hundreds of ships of all types from the north to the south horizon, crossing the Channel, and the same thing, a stream of aircraft, bombers, fighters, planes towing gliders, probably nearly half a mile wide and at one stage from horizon to horizon. That vision I shall never, never forget.

I was scared while we were making the ferry trips across the Channel. It took about five hours one way loaded and about four coming back, but it was something I'll never forget. And if I ever had to do it again, yes, I'd sign up again and do it again. It was the greatest moment of my life and I will never forget it.

•◄►• D-day Memories

Honest to god, I don't remember a thing. I remember the outfit marching down those lanes in England near the coast and then sleeping in a big hall that night and then loading up next afternoon and then going across the Channel and it was dark and you could hear the bombers going over, into France. I remember when we camped, some English school kids came along and somebody gave them a piece of chocolate out of his kit and then everybody did, and soon those kids had more chocolate than they had seen in three years. I remember one little girl ran down the road and came back with an armload of flowers—and we each stuck one in the camouflage netting in our helmets.

I don't remember going ashore. I don't really know how I did, whether we had to wade or if we just ran up the beach when they dropped the gate. If there was heavy fire I don't remember. As I said, I don't remember a goddamned thing. I once read a story in a magazine about a fighter who got a damn good knock in the second round and kept fighting and along about the eighth round he was in his corner and he asked his manager what round it was and the manager said the ninth was coming up. He asked if he was winning and the manager said it would be close, but he thought so. That's the way I was.

The first thing I remember, and this is the God's truth, I'm sitting with my back to a German tank and there's guys all around me and we're eating C-rations, you know all those tiny tins and packages and stuff. We're eating and there's hellfire and corruption all around, and some Yankee Typhoons are blasting hell out of something down the road and all you could smell is blazing diesel fuel and burned paint and there's some bodies, Germans, kind of piled in a bundle a little way down the road, and if this isn't a battlefield, I don't know what is one.

A guy named Clark, the Bren gunner, is lying on the road beside me, and I ask him where we are and he says we're past the second bridge we're after and the planes are hitting the one ahead and we'll get that one before nighttime. The sergeant comes along and asks me if I'm all right and I say, "Sure, I'm fine, and how are you, sarge?" Just like that, like two guys meeting on a street in Toronto and passing the time of day.

I ask him then about the rest of the platoon and he says some of the boys got it. He mentions a guy named Ace Johnson from the Lakehead, a good pitcher, he used to pitch for our company softball team. Johnson got it just down the road, and a few got it at the beach.

That's all I remember about the invasion. In other words, I was there and I guess doing my job like everybody else, but so help me Christ, I don't remember a thing for about, say, oh six, seven hours. I couldn't tell you about it for a million bucks. Honestly. I guess you might say, my mind didn't like what was going on and just turned off, but my body just kept on going. Crazy, eh?

•◄►• *Approaching the Beach*

I remember D-day. We were going across in this landing craft, a pretty big one. You could see there was plenty doing up ahead, on the beaches and the cliffs. The Americans were over to the right, and we were with the British. I think it was just British, Canadians and Americans, but those three words took in an awful lot of ground. It seems we had Poles with us, good fighters, wild. It doesn't matter.

A few miles out we've got to stop, and the five or six other big landing craft, we all began to circle because shells were falling around us. They weren't aiming at us, just firing out our way and hoping for a hit. But the Germans still had planes, dive bombers, ME's. They caused some trouble. Then we went in closer and the orders came over the loudspeakers. Stuff we'd heard a thousand times: keep in touch with each other, don't take stupid chances because you're only leaving your platoon exposed. That sort of stuff. Once we got ashore it was just about every man for himself anyway.

Then I was surprised because it seemed we had a chaplain aboard. He was in the wheelhouse, I guess, and after our colonel said, "Good Luck"—and as I remember he came ashore six hours later, big hero—this chaplain came on the loudspeaker and we're getting pretty close, maybe only a mile away from the beach, and he says there, "Not much time, men," but he would leave us with the words from Exodus, when the Lord told Moses to take the Israelites back to Canaan. You see, I knew my Bible then. The right upbringing, Methodist mother, Presbyterian father, and Christ, what a circus on Sunday.

This chaplain, a Canadian, he wished us luck and then he said he'd leave us with the words from Exodus, the twenty-third chapter, the twentieth verse, and I dig out my map-marking pencil and my little pocket Bible and in the flyleaf I mark Exodus, twenty-three, twenty, and then a shell from a shore battery comes zooming down and starts skipping at us and runs alongside, making one big skip the length of half the ship and disappears, and that's all from the chaplain. He's probably too scared to read the verse for us, although I'm waiting for it. We're taking machine-gun fire now, so it's that close and then we're on the beach and that's another story.

Anyway, I manage to survive and about a month later I'm not doing anything and I remember this verse so I pull out ye old Good Book and look it up and it says: "But if ye hearken attentively to His voice, and do all that I say, then I will be an enemy to your enemies and an adversary to your adversaries."

That was fine, I thought. God was on our side and was going to kick the living beJasus out of Jerry, but it didn't quite work out that way. That chaplain he should have given us some real old-time religion, you know that stuff from the Old Testament, an eye for an eye and a tooth for a tooth. That's what we bloody well needed that day!

When I first went into action, I didn't know what the score was. Nothing added up. In Canada they showed us plenty of films, but they were sweet bugger-all and we knew it. They really taught you nothing. The clock started when you got out of those big trucks and a runner from the front started to guide you towards the company position, and this was maybe eighteen or twenty days after D-day, so the shit was really flying. June and July, and boy, there was some tough going in Normandy then.

There was this little village—I mean what had been a village. There were about a dozen of us, and the captain put three of us in one platoon and scattered the rest around and told us to watch the other fellows, the guys who'd been there a few days. I remember him saying that in this place nobody wins or loses, you just survive. Well, that was okay with me.

The sergeant of our platoon, the second platoon, he was telling us his name, and the name of the lieutenant, and that things had been quiet so far that morning, and I heard an awful racket of gunfire and artillery over to our right and I asked what that was and he said, "That's an American combat team over there. Texans. It's their turn today. We got it yesterday." Casual as all hell.

Funny how you remember the little things, but this sergeant said, "You guys all got your pull-throughs? Those weapons get clogged up awful fast, so keep them clean." It seemed a funny remark right in the middle of a war, to keep our rifle barrels clean. Anyway, it makes sense now.

Just then, there's this goddamned church steeple or tower and it has been three quarters knocked over, hit so there's mostly all but one side gone and suddenly there is a *pow* sort of noise and down it comes. And then a shell lands behind us, and another over to the side, and by this time we're scurrying and the sarge and I and another guy wind up behind a wall. The sergeant said it was an .88 and then he said, "Shit and shit some more."

I asked him if he was hit and he sort of smiled and said no, he had just pissed his pants. He always pissed them, he said, just when things started and then he was okay. He wasn't making any apologies either, and then I realized something wasn't quite right with me, either. There was something warm down there and it seemed to be running down my leg. I felt, and it wasn't blood. It was piss.

I told the sarge, I said, "Sarge, I've pissed too," or something like that and he grinned and said, "Welcome to the war."

•─→─• *The .88*

Ask any tank trooper, ask anyone about the .88 the Germans had. It was a staggering thing, in size, just a beautiful piece of death and destruction for us in the tanks, or for anything. When they got it in place those Germans used it like a rifle. I think that gun was our worst enemy, and I often wonder why Hitler didn't order 10,000 of the things, train half his divisions to use it and give it to us, square and fair between the eyes. He could have won the war with it.

In Normandy I saw one knock out eight of our tanks, one after another, and they didn't even know where the thing was hidden. Eight tanks, one after another.

You can wake up in a cold sweat remembering that we were popping away at those big bastards at 1,200 to 1,800 yards, our range, and they could blow our tanks to pieces at 3,000 yards. They got hundreds of tanks, God knows how many carriers, trucks and tens of hundreds of good men.

You know who used to get most of those .88's, apart from the Typhoons, the dive bombers when we pinpointed one? The fellows in the tin hats. Yep, the infantry, they could get in close and they'd get the German crew with their whizzing tiny bullets, their little machine guns, and there we were with the firepower of a gunboat, and we usually didn't stand a chance. Yep, those little infantry bullets whizzing by usually did the job for us.

•─→─• *Horses in the War*

There was a hell of a lot of things they never told us. They didn't tell us, or maybe our famed intelligence wasn't so good after all, but they didn't tell us that the Germans used a great many horses. Thousands of horses, doing every sort of job.

So it was a shock to find them in Normandy, thousands of them, and beautiful animals too. Germany must have looted horses from every country she took over and every ally, and they died in the thousands, too.

I remember at a crossroads on the Chambois-Trun Road, just off it, a column had been caught by fighters, hit from the air, and the slaughter was bloody awful. The Jerries just fled, those that didn't die there, taking to their heels over the fields, and there must have been 200 horses. A lot dead, but an awful lot standing in harness, pouring blood, or down and slashing and writhing around. We came up right after and all I had was a .45 and my driver had his rifle, and I swear to God I killed about 30 with my service pistol, at least 30, right between the eyes, even the ones standing and not wounded too badly, because if there was no help for the men, what help could there be for the horses? Then I borrowed the driver's gun and I killed off another 30 or so, maybe more, just going from one to the other. I came from an Alberta ranch, I know good horses and I love horses, but there was not a bloody thing else I could do.

•➤• *On the Road to Falaise*

Nobody likes to talk about massacres, as if they are where women and children and old men are killed, scalped, violated. You know what I mean. But massacres are just war.

On the road to Falaise, up the road from Caen, our army lost about 14,000 men. That was in about 20 days. Big battles were fought in other places and neither side lost that many men, but they gave us the toughest job of all and we stopped and whipped a whole German Army. Thousands of dead, thousands of prisoners, stopped them in their tracks, and what was left of that army was nothing. Maybe a division, out of an army.

So they massacred us and we massacred them, but it was our victory. Baberry and Le Hamel and Falaise go on our battle flags and they get nothing. But 14,000 casualties. I told my wife this. I said, "Get 14,000 men marching past you three abreast, and how long would it take them to pass?" She said she didn't know. A couple of hours maybe. I said more like from breakfast to dinner, and she just couldn't believe it.

She said, "Now I know what war is. I think I know now."

•➤• *Everything Was Long-range*

When I volunteered—you had to volunteer—when I volunteered for the Commandos all my buddies said I was nuts. Crazy. I might have been, but I was sick and tired of sitting around on my butt. Besides, there was glamour about the Commandos. Or better still, an air of glamourous violence.

They got us into terrific physical shape and they taught us to kill. Was it 35 different ways to kill a man, or 45? I forget. The instructors told us all about the Marquess of Queensbury rules of the gentlemanly art of self-defence, boxing, and then told us to do just the opposite. We learned to kick a guy's balls off, how to use a piano-wire garrote around the neck. Many ways, and all of them deadly—popping out a German's eyeball like you'd flick a marble in a kid's game. And we never used any of it.

From D-day Plus Two until the final shot was fired I never got close enough to a real live German in action to even try to flick out his eyeball. Nobody I knew did, I think. Everything was long-range. In fact, it was rare if you saw the enemy except when he was dead or wounded or when he and a bunch of his pals were surrendering. I saw enough of them, all right. A damned nuisance there at Falaise and towards the end.

As infantry we took and held the ground, but most of the dirty work was done by the artillery. They'd just stand back, dozens of big guns, and hammer shit out of German-held ground until there was nothing left, or they'd pull out, or start coming forward waving pillow cases, surrendering. It was the artillery and the tanks that did the dirty work, the softening up, they and the fighter-bombers which would plaster the roads and Jerry's gun emplacements with bombs and that stuff that burns. What is it? Yeah, napalm. God, what a mess that would make of whatever it hit.

I'm not saying the infantry wasn't in it. Up to their hips, their chests, their eyeballs. The P.B.I. [poor bloody infantryman] took more crap and unholy corruption than all the rest of the forces put together, believe me. I've seen it. Sometimes I don't think it's possible for men to take what we took for the first two months in Normandy, Caen, Falaise, all those little villages. We didn't do too bad in the landings. We didn't lose too many guys. It was up in the farmlands where we got shit.

I'm just saying that people always have the wrong idea of the soldier. Like me. I rarely saw Germans in action and I was in action about a year and a bit. It wasn't like the 1914 war in trenches. This was a different war, but I'll tell you this. In my war you could get killed just as quickly. A bullet or an H.E. shell doesn't play favourites. What it's in line with, it hits. Believe me.

•→• *The Flame Thrower*

The thing I hated was when they'd call up a carrier with a flame-thrower to burn out one of their pillboxes. I can still turn sort of green when I think of it.

I remember once there was this pillbox, and we could hear the guys inside yelling. We didn't know what they were yelling and I told the sergeant maybe they wanted to surrender but the door was jammed. I said it might have taken a hit and buckled and they couldn't get out. He said, "Fuck 'em," and yelled to the guy with the flame-thrower to turn on the heat, and you should have heard those Germans in that pillbox screaming. God, it was awful.

•◄►• *Seven Tanks in Six Weeks*

You might not believe it but in six weeks I had seven tanks shot out from under me.

Seven. Now I'd say that's a record, wouldn't you?

When I say I had seven tanks knocked out I mean just that. Like a horse that's been gut-shot by an elephant gun, it's never going to go again. Lots of guys had tanks nicked, turret smashed, suspension wrecked all to hell, treads gone. Those you could fix up. Mine, kaput all the way.

I lost three drivers, three gunners, two loaders, and in one tank, at Caen, they all just frizzled and I got out without a scratch. Being up there I had the best chance. The poor goddamned drivers were the ones I felt sorry for. Their chances were less than anybody's.

About the fifth tank I went to the command and I asked to be taken out of the tanks. They knew I wasn't chicken, but that I felt I was a jinx. The crew didn't think so, though—I never heard a peep out of them that the lieutenant was a jinx.

•◄►• *German Officers*

This was in Normandy, a little deeper inside Normandy than the coast. This was around Falaise in August, and you've got to understand there were three German armies in there, in this trap we had on them, and they were being cut into hamburger. The Poles were in there, the Canadians closing one hook of the pincer, and one hell of a lot of Americans and the big British Army under Monty [Field Marshal Montgomery] and there was no hope.

Put it this way. All the main German strength in France was just about ready for a Burton. It was an artilleryman's dream, and you could just keep slinging that H.E. [high explosive shells] in there and you were bound to hit something, from Tiger tanks to field hospitals. It was slaughter.

What were these German officers—and I mean their top officers—trying to do? I'll tell you what they were trying to do. The dumb assholes were trying to get their loot out, and if a staff car was full of wounded, then clean it out and back it up to such and such a village back door with our shells falling all around and load the truck up and try and get out.

We couldn't figure out at first where they were getting all the stuff. Okay, the fine wines came from cellars which may have been hidden by the French back in 1940. That's true. But they had fine crystal and silverware and jewelry and boxes of clothes and hams and fine silks and even wigs and Christ knows what else. Any auctioneer would have gone nuts with this stuff. There was car after car after truck after truck and these Germans, these officers, are trying to get it out.

Where? Sure as Christ made little apples they weren't going anywhere. Maybe with a Tiger tank if they could get the gas, but nowhere in a car. Soon as they hit the road, one of those Yank planes would come down and that would be it. One minute a car, next minute no car.

We saw staff car after car, maybe 30 to 50 altogether, just in around Moissy, tires shot out, burned, busted up, all to ratshit. Some S.S. guy had figured he'd get that car back to the Rhine and across it and into Germany and please the hell out of his lady love. Hell's bells, you couldn't have got out on foot, travelling by night in a rainstorm.

That was the highly trained German officer for you. When it got down to it, to hell with his men, nuts to the war, just let me get out with my loot. Screw the rest of you. And those poor lousy dogs in the Wehrmacht—that's the ordinary German foot soldier, the kids and old men from the farm towns of Saxony, real dumb but solid soldiers—they were dying like bloody flies. You couldn't do anything else but feel contempt for those German officers, their greed. They weren't soldiers. The dumb foot-sloggers were, though.

We were outside this village which had been pounded to nothing and a bunch of Poles came up from the other side. We'd heard them popping, and we knew they weren't house-cleaning. That had been done. They were killing the German wounded. They did it all the time, wild guys, sometimes too wild to be allowed to run around loose.

There was this staff car right by one of the village wells and two German officers were arguing that the stuff inside, dresses and cameras and wine, belonged to them. By some convention of war, I guess. Nobody was really paying any attention. We were really wondering whether the bastards had poisoned the well.

A couple of the Poles were messing around inside the Germans' car, throwing stuff around, and they found some cosmetics, rouge, lipstick, and they started painting, daubing their faces like Red Indians. One of the German officers snapped out something and the Pole stopped. Most Poles understand some German and it obviously was an insult. When it comes to the Polish, the Germans figure them pretty low.

This guy had a Tommy gun stuck into his big front pocket with the nose stuck out below. A big holster. He just lifted up that, kind of tilted the gun and let fly and cut those two Germans in half. Right at the old belly button. They didn't even stagger. Just booomp, down.

My lieutenant said to the Polish soldier he shouldn't have done that, and he just shrugged his shoulders and grinned. That was all. Two less Germans. Two less thieves, I guess.

•◄►• *It Was Him or Me*

I killed lots of men and I don't mind saying it. To me, they wasn't men but they was the enemy, and that's the main thing, and it was them or me and as you can see, I'm sitting here having a beer with you, so it was them a hell of a lot more than it was me.

I killed a Yank once. In that place they called the Falaise Pocket and the poor bugger, I guess he thinks I'm a German, and I know he's going to get me. Like I can just feel it, see. My intuition tells me I'm for it, so I give it to him. Poor bugger. A corporal from some Texas outfit. I puts his helmet over his face, see, so the dirt won't get in, and goes on, but that's what I'm telling you. It was never my intention to kill a Yank—some were fine lads—but he was shooting at me as if I was a German, It's him or me. So I shoot that boy even though I know he's a Yank. Oh, no doubt about it, sir, I did feel badly about it all.

•◄►• The Maple Leaf

It was while we were still on the Normandy beachhead that Ralston [Canada's defence minister] came over with some generals and he passed the word around that he wanted a paper in France like *The Maple Leaf,* which the boys were putting out in Italy. A paper for the troops.

Ralston told this to Malone [then Lieut. Col. Dick Malone] and Malone told me, "Okay, Smitty, you're in charge. Get cracking." By this time the fighting had moved up towards Caen and we decided that would be the best place to set up a newspaper, and Malone said I was to get in there as soon as I could. I went in with the 51st Highlanders.

I hunted around and finally I found a building marked Presse De Caenese, something like that, and it was a mess. There was a big rotary press but the Germans had done their dirty work. We found the pressmen all right. They were lying around their own press and every one had a bullet behind his ear. The Germans had used this press for propaganda during the occupation, see, and when they pulled out they made bloody sure the pressmen weren't going to help us. They'd also hosed down all the paper stocks, making it useless, and taken all the type and thrown it by the bucket load out into the weeds and grass and muck of the back yard. Besides having a press we weren't sure would work, we had no type, no typewriters, no paper, no reporters and no power. No juice.

God, but there was so much to do. The engineers fished a generator out of the Orne and we got them working on that, hooking it to the press, and I got a few others cleaning up the place. I went back to England and went through the holding units and rounded up a crew, linotypers—and by the way, for some reason, the Germans hadn't buggered up the linotypes—and pressmen and reporters and everybody we needed and we had priority, which was unusual in those days, and we got them over in a hurry along with some supplies and cable for the generator.

We spent about a week with tweezers on our hands and knees out in the weeds picking up the type and getting it assembled and back in the linotypes, and we dried out the paper in the sun so it was of some use. Finally by using ingenuity and round-the-clock work we were able to pour lead.

I was manager and Malone then was editor-in-chief and we had a staff of reporters and we also had the dupes of the war correspondents. We had access to them, and also a Morse code setup from England for news from Canada and the rest of the world and the usual pin-up girls, sports scores and Jane. Remember Jane? The comic strip girl who always wound up almost nude in every strip. The troops loved her.

To make a long story short, from the time Ralston gave the order that there had to be a paper until we ran off our first 20,000, only three weeks had passed. The fighting was still going on, the Germans hadn't been routed and we were putting out a four-page tabloid and somehow getting it up to the front every day. One paper for every five soldiers and God, how they fought to get their hands on it.

When we finally got to Brussels we moved into a newspaper plant called *Le Soir*. We used their equipment, a beautiful plant and life was easy. The circulation boys were doing a grand job, everything was fine.

One afternoon the Newfoundland Regiment was in town and a bunch came and dragged me out for a night on the town and I've got this bloody awful head next morning. Just bloody awful and at the 10 A.M. briefing, Colonel Malone tells us that a ship bringing up a load of newsprint for us had been sunk.

"What supply have we got left?" he asks, and I say, "One day, sir," and he says, "Smitty, go out and find some." He was the kind of officer who damn well expected you to do your job, carry out orders, and if you did it a certain way, he'd just turn his head and shut his eyes as to how you did it.

So I've got this bloody awful hangover and I think, well, I'll take my jeep and go for a fast ride with the windscreen down, and get some cold air into my head and do some thinking. So I'm tearing along outside Brussels and then what happened is what I call The Miracle. I'm passing a convoy, British Army Service Corps, and every one of those trucks is loaded with newsprint—300 tons. I wheel around and catch up and there's a sergeant in charge. Thank God, no officer. I ask him where the paper's going, and he says to 21st Army Group, they're going to start a newspaper for the Belgium civilians, and do I know where 21st Army Group is. I say, "Sergeant, I even know where their warehouse is. Follow me," and away we go. They drive up and unload like good boys and the sergeant gives me a receipt to sign and I make a scrawl nobody could ever read. He's happy, he's got his load delivered and his receipt signed, and away they go.

About five days later I'm with Malone and others at the briefing and he says there's one hell of a flap up at 21st Army Group. It seems somebody hijacked a convoy of newsprint which they were going to use to put out a paper for the Belgiums. The shit was really in the fan. Then he stopped and looked at me and said, "Oh no, Smitty, no, no," and I nodded, and he turned away and said, "Oh my God!"

I don't know how he worked it out, but out of our next shipment 21st Army Group somehow got their newsprint back. But that was one of the ways we put out *The Maple Leaf*. It was a lot of hard work, I met a lot of great guys and it was a lot of fun.

Romance in Canada

My Handsome, Wonderful Englishman . . . Being the Good Wife . . . An Affair with the Boss . . . Drifting into It . . . Husbands Overseas, or Something Like that . . . The Girls' Place . . . Not a Typical Service Wedding . . . A Very Nice Man . . . I Guess We Should Feel Ashamed . . . A Piece of Heather

The stories of Canadian servicemen living it up with British girls and having wild old times had their parallels at home. In Canada the wives and fiancées of the men abroad were lonely, and there were plenty of men about. Every seaport had its ships and sailors, there were army camps scattered across the country, and there were tens of thousands of Commonwealth airmen in training—all looking for excitement.

One woman in Winnipeg said, "I knew what he was doing over there. I'd have been a fool if I didn't, so I had a right to live my own life too."

And I remember one fellow in Brandon who told me that the last five girls he'd taken home from dances had been married to servicemen, he said it always gave him a funny feeling to see their faces smiling out of photographs on a table, and then he said, "But what the hell."

There must have been much tsk-tsk-tsking in many places after the war and whispered confessions when the serviceman came home, but we'll never know.

•◄►• *My Handsome, Wonderful Englishman*

I was nineteen when they finished the air station and Brandon was really too far to go for a day so the young officers would come into the town and we'd invite one or two or three every weekend to stay at our home, our lovely big home, with Manitoba elms around. We had a lovely garden and large lawn, really too big a lawn, but we'd play croquet and there was the creek at the bottom of the garden. My father was a doctor.

The next summer, I'd be twenty, and I just helped Mother and her maid around the house and lived a rather sedate and genteel life, for a Canadian prairie home, I mean, and one day this chap came to the house. He was English, of course, and he wasn't in training. No, he'd fought in the Battle of Britain and now he was a squadron leader, oh, and medals galore, and was one of the higher officers at the station. I just fell like a ton of bricks. Oh, how I remember it. In an absolute dither. Now I was twenty, mind, but I'd never been in love. Never. Not even puppy love, you might say, and it was love at first sight. I guess I should say it too, but I was a virgin.

I think he felt the same way and that May and early June, just the most wonderful time of the year, he came over every Sunday and Dad liked him, and he'd occasionally borrow somebody's car and we'd drive out on the section roads. I was in heaven, although not a soul, not a soul knew. It was my secret and I think I kept it well.

While the weeks went by, I wouldn't have cared if the war went on for ever. I had my handsome, wonderful Englishman with me. We'd kiss and talk, but we never made love. I mean, of course, I was still a virgin. Perhaps I puzzled him, or frustrated him, but he was so very polite.

Then one afternoon, a Saturday, he phoned, and after a few minutes he said he was coming over in a car and he'd bring a blanket and we'd go down to a sort of lover's lane a few miles away. I protested, I guess, saying some other fellows from the station were coming and I'd have to be the good hostess, and I can remember his words: "Not tonight, my dear, and surely you must know by now this nonsense has gone on quite long enough."

He picked me up that night and, yes, we did go to lover's lane and we made love, several times, and I would be a fool not to say I was in another world. I adored him. I just adored him. And then he brought me back about midnight and maybe my eyes looked like twin stars and he walked me up the verandah and kissed me, right in front of my mother and father. Now in our family that wasn't done, unless. . .Well, you know what I mean about unless. Unless we were going to be married.

He didn't mention the next day, but often he'd have to fly, they trained almost every day, and some Sundays he'd zoom the house. He'd borrow one of the trainers and give us a scare and then about six o'clock he'd come driving up our lane. He often did that. The next day, Sunday, well, he didn't come and he didn't phone and I was beside myself and Monday, no phone call, and my mother said why didn't she phone him and ask him for dinner that night? We'd done it before. I said okay, fine.

Mother went to the phone and I heard her ask for the orderly office and I heard her talking and then she asked to be switched over to the commanding officer, a group captain, and I heard her asking questions and I guess I don't have to tell you the answer.

She said, "Thank you, yes, there's nothing you can do," and she put down the phone and came over and she said, "Betty, your English flyer went back to England yesterday. They went by train. He was taking back a group of trained men and when I asked if he was coming back, the group captain said no, it wasn't likely. He'd known for two weeks he'd be leaving Sunday."

Yes, I know, there's really not much anyone can say. I was just a little prairie flower, happy and in love.

•◄►• *Being the Good Wife*

My husband was a "Saturday night" soldier, the militia, and he couldn't wait for the war to start and when it did, zoom, he was called up right away and then he was happy.

When he was going overseas he brought me home to this town where his mother was and he never introduced me to anybody and there was no women's auxiliary or anything like that where a woman could work, and his mother, where I lived, she never introduced me to anybody and there I was with my baby daughter and there I stayed. Looking at four walls when I wasn't in the war plant.

Sure, I could have gone out partying. It was one long party anyway, but I guess it was my strict upbringing that a woman didn't go out with strange men, and my mother-in-law sure wouldn't be having anything like that going on under her roof, and the neighbourhood too. If you went out and your husband was overseas, then the neighbours would talk and talk and point at you in the streets and you were some kind of lowest of the low. You just worked your shift and came home and looked after the baby—and that went on for year after year.

I'm not bitter. I guess I could be. I know that when my husband was overseas it was just one long party. He used to write and say he was going on another leave and he always seemed to be on leave, but I stayed home and did what I was supposed to do. Be the good wife. I know, oh sure, hundreds of women didn't. Thousands of women didn't. Lots of women I knew didn't. And maybe I should have too. Maybe I would have actually have been a better person for it, had some fun. But there were too many pressures on me. Now, I wish I'd gone out and had some fun.

I got to be secretary to the wing commander at the manning pool and if I thought I was pretty big stuff he let me know ten times a day I wasn't, in front of everybody—and this was actually during the time we were having an affair. He was stepping out on his wife back in Ontario somewhere and I had a sort of arrangement with a boy I went to high school with. He was in England with the air force, and it was just a letter-a-week thing, nothing more.

When the boss went to Ottawa to headquarters, by some strange coincidence I was offered a job down there as his secretary and at better money. And even though it was only Ottawa it was a lot closer to Toronto or New York than in a small prairie city, so I went. Besides, I missed the big dumb gazook. He was old enough to be my father, but I did miss him.

Two years in Ottawa. Two years in a prison, and you cannot, you can never imagine what it was like. Same faces, same restaurants, same shows, same everything. Even the flowers on Parliament Hill, they all looked the same and, God knows, to a prairie girl like me, spring was the best time of the year. I used to date, too, but there must have been 20 or 25 girls to every eligible man and by that I don't mean the acey-deuceys at Rockcliffe or the other air force establishments around. I mean eligible men, not in the service, the men in External Affairs or Justice or staff officers, somebody with a future and a blue suit and bowler hat, and not some guy pounding a typewriter in army records or busting his knuckles on a wrench on some Anson trainer. You know. If you're going somewhere, there should be a bit of class involved.

Every landlady in Ottawa and across the river was against you. Rents high for squeaky little rooms. Houses filled with girls and creeps, and a fight for the bathroom, and if you were fourth in line, no damn hot water. God, but I used to like being invited out to Smiths Falls where I had an aunt and just get in the tub and soak and soak and soak. I'd take a pint of my liquor ration, gin, always gin, and I'd take it into the bathroom and soak and soak and drink the gin and no matter how beat I was or downhearted or depressed, an hour of that hot water and the gin drained and I was a new girl. My aunt used to go into hysterics. Here I'd come out of the tub, rosy and blooming and half jigged and she'd laugh her head off. Old Aunt Barbara was quite a girl. A widow and she had two old boys on the string and a laugh a million times a day.

My wingco found himself another, a tall blonde from Moncton named Dulcie and as he had no chance of going overseas then because he was over fifty, he decided to concentrate on divorcing his wife and marrying the Moncton Monster. I backed out of the picture, quit my job and left Ottawa on a train just jammed with troops going home on leave. This was Christmas of 1944. On that train I met the man I was to marry, about three years later. A nice guy.

•◄►• *Drifting into It*

In 1941 I was just 16 when I suddenly grew up and boy, did I ever grow up. Betty Grable had nothing on me. All over. I still have some pictures of me at Centre Island, me in a bathing suit on the beach and I was, as they say, stacked. And that's where I met my husband.

His name was Gary and his family had a small farm some-where near Peterborough. Gary was a good-looking cuss and soon I was meeting him about three times a week because he was training just outside Toronto and could get the mail truck or some truck every night and go back out with it. When I took him home my dad was in one of his good moods that night and he took to Gary. I should say my mother was sick most of the time, lying on the chesterfield or in her room, but she met Gary and said he was a nice boy. From those two, that was a compliment and a half.

Okay, quickly. I married him, at City Hall, on a Friday afternoon, and we went to Niagara Falls for the weekend and that was just about my married life. He got notice, it was posted that his bunch were going to New Brunswick for final training, and when it came time for him to come back on his embarkation furlough, he just didn't show up. I guess he found another girl in Halifax or somewhere.

Anyway, no Gary—and I can't really say I was heart-broken. Nothing like that. I guess I was more pissed off—excuse me, angry—than anything. I wasn't jilted, because he was my hus-band, but I guess you could say I was abandoned, but I kept telling myself I didn't care. I wasn't pregnant—those three days at Niagara Falls hadn't taken, and I was getting my allowance and the twenty bucks he signed over. I'd quit school, of course, and was working in a restaurant on Yonge Street and, all in all, you might say, I wasn't doing too bad. I got a letter from him saying he was going overseas. Just that. Not love and kisses, just so long. Maybe I should have been suspicious about a guy that my dad and mother liked. But remember, I was only sixteen.

From then on it was the same old story, you might say. I started going to dance halls downtown with my girlfriend Maggie Smythe, just looking for fun. All the boys were in uniform and everybody had a lot of money and there was fun around.

The first time. It was in a dance hall on the second floor and it was painted green. I always remember that. The Beer Barrel Polka was big stuff then, everybody danced it, and I think the Lambeth Walk. There were a whole lot of new dances, and all these good-looking boys. One I got to like, he was an air force something or other at the manning pool, he asked if i would go to a hotel with him and I didn't even think it over too much. I just said yes. Yes, just like that. I wanted to. I wanted him and he wanted me. So we went to this hotel just down the street. It might have been the Ford Hotel, but I'm not sure. We made love and then he took me to a nice restaurant and we had fish and chips, and that was the first time I ever tasted that kind of sauce they put on the side of your plate. I always remember that.

The next night or the next time I was there we went again and this time he gave me a cashmere scarf. Soft. I won't say that's the way it started, but a cashmere scarf, that was something. So the next time a fellow asked me I said yes, and this one gave me 3 dollars. When we came back, Maggie and I went into the little girls' room and she said, "Are you doing it?" I said I had and she asked how much and I said 3 dollars. Three dollars was not enough, she said. Five dollars, that's how much I should get.

You just seem to drift into these things. Quite honestly, cross my heart, I didn't think of it as prostitution. I wasn't hanging around the Union Station or the hotels or, well, those places. These were just real nice guys, mostly air force, who were at this dance. Oh ho, what a dumb little girl I was.

I guess it got through my thick skull what I was doing when I wasn't getting a meal or a scarf but 10 or 15 dollars a night, from the two or three guys taking me out. One night I did four fellows and I found out, I noticed, about the third guy that it was the same hotel room all the time. These fellows had come in from Trenton or someplace and took a room just for a good time.

Then Maggie came to me and she said we should rent a room by the month, the two of us and she would use it half an hour and then me, and then she would, and we couldn't get our times mixed up and there would be the rent and the hotel clerk, he'd be paid off and we'd give him some more for the police, the cop on the beat, if he got suspicious. She said, "Mary, remember, this is a business. You're not selling fountain pens in Woolworth's, you're selling your body, so you got to keep clean. Keep clean and pretty"—and remember, I was only seventeen at the time.

I think I was making about 700 dollars a month within a couple of months, working with Maggie, and I was away from home and living over near Jarvis and dressing well, and I never solicited. Just the dance halls and if some guy, usually an officer, wanted me to go down to London or up to Ottawa with him, well I did. I was a prostitute but I don't feel I was a whore. A whore, I've always thought, stands on street corners.

This went on for two more years. We never had a pimp, and when Maggie left for Halifax I kept on alone. I was never lonely and I was never arrested. You can't think of me as doing this alone. I knew lots of girls, oh hell, dozens of them whose husbands were away, overseas, everywhere, and they did it, and some right in their own homes. Some with their own kids in the next room.

Look at me. Do I look as though I had a terrible time? The prostitute all beat up by some drunks? That never happened to me, but it did to some of the other girls but I was just lucky, and I always let them know two things. One, that I was a lady, and the other was that I was the boss and no funny stuff.

We were a club too. Like on Fridays, afternoons, we'd often get together at one of the girls' apartments and paint each others' legs. You know, leg paint. They didn't have nylons then, the war, so you used leg paint. I think there were seven colours you could use and we'd paint each others' back seams and drink coffee or tea and talk and mend clothes and giggle. We'd never talk men. We weren't professionals in the sense I'd heard that kind of girl talk in cafés when I'd be in there. We were just kids, and every moment seemed to be excitement. Pure excitement. You might say, though, you had to like going to bed with a feller. You would have to say that.

Then Gary got killed in England. His plane was in an accident. I never did get the details. The chaplain's letter just didn't make too much sense, just that there had been an accident and everybody died as brave men. Some nonsense like that.

I thought it over—and remember I wasn't more than nineteen at the time—and I had nearly 5,000 dollars in the bank and 4,000 in Victory bonds and so I just quit. I just quit and I stayed away from downtown Toronto and moved into another apartment and read a bit and learned to cook and had one friend who I'd let come in. He was an officer, a nice guy. After the war I took a trip across the country and on the train coming back, the C.P.R., I met this guy who got on at Banff and we hit it off and I married him a month later. I told him my money came from my aunt's estate and I had no other relatives, and really I didn't, far as I was concerned, and that's about all there is to say about it. I'm happy now.

•◀▶• *Husbands Overseas, or Something Like That*

What I remember about the war probably isn't what you're getting from the other guys. I remember girls. I never asked myself whether it was because they were doing their patriotic duty, their bit for the boys in uniform, or whether they just loved to screw.

I was a wireless instructor at Vimy, at Kingston. No point staying around Kingston on a leave. We'd go into Toronto. We'd take the afternoon train, getting into Union Station about seven o'clock, and usually you had a place to go. A friend's place, or the Y.M.C.A. or Sally Ann would find you a place. There were plenty of places. The guy in uniform got treated well in Toronto.

Then. Yep, then. This would be on a nice sunny day in spring, summer and into fall, but at noon we'd stroll around to College Street, where the new Eaton's store was, and there would be the gals. Lined up, on either side of all the doors, all nice girls, but lined up like whores on Shaftsbury Avenue or Piccadilly. And along we'd come. I was a corporal, my buddy was too. Boots you could see your faces in. Creases sharp enough to cut you. Everything perfect. When I come to think of it, we were dazzling, far better-looking than the girls.

You could have your pick. Maybe you saw an old friend, somebody you'd had before, or maybe it was somebody new who caught your eye. There wasn't much dozie-do about it, not much of what you'd call flirting. Hell, there was none. You'd ask if she was busy that night and of course she wasn't. If she had been she wouldn't have been out there. You usually clicked nine times out of ten, fantastic, and they were all nice girls. I mean good-looking. They took care of themselves.

They didn't get to buy much lipstick or nylons or good clothes, everything was short or rationed, or both, but they did their best. You had to hand that to them.

The next thing was to arrange to meet them at five-thirty, usually right where they were standing, because they usually brought their good things to work with them in a bag, so it was away we go.

But first you went over near the old City Hall and got a room. There were hotels that did only a full house on Saturday nights, and maybe Thursday if a guy was on a 72. Next step, if you hadn't already done it, was to line up a bottle and then a party. But if there was no party, then you'd take her to dinner and maybe a show, but usually dancing. But I've had girls who didn't want the dinner or the show or the dancing or even a couple of drinks to warm themselves up, something I always had to do. All they wanted was to get up those stairs and into that bed and stay there. It was a grand life, and too bad it all ended.

I want to make one thing clear though. These girls weren't chippies. They weren't whores. They were just shopgirls who worked at Eaton's for maybe 17 dollars a week and lived at home, and life was pretty dull for them. It was fun for them, and for us. I don't think there was much of this eat, drink and be merry for tomorrow we may die stuff. None of that French Foreign Legion baloney. These girls liked a good time. Why, a lot had boyfriends overseas or somewhere and you'd be surprised how many of them were married. Husbands overseas, or something like that.

•◄►• *The Girls' Place*

Say what you will, but I always thought it was asking just a bit too much of wives, leaving them at home for two or three years during the war, cooped up in small houses somewhere with hardly enough money, and getting letters from our husbands saying what a good time they were having on leave in London.

I didn't have to read between the lines to know that there was jiggery-pokery going on. After all, they were healthy young men and London was London, and I didn't expect my Alex to be playing checkers at Canada House or, after the first time, visiting the Houses of Parliament. Oh, I knew what he was doing. He was always complaining about no money, not having enough money, but after the war he told me about the motor oil and gas and tools and tires he and his friends used to sell to the English. To cab drivers and farmers. There was money coming in.

And us. Did you know what a sergeant's wife made? Don't even think of a private's wife. It was scandalous. How they expected us to live I don't know, and it wasn't much easier either, I'll tell you, when they gave us the children's bonus in '44. You could just get by, and that was being generous. Without my parents, my sisters passing down shoes and clothes for the kiddies, I couldn't have done it, and none of my friends could have. I used to go to church, when I used to go, and hear Mr. Macdonald up there in the pulpit like some sort of god, telling us about the sacrifices our husbands were making. Well, what about the sacrifices *we* were making, sitting out on the bald prairie in some little wooden house with the wind howling around, and digging out our own walks so the kiddies could go to school and oh, I could go on. And do you think anybody ever came around to help out? Not a chance.

That was the way it was the first two years, up to about school's-out time, June, in 1943. I had these three friends, and we were sitting on the lawn one afternoon slapping mosquitoes and drinking lemonade and just plain bitching, I guess you'd call it, and somehow I guess we were all thinking about the same thing, and when it got down to brass tacks I guess we had decided to rent a cottage for a month at Sylvan Lake.

If I remember, the rent was 20 dollars a week, and if one of us rented it then the other three girls could move in and I think we had, oh, let's see, nine children among us and all about four, three, six, in there, and 20 dollars split four ways was 5 dollars a week and what the landlord, the owner of the cottage, didn't know wouldn't hurt him. It was nice, big and roomy and a big verandah, and we put out two big tents behind. In those days everybody had tents because that's the way you took your holidays, with a tent beside a lake.

That was a summer, let me tell you. There was an air force training station somewhere near and the boys used to come for weekends from the army camp. It seemed the place was always full of men, young ones and full of the old zip, and there was an outdoor dance hall at Sylvan Lake, and these guys could always get booze. What our guys in England were doing, well, we couldn't care less. It was what *we* were doing that was fun. I'm not going to tell you what went on, but plenty did, and all we had to do was make sure that the fellows used . . . those things. We made sure of that. Darn sure of that. Fun was fun, but a baby was a baby.

There was rationing, but what's rationing when one girl had her own farm and Josie's father had a farm, and we'd say to the fellows that they had to pay tickets, buy tickets at the door, and we didn't want money but vegetables and milk and cream and booze would do very well, thank you, so we never went hungry.

This cottage became known around as The Girls' Place. I imagine it was called other things too—that I prefer not to go into—but The Girls' Place would do, and it was quite a place. We had no trouble from the police. Half the nights you'd have a police car parked tight up against the back window with the window open and their radio set turned up so they could hear.

That went on next summer, all next summer for two months, and my husband came home in March of 1945. He wasn't in the beer parlor one night before he heard about our goings-on. He came home drunk or three sheets to the wind and he wants to know about it and I said, "Fine, and tell me about Piccadilly, and how was the squiff in Glasgow?" That shut him up, so I knew I had him dead to rights and the next night, he's back and he's been over at Bentley snooping around, or over at Red Deer which was near Sylvan and he says, "You've been running a whorehouse, you bitch," and he's so mad he's going to bop me one and I pick up a frying pan and I say, "One more crack like that and I'll flatten your nose. I mean it, Jack, I mean it."

So we've got this truce. I don't say a word about what I've done, and I don't ask him what he's been up to, and we get along. It's not perfect, but we get along. Things worked out, but if others had done it the way we had, then there would have been fewer divorces around, and in that one part of the country alone, I can think of six or eight right off who got divorces.

Far, far too many quick marriages, you see, a couple of days together before he'd have to go back to camp and then three years, four years, two years away. What else could you expect?

Why, I knew the clerk in the general store in town far better than I knew my own husband, and I never was closer to that kid than with the counter between us and me asking for a bar of soap or a can of tomatoes. They were hard times for all of us. Unnatural times would be a better word.

•◄►• *Not a Typical Service Wedding*

I nearly didn't get married at all. We were in Victoria and we'd set the date, December 29, 1941, and we had it all arranged for the Douglas Hotel, just a few people. About 15 or so. My husband was in uniform then.

Then the minister phones and says he can't make it, and that set my husband off and he said we should have a few drinks while he figured things out, and about half the marriage liquor went while he figured things out. So we call this other minister, a civilian, and he said he'd do it, but we'd have to go to Esquimalt. So away we went, and the boys were getting pretty high by this time.

Anyway, we get there even in the blackout and it's as dark a night as you'll ever see, but we get there. And just as we go in the minister's house, well, the damned air raid warning went. It was a phony, naturally, but they were always pulling these stupid stunts. Who'd want to bomb Victoria anyway? So the minister says sorry and grabs his tin hat and rattler, and it turns out he is an air raid warden and he's got to be at his post to do whatever they were supposed to do. Direct traffic or stand on his silly head. Something. So my husband says we should have a drink on that, wait until the minister gets back.

In about an hour he's back but the wedding liquor is gone by this time and my husband is feeling no pain whatsoever! Believe me. He's about ready to pass out, and the best man is staggering. The minister says he can't marry a man in that condition. Wrong in the eyes of God or some damned thing, and I said he'd marry us or I'd see to it that he'd never marry another person. I think I even threatened to burn his damned house down.

Well, his wife is there and she tells him to go ahead. I guess the old silly wanted to go back to bed. It's late by this time. So we get married.

Then the old boy—in fact he's so old he doesn't even have a church any more—he said he'd like to toast the bride. He always did it, he said, and what does he do but reach down into the cabinet of a gramaphone and haul out a bottle of rum. Not even touched. I can see the way the boys look at it that he won't have it long, and the best man grabs it from him and hands him a 10-dollar bill and says, "Thanks, Rev. Two bucks for the wedding and eight bucks for the booze, and thanks," and we all high-tail it out the door with the minister looking at the 10 dollars in his hand.

I knew then that if I was going to have a wedding night I'd have to do something quick before Johnny and Mike got on the outside of that bottle. So when we're hoofing it along back to Victoria looking for a taxi, I accidentally on purpose slap my hand down and *kerplunk*, crash, there's the rum bottle smashed. No more rum.

It's so dark, you see, that nobody can see anyway. We're just stumbling along and Mike is cursing, God, but that man cursed, and he is cursing at me and there's Johnny and the rest just standing there and they don't know what's going on, and then Johnny gets the drift and he wallops Mike and gets a good one back and soon the whole bunch are fighting. In the dark, mind you, and we girls are off to one side and when we get it straight the guys have got **bloody** noses and their uniforms are ripped and it's a mess.

As a service wedding, you can say it was kind of unique, wouldn't you say?

•◆• *A Very Nice Man*

I wrote him every Monday, Wednesday and Friday. Those V-mail letters. Remember the blue ones? Three times a week, with what was happening and he wrote three times a week and never about the raids. It was just a sort of casual talk between two good friends, I guess. This was in 1943.

Remember that year, the year of the huge daylight raids over the German cities? It was inevitable death for so many of our men because you just had to look at the casualty lists to see what was happening. Maybe they shouldn't print casualty lists in the newspapers. It was slow death for us at home too. I knew one day the big black car would pull up in front of my house and the chaplain would get out and that would be it. Dick would be dead, another bomber pilot lost. I'd seen it happen twice on our street already.

He came, of course. An older man and very grave and I had the feeling I wasn't there but somehow hovering up in the air over our heads and hearing him say the right words. Over Dortmund. Courage, my dear. A brave soldier. I dried my eyes and thanked him and then thanked the Lord he hadn't given us a child. Knowing Dick only a year and married only five months, somehow, well, things would get better.

I moved into an apartment and then I took a job in a war plant welding things to things for radios, and about six months later I put his pictures away. The war ended and I stopped thinking of my dead husband, Dick, the good hockey player, the skier, my lover and husband. After a while I'd try and remember his face and I couldn't, and finally I could only think of him as a very nice man I'd known for such a short time.

•◂▸• *I Guess We Should Feel Ashamed*

The things we used to do. I guess we should feel ashamed. I guess we just didn't care. Not in those days. There were so many men.

There was this one fellow. Good-looking. He looked so good in his uniform. Big. A lieutenant. He was all man. He wanted to marry me before he went overseas and I said no, I'd take a rain check. I said I had to think about it, or something like that. I had him dancing on a string so much he'd take any excuse, and even if he didn't believe it, he'd make himself believe it.

He wrote every day. Every bloody day, mind you. At first I'd read them and answer, maybe one to his three, but what could I say? That I was going out with every Tom, Dick and Harry, my boss, the engineers in the plant, anybody who asked me? For Christ sakes, I was having the time of my life. I hadn't had much fun in my life and now it was a full-time job, you might say.

Working eight hours, playing . . . uh, about ten hours and sleeping about four—and I loved it. It was whoopee all the way.

Sometimes I'd get seven or eight or twelve letters from him at a swoop. Depending on how the ships sailed, or the planes or however those blue letters got back. They'd be lying on the hall table in my apartment and somebody would come to pick me up and see them and I might make some crack like, "Oh, letters from an old boyfriend." Sometimes. Or, "They're all crazy about me." I wonder now what those fellows thought of me. I mean, letting some soldier's mail just lie there. I was too young and too giddy to even think about those things.

And something else. Oh yeah, this was really something. This overseas lieutenant had been a commission salesman and he had connection somehow. Don't ask me how he did it but every so often, maybe once a month, a little guy would come up to the office of the plant and to my desk and he'd hand me a parcel. Just that. Walk up, hand me this parcel, maybe give me a little smile and away he'd go. There would be half a dozen silk stockings, silk panties, lingerie. Real expensive stuff. Now let me tell you, in those days, silk was class, baby, and here in the war with no silk anywhere, this little guy in Edmonton seems to have had his mitts on some. Maybe not much, but enough for this gal.

So I'd write the poor guy another lovey-dovey letter. It was sad, really. A kid of nineteen, which was what I was, without two brain cells to rub together, and putting a very nice guy through the hoops.

You know, finally I couldn't even stand to see his letters. They'd come and sometimes there would be so many, ten or fifteen, that the post office had put a string around them, and I'd just throw them in a cardboard box in the closet. Honest to God, that's what I did. I just could not stand the sight of them.

My conscience, of course. I know that now. I was being the proper little bitch . . . oh, yes, don't deny it and I just couldn't face up to it all. But I wasn't the only one. To hear the girls talking in the canteen at work, it seemed half the guys overseas must have been jacked around by someone at home.

This went on for two and a half years. I don't think he missed 20 days in all those years, and one day I was clearing things up and I decided, well, I just burned all those letters. Threw the box in the garbage, and then I was going to write him a Dear John, tell him to get himself a nice Scottish girl like my mother must have been and forget me.

I didn't, of course. I know now why. Maybe I didn't know

then. I wanted those little parcels to keep coming, that's what I wanted.

I didn't have to write that letter. He was killed. A friend of a friend was in the same place, and he wrote and said Harry had been killed in a bomb explosion in France. I guess I haven't done much thinking about it for a long, long time. But I know this now, I wouldn't do now what I did then.

•━━• *A Piece of Heather*

It was a day like today, actually, a bit windy and the sun was shining, the morning, and I was sitting in this little restaurant on Fraser Street. I think it was called Triget's or like that and this soldier came in and he recognized me from being on the baseball team at school because he'd been on the senior boy's team. I didn't know him, but he came down and sat with me and talked with me and said that he was going overseas and would I spend the day with him. At first I thought no, and then I thought I believed him, and so we went for a drive in his dad's car and we went down to Point Roberts, and we sat on the beach for a couple of hours and we walked around all day and just talked.

It was all boy-and-girl conversation. We talked about the future and dreams for the future, and I was doing most of the talking about the future and I asked him about the future and he said no, he didn't think about the future because he said he wasn't coming back. Of course, your first reaction was to say, "Don't be silly." And he said no, he had this feeling that he wouldn't come back, and he said that he would send me something from over there to thank me for spending the day. And then he said that if anything happened to him, he was going to give his mother my name and address and she'd tell me.

And he did. He sent me a piece of heather from Scotland that he'd picked when he was on furlough. And then one day in the spring, just before the war ended, his mother phoned me and told me that he'd been killed in action. I kept the heather for many, many years after, and then I don't know what happened to it.

It was not a love thing. There was nothing involved. There was not even kissing in it. Just talking, communication. In fact, hurried communication, because the next day he had to go back to his base to go overseas.

I think he felt that day that everything he saw with me, everything he saw at home, the sky and the sea, he must have thought, "I must have a real hard look at this, because it will be the last time I will see it."

That is why he asked me, I'm sure. He wanted someone to share it with him. He didn't have a girl but he wanted someone not his family who he could write to, to tell what he thought. Because, afterwards, he knew he was going to die.

Above: The sign certainly is explicit enough in this shelled Normandy village on June 23, 1944.

Below: Street by street, house by house, often room by room, Canadians moved through Normandy, clearing out Hitler's self-proclaimed "master race" of tough soldiers. This action took place July 10, 1940, at Caen, the northern French city the Germans fought hardest to hold to protect their line. It was shelled and bombed to rubble.

Above: Three Red Cross nurses just behind the lines at Arromanches, Normandy, on July 23, 1944: H. O'Donnell, T. N. Woolsey and J. Mackenzie—and have you guys thought about a reunion?

Below: Provost Corps soldiers Chess Groves, Art Geddes and Aime Cyr get a big welcome from the girls at Fleury-sur-Orne in Normandy in late July. Where are they now, the soldiers and the girls?

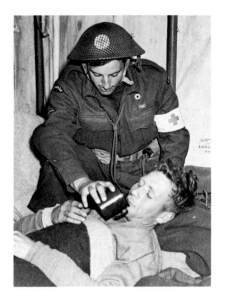

Left: The casualties? There were thousands, usually from mortar and shell, and it was the policy to air-lift all wounded back to England within 48 hours. Treatment was the very best and the recovery rate was highest of any war to date. Private R. Weaver gets a cup of water from corpsman M. J. Marantette prior to an aeromedical flip to England.

Below: Not forgotten. Three Frenchmen place flowers on the grave of a Canadian soldier at Bernières-sur-Mer while the fighting rages not far away. Every summer, hundreds of Canadians make pilgrimages to graves in military cemeteries throughout Italy and north-west Europe.

Above left: By the very nature of war, every nation consumes its youth with ferocity. This soldier, a fighting man in France, was like countless thousands of other young Canadians, caught up in a struggle he probably did not understand. Getting home again was his main objective.

Above right: If there is only a horse-trough available, that will do. Captain E. W. Owenship lathers off the grime of battle at Fresnoy-le-Puceau.

Below left: Rosie the Rivetter was an American term, but it applied also to tens of thousands of Canadian girls and women who worked for years in war plants. Through it all they laughed and smiled—and loved the good pay and the independence it bought.

Right: The Mighty Lancaster. The four-engined bomber that carried the horrors of the London Blitz and Coventry back into Germany's heartland with heavy bomb loads. A grizzled Lanc skipper said, "Such a sweet airplane. I'll love her forever."

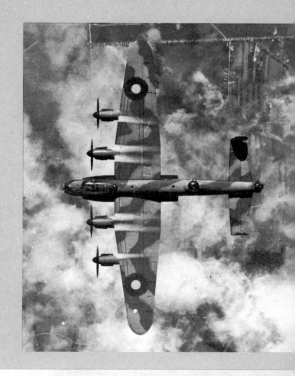

Below: Hamburg! As well known a target as Berlin during the war, it was hammered relentlessly by British and later American bomber fleets to cripple its huge military production. When war ended, the city was rubble but quickly bounced back in the remarkable post-war West German resurgence.

Opposite page. Top: German guards rummage in a garbage dump in a P.O.W. camp for scraps from Red Cross food parcels. They were often as hungry as the prisoners. This picture was taken with a camera swapped for food from a guard.

Middle: The Gondoliers *was a favourite production in Allied P.O.W. camps. Sets and costumes were extravagant.*

Bottom: Fully confident they would survive, two Allied P.O.W.'s wrote a book called Barbed Wire *about life in a German camp and took advance orders in their camp. It is believed about 5,000 were printed in England and distributed after the war. Some copies exist in Canada today.*

This page. Below: On a bits-and-pieces clandestine radio, men of Winnipeg and Quebec regiments listen to news of the Japanese surrender. Many prisoners of the Japanese worked for years on barely subsistence-level rations in coal mines, airport construction sites, steel mills and shipyards—all contrary to the Geneva Convention.

Right: Remember the war bride? In the few months following the victory in Europe, more than 43,000 brides of Canadian servicemen arrived in Canada. Some, disillusioned with their new home, went back to Britain—but the vast majority stayed.

Vancouver Province

Below: On October 26, 1945, the H.M.S. Glory steamed into Esquimalt, B.C., harbour with the bulk of survivors of two Canadian battalions captured by the Japanese at Hong Kong at Christmas, 1941. Three wives stand dockside welcoming their men.

Bomber Command

You Never Got to Know Them . . . "Goose Pimples in My Gut" . . . A Rear Gunner . . . Like a Football Game . . . The First of the Real Big Raids . . . Evasive Action . . . "Flak!" . . . It Was Bad Every Time . . . Collisions . . . A Most Interesting Chap . . . In the Cemetery . . . All Shot to Pieces . . . Dresden . . . Writing the Letter

---

The operational record of 514 Squadron between its first mission to Düsseldorf on November 1, 1943, until May 24, 1945, was 3,800 sorties, 73 Lancaster aircraft lost, and more than 12,000 tons of bombs dropped. The target list reads like a map of Germany: Mannheim, Ludwigshafen, Frankfurt, Dresden, Wiesbaden, Koblenz, Stettin, Dortmund, Munich, Augsburg, Hanover, Kiel, Bremen, Cologne, and on and on and on.

That was just one squadron with Canadians.

More than 10,000 R.C.A.F. personnel were lost in Bomber Command. More than 10,000 out of 41,000 fatalities for all of Canada's three services.

There was never all that much publicity about them. The night-by-night duty of going there and coming back (if you were lucky) did not make especially dramatic reading. But those who were perceptive and could analyze the casualty lists could see that the death toll in Bomber Command was fearful.

Through the deadliest flak fire ever thrown up, evading searchlights and the Messerschmidt and Focke-Wulf fighters, night after night the great streams of bombers crossed the Channel and sped deep into Germany; and so many did not come back.

•◄►• *You Never Got to Know Them*

Every squadron had a bulletin board. Orders, news, bits of this and that. You looked at it every day. What used to get me was if you saw that a new crew came in, and they'd come in together. So there would be seven new names and they'd be under the title "Arrivals" and then you'd see, sometimes, those seven names, bing, bing, bing, bing, all seven, and they'd be posted under the title "Missing In Action." Same board, same day, you understand.

In other words, one operational flight, one kick at the cat, and that was it. They never had a chance to learn what it was all about. Just one flight and down. Maybe safe, Holland, Germany, in a camp somewhere, but more likely a million-and-one pieces mixed with the ship.

You never got to know them.

•◄►• *"Goose Pimples in My Gut"*

I always had just one bad moment, just at that time we're on the line and getting the go-ahead and those four Merlins are roaring away and the full power is on against the brakes and all I do is let go with the brake and we're heading down the runway, building up to 90 knots, and there's a six-ton cookie in the belly and enough incendiaries to burn up Dortmund or Essen, and over the fence, over the valley and we're on our way. From then on, it's okay. I can get along. But just back before the brakes come off, that short time, and my guts turn to mush. Every time. Fifty-two missions, and 52 times I get stomachy mush.

We had this American kid at Tail-end Charlie and he was a cocky little bastard and just at that time, every time he'd turn on his I/C [inter-communication] and he'd crack: "Nobody can kill us. One day the crew of old G for George will rule the world." Always that, and the mid-upper would say, "Fucking right, Barney," and that would kind of ease the tension. I never loaded it on those two, because gunners don't have a very happy life, and especially Barney out there in the tail—that's the end of the world as far as I'm concerned. Bloody cold and bloody lonely out there in the tail section, with the glass out and dark all round.

It got to be a thing, those two guys, Barney and the mid-upper, and if they hadn't given their bit of repartee just before take-off I think the rest of us would have felt, "Oh oh, bad luck. Breaking it off. Bad luck." But they kept on, and we started as a crew and we finished as a crew and kept lucky. But there wasn't a day, not a night, when I didn't get those goose pimples in my gut for those few minutes. And let me tell you, the last operation, into Bremen, that was the worst. The very worst. The last, always the worst.

•◄►• *A Rear Gunner*

You had to be a little guy. At least it gave you more room to move around in the rear. I always felt a rear gunner was the next important guy to the pilot. More than the bomb aimer, hell, all he did was dump bombs where everybody else was dumping their stuff.

But me, and the guys like me, we were the eyes of the pilot for behind, above and below, and mate, that took in one Christly lot of sky—and at night, wow, that was a big sky.

Brunswick, Düsseldorf, Kiel, Berlin, even Paris, I was over them all in big raids and small ones, always me alone in the little turret. I tell you now, if they had asked me to redesign that turret, I'd 've taken them up on it. Lot wrong with it, lot wrong, mate.

But there we'd be, and an Me-109 would be streaking out and down at us. Say we're over Osnabruck, some place like that. I can see the Jerry but our pilot can't. So I'm his eyes. Now what are my chances of knocking him down, scaring him off? Well, let me put it this way. Not as good as his chances of shooting us up, or down, whatever way you like to put it, and I've got this big piece of equipment to think of, and my buddies, so what does Izzie do? Sure, I start firing at the Jerry, but I'm yelling over the intercom for the pilot to take what we call evasive action. That means throw the damned aircraft all over the sky, to port, fall off to starboard, dive, zoom, twirl and twiddle, do everything that Flash Gordon in one of his moonships would do. It was me and the pilot, the pilot and I, who were saving that kite. Believe it. You'd better.

I'd yell a direction and old Smitty would sock the kite around, up or down and we'd keep doing this. On the way home when we had more control, no bombload you see, I've seen two of the buggers on us one time and we fought, or evaded them, for a hundred miles. No, probably only 40 or 50 but it seemed like a hundred and we must have gone from 13,000 down to the deck, maybe 3,000, and up and down like a Chinaman's yo-yo on Saturday night. A regular elevator.

After that one, and we only had a few holes, nobody hurt, and I had to write negative on the report as I always did about how many bloody Focke-Wulfs I'd shot down, how many Messerschmidts. The skipper goes down to our pub in the village and he calls me over from the pub part of it. He wants to buy me a drink, whiskey. He can't come to the sergeants' mess and I can't go to the officers' mess and there is a posting at the station an officer has to drink in the saloon bar of the pub, so I join him there and this chap named Smitty, Flying Officer Smith, with a medal too, he doesn't say why he's buying me drinks. We just talk about the squadron and Canada and have a rare old bloody time and I get good and proper drunk. But we both know why we're drinking and the other lads aren't with us. It's because him and me saved that aircraft, and their lives.

You know, when you're on a bomber after a few missions

you're like a bunch of boys, like a little club, and it's him for me and me for him. Kind of like you're a family, even though one guy may be a Pole and another a South African or an Aussie and the rest of us Canadians. So I knew why Smitty was getting me drunk. The big gink was bloody well thanking me.

•◄►• *Like a Football Game*

There isn't all that much to tell. Not then. If I'd known what I know now, that half of all Bomber Command, R.A.F., Canadian, were killed, wounded, missing, screwed up, half in all the war, then my thoughts might have been a hell of a lot different. Remember, I was just a kid of twenty.

It was like a football game, or maybe a prize fight. C'mon, let's get going. Let's get this kite in the air, let's get up to 18,000, let's get in the stream, let's drop the stuff and get home.

There was a sort of anticipation, like the warm-up on the field before the game. That's Briefing. Met. Intelligence. Good wishes and all that crap. Then getting J-for-Jig off the ground. What an old beast. A bit of pep talk from Graham, the pilot, and near the target instructions from the Pathfinder, the guy who sat up above it all and dropped the flares. Somebody once said he was like the guy who pinned the white paper over the heart of the guy who was going to be executed by firing squad.

Then let the load go. We didn't care where it hit, on target, two miles from the target. They used to say we were always going after some ball-bearing plant, railroad yards, explosives plant, bridges on the Rhine, but I always figured that was so much baloney. The flares always seemed to be dropping on houses and apartments and parks where children played next day.

Who cared anyway? They were Germans and we were us. They socked London and Coventry and Liverpool and half of England when we couldn't sock them, so now we were socking them. But good. Imagine a thousand bombers, flying in formation, squadron after squadron, taking maybe 20 minutes to dump, and then the next bunch comes along just when people were poking their noses out of their shelters and wondering if we'd split the sauerkraut barrels. That was a joke on our station. How many barrels of sauerkraut did we split open? The Germans eat a lot of sauerkraut, you know.

The flak was rough. They had good gunners. Some of the planes used to come home riddled. One was so badly shot up the sergeant of its maintenance crew said it looked like a player roll on a player piano. You know, those hundreds of little holes. And nobody hit. A damned bloody miracle.

What used to get me was to see a ship get it. I don't mean to start down, because you figured the pilot still had some control and if he couldn't baby-sit the goddamned thing home, or at least down, the boys would be able to bail out. What would get me would be to see a Lanc take a direct. Pow. There it is in front of you, and then, just flame and smoke and debris and no parachutes. If they were like us they didn't wear them, anyway. Wasn't worth it. If you had to jump, there was always time to put one on, if you remembered how.

•◂▸• *The First of the Real Big Raids*

Cologne. Yes, the bombing of Cologne. May 30, 1942. I think it was the first of the real big raids. You know, a thousand planes. Cologne was just the start, to show the Germans we could bomb the living Jesus out of any of their cities. Berlin next, so to speak. "Bomber" Harris [head of Bomber Command] even sent us off with a nice message. "Press home your attack," he said. I remember that.

The Luftwaffe must have known we were coming because the bastards were everywhere. And the flak! We lost 44 planes on that go-around, but sometimes I think it was worth it. British squadrons, Australians, Canadians, and naturally Newzies and South Africans mixed in, too, so it was a real big Commonwealth show. Wellingtons, Stirlings, Halifax bombers, the whole bit, and you could see them all around you because there must have been a thousand searchlights down there. Like day I'd describe it.

We were dropping the first of the big babies and when we let them go, you'd feel the aircraft go whoosh, up, up, and those big ones were really doing the damage. Let's face it, civilians are civilians, but when you start levelling factories, factory after factory, that's when you start fighting the real war.

You'd look down and it was like looking into a blast furnace. Like an inferno. Not just flames, no, not flames, but the whole area everywhere was just a red, red glow and you knew the frigging damage was everywhere. It lit up the sky. Going home, hell, you could see this big red glow for miles. To the Dutch coast, I guess. Maybe 100 miles, and you'd bank a bit and look back and there it was.

Two days later, they'd tell us, the ruins of the city were still smoking.

•◀▶• *Evasive Action*

After we'd dump and head for home, some pilots would put on the automatic pilot. Of course it could fly a course better than I could, but I never put it on automatic. Never. And I'll tell you why.

Because, in that split second it took you to disengage the automatic pilot, you could be shot down. We flew at night. You only had a split second, usually, if a night fighter came at you, and that meant life and death. By the time you saw a night fighter he had seen you and was closing on you. The standard evasion tactic was, well, take the rear gunner, his patter would be, "Fighter, fighter, prepare to corkscrew, starboard corkscrew, go!" and that was okay, and then you'd turn and he'd have to turn in on you and you'd catch him and the slipstream from your four engines, they'd roll him over. Four engines would just rock the hell out of a fighter, and sometimes that would give your gunners a good chance at him. Not often, but occasionally.

But usually the manoeuvre was so violent that nothing would happen, and usually, instead of the gunner giving his set patter, there would be a yell, "STARBOARD GO!!!" and you'd just wheel over and dive like hell.

Like that, with all your strength, and there'd be yelling and shouting over the intercom and I'd have to yell back and say, "Shut up, you guys, shut up." And you'd get to the bottom and you'd roll in, this way, and then roll that way and then you'd climb, and then you'd roll and dive and, if the fighter was caught in the slipstream, he'd be bounced all over the sky so that if he didn't get you in his first burst, way back there, the chances were pretty good he wouldn't. That's called evasive action. It was only learned by experience, and I'm sorry to say a lot of good lads never had a chance to learn it.

•◀▶• *"Flak!"*

Flak? It was two different things. At night it was one thing. If it was a clear night you could actually see the .88-millimetre cannon, the classic German aircraft cannon, firing at you. You could also see 20-mm. and 30-mm. cannon firing at you. It was even a bit nerve-racking with that light stuff, even though you knew it wouldn't quite reach you. But the heavy flak, the muzzles of the guns belching below, and then the crump of the explosion, and if it was very close you'd hear the metal rattling like heavy hail against your airplane and sometimes actually punching holes in it—that was terrible.

If you got a direct hit, which you could, and survive, it would actually seem like the plane might be coming apart. Of course, if the hit was in a vital place, then that was it. The game was over. It could be sudden, fatal, all over with, or it could be drawn out and you'd head for home with your airplane falling apart. But it often was fatal.

And in daylight, and especially in our particular operations, the flak was very nerve-racking because you just had to go down the old slot with our gunners calling out where the bursts were, coming in on you, closer and more accurate as the gunners down below got you in range, and I would sometimes yell, "Shut up! I don't give a damn where they are! There's nothing we can do about it." In other words, we had to fly that one track in on this precision bombing, and so I'd say, "Shut up, I don't want to hear about it."

But the rest of the crew, they'd be so tight about it— because it's a hell of a feeling to see this stuff coming up at you and the next one could destroy the airplane and everyone in it—they just felt they had to communicate. You see this hairy great ball just out there, and the next one bound to come closer, and you feel you want to warn everybody about it.

I remember the tail-end gunner once, and that's a hell of a lonely place to be, he once said over the intercom. "But I can't keep quiet. I've got to say something."

I remember once just after the war and my brother and I were sleeping on this porch at the cottage on the island, and suddenly there is this lightning and it must have landed very near, and he said I just leaped straight out of bed and screamed, "FLAK!"

•◄►• *It Was Bad Every Time*

I've seen it happen many times and it might take you a week to get over it. They'd be coming back from targets in Germany, and coming home it was usually every man for himself. Once they dumped, they'd just come home.

Sometimes there were stragglers, and if they weren't ordered to bail out over the Channel or a closer field, they'd come home. You'd be surprised how many wanted to just get home. Maybe because of a girl they were to meet at one of the village pubs, but usually just to get home. The base was home. Often, we'd be in the tower an hour after the last one came in, because there were still two or three not accounted for.

The fighters would nurse them home, but often it wasn't enough. They'd make the circuit and come in over the fence and their landing gear would still be up. A cable shot away. We'd order them up and away, over to the Downs to bail out and hope for the best. But if they were too low over the fence and they were on two engines they might not have enough power to get up again.

I've seen them hit. Just a pancake, sparks and then, Christ, you should have seen it, like an atom bomb had exploded. Just smoke and flame and nothing the trucks could do.

When that happened, I often would have to take charge. The English girls on the phones would be crying. Maybe they didn't know the crews, probably not, but half a dozen men were burning to death just half a mile away, and they'd be sobbing, crying, hysterical. It was bad every time. Those girls on the phones really suffered.

•◄►• *Collisions*

Collisions. Nobody talks about it, even today.

When you were going over, I liken it to goldfish. You know how they keep together, going this way and that way in perfect formation. Or, another way, when you were all in the bomber stream, from maybe 70 to 300 aircraft, you were in the womb of the bomber stream. You were pretty darn safe. Flak, yes, but no German aircraft could really get at you effectively.

But. The big but. When you came towards target, in a place like the Ruhr, there was several targets all equal distance apart, and the enemy never knew which one you were going to hit, but eventually there had to be a turning point. A point where you went due south or southeast or south-by-southeast and roared in. That's where the danger lay.

When it comes time to turn, the first guy turns, you see. But you're flying close, and in fact so close that you'd sometimes feel the slipstream of the guy in front, and then you knew you were too close. This was at night, you see. And the danger of collision was tremendous, and it did happen. Oh, yes.

I can remember my mid-upper gunner saying to me once: "Skipper, we're coming up to the turning point. I just saw two kites collide." Well, when two Lancasters collide, it's game over for them. And the navigator said, "Who's navigating this bloody aircraft, me or you?" As a kind of joke. It happened all the time.

You won't get anybody to say this but I'd estimate that we lost about as many aircraft in collisions, I would think, as we did to enemy action. Maybe not. But a great many.

•◄►• *A Most Interesting Chap*

One of my crew, a New Zealander, he got the D.F.C. when our squadron was jumped by a whole bunch of Focke-Wulfs. This mid-upper gunner got the D.F.C. because our hydraulics were shot out and he had to handle the turret manually, which is quite a job in itself, and the Focke-Wulf was right in, you know, as close in as across that road, and blasting us with his cannons and this air-gunner shot the Focke-Wulf with his pea shooter and it exploded and the propellor cartwheeled off and imbedded itself in our fuse-lage. We got home, though, and made it a squadron trophy in our mess.

This New Zealander, by the way, was the only guy I've ever known who could stand on his head and drink a pint of beer, bottoms up. A most interesting chap. He would take his hat off, put it on the floor, stand on his head, feet against the wall, hold this beer and I can still see him going *"ulp, ulp, ulp."*

•◄►• *In the Cemetery*

On this one raid, we'd lost three engines and we were down to one engine, the inner port, coming home. And the inner starboard engine wouldn't feather. It was windmilling, and it was setting up vibrations, and the vibrations were so great that the instruments popped out of the panel. I was with primary instruments in this four-engine Stirling and I was really too short to fly this plane so I'd put an extra parachute at my back to put me forward enough, and this always made me furious, and so here we are and I tried to bail the crew out.

In this sort of a deal, the crew go by you to get out, and as they pass they tap you on the shoulder and say, "Navigator out," and so on and in series so you know everybody is out. But the first guy, he blew his parachute in the escape hatch and there he is, hanging down in the sky, and the guys pull him back in, and by this time we're at 400 feet and the guys all take up crash positions, behind the main spar, so we just landed straight ahead. I had no alternative.

Well, in a sense, I brought it in. We went through a forest and actually we knocked the top off a little church and the wings shed, and the tail shed, and the fuselage cannoned on and the remains of the petrol was everywhere and we landed the thing in a cemetery. I've just forgotten the place.

We weren't far from this American base I'd been trying for, and they sent out their crash vehicles, et cetera, and these guys all converged on this cemetery and they are all smoking Lucky Strike cigarettes and wading around in all our fuel. The ground was soggy with it, and how the damn thing didn't go up, I'll never know.

We were terribly fortunate. I was knocked out and buggered up my leg, which gave me problems in my spine for years after, but we had only one real casualty. Sometimes you wonder, you get sort of superstitious about it all. I mean, "Why me?" Why should I survive?

•◄►• *All Shot to Pieces*

We used to watch them coming in from those big raids deep into Germany. Our station was in East Anglia. Not many flew in formation. It was rather like every man or plane for himself and of course, the fighters were bringing them home, but that didn't help them against their own internal problems, so to speak.

One engine. Two engines. All shot to pieces. Some with smoke coming from them. When they hit the coast some men would parachute and the pilot would get it in alone or take it out to sea and ditch or jump himself. I've seen Wellingtons come back, no skin on them at all. You could see the crew inside, at their guns and so on.

An awful lot of good young men died in Bomber Command. A lot of them needlessly. Inexperience, that caused a lot of it. You know, many a crew got shot down on its first operation. But the hard ones, the ones that really hurt, were the crews that got it on their last mission. You know, three to go, two to go, and then the last one—and then on that one they got killed or captured. That really hurt. Going through a war and going for a Burton on the last trip. That hurt.

I participated in the Dresden affair, which was a terrible thing. The fire raid. I understand there were about 135,000 or so people killed in that raid.

We were told that the Russians were advancing and the Germans were falling back into these cities and when the Russian armour went by, the Germans would fan out and cut their supply lines up, and for these reasons, certain cities had to be obliterated. This is what they told us.

And then it started to filter through later that this wasn't a tactical thing. What I think really happened was that the Russians were moving very very rapidly and the Allies decided they would show the Russians that even though we had a tremendous army, we also had a tremendous air force, so don't get too cocky, you guys, or we'll show you what we could do to Russian cities. This was Churchill and the rest. This was a calculated atrocity, no question in my mind.

We weren't in the first phase, we were in the second. Even then, the city was burning. We could see the great flare in the sky for a long way out and we knew that was Dresden burning. Burning cities is a technique, you know. You didn't need any atomic bombs; you could create what is called a fire storm. You had incendiaries and then heavy bombs and this would create an artificial wind roaring up the streets and it sucked the oxygen out, and people didn't die, or die all that much, of fire; they died because the life was literally sucked right out of them.

We went there at night and the Americans went there the next day and they had the long-range fighters protecting them, and strangely, the Germans had fighter protection for the area, but the order was never given and so their fighters sat on the fields. The American fighters went down and strafed the poor bastards in the streets who were picking up the corpses, and this German who told me this after the war, was very bitter about that.

This strafing in the streets, by the Americans. That was a beastly thing, wasn't it? Our guys didn't do that, did they? Only the beastly Huns did that, didn't they?

We carried incendiaries over Dresden, and the Pathfinders were leading us into places where major fires hadn't started yet. I mean, there would be a patch over here, say some residential area, and the Pathfinder pilots would scoot over there and drop their markers. It was wholesale destruction of a city, using the latest in city-burning techniques.

It was indescribable! When we saw the photos two days later, it was dreadful. Dreadful. It was then that I felt we'd all been had. I thought it was a pretty . . . Dresden was an unarmed city. Maybe a couple of battalions of home guards or Boy Scouts or something, and there was no military justification for that. As far as I've ever been able to find out later, I was right. A straight political destruction of the city. No tactical advantage. The straight politics of destruction.

•◄►• *Writing the Letter*

It wasn't part of my job writing those letters—The Letter, we called it—telling his folks he was dead, missing in action or what. It was the chaplain's job, but when the station might lose three or four bombers in a week, which thankfully happened only once in a while, then the chaplain would be pretty busy and I'd take over.

They were pretty routine, you know. In 1944 we had a lot of replacements, filling for men going home after finishing their tour, or transfers to other squadrons for any reason, furloughs, what you'd call combat fatigue and, sure, the dead ones and those missing. So you never got to know all the chaps. They might be with you only a week or two, a face seen at the mess or bellying up to the bar when the whiskey came on at six at night, and you couldn't say you knew them. The letters were routine, something like:

Dear Mr. and Mrs. Smith:

I don't think you will ever know the grief I feel in writing this letter to tell you of the death of your son Kenneth over Dortmund [or Berlin or wherever].

Ken was a fine lad, liked by everyone who knew him and he died with his crew mates with courage, for Canada and as a Christian . . .

And on and on for about four more paragraphs.

Hell, you never knew the kid, except from what you could maybe glean from his kitbag, his possessions, and if you asked somebody in the same squadron, they'd probably say, "Smith, oh yeah. Nice guy. Hear he bought it. Tough luck," or something like that.

No, the letter had one purpose and that was to try and lessen the grief on the family. Fat chance there, I guess, but at least this letter from me, the squadron leader, would follow up the Department of National Defence telegram and make death somehow softer. Something that the minister of their church could read at the memorial service they'd probably have in the small town where he lived. That's what it was for.

That's why I put a certain amount of care into them. It was a chore, yes, that's true, but remember, I had a mother and father too, and I think I'd know how they'd feel if they got a sincere and sympathetic letter.

I'm not telling this too well, but when I say I probably never knew these kids and the letter wasn't actually sincere as far as I was concerned personally, it *was* a sincere letter and something far more important than the telegram from Ottawa saying sorry but your only son is dead.

A Lovely War — at Home

*"When War Come, I Was Glad" . . . Spend, Spend, Spend
. . . Jobs Everywhere . . . The Money Just Rolled in . . .
Good Years for Everybody . . . A Fabulous Steak—One
Dollar . . . Some Kind of Las Vegas . . . We Made Good
Money . . . Selling Was Easy . . . The Best Farm in the
District*

---

*Canada was never really threatened by any foreign force. Jobs were
plentiful, and although in many cases wages were frozen, others
were doing very well. Since the cost of living only rose about 20
percent in five years, there was lots of money to spend, although
not always much to spend it on. Booze was rationed, of course,
but everybody seemed to get enough, somehow. There was plenty
of food, and enough gas for rather stringent use of the family
heap. Sugar and meat and . . . well, some things were rationed, but
who cared?*

*The country ran better than ever. The Depression, and its
600,000 to 750,000 unemployed men, was a thing of the past.
Everybody was buoyant, and only the politicians really worried
about the actual running of the war and how the country would
absorb a million servicemen and women back into civilian life and
the big question: would there be another Depression?*

*It would be wrong to say that the whole country had an
"eat-drink-and-be-merry" attitude, but there certainly was some
truth in the song, "Happy Days Are Here Again."*

•◄►• *"When War Come, I Was Glad"*

When war come, I was glad. I knew that they'd be building ships
on the West Coast, there'd be jobs for all. In December of 1940 I
packed up the wife and kids, just packed up. I sold the farm and
got 3,000 dollars cash and I told the elevator company to take
everything on it. Every last blamed thing. For all I cared they
could have taken the clothes drying on the line. We piled what we
could in the truck and hoped the truck would get us there, and we
headed for Lethbridge and then down over to Spokane and came
up through Seattle into Vancouver. That was just after Christmas,
and everything was green.

I went to the hiring place and the guy started to fill in

papers and he said things like, can you do welding? and are you a carpenter? and ever do any plumbing? Sheet metal? and on and on, and I gave him a yes to every question and finally he said was I a shipwright? And I said what's that? He looked at all the yeses on the list and he said, "Yes, I guess you're a shipwright too." That was on a Friday, I think, and I started work on a Tuesday.

My first pay cheque was 72 dollars for the week and multiply that by a month and you're up around 350 bucks—and that was more than I'd see for any whole *year* back in Saskatchewan since about '32.

I worked real hard and I did a lot of work and then in about a year they gimme a promotion and so I was like the rest of the bosses, I could go around singing that song:

"Now the labour union can kiss my ass
I got my foreman's job at last."

Now, I'll tell you, them were the days.

•←→• *Spend, Spend, Spend*

People tried to spend their money. I know I did, and I know others did. Kind of spend, spend, spend because it was shortage.

My folks had come from Saskatchewan and when we moved to Edmonton my dad got a good job. He was in construction, helping to build an airfield, and instead of 15 dollars a month coming in for relief, and that was for a *month*, here were the Hiltons with 50 to 60 dollars a *week*, and more if he wanted it. Dad was a foreman by this time because anybody who could hit a nail was a construction man, and if you knew a little more, then they grabbed you.

You wouldn't believe the stories he told us about stealing. Right, left and centre. Gas, wood, nails, tar paper, plumbing fixtures, pipes. People actually stole for the sake of stealing. I think it had something to do with the Depression, where you had nothing for many years. Then there was everything around just waiting to be picked up. People had basements full of pipes and bags of cement. Somebody once even stole an earth packer from the station and they found it way down by Cooking Lake, and that's a long way away. Just lying in the bush.

My mother was different. I remember she and Dad used to go driving on a Saturday, a Sunday, and she'd be prowling through all these little stores in the country. She'd buy anything, anything that was there. It didn't have to be cheap. She once brought home a big box full of 144 rubber spatulas. You know, crazy things like that. Dad used to humour her. I asked him once and he said she had such a hard time during the Thirties at Marion where we once lived, that if she wanted things, well, she could have them.

•◄►• *Jobs Everywhere*

Shit, there was jobs everywhere. There's a long street leading out towards the Winnipeg airport and there was a lot of businesses on it. Oh, offices, small warehouses, manufacturing, coal and wood and ice yards, stores. You could call it a typical junky, ugly street, I guess.

I come in from Sudbury that morning and where three years ago there might a been 100, 200 guys on top of the cars, there only is a few now. Ten, maybe. You got sort of lonely, and I figured the C.P. would have the usual number of bulls outside the yards, so I hop off a few miles out. Figure a bit of walking won't hurt the old stud nohow.

Guy picks me up, asks me if I know anything about roofing and I need a job, I'm flat, so sure, I said I roofed the Empire State Building, Buckingham Palace, you know. Just kidding. He says okay, you're hired, and we go out to the job. He's driving to work, see, and he takes my name and shows me the foreman. Well, we're working with gravel and boiling tar and you've got to hoist gravel and tar up about 40 feet. Now in all your life can you imagine a worse combination? Christ.

About ten I go down the ladder and across the street where there is a kind of community water tap or something and guys are around it, and I take a drink and get talking and before you know it, a guy asks me if I know carpentry. I said I'd framed houses from Victoria, British Columbia, to Halifax, Nova Scotia. He don't believe me, of course, but do I want a job? Ten cents more an hour than spreading tar. Damn tooting! So now I'm working for Birdsall Construction. Some name like that. There's a bastard of a foreman and he keeps yelling, "Get a leg on, you guys, don't you know there's a war on?" Bloody well do I know there's a war on.

By this time it's getting on to noon and I'm not sure I was cut out to be a carpenter. Okay for Jesus, maybe, but he was just biding his time. That goddamned foreman is just about hoarse now, trying to win the war all by himself.

At noon, there's about 40 guys around this outdoor tap and I get talking to a guy and he offers me a sandwich, and I ain't eaten since the day before. I get a pour from his coffee jar and half an apple and then he offers me a job. I'd clean streets by this time, that foreman is getting me down.

Welding. I tell him I don't know nothing about welding, but he says nobody does at first. You start out as assistant and in a week you're up in the big money—$1.50 an hour. I can't believe that—it comes to about 75 dollars a week, and that's more than a brigadier makes. Boy, you should have seen my smoke grabbing that job. So I'm assistant, and once I get going I find they're teaching me like in a school. We're not making things, we're just doing things over and over. I don't get it, and I ask the young fellow I'm working with and he says, "When we finish this course, then we get shipped out." "Oh," I says, "and where do we get shipped out to?" He says, "Well, the bunch on this two week course goes to Norman Wells, the army's building a oil pipeline there." "Now that's interesting," I says, "and where is Norman Wells?" The kid snaps off his flame and says, "Somebody says it's up near the North Pole."

I said goodbye to the kid and walk out and down the street and it's about three then and there's guys around getting a drink and rolling smokes and one says to me, "Looking for work?" "You bet," I says. "Lead me to her." "Drive a truck?" I laugh and say there ain't a truck that can't be rode. Gravel trucks, pick-ups, stock trucks, pulp trucks, I drove 'em.

This big guy tells me to go over to the office and he points to a big garage down the road and I go over, you see, and there ain't nothing there that can't be rode. Mechanic tells me they haul airplane parts from the C.N. and C.P. yards to some plant, some outfit at the airport making planes. No problem there.

The big guy comes over and explains, it's a buck an hour first two weeks and up from there. I can see big money ahead. Can I drive this thing, and he points to a big G.M.C. Shit, I could drive that over Niagara Falls, I tells him. Duck soup.

Okay, and he tells the office boy to go the first trip with me, show me where to load and unload, how to sign the papers for the stuff, no problem there, and I drive out the yard and onto this main street and I'm looking east towards town and Christ, out of nowhere, out of no bloody where, this big tanker comes along and takes out the front end of my outfit. I wind up looking like the elephant what's lost his trunk.

Everybody's running and I get out, tip my hat to the boss, who's running the hardest, and I take off down the road. I'm not running, you see, because there's my dignity involved, but you could say I was making good time. Soon I'm out of sight, I guess you might say.

That's what I meant about jobs. There were lots of them in those days. Every damn fool wanting to win the war, and as I remember, it took about another three years to win it anyway.

•◄►• *The Money Just Rolled in*

I am seventy-five years old now and in the Depression I was a Returned Man, but that never did cut any ice with the government and me, not when there was no work at all. I reckon that with everything coming in, my oldest boy having a *Star* paper route and what I could get shoveling snow in winter and getting some lawns to cut in Rosedale summertime, and my wife getting two weeks' work at Eaton's store at Christmas and the relief, about 10 dollars a week for everything, I reckon we got by on about 700 dollars a year. That didn't count the rent. It was 15 dollars, only we never paid it.

The war came and I being a Returned Man I went down to sign up, figuring they'd want men with experience. But you see I'm about forty-two by this time and they wouldn't even let me in the front door.

Oh, I wasn't complainin'. An Old Soldier knows they'll want the younger men first and my turn would come. I figured if the war lasted more than a year I'd get over to London and see the old sights again. Well, you know what happened.

There was still the relief, but the wife got a war plant job and a company what was putting up air force stations, they put in the *Star* for workers, and I could drive a truck and I got a job. A good job. Billy came up to eighteen and he joined the navy down at the navy base, called York in them days, and he was sending half his pay home and the money was just rolling in.

It wasn't long before the landlord came around and wanted his rent, all of it, so we just moved out to a nice place. I can remember having a whole case of beer on Saturday night, and for my lunch the wife would put in chicken sandwiches and a quart of cream and two or three big handfuls of them shiny Spanish peanuts and that would be my lunch, and I tell you, me and her was soon getting fat as a pig. I'd say, "Mom, we're getting fat as two pigs," and she'd say, "Don't see what right not to. We been starving for the past eight years," and that was right.

We bought some house furniture and a big second-hand radio this high and this wide down on Spadina, and we went to Prescott for a summer holiday and by the living Jesus, we were living. She working and me working and overtime, and the money just rolled in.

The gist of it is, once I got to having them chicken sandwiches and cream and Spanish peanuts for lunch, I never wanted to go to war anyhow. So as the gentleman says, I did not offer my services to my country again.

In the war we lived good. Real good.

•◆• *Good Years for Everybody*

All the houses in our block were pretty much in a mess. An awful lot of people had been laid off in the Depression or they'd had to take big pay cuts and there was just no money for repairs. Everything went on hamburger and potatoes and taxes. Oh yes, they still kept collecting taxes. Did they ever! But now people were getting jobs back on the road [the railroad] and working for the army or the government and in stores, and there wasn't all that much of an unemployment problem any more and there was money around. People were buying those war bonds just because they didn't have anything to spend their money on.

Neighbours started to come around to Dad when they saw how spic and span our house was after he had fixed it up. He was a carpenter, you see, and he'd kept his tools even when we were half starving. We lived on the South Side, a nice place, and people, you know, have a pride of possession, and now that they had money they wanted their houses to look nice. Soon Dad was working all the time he could, 10 or 12 or 14 hours a day was nothing. I've always said he was a compulsive worker and he always said those two years at varsity had spoiled me for ordinary conversation. Then he had too much to do, and he recruited me, and my mother told him that girls don't work painting fences and I remember him saying, "At a dollar an hour they sure as hell do," and my younger brother worked until he joined the air force as a gunner and my sister, even when she could hardly swing a hammer, was out straightening old nails on an anvil because with the war everything was shortages.

Within a year Dad had six people working for him. My cousin came up from Chilliwack because he could make more money working for Dad than in the shipyard, and another cousin came from Red Deer, and we were a going concern.

This went on for a year, and then another year, and then I got married to my husband, he was in the air force, and by that time Dad was pretty worn out, but he had made more money than anyone I know. People just couldn't hand him enough money to get jobs done, small jobs or big ones. Not building a house, mind you, but we could sure take a house apart inside and put it to-gether nice in a hurry.

Dad made thousands. No, he made tens of thousands, and you would wonder just how, all that money coming from what would be considered now an itsy-bitsy contractor, such a little guy that they wouldn't even be bothered by the union to sign up. He made thousands, and everybody got their money's worth.

Yes, we were on the Home Front. For that matter, you could say everybody in Canada was, one way or another. Wouldn't you say so? Even the black marketeers. They had a usefulness. Often we'd have to buy nails or windows or something from them and at their prices. There wasn't much bargaining with a black marketeer, but we figured the means justified the end. If it was housing for a woman with five kids and her husband at the war, that kind of thing. Oh, I could give you a hundred other examples.

I think the war years were good for everybody in Canada. I think everybody enjoyed them. Like a big adventure. An exciting experience.

•◆• A Fabulous Steak—One Dollar

I remember in Winnipeg there was this small restaurant, and it seems to have been maybe 15 feet wide but long, quite long, and the owner, boss, cook and bouncer was a big man, really a big man. Not tall, but like a barrel through the chest.

I have a feeling the place was named Mike's and he was Mike but this was about '43, 1944, so I'm not sure. But when you went in, he was at your left in front of a big gas burner stove, a big black thing, and in front where the cash register was, although this character used an ordinary kitchen table drawer, in front were the steaks. Not runny little things, but big chunks of steak, well marbled, maybe half a pound each. You pointed to the one you wanted and he'd flip it out with a long fork and say "7" or "14" or whatever and that's the seat you took at the counter.

There were always these grunts from up front and that was Mike saying a steak was ready, and like grizzly bears who under-stand each other in grunt fashion, the waitresses did too. You'd get steak, medium, never rare or well done. I often wondered where he got the steaks, it being wartime, but he seemed to have plenty.

With your steak you got about three big chunks of potato. Just that and no more, but he could do things to a spud I've never seen done since. And a piece of pie. If you didn't want the pie, you didn't eat it, but you got it. Apple pie. Always apple pie. And coffee.

When you finished this fabulous steak, you walked to the front and you gave him a dollar. That's the point. *One buck.* A dollar, and you got the best meal you'd eat that week, and it was steak, potatoes, bread if you asked for it, pie and coffee. It was fabulous.

After the war I came home and one day I went down for a steak, but the place had closed down.

•◄►• *Some Kind of Las Vegas*

The big money was on the North Van ferries coming back, going over, pay night and the day or two after. These gamblers, out from Montreal, made a killing, and it wasn't called the Klondike gold rush. No sir, just the North Vancouver ferries, some kind of Las Vegas.

Why, there was people from all over Canada, people who'd come off the farms, people on them farms who'd never had 2 dollars to rub together. You see, you gotta remember there was the Depression, and if you don't think the prairies wasn't hard work, then you got another think coming. So when the shipyards open up here, there's jobs. Ads in papers in Regina and Calgary saying come to Vancouver, work in the shipyards, help build ships, big money. There was big money—and there was the smart boys to take it away from them.

Oh, it was like fleecing. What does a farmer from Prince Albert know about shaved dice? Slow rolls? What a real shooter can do on a blanket? He might know about pea pool or snooker, but about dice, he doesn't know from nothing.

Some of those people were getting 60, 80 dollars a week and that was big money, likely three times as much as they got before the war. They couldn't buy booze, rationed, and not many had a car, and you just couldn't spend it all. Now that's a fact, believe that, and so there would be six or eight of these games around the deck and three or four more in the cabin. Seven or nine people in each game, bouncing the dice off some guy's lunch-pail and a heap of money in the centre, and always one gambler. Sometimes two because they'd work in pairs.

Those guys could palm and switch faster and smoother than anyone I've seen since. They were real dice mechanics. They had shaved dice and Tops and Bottoms, that's dice you can only see three sides of unless you can see around corners and you can't win. And then they had Hits and Miss-outs, and, well enough of that. You get the idea. It was sharks among goldfish, and there was no way the gamblers would lose. They'd lose a bit, get up from a game and say they were busted, that sort of thing, and move over and get into the next game.

I'm sure the police were wise, or they suspected, but what were they going to do? Gambling was illegal, but these guys were working 10 hours a day and hard work building those Liberties and warships, and to start telling them they couldn't have a bit of a crap game, why, don't you think you'd have a riot on their hands?

This happened time after time, week after week, the gamblers skinning the suckers. Oh my, how they skinned them. Thousands of dollars a week. Figure it out. There are hundreds of people making good money over there, and two shifts and there are all these ferries going to work month after month. A lot of people got cleaned. Why, if you wanted you could blow a cheque in one roll, two rolls, three. You'd always get money to cover you.

Remember, those ferry rides took about 20 or 25 minutes. The farmers wanted action fast and so did the gamblers. Bing, bing, bing and then bang! Somebody wins, somebody loses. Bing, bing, bing, and bang! Murder, plain murder.

•◄►• *We Made Good Money*

Denny, my buddy, used to be a foreman in North Van. In the war, in the shipyards, we used to get paid by the inch, so much to weld, on these Victory ships they were turning out. He was on the night shift working on one freighter.

We used to put the rods in by the handful in the weld and then we'd just make a pass over them with the torch and go on, doing more. We made good money. This one ship, it split up before it got to Alaska and they towed it back to Vancouver in two pieces. Bow end and stern end.

We made real good ships in them days. It's a fact, that's right—as long as you didn't have to sail in the damn things.

•◄►• *Selling Was Easy*

I was selling toiletries, notions, children's clothing, and everything except farm machinery, I guess; not food although I did have a small line of cat and dog food. Speaking of that chow, I've seen a grocer pass over necessary things and swap around to get a bigger order of cat food because he'd have a bunch of old biddies as his customers who had cats who would pay double, triple to get old tabby's special food. Crazy.

Anyway, you had a route book which gave you the info on every store in your territory, from Winnipeg south and over to Brandon and south from there and it kept you humping and before the war, you had to sell. I mean get in there and keep throwing strikes. Hard work.

Then the war came and they fired the guy west of Brandon and gave me his territory and about the same time they said I couldn't drive over 40 miles an hour. Or maybe it was 45. I forget. That way I'd save gasoline, which was rationed, and tires, which were impossible to get except on the black market, and Detroit and Windsor were making jeeps and tanks instead of cars. One guy in Saskatchewan was fired when he was caught doing 60. I was pretty careful.

Still, it was a snap to cover the territory. 'Stead of once a month, every two months. Tell them to order double and make up an order for say, the month of March, and send it in, and in April I'd sit at home or in some apartment, and I had a friend who was a salesgirl at Eaton's and I stayed there, so I made up April's orders in a big easy chair. You could work it. You just had to be careful, a bottle once in a while to the guys in the order department, and another in shipping. You also checked once a month by phone and that was a snap, too.

Then they took me off the road and I did miss that. I had a lot of good memories. You know, there's far more free tail in those small towns than any city fellow ever really quite realizes. You got to know them. Usually a school teacher, a nurse or some gal whose husband had got stupid and gone off to war. In that case, it was strictly a back-door deal, sneaking in the back door. So there I was, in the office down on Ellice Avenue, at a desk, white shirt and tie, phoning, making up orders and doing exactly what I'd been doing in this girl's apartment.

The thing is, you didn't have to sell. Walk in with a gross of those Australian throwing things, banjos, and he'd say, now, what do I want them for, and you'd say, "You want soap, don't you? Olive oil. Okay, you want banjos too." Hell, I mean boomerangs, not banjos. So you didn't have to sell.

•—→—• *The Best Farm in the District*

Call us Ruthenians, or Galicians. Actually, though, we're Ukrainians. You could make it easier on yourself by just writing down the word "Hunky." I won't mind. Nothing can change the shape of my head, and I couldn't care less, although one of my boys might take a sock at your nose.

When I was eleven, in 1932, the old man bought 160 acres in Alberta for 50 dollars. That wasn't any bargain either, not being cleared, but it had a lot of good timber on it and some open pasture, a slough, so it meant we didn't have to work for anybody any more like in Manitoba. We lived all that spring in a tent and we built a good house and barn out of logs. You can still see some of them up that way even today. Ukrainian houses they call them. Let me tell you, by the time you've got the logs in and a roof and a loft and you've made yourself a horse trough of mud and water and cow shit and swamp grass, the long tough stuff, and slathered it on the buildings and they've dried for about a week in a hot prairie sun, you've got yourself a house like Gibraltar.

We didn't have no floor, just hard dirt, but one of my sisters swept that floor twice a day, after each milking, and it was hard as a bowling alley and just as shiny. It took two years to get wood for a floor, and even then I didn't like it. My mom was always having babies and each baby, after it left their bed, slept on a kind of bed on top of the stove winter nights. Warm as a bug in a rug.

What happened? Well, damn it all, we worked. Don't ask a Ruthenian what work is when he's working to start a farm. Fifteen-hour days? Nothing. Sun-up to sun-down. The whole family. At one time we had eight hands, including my sisters, but not Mom. I never knew how we were doing because I never saw any money, just a dollar a week, but it must have been piling up. None of us left, myself or Rudy or Alex or Nick or none of us. Just stay and work.

The war. Well, how are you going to get out of that? Five of us boys left, all in the army except Rudy, air force, and that left three boys home and the girls. I was away four years. The only one even wounded was Nick, and he got killed with the Calgary Highlanders.

My sister Reba, she'd keep writing. Dad and Mom couldn't, but she'd say things were going well. Prices were high, you know, and a neighbour was too old and they'd bought out his land. I never paid much mind. I knew that piece of land, and it was mostly bush. What I didn't know was they had these new machines, two big cats with a huge chain as big around as a man's thigh and weighted down by balls that rolled along, and where it took a man and a tractor and two helpers a month to clear off a few acres, that machine would just go through like you was cutting hay. Just swathing those poplars down. Ripping them up. Rip!

Maybe Dad was, well, he couldn't read, but he could think and he knew what a dollar bill was, and he put everything into those machines and everybody was burning and breaking land and the government was buying everything, everything you could grow, and prices was good. It seemed like the Depression had never been.

I was first home, first in, first out, and you wouldn't have believed it. A new house. A new barn, and our own portable sawmill done the lumber and cut for the neighbours' too. The half-section had grown to two sections. A big herd of Holsteins. Christ Almighty, but it was a real farm now, and one of the best in the district. That old man, my mother, three young boys and the girls. How they did it, Christ knows.

When we all got home we had this big party, and the reeve and his council came and half the district and it was like some kind of government affair, just as dignified as you can imagine, all done up right and in style. Everybody made speeches and some telegrams were read. You'd have thought it was a Coronation.

Then Dad gets up and he says his lawyer had done him a bit of a job, and we find that the farm—the best in the district, mind you—he's put it under a company name and we're all owners. All the family, and that's not like a Ukrainian way to do things. The old folks always want to hang on, running things. So here we're getting about two and a half sections of the best land in northern Alberta handed to us on a silver platter.

Well, that's the way it was. The folks moved into a little house in town and we ran the farm. Rudy went off to school and became a doctor, and the girls married, and one way or another, everybody sold or bought out everybody else's share and there was no running around to lawyers and to courts. Everything worked out fine, and you asked, that's what the Depression and the war meant to me.

Oh yeah, one other thing. You see, when a person leaves the Old Country they bring a handful of soil with them and when they die in the new country, that's Canada, we sprinkle that bit of soil on their grave. It's just an old custom. Kind of nice. Well, just before my father died he said, in 1956, he was seventy-two, he said, "Basil, don't put soil on my grave. There's no old or new country. Just Canada. This is my country."

Us and the Yanks

American Volunteers in Toronto ... Negroes in Winnipeg ... We Didn't Like the Americans ... In Joint Flotilla ... In an English Pub ... The Biggest Aircraft ... They Bombed Everything That Moved ... The G.I. Was a Good Guy ... "Tough Guys, You Canadians" ... The Navy Against the Army ... A Group of Them ... The Yanks Couldn't Navigate ... The Dutch Victory Parade

The material in this chapter surprised me greatly. I had my own opinions of our American neighbours in wartime, but I judged each individual as a person, and stayed away from generalizations. But I was not in any sort of close competition with Americans for girls, accommodations, meals, and so on, as so many of our servicemen were, so I did not notice the flaunting of their dollar as much as those who speak here.

I also suspect that many of the incidents related here stem from the fact that the Americans in Britain felt themselves to be in an alien environment, while our own servicemen felt more at home, which made the Americans feel defensive.

As for battle, on the ground, at sea and in the air, there seems to be a consensus that the American was a brave fighter, but would have been a better one if he had had more discipline—which goes back to training—and had been better led. In other words, Americans took casualties needlessly.

But I think this chapter should stand without further comment, and that every reader should judge it for himself.

•◆• *American Volunteers in Toronto*

We had Americans joining up long before Pearl Harbor Day. Ninety per cent air force. None of this foot-slogging for them, I guess they'd heard too much of that from their fathers.

They were good chaps, mainly, and mainly officer class. I mean, university, either graduated or nearly finished, and they'd get it into their head to get into the thick of it over there. I don't think there was any of this Roosevelt b.s. about saving the world for democracy. They just wanted to get in on the fun.

When I was recruiting in Toronto, I guess I handled 300 or 400 and I was always amazed at how many of these fellows showed up drunk, half-drunk or with a hangover. An awful lot did.

Finally I asked one young fellow about it. Well, he said, he and his friends had been at this big party down South, Mississippi. and they got talking about the war and about how the United States should be in it, on and on, and somebody said, "Well, why don't you then? Canada's up that way. They're in it." Something like that.

One of the fellows had a plane, and they spent the night and part of next morning toodling along, stopping at this cornfield and that one for gas, and they had two or three quarts of bourbon with them, and that was about it. Here they were, looking like death warmed over, but ready to do or die. We put them through, of course, and that's the last we'd see of them.

But you often wonder what happened to those fellows. Some switched back to the American Air Force when Roosevelt declared war, some probably stayed with us. I guess some died too.

•◀▶• *Negroes in Winnipeg*

We used to go downtown and go to the big dance halls. We'd say we were eighteen when we'd be sixteen or maybe seventeen. Even fifteen. Some girls could get away with being fifteen and saying eighteen. That's where the fun was. I mean, the guys came in from Shilo and Macdonald and there were several camps around Winnipeg, quite a few, and there were some camps in North Dakota, in Minnesota, and the guys used to come up to Canada. I remember one fellow I was dancing with and he said, "Ma'am, this is a real nice little country you got up her," and I said, "Soldier, you looked at a real nice big map lately?" He was from North Carolina, South Carolina. A lot of them were, and they all had bottles. That's where I first learned to drink Southern Comfort right out of the neck of the bottle. My, oh my, but we had some good times. Those Americans were a lot of fun. You see, it was too far to go to Minneapolis or some other big town, so it was Winnipeg for them. They liked the place.

The fact of the matter is, until they started coming up I don't think I had seen a Negro except on a train. The few in Winnipeg, I think they lived up around the C.P.R. station. Porters on the trains. The Negro soldiers were nice guys. Young, like us, and there were more good ones than bad. I got to know one named Ray Durban, I used to meet him at this dance hall on Maryland Street but I didn't take him home for dinner. I just didn't. My mother didn't like Jews, she didn't like Ukrainians and her father lived with us, an old Scotchman with a fierce face, and he just hated Englishmen. That sort of narrowed the field, wouldn't you say?

This Ray Durban, he said that in Grand Forks or Minot or wherever they were stationed in North Dakota, they couldn't even get a meal in a restaurant. This would be in '44. Or go in a bar, or, heaven forbid, go to a dance hall and dance with a white girl, and as there were no Negroes, civilian Negroes, in North Dakota, that put the military Negroes in a tough spot. That's why they loved Canada. We danced with them, went out with them. I didn't care. But then, they were just young guys, lots of fun and really terrific dancers. They could really dance.

Well, it wasn't the Canadians, the air force and so on, who objected to us going out with the Negroes. It was the Americans themselves. The young white ones, like the ones from the American South mostly, but the Northerners too. They hated it. Oh, how they hated it. They'd get in a corner and just give us, the girls with the Negro partners, they'd give us a real stare. I once asked Ray if he wasn't scared. I was, so shouldn't he be, and he said he was scared out of his boots. I remember what he said. He said that if he kept coming to these dances he was going to get killed. I said how, like meaning a gun or knife, and he said no, with boots. I said why, and he said, "So everybody will get a crack at me."

It never happened, but some girls walking down Portage Avenue after a dance, they'd had the colored fellow who was with them yanked into an alley and he'd get beat up something fierce. It happened a lot. It never got into the papers. Nothing ever got into the papers in those days, but there were a lot of beatings.

I remember asking this Ray friend I had why they didn't do something about it. You know, he and his friends fight back. He said that if they did that and there were ten white American soldiers in that dance place that night, then next week there would be a hundred. I remember him saying, "It's just something you live with. I'm used to it."

Anyway, these colored soldiers sure liked Canada. They talked about moving to Winnipeg after the war but I don't think they ever did. I know I never heard from any. They were just kids and at that age, they'd just say whatever came into their heads. They were so grateful that somebody treated them as human.

•➤• *We Didn't Like the Americans*

Initially we didn't like the Americans. This the British sometimes found difficult to believe, same language, practically the same culture and the same continent, of course, but principally it was money. We had only X amount of it, having to sign over part or most of it to mother, wife or savings account, and they came in throwing their money all over the place.

So this sometimes led to fights in London with the M.P.'s of both nations whaling in busting heads, Yank and Canadian, with equal vigour, but it all worked out. But it used to brass us off to see some Yank come in to a pub flashing 5-pound notes, and try to buy the one bottle of whiskey in the place plus a place in the dart game plus the barmaid plus everything. I'd say most of the fights occurred because the Yanks had too much money and didn't understand the climate of England in those days, and they often got their faces pounded in for it.

I remember once seeing a wounded British army captain. He had a cane, and he's standing outside Victoria Station looking for a cab. Probably back from some war zone, all shot up, and this cab shoots by him and stops in front of some American P.F.C. who's waving a quid in the air. Now that is pretty much.

We didn't like him for his money. Every day was Christmas for the girls in London when the Yanks came. Prices shot up, for girls, for everything. And we didn't like him for his medals. We didn't have any, and he'd get one for keeping his rifle clean or showing up five days in a row for breakfast at the mess hall. Meaningless. But they were ribbons and pretty ones too, I must say.

But in action, they were like most soldiers. Not as good as us, not as good as the British or the New Zealanders, but they were okay and now that I look back on it, that war they fought in Southeast Asia must have been a real killer and they did very well in that. I wouldn't have wanted any part of it.

So now, I regard them as troops like any other. They were not too disciplined, and though their equipment was the best, they didn't use it too well, but their expertise at logistics and their sheer wealth of material was unbelievable. Their tactics were not as saving on men as the British and Canadians. They were too wasteful of men.

•◄►• *In Joint Flotilla*

We worked with both the English and the Americans on coastal patrol. Literally, we operated in joint flotilla even though the American admiral and the English admiral back at the base weren't even speaking to one another. We had great admiration for them, a liking for them, but I will still take the British sailor over the

American any time. The idea in the American's mind as to what his duty was was completely different from that of the British sailor.

Our crews were, in a sense, scraping the bottom of the barrel. After all, we'd been fighting for three or so years by that time, while the American crews were specially picked. Most of them from university. Prime beef, you might say. But I would take the Canadian any day, just because of his attitude. They were cool in action, calm, ready to wade in with everything blazing away. No fear. And this attitude by a process of osmosis seeped into our way of looking at and acting in battle.

And what was the Americans' attitude? Fire your torpedoes by radar from a mile away, then get out of there. Fast. That kind of thing. Or if we took out an American boat to guide us because they had radar and we didn't, when we were driving in to attack, the American boat would disengage. He wouldn't want to get involved in this close stuff, ship to ship at a few hundred yards, or even much less.

The reaction of the British seaman to this, needless to say, was strong and forthright.

•◄►• *In an English Pub*

Once, I remember, in a little pub down in Surrey, these Americans come in. Typical. Young, mouthy, tunics not buttoned, caps every which way on their beans, cigars in their mouths and they sit down, about six of them. It takes only a few minutes to find out they'd just arrived, about two weeks before, and this was their first time out. They thought darts was a silly game and said so, out loud. They called the barmaid "Hey, you," and her name was Mildred. They wanted rum and Coke, which they couldn't get, but they didn't like the English beer and it happened to be a local brew and bloody good. They were boors, and I was getting some glances from my English friends, farmers, village people, the like. A village pub to me is heaven, but usually a bit small. So one of these soldiers looks over and sees my Canada flashes and he calls me over. He said something like, "Hey Canada, c'mon and translate Limey for us." There wasn't much I could do. A small place, you know. So I went.

Bitch, bitch, bitch. Saviors of the world. They didn't like the left-hand driving and said they had been told in the States the system would be changed. Just for them. I had a hard time believing what I was hearing. And they didn't like Spam. They didn't like evaporated potatoes, they didn't like dried eggs. Christ, England had been living on the stuff for two years or so. They said they had been told in the States that the Spam and dried eggs would be for the British and they'd get the ham and fresh eggs off the English farms.

But that wasn't the clincher. One kid, and these fellows were no more than twenty or twenty-one, he said they had been told they wouldn't be living in barracks but in seaside hotels. And it went on. They were going to be treated like conquering heroes, with the conquering still to be done. They believed it. Somebody had been peddling them a load of bull and they believed it. I didn't try to set them straight. That's what they had chaplains and psychologists for.

Anyway, after a while, and the whole pub was listening, getting their first taste of Americans, I got up to go and I went to the bar, and even though my old man was Polish and my mother German and they still nattered at each other in some crazy bastard of the two at home, I was a Canadian and I went up to the bar and I said loud enough for everybody to hear: "Canada buys a round for the house." I just wanted any strangers to know bloody well who I was.

The American soldiers, of course, let it slide over them. They didn't understand, but Millie the barmaid, a real decent soul, called out, "Canada orders drinks for the house, gentlemen," and then she says to me, low-voiced, "And I say the drinks are on them. They don't know pounds, shillings and pence, darling, and I'll stir them around until they don't know what they've paid for." We both laughed at that.

They learned. Most of them learned. But it did take time, and I imagine more than a few training and orientation movies were shown, but they did make a lot of enemies. Maybe that's too strong a word, perhaps dislike would be better. It was too bad. Canadians and Americans, just a border there, and so different. It was the empire thing, King and Country, I swear it.

•◄►• The Biggest Aircraft Factory in the World

I knew we were going to win the war when I saw the Willow Run aircraft factory outside Detroit. My God, but it was a big one. The biggest in the world, unless the Germans had a bigger one. But that's not what was fantastic about it. They had a sod turning, you know, the official start with Ford Company officials and big shots and Hollywood stars. What was amazing was that here they built the biggest aircraft factory in the world, to make Liberators, a big four-engine job, and *one year* after the official opening, the first Liberator was produced. I'm not joshing you, I'm telling you that that is one of the most fantastic production feats in the history of the world. Yes, the history of the world. One year. Twelve months. One year.

They wanted people to work as foremen, to train others while the plant was being built and I went down and I got a job. I was a trouble-shooter, going from one part of the plant to another, settling problems and just looking for ways to speed things up. The place was so big I even had a little electric cart like one of those golf carts to get me around. Zip here, zip there. A lot of people got to know me. They called me "Jolly Canuck."

I remember some things, like the plant took up 1,300 acres and there was parking for 15,000 cars. There were thousands of workers. Dames who'd never seen a screwdriver, there they were working on engines, radios and fuselages. One of those big babies had more than 600,000 rivets, and those women socked home every one of those rivets. It had four Pratt and Whitney engines and could do 300 miles an hour. I think the Lancaster could only do 200. It was a mighty fighting machine.

You'd see those Libs come out the end and they'd be gassed up, no fooling around, and given their tests right there and then. Right from the factory to the test pilots, and off they'd go. It was fantastic. You have to know something about manufacturing to realize just how fantastic it really was.

They'd just keep rolling those big buggers out of the end of the assembly lines, and they'd just keep coming and coming and coming. As I said, when I'd worked in Willow for a while, I knew that Hitler and the Japs could never win the war.

•◀▶• *They Bombed Everything That Moved*

We never wanted the Yanks around us, their air support. What those stupid bastards were going to do next, I don't think even the Lord on High knew.

In France they'd bomb anything. A jackrabbit in a field. Anything that moved. They bombed Germans, sure, but Canadians, British, their own, the Poles, anything that moved. If a unit wasn't exactly on the point where it was supposed to be, if that unit had moved a few hundred yards, boom. Bomb, bomb, bomb. Everything. An old peasant woman going into the field to get her cow. Hit her. I'm exaggerating a bit, but I sure as hell know where they got their bombing tactics for Vietnam. Right out of the book their generals wrote for them in Italy and Europe.

And the thing is, they couldn't hit anything. With the fighter bombers it was visual bombing. Map coordinates, a house, a tree, a road, and you find your target from there and go in. They couldn't do that. The mediums were a little better, but the big boys, just dots up there in the blue, there'd be this village here called Abbeville or something and 500 yards away there'd be another tiny one and bang, they'd try for Abbeville and get the other one. Why try for either anyway? It was just a bomb-the-goddamn-hell-out-of-everything philosophy.

Us? Oh, yeah, they knocked us around three or four times. Accidental, of course. Always accidental.

Then you'd see these little snotnoses swaggering around the streets, these fighter-bomber kids. Waving 50-franc notes, playing the big shot. Right out of South Chicago high school or Minneapolis high school. Many a kid, those kids, went back to his mess later with his nose three inches wide and flat. Not us, either, their own guys. Some of those Texans and that, those combat teams that were knocked around, they just weren't prepared to take that kind of crapola. Not when the German was giving them more of the same.

Say, if you ever see a guy of about forty-seven or fifty walking around with a nose all over the place, ask him if he flew bombing runs into the Caen and Falaise areas of France in '44. He just might be one of those guys.

•◄►• *The G.I. Was a Good Guy*

I think the Americans suffered a lot from titles they didn't deserve, and I mean that. A lot of guys knocked them who didn't know them. The Americans were top dog over there, best equipment, most men, best conditions, so everyone wants to take a shot at you, eh? I think, and English guys who fought in North Africa with them, said they were terrific soldiers, so that's two of us. I met American tankmen I thought were the best goddamned tank men I ever saw. And the American G.I., he was a good guy.

•◄►• *"Tough Guys, You Canadians"*

We were shipping a cargo of mutton and wool from Auckland and we were glad to stretch our legs ashore when we got to Bora Bora. The island paradise. My friend, then it was the asshole of the world. About 10 feet above the water at most, and most of it swamp and bugs and no booze, and the women are no screaming hell, and what's worse, the Yanks are there. The Seabees, that's the construction corps of the army. Or the U.S. of A. frigging Marines.

Everything comes off by barge so we've got a couple of days and the second day we go ashore, about 25 of us. Looking for booze, women if they're not hiding. And on the road what do we meet but these Yanks. I find out later they're a very pissed-off lot because the women are no good or something and the old war has passed them by and they don't know what they're doing on Bora Bora, just washing laundry and playing poker. Lord, you know, you can only play so much poker.

So they meet us. About 50, 60, 75 of them and one guy comes forward and he says how many? He means how many of us. I say, just a guess, oh, 25. But he wants to know exactly. What the hell. I count. Twenty-three. So what it turns out to be, he calls out 22 other guys from his bunch and we're gonna fight them. All together, boys, all friends together, but man for man and every man for himself. Oh, we're willing enough. We're pissed off too, not being allowed ashore at Auckland. So I says, like, who starts this fight? He says, "Buddy, you and I start." And he charges. And it's on. I won't give you blow by blow, but you can pretty well imagine it. Broken noses. Black eyes. Guys spitting teeth. Kneecaps half kicked off. Those guys could fight dirty, but so, for Christ sakes, could we. Twenty minutes later, or maybe ten, somehow we all decide it's gonna be a draw, so we quit.

That's all, we quit. The big guy says, "Tough guys, you Canadians," and I say, "Tough guys, you Yanks," and we go back to their barracks, their canteen and drink about 15 cans of their Schlitz beer each. Everybody's patching everybody else up and we're all friends.

They just wanted to fight, see. Just fight. The place was boring them to hell and we came along and gave them some entertainment. That's what a goddamn tropical isle could do for you.

•◄►• *The Navy Against the Army*

There were thousands of guys waiting for the boats at Liverpool to take them back home and there was nothing for them to do, and I remember one fight and by God, there must have been hundreds in it. Just like one of those barroom fights in the movies, except you multiply it by a hundred or more.

If you came around the corner into this area, you'd think it was Canadians against the Americans, but if you looked closer you'd see it was different. It wasn't Canada against the U.S., but the navy against the army. So, there were American and Canadian navy types fighting American and Canadian army guys and oh, what a battle. Broken noses, broken arms, a few guys half-kicked to death. Some in pretty rough shape, let me tell you.

This wasn't one of those Canada-against-the-Yank things. No, this was just like a brawl, the guys fighting, beating the hell out of each other because they had nothing else to do with their time. So it was easier to just pick out a navy uniform and bash what was inside it and then hit the next one than go looking for an American uniform or a Canadian uniform. It made it that much simpler.

•◄►• *A Group of Them*

I didn't like the Americans. You give me one American, he's a helluva nice guy. Drink with him. So on. Two Americans, you've got opposition, because there is nobody half as good as the Americans, and they have to keep telling themselves that to believe it. Three Americans and you've got three stupid buggers.

Christ, we had Americans who hadn't been in England two weeks, sitting in pubs with English guys, Australians, Canadians, and we'd been to Dieppe and on raids on the coast, and a lot had come back from North Africa, some had been in Norway—and there we would be sitting in the pub and listening to these guys say that if it wasn't for the Yankees, none of us, including England itself, would be there. They hadn't even set foot in a battle yet, and they had practically won the war.

You get three Americans together and they're pretty obnoxious, and get in with a group of them and you usually wound up in a battle with them. And don't think that didn't happen, because it did.

•◄►• *The Yanks Couldn't Navigate*

After the Americans came in, after they got their aircraft plants going and their crews changed, they started ferry operations. Some down to Brazil, over to the Azores and up to England that way, but an awful lot to Gander in Newfoundland for refueling and then the one big hop, or to Iceland for a fill-up, or Greenland and then in to Scotland. It was a simple operation.

Except for one thing. For some reason the Yanks couldn't navigate. Now you take a squadron lost 100 miles somewhere off Iceland. That is one hell of a lot of planes going to hit the drink somewhere in that cold old Atlantic. This was happening, and nobody was saying anything about it, but often one or two Flying Forts, B-29's, others, wouldn't make it with the rest. That is one hell of a way to die, ditching in the Atlantic.

This buddy of mine named Watkins, a navigator, his crew was at Iceland flying V.I.P.'s home this time and the word was out that about 18 American bombers were lost, and the way he puts it, in his own descriptive language, he said, "And Bunny, I mean good and bloody lost." The upshot was, somehow back-tracking on their flight plan and figuring the winds, drift, magnetic variations, his crew went out and found them, and they were hell and gone, north by northeast above Iceland and heading for Santa's home. Fifty or so miles off. They'd missed the base completely.

This was happening far too often. Losses, you understand, weren't all that heavy, just a few, but there was going to come a day when a whole squadron or more, maybe two or three, were going to follow the leader right into that North Atlantic soup and that would be that, and God only knows, Britain, the war effort, needed those planes.

The upshot was, on the big ferry hauls where there was no trained navigator, they were putting Canadians on as head navigator. Like, follow me boys, just follow your leader—and they'd always get there. It was like a drunk going home. I think there only were six or seven course changes, and any kid who'd ever handled a sailboat could get them right.

•◄►• *The Dutch Victory Parade*

Tell you the difference between the Yanks and us. We're in Holland and the Americans, this army of theirs, is near us. We've practically got the same front, you understand. So the brass decide there's going to be a big victory parade in this town. Not in one of their big cities, Amsterdam or Antwerp, understand, but a smaller one. There's the Canadians and the Yanks and a few British units around, special outfits, and airmen, and we'll all be marching in the big parade and there's a real proper place as I understand it, just behind the flags, for the Dutch underground. Good boys, good fighters. Took a lot of shit too.

Day of the parade, we're like we were having a ceremonial in Ottawa before all the high mucka-mucks. I hadn't polished a button for months but there we were, all of us, polishing. Where they got that filthy blanco I'll never understand.

A big victory parade, you understand. Thousands of guys, and they're flying in a band from England for us, and the Yanks had their own. A big day and it's a wonderful day, understand? May, weather just lovely.

Two regiments are chosen, and away we go to the marshalling site, about 12 miles away, left, right, left, right, cadence count, you know the old bullshit. Just like in training. Then we're there, and the army's the same as ever, run to get there and wait for 2 hours until somebody tells you to do something. Understand?

Officer says we're waiting for the bloody Americans. Parade can't start without the bloody Americans, and they're only 6 miles away. So here they come, and, boy did they come. Could they march 6 miles? Not those lads. Jeeps, little trucks, big trucks canvas-rolled, half-tracks, every bloody thing that moved was filled with American soldiers, and so help me Hannah, in their walking-out dress. Where they get walking-out dress on a battlefield I'll never know. Any G.I. I ever saw was usually a walking pile of dirt and beard. Anyway, they sure looked pretty, and they've got a couple of bands.

Off goes the parade, our general, their general, the mayor, some guy who is probably the governor, and then the Dutch underground and they look like a bunch of farm laborers, which many of them were, you understand, and then us guys. The Canadians, there we are slogging along with rifles just as if there was a bloody war on, and the British boys, they're there too, and some air force guys from somewhere. And then come the Yanks. Rah ta ta ta ta tah! Give them bugles, lads. There come the Yanks, *riding in their bloody vehicles.* Fancy little hats, laughing and joking among themselves and some drinking out of bottles. Paying no attention to the Dutch people all standing there and waving their little flags and cheering. Couldn't even march more than a couple of miles in a parade. We all thought that was pretty bloody lousy.

The Dutch people saw us, and then they saw this great big bloody convoy with these pretty soldiers sitting in the trucks, and when we ended the parade in their big city square you can guess who got the cheers and the invites home to dinner and the big eyes from the girls. Yep, I felt good being a Canadian that day. Those Dutch people have never forgot, you know. Go to Holland even today and say you're a Canadian and you get the welcome mat put out for you.

---

295   *Us and the Yanks*

Liberators

*"We Love You, Canadians" ... Losing So Many Wars ...
Their French and My French ... Sounds in the Orchard
... Business as Usual ... They Strung Them Up ... In the
Town Square ... Little Jan ... A Canadian Boyfriend ...
Conquering Heroes — Then a Nuisance ... The Six Germans
... The Josephine Baker Incident ... "Oh, That War"*

*Everyone has seen movies of Allied troops liberating European
countries that had been occupied by the Germans. There is no
doubt it is a heady and affecting image, the grimy soldiers being
greeted with parades, flowers, cheering crowds, girls eager to kiss
them, wine and smiles. But that sort of enthusiasm cannot be
sustained, and the Canadian liberators found that in France and
Belgium their welcome soon wore out. It was a strange feeling,
fighting to free people and then being made to feel unwelcome;
but perhaps over the centuries the French and the Belgians have
seen too many armies on their soil to regard soldiers as anything
but nuisances.*

*In Holland things were different. The Dutch were con-
stantly welcoming and grateful, and for some months the
Canadians lived with the Dutch. It was a good feeling, having a
home away from home, and even today the Canadian traveller
finds a wellspring of hospitality and kindness when he visits the
Netherlands.*

•◆• *"We Love You, Canadians"*

When the Canadians went into Amsterdam—it was on May 5 as I
remember—half the town came out into the Dam, the big square,
and it was like a picnic ten times over.

I've still got some little pieces of paper that little children
gave to us. They were just pieces of paper and they said, "We Love
You, Canadians." These little kids running around giving us these
pieces of paper, and I'll bet a lot of them hadn't even been born
yet when the Germans took over the town back in '40.

They knew it was the Canadians who would liberate them
because our First and Fifth divisions were moving. I guess they
made their little signs in school or kindergarten.

As I remember the kids looked pretty well. Not starving
anyway, and shiny and clean. It was us and the British with us

who looked like men from the other side of the moon, dirty, stinking. We were a tough lot.

•◄►• *Losing So Many Wars*

One thing I sure didn't like when we got to Paris a couple of weeks after the Germans had left it on the run, and that was the signs on buildings and sidewalks, painted in white lime or white paint and the signs said, "A Bas Les Juifs!" Put there by the French.

Your French doesn't have to be all that hot. It meant "Down With The Jews!" and I told my buddy I thought that's one of the things we were fighting the war for. Against that kind of thinking.

I was wrong. You never can figure out those French. Next time we were there you could still see the Jew signs, but you could also see signs telling the Americans, the Canadians, the English to get the hell out. "A Bas Les Canadiens!" They're a funny bunch. I don't know what makes them that way. Maybe from losing so many wars.

•◄►• *Their French and My French*

It was a funny feeling for me to go through Normandy in a Bren gun-carrier. Here, my family, the Fouquets, had come to Canada from Brittany in the 1600's, about 1670, and my wife's people, the Provenchers, about 50 years later and here I was, liberating France.

I didn't feel anything. I tell you, not a damn thing. I thought I would. Oh sure, I thought I would, but those people, looking out of their windows at us, looking at us in the street, they had nothing to do with me. I felt nothing for them and I know in just a day or so it was for them, "Ho, here is another Canadian. How can we separate him from his money? Some calvados, maybe? Some rolls and butter, maybe? A girl, maybe? Madeleine. Josette. Who would he like?" That sort of thing.

One day we are heroes, talking to them on the street and getting along okay in their French and my French and we're friends, see? Next day, they are out to get us. I was told prices they charged the Germans in the cafés, they're lower than they charge us. The Germans, they're in charge, see. They're the boss. They're scared of them. Canadians? We're friends. From Quebec, so even more friends. Okay, papa, charge them the sky.

That's the Frenchman for you. All money, all business. Mama sitting at the cash register like a big eagle, Papa doing her orders. It was always the same. Out to get you, and every time.

That's one reason. When I was a kid I always thought France and the people, were pretty big stuff. When I get there, when we're chasing the Germans out, we mean nothing to them. Just foreigners. I don't think they even liked us, even French guys like me. They only liked themselves, and all the time. Soon they mean nothing to me either.

•◄►• *Sounds in the Orchard*

I can't remember the town. One of those little villages, south of Caen, between there and Falaise. One of those American combat teams had gone through after their artillery had banged the place around, and then they'd moved out and we'd moved in. I think it was just for the night.

Some Polish had been in a fight in the orchard next to us, there were a lot of dead Germans lying around and a lot of horses, and this was about three days later. Three nights—and it was hot, bloody hot—and some of those bodies were getting pretty squishy. The smell, Christ!

One of our patrols heard this sound out in the orchard. Most of the trees were banged up, but there still were trees, and we heard these sounds. I said, "Somebody's cattle," but we heard voices. Low. You couldn't make them out. Low, like muttering.

We had these big searchlights and somebody cranked one down and turned it on, and by God, right in among those stinking horses and those corpses—and some had been dead for three or four days—there were French people. We told them to come forward and checked them out, and they had harness, saddles, anything they could get. They had German rifles, pistols, billfolds, rings. I woudn't have been surprised to have seen gold teeth, but if I had, maybe I'd have tossed up my cookies. They had uniforms, the jackets, water canteens, ammo.

To put it this way, they were going through that stink and squishing flesh like monkeys looking for lice. Anything they could get, what they thought might be valuable, they were taking. It wasn't looting, so much as being just downright disgusting.

They stank of decaying flesh and shit.

We all might have felt better if one of them had said that they were taking this stuff off the dead because the Germans had been terrible to them during the occupation, but I can't even say that. They just looked at us like dumb animals, and finally our captain gave them a gesture. You know, "Bugger off," and we turned off the lights, and I could hear them for about another hour messing about, feeling, looking for something they could use or sell.

•→• *Business as Usual*

Those Belgians used to give me a charge. I didn't like them, I never thought they were trustworthy but that's personal, and I'd get a charge out of how it was all business as usual for them. German or Canadian, Yank or Englishman, it didn't matter who you were, just so long as you had the bucks. Any kind of currency would do, except when we went through, the mark would be out. I don't think they ever expected to see a German soldier again. They were pretty realistic people. Pretty hard-headed.

I remember one day we were chasing Jerry and they made a bit of a stand just outside this town. It lasted only a few minutes and then they took off through the town and joined up with the rest, and there was a bit of a scrap again there but nothing heavy. I think they were short of ammunition. They were certainly on the run.

Our company was sent back to clear out the town if there were any snipers left behind. I guess there were none. We saw none. It's about four o'clock when we're finished, so we're just hanging around this square in the town. Nothing doing. A few shops open and townspeople shopping. You'd never think there had been a war on, occupation, German domination for more than four years. It was like my home town on a warm Friday afternoon.

Yet, to the east and south we could hear the big guns. You know how they rumble away, sort of like thunder on a hot summer night on the prairie when it's a long way away. It was probably the first time the people of this fat-cat town had heard guns, except for maybe in 1940, but for all they were concerned it could have been summer thunder. Maybe they thought it was.

I saw a shop which looked like a sporting goods shop, with things like fishing poles and the like, and I wandered over. And as I get near I see this heavy curtain just flick a little, just as if somebody was watching me. Now it could have been anything, or it might have been a Jerry. We actually hadn't done that good a search, and not in the square where the townspeople were. Not too good.

I yell at the sergeant and I crouch down below the window, and the sarge brings half a dozen guys over and we wonder, should we kick in the door, bust a window and grenade the place or what? By this time there wasn't a town person in sight, and our guys are meaning business now. The company interpreter yells in German for the Germans to come out, hands up, and I knock out a small pane of glass to show them we mean *them*. There's a long wait, maybe a minute, and then the door sort of creaks open, slowly—and out comes this old lady. She's eighty if she's a day. A real great-grandmother type. What the hell.

Anyway, we search the place and there's nothing. Just an old lady's living quarters above a little store filled with junk. There's a picture of a man and she points to it and says, *"Mon fils. La guerre, m'sieu,"* and holds her hand over her heart. Her son, dead, killed in the war.

The sergeant says, "C'mon, you guys, get the hell out of here. The old babe is starting to cry," and so she was and we start out and I'm the last and she takes hold of my sleeve and holds me back, and she's pointing at a box. She takes this box and opens it and there's a little knife in it. What you'd call a skinning knife on the prairies, I guess, and the handle is covered with fur and so is the sheath. Cat's fur, I think. Don't they eat cats, breed them for eating?

I mean I don't want this. It's cheap steel and it looks corny, that fur. I can't see myself going on a deer hunt up in the lake country at home and carrying that on my hip, but she's fondling it like it was a treasure and saying *"Pour votre fils, m'sieu."* For my son. Buy it for my son, and I look at the old girl and there's still a couple of tears running down her old face. Christ, but she had an old face. Right out of the ice age.

Okay, it'll make a souvenir for somebody, so I ask, you know, gesture how much and she shows me by fingers it is 35 francs. That's no good, and I show her 20 and we're haggling back and forth and she's still crying a bit and finally we settle for 30. I forget what that comes to. It was no bargain anyway.

Once the deal is made, she whips out a piece of newspaper and wraps it up and grabs my money and makes some quick change and she's got a big grin on her face, and she sort of pushes me up the stairs back onto the street, and just before she slams the door in my face she grins again and says, *"Adieu, adieu."* Then bang goes the door.

I walk back to the patrol and the sergeant asks what I'm carrying, and I show him and he's been around, trapper somewhere in Northern Ontario for one thing, and he hefts it and tests it with his thumb and hands it back and says, "Marty, why in hell would you buy a piece of junk like that?" and to tell you the truth, I didn't know.

•◄►• They Strung Them Up

Our squadron came into this Dutch town just after dawn this morning and Jerry had pulled out the evening before, or during the night. One of the Dutch underground guys came out to tell us the way was clear.

The Germans had been in that town for three or four years, I guess.

When we turned our tanks into the square there were four bodies hanging from lampposts. Three from posts and one from a kind of arch into the middle of the town. I thought, "Oh ho, the underground picked off a few Jerry stragglers. Good for them." One of the guys took a potshot at one of the bodies. Just for the hell of it. You know, there's always some guy like that in every outfit.

A couple of Dutchmen came running up, their arms going like windmills and the one who spoke English gave us the word. The bodies weren't Germans. Dutchmen, from the underground. The day before they'd come out a bit too early, thinking we were just down the road, and when they started to bang away at the Germans, that was it. They strung them up, women and kids and everybody standing around too.

It was sure tough, I mean if some of the guys had relatives, wife, kid, hanging around. But it doesn't say a hell of a lot for their intelligence. Not much at all. Nobody had to die in that town.

•◄►• In the Town Square

In the spring of '45 we were in what they called Buzz Bomb Alley. All the V-1's and V-2's were going right over this little Belgian town we were in and this morning they're coming over thick and fast and one lands right in the square. Of course, the whole battery is turned out and pulling out bodies and the wounded and it was a mess, a bloody mess, and the whole town was in a panic.

That afternoon the things are coming over just as heavy, and the major orders us out, all polished up, all slicked up, parade ground inspection type of thing. And we march into the square and we stand there at full attention for two hours, with at-ease periods, naturally—but we stand there for two hours just to show the civilians that if another buzz bomb dropped there, we'd be taking it along with them. It was a show of what Canadians were like, and a morale booster for them. Those bombs were going over all the time, and we stood there, and I think it gave the town people a real boost.

You know, there are some things in a war you can be proud of and that was one of them.

•◄►• *Little Jan*

There were cases, you know, where boys would attach themselves to our units. I guess they did it to American and British outfits too. Maybe a kid was French or Czech and his family had been wiped out. Jewish kids, I'm mainly talking about. Twelve, fifteen. They'd hang around and be fed, and usually somebody fixed up a uniform for them.

There was this kid we had, an Austrian Jew. His name was Jan. They brought in this prisoner and the major was interrogating him and little Jan, who was about so high, was doing the interpreting. The German lieutenant was being snotty. In a case like that, you do your best, but if he's adamant, then turn him over and somebody will escort him to a P.O.W. cage.

There were five of us in the room of this house, the major, me, the guard, Jan, and the prisoner. The major says to me, "We're not going to get anything out of this shitheel," and Jan, without a word, grabs up the major's Luger, which is lying beside him on the cot where the major is sitting, and bam, he blows this Jerry's head off. I mean, what there is left of a head, well, it wouldn't fill a can of soup. Don't mean to be crude. There's blood all over the place. Everywhere.

What are you going to do? Shoot the kid? You don't court-martial him. No, the major says, "We'll forget this ever happened," and the guard and I agree. No use asking Jan to agree to anything. Those little bastards were tougher than any troops I ever commanded. You know the old saying, the only good Indian is a dead Indian. Just substitute the word "German" and you've got their thinking pretty close. Hard little nuts.

•◄►• *A Canadian Boyfriend*

Canadians were big stuff in Holland. We'd liberated a lot of it, you understand, and their Queen Juliana had been in Ottawa during the war. Everything worked together, and we all got along fine.

Our artillery bunch had been pulled back and we were at rest in a large building. Anyway, nearby was this Dutch farmer's house. There was this old man, Van Voort, the mother, a grandmother who didn't say much, and three daughters. One son was with the Royal Dutch Air Force and the other had just disappeared some time ago.

When our outfit went back up, six of us, a sergeant, a corporal and four of us, we were left behind and this place we were in became kind of a rest area for our battery, and others. We kind of ran it. There wasn't all that much of a war that winter, so it was a good life for us.

At night some of us would go and sit in the farmhouse kitchen and yak. They spoke good English. Most Dutch people spoke some, but the Voorts were good. We'd bring our goodies from the kitchen and they'd share, and make special soups and stews with chunks of meat and big fat dumplings. They knew how to eat. They also know how to entertain, and we'd have rare old times. We spent Christmas with them and exchanged presents, things we'd bought on leave in Amsterdam, and they gave us socks and I got a wool vest.

One of our guys was Keertbergen. He spoke French and Dutch but he never let on. When the mother and dad would suddenly break into Dutch and talk, or the girls did, well, old Keert was there, ears all pricked up but not letting on.

So one night back in our quarters we're melting down some chocolate bar for a drink before dinner and Keert is snickering away, and finally he says, "Tim, they've got Anna staked out for you." Anna is the second, about twenty-two then, and I've got to say it, she was quite pretty. Big like a lot of Dutch girls are, bigger than her sisters.

I said what the hell are you talking about? He laid it out, line by line. I was good-looking, and I said well, thanks. I had a good education and my father was wealthy. So, Anna would try for me. She'd shoot for a Canadian boyfriend.

How the hell did he know all this? He said two ways. He'd listened to the old people talking, you know, when they would suddenly start speaking Dutch, and besides, Katie had dropped a hint along the line. This was the first I'd heard of him making up to Katie, because with the old folks there, it was strictly chaperoned.

And how did they know my old man was wealthy? I said, "Christ, all he is is a manager of a small department in a big Eaton's store." Keert said *he* knew that, but to the Dutch a manager meant something more, like a works manager and that meant a factory, and if that's what my dad was, then he was pretty big stuff. Anna would be making a real match.

From then on, he said, the heat would be on. The old folks would leave about nine or so, and if I had the inclination, and so on and so forth, it was okay with them. Apparently it was just fine with Anna, although you couldn't have told it from the way she'd acted the two months or so we'd been going over there. Just a good kid, that type of thing. But I thought, maybe she knew how to play it smart a long long time before I did.

That's about the way it was. Play the game, I figured. If she'll jump into the hay, fine. Maybe we wouldn't be around that long. I was a pretty young soldier and I didn't know much about sex, so, what the hell, I thought, catch up on the game. On Sunday we'd go for walks, just like I would have in Toronto. Over to a village three miles away, a hot chocolate. Holding hands. Kissing. That sort of thing. Then quite a bit further than kissing, and momma and poppa and oma, her grandmother, smiling quietly and Katie being awful nice, too, and her other sister, the youngster, whose name was Jay-Jay.

I don't want to dig myself in any deeper than I am, so I'll just say this. We got shipped home in July of '45 and we were supposed to go to Japan but that finished up, too, so about November, Anna came to Montreal on a ship and I drove down to pick her up and back here to Toronto and we got married and it's worked out pretty well. I've got no complaints and that was nearly twenty-five years ago.

•◄►• *Conquering Heroes—Then a Nuisance*

If you were out of the line of battle the French life went on. They could hear the guns, sure, but they still had grain to take off and cows to milk and they have very good orchards. I think the Normandy peasant will survive long after the last other man is dead.

You could get a jeep and high-tail it across the country, and when you got out of the range of guns and stray German units, it was pretty country. In fact, in August it is lovely country and very bountiful. Very lush. Huge crops.

The first time you visit, everybody is rushing out into the streets, and the next time it is big smiles and "Welcome, welcome, come in." This is in the villages or those big farms. The next time, they want gas from you. Gas for their machines, their engines. So next time you bring gas, a few cans of it and you're a hero. But more next time, and more. A very demanding people. Sincere at first, and then very mercenary. Okay, you were conquering heroes then, but now you're a nuisance.

A friend who had been there before the war said, "When you go into a bar and the wine or brandy you get makes you want to spit it out, then you have outworn your welcome. You are no further use to them." And then he said, "And it won't take long."

Right. Right. After about a month, four or five visits, the wine, you couldn't drink it, and there were no smiles. What they were saying was for us to get out. War's war and peace is peace but we're busy people and we've got to get back to the business of making a living. So vamoose.

I think that is why the Canadians like the Dutch much better. Not the Belgians. A Belgian is just a Frenchman, only worse. And I have a sneaking suspicion that our boys liked the Germans in the villages and towns better too. Funny thing, isn't it? One year the German is the lowest thing on the face of the earth and the next, well, living in Germany for the few months after the war as I did, I enjoyed myself and the people too. Nice people.

•◄►• *The Six Germans*

We're in this salient. Part of it is in one of those man-made forests the Dutch plant, and it's quiet. Almost Christmas Day, and who wants to get killed at Christmas? That's part of what I'm saying.

Anyway, we have patrols out and you've got to figure the enemy has too, but we're out all morning and nothing's moving and we bog down at noon at the edge of a little clearing in the forest. It looked like the foresters kept equipment there, and it's about 100 yards across. We're lying around in the snow wondering if we're going to get the turkey and trimmings bit the next day. The bumff from down the line said we were.

Okay, there we are and wham, there's a shot. Just one. High and to the right. It's gotta be a German patrol and they must have seen our smoke. One of our guys smoked a pipe. You know how pipe smoke is. Blue and heavy.

Then another shot, low and inside so to speak, and too blasted close, so the corporal says to start fading back among the trees. We don't want to fight, and it looks like they don't either. Else they'd be down on us like a ton of bricks with everything they had. They'd spotted us, sitting ducks.

Now what happens? Damndest thing I saw in the war. We're almost back in the heavier timber and across this open meadow these six Germans charge. *They get up and charge.* I couldn't believe my eyes. There they were, wearing those damned awful tin hats and greatcoats all buttoned up, and here they come thundering across the plain. I mean, you don't know what to think.

Your experience says to kill them, but there's a flash in there that says something is awfully wrong. These guys must be playing a game.

We've got this big guy with us, from Fort William. He's black and big and mean, and I think everybody up to the brigadier at one time or another tried to get him to shave. He says, "Shit, let me have these daisies," and he stands up. He's got a sniper rating, by the way, but that doesn't matter a hoot here. This is a turkey shoot.

He just keeps slamming the full clip at them, one to each Jerry and each one right in the brisket. You see, it's a flat shot, no trajectory, like firing across your lawn. The last one falls about 20 feet from us. They're all dead, of course. The big bastard couldn't miss at that distance.

The four of us move around, around the perimeter of this clearing, but there are no more of them. Just these six. Then we walked back and checked each one, and they were all from the same regiment. Hans this and Horst that and Wolfgang something or other. Just kids, all under twenty or so and their uniforms were clean. Probably the first time they'd been in action, if you call that action.

They didn't do anything right, and they had the drop on us. We were sitting ducks, lying there smoking and bullshitting. We were doing everything wrong except singing "Roll Out the Barrel." And they charged. Straight up the spout, no evasive tactics. Nothing.

Blackie, the great marksman, said, "Okay, you guys explain it. I can't."

I remember thinking, somewhere in Germany in a few weeks, six mothers are going to learn that their sons died in a battle in Holland. And if they're going to wonder what it was all about, then the only thing I could tell those ladies is that their sons died as stupidly as six men ever died. That's all you could say about it.

The Josephine Baker Incident

A pal and I, we got drunk in Brussels and somehow we wound up in a whorehouse that the Germans had set up. The girls were gone but the madam was still there. God, an old hag, but real interesting. What she could tell you about the Germans. So we're drinking her wine and she says she's under house arrest unless troops are with her; for some reason this was the setup. Canadians were kings then, we could do no wrong, so we say to this old girl we're going to take her to the fanciest nightclub in Brussels, and God, she's happy, so off we go. She's got this huge car, and a chauffeur.

So we go to this nightclub and it's full of officers, and here I am, a corporal, and my buddy is a sergeant and we've got with us this old bag in an 1908 gown and behind her is her chauffeur, and he's lugging along a case of the best champagne in all Belgium. Ten years old maybe, and everybody else is drinking raw wine. Whoo!

So I dance with the old madam, and about the third time around this tiny floor I see a coloured girl at a table and she's with two Arabs, in those long white burnouses, you know, and I don't know them, but I recognize her. It's Josephine Baker [a famous American jazz singer]. So when the music stops I send a bottle of the bubbly over to their table and about 10 minutes later I ask her to dance. Me, a bloody corporal asking Josephine Baker to dance with me! So we dance.

Oh, the two guys in Arab clothes. Hell, they were Americans. Negroes. Sergeants in some regiment, but there was so much racial discrimination in the American Army that this is the way they had to go. Negroes, no way. Arabs, sure, come on in.

So I get back to my table and there are two American field officers next to us and high rank. Colonels, I think. And one starts to give me hell for dancing with a Negro. Josephine Baker. To me she's a great artist, to them she's shit. So I put up with this crap for a bit and then I got up, knocked off his hat because the silly bastard was wearing his hat in this nightclub and I pasted him one. And another. Right in the chops. And when his pal got up I knocked him on his ass.

And by the time the police got there, if they ever did, my pal and me and our madam and her chauffeur were hell and gone away in that big car of hers.

•◆• *"Oh, That War"*

I met this American admiral in Phoenix after the war, years after the war, and we were talking about the old days and he said something about when the war started and he mentioned December 7, 1941.

I said, "I always thought the war started about September 1, 1939," and he looked at me absolutely blank. He didn't know what I meant. I said, "When Britain and France went to war against Germany. You know, the second world war," and he said, "Oh, that war." And he was an admiral. So many Americans think the war started when the Japanese bombed Pearl Harbor.

Booze

Perhaps it was a reaction to the Depression, perhaps it was a response to the excitement of war, perhaps it was simply because the stuff was rationed; but in Canada during the war, everyone seemed to go loony about booze. It came out loud and clear from dozens of interviews, people vividly remembered the importance of beer, wine and spirits during the war.

Perhaps some sociologist will write a book to explain why and how this national craving seized the country. But I know that it affected me. One of my saddest experiences was dropping a quart of rye on the sidewalk outside a Montreal liquor store on weekend leave. I still think that I showed great manliness in not crying.

•◄►• A Personal Relationship

My sister and I lived with this old aunt, a dear sweet thing but very, very unworldly, you understand, and this Christmas Dorothy and I decided we would have a party and invite all the young men from the base who had taken us out in the past few months, and of course we needed liquor for the punch because we decided we would make a punch, as potent as we could.

This dear old aunt didn't have a liquor licence. Everybody else did, but not Auntie Nan. So the first thing, we got her one. We had got our November quota, my sister and I, and now we would use our December Christmas quota, and with Auntie we felt, well, there would be enough for an interesting punch and who could tell?

We coached her, the dear old thing. Getting liquor in those days was unlike any shopping she had ever done. She was English and shopping meant a personal relationship with the butcher, the greengrocer. You know. We said, "Now, Nan, when you go in, just ask for Seagram's V.O. One bottle of V.O." And we had her repeat it. What a joy she was, the dear soul.

The day arrived and we walked downtown and to the liquor store and there is a line-up around the block, a long line-up, and the three of us get in it and wait and move forward and wait, and it is cold and rainy but it is not unlike an adventure for Auntie and then she gets to the counter. We're right behind her, of course, but now she is on her own.

She looks at the shelves, she looks at the fellow behind the counter, she looks back at the shelves and then she puts her elbows on the counter and I thought, "Oh God," and I was right, for she said in a friendly voice like she was talking to Mr. Grantham at the butcher shop, she said, "And now, young man, what have you got today that's nice?"

•◄►• *Cider for Pigs*

When the war came you couldn't say the Depression was gone from the Annapolis Valley, but there was jobs in Halifax and Dartmouth, and a lot of fellows went up to Canada to work. They got a chance to see the world so they didn't stay down home. Then, all the lads were joining up, in all the regiments, and the navy over at Halifax, and some joined the air force, too.

In about a year you didn't see no more lads on the roads looking for work or coming round to the back door asking for a feed. They was all gone to the war or to jobs, and the next year it was worse. We all had good loads on our trees, they was heavy, and no pickers. First, we had all the pickers in the world and couldn't pay none, and then no pickers and we could pay them because they was sending an awful lot of our apples to England.

Feast or famine, you might say, and how do you stop apple trees from growing? You can't talk to them.

I had this big windfall. Every inch of ground was covered with those apples, all over the place so you couldn't walk within them, always stepping. I put up a sign that said, "Free Apples, Just Pick Them," but there were so many others, nobody bothered.

One morning my wife says, "Jock, you know you could make a little cider," and I'd had the idea too, so I got out the stone boat and put three barrels on it and got a six-tined fork and away I went, and in a week I'd cleaned up that whole orchard, all six acres of it, and what was left I turned my two pigs in on.

Oh yes, when I'm cleaning up, the young Mountie from town drives by and stops and he says, "Morning, Mr. McIvor, a nice crop. What will you do with it?" and I says, "For the pigs this winter," and he says, "I didn't know you had a herd of pigs," and

I says, "Everybody's got pigs," and he laughed and, you see, I didn't give the game away. I didn't say I just had two pigs. I just didn't give him the sure right answer.

It takes another two weeks to crush and separate that pile of apples, it must have been 10 feet high, and by November end we've got our cider. Barrels of it and I've a mind to run it through again so I do, and this time it's real skull-cracking stuff. It's not cider any more. It's the real stuff, hit you in the jaw and drive your teeth up into your skull.

The word gets around, you know. Jock's got some pretty good stuff, and soon somebody wants to buy a quart and I don't know the price, but I figure 5 dollars, and of course it was high but whiskey was pretty scarce. Law of supply and demand, it works for the farmer sometimes too, you know.

Before you know it, I guess, I'm in the bootlegging business. I'm smart enough to know that it will just be for one year because everybody in the county will see how Jock McIvor did so well in applejack, and everybody will be selling applejack and that's when I *won't* be selling it, because it will be down to about a dollar a bottle and I'd rather make ice in the curling rink or work for the government or something than sell at that price. I'm selling right and left and it looks like the best year I've ever had with that orchard. My father who planted it would have laughed himself into a coughing spell should he have known, but he was dead then. Every day I'm selling maybe two or three bottles, and only to friends or people from town I know. Even the doctor in town comes and gets five bottles, he says, for his friends in Halifax.

Just before Christmas there's this knock on the door and when I open it there's the young Mountie and he comes in and chats, talks about things country, and then he says, "Mr. McIvor, how are your pigs making out this winter?" and I don't get the track of his talk and I said, "I butchered them. I always butcher in the fall," and he says, "Fine, in that case I'll take some of their feed home," and I still don't get the track of what he's saying. And then he says, "Mr. McIvor, look, I'm taking off my hat," and he takes off his Mountie hat and he says, "That means I'm not in full uniform now, so I'm not really a policeman"; he nods and he says, "Okay, can I have two bottles of that pig feed?" and then I get it. Two bottles of applejack. He wants two bottles of applejack.

Well, there I am, a policeman in my parlour asking for some of the booze I'm bootlegging, and so I figure, the lion shall assimilate the lamb, nothing much I can do, so I go out in the back and bring out two bottles and he has a 10-dollar bill in his hand

and he says, "Ten dollars for two bottles of pig feed." I hand over the bag, and he gives me the money.

He says, "Merry Christmas to you and yours, Mr. McIvor," and I say the same thing, and that's all there is to it.

He was a smart young fellow and I don't think what he did was something they taught him in the training school they go to in Regina.

My wife is in the bedroom off the parlour and she comes out, trembling, and I says, "Mary, don't you worry. He's a nice young man. He took off his hat, didn't you hear, and not once did he mention whiskey or spirits or applejack. All he bought was two bottles of pig feed and I never heard of a law against that, did you?"

•➔• *Washroom Booze*

I took my training, air force, pilot, and they said, "Boy, it's instructing for you," and they sent me to the I.T.S. school at Edmonton. What a hole in those days. A small town, you know. Now, it was rationing, and you needed a permit. I'd tell my class to go down and get a permit for liquor and, you see, the classes were only for 10 weeks and the permits were good for a year, so there was a lot of time left and when they'd move on to the next station, you see, I'd get their permits. They'd give them to me, although some guys might sell them. Two bucks. Five bucks. So what? So there never was a time I didn't have 20 or 25 permits on me, and I'd buy mickeys.

This was when they were building the Alaska Highway, and the Yanks, soldiers and construction guys, would be coming down the N.A.R. [Northern Alberta Railway] to Edmonton for a blowout, or just going back home. Christ, the wages those construction guys were getting, about 600 or 700 bucks a month and nowhere to spend it. They didn't allow booze on that road, officially, and no whores. So poker—that was all, poker. And these guys were coming out with thousands.

The word was, you see, that the booze was in the men's can in the N.A.R. station and that's where we'd be when the night train arrived, and you'd have 30 or 35 guys lined up to buy your booze out of your kit bag, and there wouldn't be only me, because there would be maybe four or five other guys selling too. It was nothing for a guy to buy four or five mickeys just like that, and we charged between 20 and 25 bucks a mickey and, my God, I'm telling you, it was real rot gut. Real wartime stuff. God.

I don't know how much I made. Thousands—oh, yeah, thousands. I'd send a hundred to my folks, and this was when my old man was making maybe a hundred and ten for the railroad, so a hundred more put them on easy street, and I don't know what I did with the rest. Women, gambling, and well, you know, I just don't know what the hell I did with all that loot. Spent it.

•➤• *The Famous Toronto Party*

This was at manning pool in Toronto in 1942 and there must have been 10,000 guys there. Well, at least 5,000, and this C.O. decides for some damn-fool reason he's going to throw a big party at Christmas for the guys that couldn't get home for Christmas. That meant just about everybody who didn't live in Ontario or Quebec, so he arranges this party and Christ, he must have looted every mess fund in the country, but he threw a party. God, anybody who was there will never forget it.

There was grub and booze galore and entertainment and I think just about half the C.B.C. was there and a bunch of entertainers from the States, because if you didn't do your bit for the boys, why, you were dead. They'd bloody well blacklist you. It didn't matter how big you were, Bob Hope or Jack Benny or what. If they asked you, even up to Canada, you got your ass up there.

And this C.O., and what a randy old bugger he was, he brought in girls. Busloads of them, truckloads of them. I don't know where he got them, but he did. And most of them were pretty good lookers too. Some were smashers.

Well, there was food and booze and entertainment and dancing and, well, what it really was all about was screwing. I remember next morning you'd see girls staggering out towards the main gate, no stockings, skirts ripped, looking like death warmed over. I took a detail through the huts at noon and, believe it or not, there were still girls in the sack. Not screwing, just sleeping. I think we rousted the last one out and got her dressed about two o'clock. Found her sitting on the can, sound asleep.

•➤• *No Trouble Getting Booze*

The bootlegging. We got a big bang out of it. There was always an Uncle John somewhere, and you'd go off on a country road and the cars would be watching down the road to see if a police car was coming and the others would go into a house or a barn and pack the stuff away.

It came in big jugs, those stone jugs or the big clear glass ones. You never bought it in quarts or bottles like in the liquor store. It was just in big jugs of gallons, and this was because the bootlegger would be making so much of it that he'd try his best to sell it as fast as he could.

Some of it was white, and if you shook it up, the guck from the bottom would come up and it would become milky, chalky, but we used to mix it with anything. I once had a party for half the town with three or four gallons of this stuff mixed with peach preserves, Coke, molasses and God knows what else. You know what the party was? A christening. Everybody came. I called it peach punch and I served it in a washtub.

You couldn't get sugar. Not if you were just wanting to put down some fruit or something, but if you were a bootlegger there always seemed to be lots of sugar and everything. Some of the stills were quite elaborate.

There was this air station about 25 miles away and they used to tell the pilots, the trainees, that if they could spot the smoke from a still in the bush they would get a reward. The planes they practised on flew very slowly, and low. I think they found some stills that way. Just family stills. I don't think they ever found the big ones. The police usually got those through an informer. Somebody who had a grudge.

It was no trouble getting booze. The lady in the post office if she knew you, would tell you who had just run off a batch, or the filling-station man, the baker. There aren't many secrets in a small town.

•◄►• *In the Baptist Church Hall*

Oh my, oh, those days. The church had this old peoples club down at the hall, just for old people, to go and meet and talk. It was sort of a club for people getting on, you know. None of us had any money. Well, not much. Remember now, there had been a Depression, and Mr. Bennett and then Mr. King, they never allowed us very much. I think it was 10 dollars a month for everything, and that was all.

But there were all of us at the church hall and a young fellow came in and he told us, right out like I'm telling you now, no going sneaking around the corner, that if we gave him our liquor books he'd give each of us so much. I forget. Fifty dollars, I think. Well, sir, you never saw such a rush. He bought I guess two dozen and that helped a lot because he did it every year, for four years as I remember.

Oh, I guess he had some arrangement with the man at the liquor store. We never signed a blamed thing. Just took the money.

The tee-hee-hee was on him, because Mrs. Adams and Mrs. Ireland and Mrs. Gill and Mrs. Johnson, these ladies were all my friends, we never drank anyhow, and so the 50 dollars was free, because we would never have used the stuff anyway. Our church was Baptist and I don't know too many Baptists who do drink. But imagine, coming right up to us in our own hall and saying he'd buy our books. The nerve of him.

•◄►• *A Bitter Disappointment*

My husband sent me down for this bottle of liquor and when I got to the store there was quite a line-up, so I went across the street and did my shopping and then I came back and got in line again. When I got my bottle of liquor I put it in a sort of straw purse I had over my arm and I was carrying my shopping bag, and just as I got out the door this guy came up and he threw a 5 dollar bill into my shopping bag and grabbed a big bottle that was poking out of the bag.

Then he took off down the street with my bottle. Except it wasn't my bottle of liquor. It was a bottle of vinegar I had bought.

•◄►• *Christmas Eve Cocktails*

Wasn't there a deal once at Winnipeg during that time when a bunch of air force people at Christmas made a cocktail or punch out of glycol, the stuff that they used as de-icing fluid for aircraft windshields, and a bunch of them died?

Didn't they get this fluid and strain it out for impurities and thought they had straight alcohol and they mixed it with orange juice and Coca-Cola or stuff like that and five of them died, and a bunch were blinded for life?

This was on a Christmas Eve, a party they were holding out at Stevenson's Field and they had no booze, so they made their own. They sure did. I can't remember the sordid details, but I had a cousin who worked out there as a fitter and he told me about it. Apparently it is a horrible way to die.

•◄►• A Lonely Life at Sea

Remember the midnight boats, the Canadian Pacific's boats to Victoria? If a guy had a bottle of whiskey and a cabin he was king. Just walk around the deck waving the bottle and he could have his pick of the girls, and I don't mean just girls either. Housewives with husbands in the army, husbands overseas. If she wanted to, a woman could make quite a few dollars on the weekend midnight boats when they were loaded down with air force and navy boys.

I remember one night the captain of the ship tried to get me into his cabin. He wanted some fun, I guess, but I wasn't having any of that. He tried several ways to get me in, short of dragging me in, and then he said that he was lonely. He said command was lonely and it was a lonely life at sea. I nearly fell down laughing. Here was the old goat—and if he looked backward he could practically see Vancouver if it hadn't of been for the blackout and if he looked forward he could nearly see Vancouver Island—and here he's yapping about it being a lonely life at sea, like it was the North Atlantic.

But no kidding. Anything and everything went on those midnight boats.

•◄►• Flying the Beer Patrol

I remember once the beer ship didn't make it to Newfie. A whole ship of beer. Heavy ice, icebergs, that sort of thing. It went back to the mainland and somebody else must have got their hooks into it. Anyway, it didn't make another try, so the services on Newfoundland were pretty short of suds for a few weeks.

I was flying with Number 10 B. R. [Bombing and Reconnaissance] on B-24 Liberators. Out of Gander or Torbay, I forget which. The next time the beer ship is heading for St. John's, we get orders to fly the beer patrol. Fine, so up we go.

The problem is to spot the ship and identify it and then fly ahead and spot loose ice, big chunks and if they were there, then guide the beer ship through the ice. In other words, find a channel for it. This was in the months when the ice was coming down from Greenland and there still was a lot of it around. But we made it, we made it. Got the ship through and the boys got their beer.

•◄►• Granny Was Ninety-five

My grandmother's name was Charlotte Currie, and if she had anything stronger than a few sips of wine at a shower or a christening or a funeral, then I never saw it, and I don't think anyone else did either.

Then comes rationing and I said to her, "Maybe you don't drink, but I do, and you're entitled to a rationing book just like everybody else, so why don't I drive you down and you pick one up." I expected her to raise an unholy fuss, but she just said for me to get her sticks and bonnet and away we went. I took her in and she's moving about 100 feet an hour and the guy at the wicket, he's winking at me, but by God, she gets her booze book.

Then she wants to know what to do with it, and I tell her that when I want a bottle or some beer I'll come over and drive her over to the liquor store and we'll fill up her quota. And that's what she did.

That was a sight for you. Granny was ninety-five, I'd say, and she'd totter into the liquor store with her two canes and get the bottle and stick it into a bag she had around her neck and totter out again, and when we got out on the sidewalk she'd give the bottle to me and I'd pay her, and that's the way we did it.

Once I got curious and asked her what she thought about it, being a messenger for me to the liquor store and she said—she was Scotch, you see—she said, "I don't care if it's right or wrong or not. I'm entitled to that stuff and I'm sure going to see I get my right share. Remember that."

•◄►• *A Roadside Party*

This night I'd driven two officers over to Fredericton and I was coming back by myself, and suddenly on that stretch down to Moncton everything went whirlygig and when I opened the hood the carburetor was loose and spinning on one nut and the rest were sheared off or had dropped onto the road. The screws, I mean. It must have been on two screws for some time and that's the story of navy vehicle maintenance for you. I wasn't going anywhere and it was getting dark, so I pushed the jeep partway off the road and figured I'd just tough it out until daylight when I could get to a phone somewhere. There's not much on that road, only at crossroads. Everybody's back in the bush. Cutting pulp or making potatoes.

So a big truck comes along and he stops and looks at my rig and laughs and says he'll tow me but he's going the wrong way, so I give him a drink out of this mickey I've got and we stand there chatting. And soon a car comes along and two guys pile out and we have another drink and they haul out a bottle of goof.

Then in a few minutes along comes a man and his wife from a house just a bit down the road that I didn't even see going by it, and they take a snort and we're shooting the shit, like I'm from Chilliwack and these cranberry boggers ask where is Chilliwack and, hell, they hardly know where British Columbia is. We're yakking away and the guy sends his wife back to the house and she brings back a lantern and half a gallon of old popskull, and by this time, a couple more cars have stopped. Local people and a long-distance hauling truck, and now there's about a dozen people around and three or four jugs.

We're telling jokes, and down in that country they've got their own kind. I guess you'd call them hillbilly jokes. They're really a poor lot, you know. I mean, poor when it comes to money, and to get ahead they want to send their kids to Montreal and Toronto. Toronto they still call Canada.

So more and more cars and trucks are coming along and stopping and I never saw so many bottles, and two young fellows start a fire on the road allowance and I say, what about the Mounties? and the first truck driver who's getting pretty drunk, I remember him saying, "Let the bastards come. We ain't hurtin' nobody." Well, the cars and trucks were off the road, so he had a point.

Everybody laughed and one guy had been to town to buy food and what the hell, he hauled out cookies and cucumbers and loaves of bread and a can of molasses and everybody was eating and there was plenty of booze. The guy from the house close by went and got his fiddle, and one guy could make a whomping sound by banging his cupped hands together and blowing into them, and a couple made kazoos out of combs and newspaper, so there was a regular orchestra and sing-song going. They were a musical bunch and they'd dedicate every number to me, "And now a little number for our friend the sailor from Chilliwack in the Western Canada mountains," and away they'd go.

This was in May or June as I remember and it was a nice night and I remember waking up about four o'clock, four-thirty, and Christ but I had a head, and there were two guys mucking about with the jeep engine—there were parts all over the god-damned place—and they were drunk. There was a jar of white stuff balanced on the fender and when I climbed out one of them handed it to me and I was going to drink but then I noticed the stuff was kind of cloudy, sort of foggy, and I knew if I took a snort of that I'd be pissed for a week. I told them I had to get a phone and they said not to worry, cap, don't worry, cap, we'll get her going for you, and I said it was the carb that was fucked up and not the engine itself and they said, the big lanky one said, "Yeah, cap, we know, but before we fix that we just wanted to see what makes this here little bugger tick."

The nutty part of it was that these two guys hadn't even been at my roadside party when I called it quits about one in the morning and sort of passed out in the front seat. There were still a couple, three cars and a truck around and everyone asleep, and the two super-mechanics got the block back on the engine together, but I told them to leave the carb as it was, because that was the only excuse I had for not making it back to base the day before. I was smart enough for that.

The gist of it all was, we had this big party on the highway with booze galore, and none of it had that old government stamp on it and we had food and singing and girls and music and by God, I wouldn't be surprised if a couple of bang-bangs hadn't taken place somewhere close. There must have been 25 or 30 people there, more or less, and it was one of the best goddamn parties I'd ever given.

Officers and Men

*Officer Material ... Two Drunk Generals ... Some
Officer, Some Leader ... In the Mess Tent ... Killing
Officers ... "At Least an M.C. Here" ... The C.O.'s
Parade ... The Jewish Captain ... The Real Heroes ...
The Padre Who Wanted to Kill ... Generals*

---

*One of the most common themes to occur in my interviews was
how much the men disliked the officers. Again and again, old
soldiers, airmen and sailors would harp on the fact that there were
very few officers they respected, and would claim that they knew
better natural leaders in the ranks.*

*Obviously every military force needs officers, and, men
being what they are, it is unlikely that officers will ever be
admired by all of the men in their command. But perhaps this
constantly stated belief "I'm as good a man as he is" says something about the Canadian character. Canadian troops actually
booed Prime Minister Mackenzie King when he inspected them at
Aldershot in England. Certainly, troops on parade who boo their
Prime Minister are not the most submissive people on earth. As I
say, perhaps that tells us a lot about Canadians.*

•◄►• Officer Material

Our officers, right from the brigadier general—if that was what he
was—down to the second lieutenant, were a pretty poor lot. Pretty
poor. Ask anyone.

Take my company, an infantry company in a prairie regiment, but it would work for a B.C. outfit, the Royal Twenty-
second from Quebec or some Maritime outfit, say those crazy
Cape Bretoners. About 200 guys when we were training in
England and by the time we got to the islands [Walcheren Island
in Holland, a major Canadian campaign] we were down to about
50 of the old guys left. The rest, dead, wounded, missing, pro-
moted, fucked off, I don't know. But those 50 guys, man, they
were tough. They knew everything there was to know about the
kind of fighting we were doing, day to day, on foot, cleaning out
pockets, tank and carrier support, killing Germans by the dozens,
and I myself must have waved about 2,000 of the bastards back to
the rear, lucky bastards, a warm billet, warm food, no more shooting.

We'd lose an officer, and a new second lieutenant would come up with the mail next day. I got to calling these new guys the Pony Express Kids. They knew sweet bugger-all, and I mean that. I also mean, how could they know anything? What does a kid of twenty-one right out of Queen's University know about nothing? He's only been trying to avoid being called up. Or what does a school teacher know? Sure, he may be thirty-five, but he has an education, and those nine-year-olds in some Winnipeg school sure jumped at his word, so he's officer material.

They were quite useless. If you tried to train them it was kind of useless. Like, "Look, sir, if we advance here and the Jerry has a tank in this bit of woods and it comes out, we're dead. The whole section is dead. So why don't we shell that wood and then put the anti-tank here and go in, and we'll see what happens." Things like that.

Most times the sergeants in our battalion would just take over, at the platoon level, I mean, and if the sergeant had been gut-shot, then a corporal would, and the lieutenant could string along and see what was doing, learn by watching, or else he could go back to Old Broadway for all we cared.

Mind, it wasn't that we didn't like these guys. No, not at all. We just didn't get to know them, and they couldn't get to know us. The caste system, you know. Along with stripping a Bren gun in the dark at wherever they'd been trained, mostly in Canada, they were also told that the caste system had to be enforced. Master and slave, that stuff. Army wouldn't work without it.

•◄► • *Two Drunk Generals*

I took two drunk generals on a trip once, south of Halifax. The roads were all closed up, a hell of a lot of snow.

I know a bus followed me all the way up, about five miles an hour. He couldn't pass me, and I couldn't get out of the way. I finally got into Bedford, and the road was clear and slick, sheer ice. I just went into a great spin and right off the road and right up on my back bumper, like that. Standing on my rear bumper. Straight up. They sat in the back seat, still straight up. They were both absolutely sotted. I got a tow truck and he got hold of my front bumper and let me down carefully, and these two guys still sat there.

When the truck was coming, one general, he was about 300 pounds or something, he said, "Driver, why are we stopped?" and I told him there had been a small accident but it was nothing.

When I got going, I drove them to where they were going in Bedford and they both got out and the fat one thanked me for a pleasant drive and they staggered off to wherever they were going.

There were some dandy officers in the Canadian Army and I think I drove a lot of them. Drunk, sotted at two o'clock in the afternoon.

•◄►• *Some Officer, Some Leader*

Too many officers received too many medals. I've seen them handed out indiscriminately, stupidly too.

I remember around Caen, I was in charge of two troops of tanks from our squadron, and this battle went on morning and afternoon. It wasn't a major battle, but for what it was, it was a decisive engagement on our section of the front. It was a bloody little one, Shermans, infantry which was rather disorganized as some outfits had been decimated, and some artillery, but our tanks were the decisive factor.

This commanding officer, he was far from the action. I tried to raise him all day and got him a couple of times in the afternoon, but he made no effort to move up to help us. He showed up about 6 P.M.—after the engagement was all over, of course, and our troops had routed Jerry.

And you know what? He was given the D.S.O. And he hadn't been within miles of the fighting and hadn't wanted to be. I was quite sure he could hear us calling him on the radio. I'm not saying our action was worth the D.S.O. or whether I should have got it or not, but it was given to him, although he was miles from where any of the fighting was and quite preferred to stay there until it was over, one way or the other.

Another time we were in position and this same officer called up this other chap and me on the radio and said he wanted to see us. We couldn't use the tanks because we were dug into a defensive position, and besides, our glorious leader was only about 150 yards behind us, very well dug in, I might say. We had to take extreme care because our squadron could come under direct fire from Jerry at any time. We found his tank, all buttoned up, not a sign of life around, and after banging on the side with our pistol butts, he sticks his head out and the message he had for us was that we're under German observation, some activity was expected that night and we were to be alert. To be alert! For God's sakes! Here he was talking to two officers, tank corps, who if they didn't know how to be alert by that time in the war would have been dead.

As we walked back, there was this German sniper in this tree and he shot my friend. The bullet went in his shoulder and passed down and came out through his buttocks. Well, by the time I had rousted the fellow out of the tree and disposed of him, and rustled around getting men to carry my fellow officer's stretcher to the rear, it was getting on. And you know, that officer, our leader, he sat buttoned up in his tank and watched all this happening, the shooting, what went with it, me trying to help my friend and all, and he never once popped his head out of his tank, let alone got out to give me a hand.

Some officer! Some leader!

•◄►• In the Mess Tent

The only officer I would fight and die for was a rather sissy type of guy from Montreal who one day got so mad at the slop they were feeding us this day at supper that he walked down our tables in this mess tent and took every man's mess tin and dumped it on the floor. And then he marched us all down to the pub in the village and he paid while we cleaned it out of beer and pasties and sausage rolls and everything else eatable that the pub had. His name was Davidson and in about a week he had been transferred. The orderly officer of the day had seen him throwing this shit they called food into the grass, and he put him on report. We never saw him again. A good guy.

•◄►• Killing Officers

The American solders in Vietnam had this word, "fragging," and it means troops killing their officers. Wounding them or trying to kill them.

They talked about it as some sort of a new thing. Hell, ask any soldier. It happens in every war. It has to. Check back to the Roman legions and you'll probably find it happened. You get an officer who is a pure unadulterated son of a bitch and it is going to happen.

I know it happened in the Canadian Army, and when it was done we didn't miss either. We got the son of a bitch cold. I personally know of two cases, and I was just in one company of one battalion of one division, and both guys deserved it and they got it.

One guy was a famous athlete, a hero, so to speak, and he got it during an attack in France. The first bullet hung him over the wheel of a farm wagon, we all saw the guy who did it because we were all with him. And every guy who went by him—and we all did—we all fired a round or two into him, and one guy with a Sten gave him a full clip. The bastard must have weighed 10 pounds heavier when we finished with him. My mother sent me the clippings from the paper and they made him into ten different kinds of hero.

•◄►• *"At Least an M.C. Here"*

There was one hell of a battle around Ortona and we'd just about had it, and the Germans had just about had it and all around for miles there were wrecked tanks, turrets shot off, burned out, personnel carriers, guns and trucks, theirs and ours, and just the old house left standing but ready to fall down any minute. The battle I guess you could say was over, but this is what is always left. The debris of war.

We'd lost one hell of a lot of men and new guys were slow in coming up, and Jerry was in worse shape than us but he still was hanging in there. It would be a bit before we moved him out.

We get the word a new company commander is coming up. I'm senior sergeant and then there's just nobody above me but a couple of lieutenants and they are new guys. The new officer comes up and he's a captain. He's a bastard, all spit and polish, and the company clerk said he's spent two years at Kingston in administrative work, so naturally he knew all about war. His name was Knight or something like that. Right off he puts on the big act and asks what we are doing. Jesus Christ. Here we are, a company of maybe 60 men and we should be about 150 or more with support, and he's asking foolish questions.

I said we were doing patrol at night, and doing some training on the new replacements when we got them. Trying to get ourselves into a unit again. That's about all.

Then he wants a tour of our front. Well, Jesus, there ain't no front. It was all higgledy-piggledy. The Germans knew where we were, and we knew where they were, and occasionally somebody would throw a few H.E.'s over to keep the other guy honest, but there was no front. The frigging army had a front along a ridge and river line, but Company C sure as hell didn't have one.

Anyway, I take him up a bit and he looks around and there is all this crap and corruption, corruption and crap. There must have been a million bucks in wrecked and burned-out equipment just in front of us.

This Knight guy, or Wright, I forget, he looks it over with his shiny new fieldglasses and then he says, "For a person with imagination and with proper planning, there should be at least an M.C. here." I thought, this guy is nuts. Why doesn't he go for a Victoria Cross while he's at it?

To make a long story short, I tell him there will be no attacks or monkey business without my say-so, and he looks at me in his best Canadian parade ground manner and says he could have me court-martialled for that remark. I say go ahead, talk to the old man about it, and that finished him. He didn't go to the colonel. Didn't have half the guts needed.

After that, it was just a case of waiting. A horse's ass like that is going to get it anyway. He's just going to do something stupid, and I guess it was about five or six weeks later, just when I was starting to teach him a few things, he got it. This arsehole was walking around where he shouldn't've been and a sniper with one of those super-rifles they used to have—blat, one shot is all they get, you know—and that one shot caught Knight or Wright in the chest and that was the end of him.

He didn't get his Victoria Cross, and he didn't get his Military Cross. All he got was a bullet. Most officers, once you got them straightened out, were good guys; but once in a while you got one like that fellow and nobody could ever feel sorry for them.

•◄►• *The C.O.'s Parade*

When you put a uniform on some men and put them in command, something happens to them.

We were at Boundary Bay, and the C.O. was going to have a parade. A C.O.'s parade is nothing but an ego trip. Several hundred men and women spend a whole day or two getting ready for it, and when it's over the only one who feels good about it is the commanding officer. Nothing useful in one.

Anyway, the C.O. ordered one, and it was a very hot day. The M.O. [medical officer] said it was too hot, that people would be fainting and falling over the place, and he ordered it cancelled. The C.O. was mad, but the M.O. put his thermometer on the tarmac and showed him how hot it was.

The next day it was even hotter and the C.O., who was a pig-headed idiot, ordered another parade and the M.O. cancelled it again. By this time the station commander was blazing.

The next day it was just as hot, or hotter, and the medical officer says no parade, and the C.O. says for him to look out the window. There are the station's fire trucks hosing down the tarmac, and the C.O. says, "Put your goddamned thermometer on the tarmac now, Mr. Medical Officer," and so we had the parade. You see what I mean about stupidity?

•◄►• *The Jewish Captain*

Everybody seems to think most Jews got commissions in the air force or posh jobs in the army, doctors, dentists and in the orderly offices and things like that. That just isn't so. I ran into quite a few Jews in the army, and they certainly weren't all officers. In fact, a lot were riflemen and sappers and just doing the joe jobs.

One day in December our attack went across this small river, and we dug in. During the night the engineers were supposed to throw a bridge across the river. But the Germans were wise because they knew the only place where a bridge could be put across, and they lumped it with machine guns and mortars. So no bridge. That meant no tanks for support for the morning attack out of this bridgehead and so we get the order to just hold. But we find the Germans, about a company or so, had got behind us between us and the river, and so we've got to fight our way out.

This Jewish captain is leading us, and we get mortared and he's down, and when we fight back across the river I say that Captain Blinder, and I think that's his name, I say he's dead and we left him back across the river. I was sure he was dead. Positive.

And then we see these two guys coming across the river and Jerry is plastering them but somehow they miss and I don't know how the hell they could. And these two guys are carrying this captain who is not dead but so damn near to it that you couldn't tell. They had made a stretcher out of sticks and battle dress, as I remember, and for about 300 yards they'd walked or half-run through thick and thin, all the shit in the world flying about, and they'd made it back.

The two riflemen were French Canadians because the R.C.R.'s [the Royal Canadian Regiment] was mostly a Montreal regiment. That's why it had a lot of Jews, too. The major said he might put them in for M.I.D.'s, although he never did.

Anyway, the captain died, and one of the officers came into our quarters and made some remark like, "Well, the Jew captain has gone," or something like that, and the major gave him the dressing down of his life, really up one side and down the other, and he wound up saying that this captain was the best officer our battalion would ever see, no matter how long the war lasted.

•◀▶• *The Real Heroes*

Why were the medals always given to the warriors, in the sense that a man who stupidly led his company across a bridge swept by German fire and took the gun, even though a third of his men were lost—why should that man get the Victoria Cross? Shouldn't he have called in artillery fire on the position, because artillery was available? Shouldn't he have been court-martialled?

Or the man who sneaked up in the dark and garrotted three Germans on sentry and then wiped out a company head-quarters in a cellar. A fine piece of work, of course, but was it worth a Military Cross?

What I'm trying to get at is this. Why medals for the bloody types? Why were the heroes men who killed and killed again? Yes, I admit killing is what war is about, the end result, but there is something else.

And I'm not talking about colonels and brigadiers and others up the ladder who got medals just for being there, even if most of them were useless, as they were. I'm now talking about the men in battle. In the line. The men up front.

What about the artillery who would pound a German position for 24 hours, no sleep, moving the guns, devilish hard work and dangerous too. Did artillerymen ever get medals? Or sigs? How many signalmen up almost within sniffing distance of German positions ever got medals? The guys bringing hot meals up. The medical corps, right up in the front and often much more exposed than the guy with the rifle. I could go on and on. Truckers. Engineers. There are some of your real heroes, the engineers. Hell, anybody who was there could go on and on, but the medals went to the guy who wiped out or captured a .88. Well, maybe he deserved a medal. That guy, yeah, maybe a medal.

The officers. The n.c.o.'s. The sergeants, especially. The officers and sergeants who worked harder and felt harder for their men than they did for themselves, they were the real heroes. I can name you a dozen officers, a dozen three-stripers I served with and under who were the heroes. Not heroes in anybody's M.I.D. [Mentioned In Despatches] but heroes to their men. That's where it counted, my friend.

An officer who would see that his men were fed and bedded down right, and that they got hot meals if there were any hot meals, and got their mail and would talk to them, be kind of a big brother, a father confessor and a good guy, they were the heroes. You found this kind of man up in the front lines, with the infantry, with the tank squadrons. I can't recall ever seeing this kind of officer back at regimental headquarters, back at div. The officers who were soldiers were up front with the men, and the officers who were politicians, right down to the last little ninny of a lieutenant, they were back out of range. Happened every time.

No, give me two Victoria Crosses, six D.S.C.'s and three D.S.M.'s and a dozen Military Crosses and medals to pass out and I'd know where to pin 'em. Yes, sir, you bet, right on the guys who knew what war was all about. Those officers and sergeants I've been telling you about.

•◄►• *The Padre Who Wanted to Kill*

There was this chaplain, and I'll call him Martin for the sake of narration, he came to me one day as I was his superior officer and he requested a transfer into the infantry. He requested infantry, but he indicated that any branch would be suitable.

I naturally was astonished. I think anyone would be. A United Church minister before the war, a man of probably thirty-five years of age, and requesting a transfer, to get into action. Frankly, it was unheard of, at least to my knowledge.

Naturally we sat down for a chat, not officer to officer but man to man, and I asked him why. He said he had lost the loving spirit. In his way of looking at a minister's task, and a chaplain's task, the loving spirit is the most important of all. He never did define it, this loving spirit, but I think I can. He meant a love of mankind. The Ten Commandments, I suppose.

He told me he wanted to kill Germans. And we were still quite a ways from any combat. It was a strange feeling to be sitting having a drink with a chaplain and hearing him say he wanted to kill, to throttle Germans with his bare hands, bayonet, that sort of thing, and in a perfectly calm voice. Cool as ice water. There was a moment, I will admit, when I thought he was around the bend, but, of course, he was as sane as I was.

It turned out, of course, that there was a great deal behind it, much more than this loving spirit thing. His younger brother had been killed in an explosion when his bomber crashed while landing. It had been shot to pieces somewhere over France, Germany, across the Channel. So there it was. The old reason, an eye for an eye. He wanted revenge, and he wasn't going to get it giving church parades for a bunch of soldiers.

I signed the transfer. There was nothing to be gained by not doing so. You learned one thing in the army and it was that if a man was a liability, he had to go.

•◄►• *Generals*

All in all, when you take everything into the plan, think of every consideration, I guess you could really say the Germans lost the last war because they had lousier generals than we did. If you thought there was unbelievable pig-headed thinking on our side, there must have been more on the German side. Stands to reason.

I don't know who said it but war is far, far too important to leave to the politicians and the generals. That's what I believe.

Zombies

They Were Okay ... Terrace Was Useless ... Incidents Almost Every Day ... Ill Feeling ... We Called Them Cowards ... A Form of Punishment ... The Assault on Kiska ... A Very Canadian Mutiny ... They Used Bull-whips ... A View from the Front ... A Passage to Vancouver ... Pity for the Zombies ... We Didn't Want Them ... Darn Good Soliders ... No Right to the Battle Medals

---

A Zombie was not a cocktail, or a creature in a horror film, but a creature of the Liberal government created in 1940 when Prime Minister Mackenzie King decreed that Canadians conscripted into the army would not be sent overseas to fight. That cast the die for what, five years later, was called the greatest constitutional crisis in our history.

Briefly, the term "Zombie" described the soldier who was conscripted under the National Resources Mobilization Act (N.R.M.A.) for 30 days, and later for four months, and then for the duration of the war. However, he was conscripted only for home defence. About 57,000 of these men later volunteered for active duty, overseas, but about 70,000 didn't. About one-third who didn't were from French Canada, Quebec, but many thousands were also from the rest of Canada.

In 1942, after Japan entered the war, the King government called a plebiscite asking Canadians, in effect, to relieve him of his pledge never to send these N.R.M.A. men overseas. English-speaking Canada overwhelmingly voted that pledge but Quebec— by a vote of 993,663 to 376,188—refused to give King the chance to sneak clear. However, the total vote in Canada still supported King handsomely. That wily gentleman, however, saw clearly that if he did send the Zombies overseas he was certain to lose much of his support in Quebec. So he refrained from doing anything.

But by August, 1944, Canadian infantry fighting in Italy and France were badly overstretched; death, wounds and sickness had thinned their ranks and the support and supply troops who were thrown into the regiments were described as badly trained. The situation was grim. Meanwhile, over the many months, anti-Zombie sentiment had been growing in Canada. More and more were demanding that the Zombies be sent overseas to thicken the fire instead of sitting uselessly in camps in the West, mainly in

British Columbia, waiting for an attack by the Japanese army,
which was 7,000 miles away.

The Zombies in these camps were restless, too, and had
been for years. They felt they had been betrayed by the N.R.M.A.
and were wasting their lives away—which they were. Desertions
were high, discipline was poor, morale nonexistent. Clearly,
trouble was coming.

But still the Prime Minister refused to budge, although his
cabinet was split. Then Minister of Defence Colonel J. L. Ralston
was forced out on the reinforcement-conscript issue, and a panic-
button active service recruiting plan failed most miserably. Finally
the Prime Minister approved the shipment of 16,000 Zombies to
Europe to fill the reinforcement pools. About 13,000 went, and
soon afterwards the war ended. So the potentially explosive issue
never did blow up—but it is not a happy chapter in our history.

•◄►• *They Were Okay*

I didn't hate Zombies, I think, because I didn't really think of
them. They put them in different camp areas, like in Shilo they
had them down in a few huts called The Swamp or The Slough,
low-lying ground where it got pretty wet in the spring and
during heavy rains. I'm not sure whether that was a form of
punishment or not.

They were just guys going the other way, and they were
using the system. If Mackenzie King was too goddamn chicken to
change the overseas draft law, if that was what it was all about,
and wanted to pick up votes in Quebec, then it was Mackenzie
King's goddamn fault and not these guys'. Some guys just work
within the system.

I never thought much at all about the Zombies, although
now, I guess somebody thought about them an awful lot to give
them such a rotten name.

•◄►• *Terrace Was Useless*

Terrace was a small, quiet hick town with two or three hundred
people and a Liquor Commission and a movie theatre and a few
stores, and this is where they dumped thousands of troops. The
troops were permanent force or volunteers at the start, I believe,
and then they brought in some of the non-active regiments. They
were to be used as a back-up force for the defence of Prince
Rupert if the Japs landed there.

Now, tactically, you must realize that there was no road from Terrace to Prince Rupert. Just the C.N. railroad and I think there were 68 bridges on that 35 miles of track. Nobody gave a thought to that. How in Sam Hill were we to get out to defend Prince Rupert if the Japs suddenly attacked, a sneak attack? How? Why, all they had to do was dynamite just one of those bridges and that would stop us cold until they took over the whole coast.

There was a conference of command officers in Vancouver and they asked about our problems and I told them some of the problems of Terrace. No road. The railroad. All those vulnerable bridges. I said we should move out and put the bloody regiment at Point Edward, and that would let us cover with fire virtually all of Prince Rupert except about an eighth of it which would have been dead ground. At least we would have been there, we'd have been able to fire on the buggers.

And all those brains of the Canadian Army said, "Oh no, no, oh no." Couldn't be done. Impossible.

So that's the way it was. The regiments at Terrace were completely useless. In fact, they just used it as a dumping ground for Zombies.

•◄►• *Incidents Almost Every Day*

You heard things, of course, but nothing you could actually pin down unless you were right there, right on top of things, so to speak. Of course, there was that affair up at Terrace, which could have been very bad but wasn't, because everybody seemed to have the good sense not to let it happen.

There was a riot at Drummondville, east of Montreal. Several people were hurt. You see, most of these things happened when the R.C.M.P. and the M.P.'s would go into a town trying to scoop up draft dodgers or Zombies absent without leave. The townspeople or the man's family would become irate, words would fly, then fists, night sticks and so forth, and you had a real schmozzle on your hands—and then it would have to be kept out of the papers.

I heard of one blow-up at a camp at Gravenhurst, in Ontario, where one Zombie was actually shot to death. An accident, I believe, but regardless, a man was dead. That was hushed up, too.

At Shilo in Manitoba, there always were incidents and there was trouble at Vernon, in British Columbia, where there were a great many N.R.M.A. men, and at Prince Rupert, and up and down the B.C. coast.

I was in an office in Ottawa, Intelligence, where these reports would come in, so I was in a sensitive position. Low on the scale, but nevertheless, the word would go around. But even I did not know the full extent. There was great secrecy. The iron fist of the Great God Censorship, you might say.

There were incidents almost every day, but the public never heard of them. Not a word. There were rumours, of course, but there always are rumours, that's the only commodity in over-supply in a war. Rumours everywhere, but I do think a lot of them were true. It was a nasty business.

•◂▸• *Ill Feeling*

The Zombies antagonized a lot of people. They did what they wanted to do, and nothing a civilian could say would stop them. This was when they were in Terrace, for months and years waiting for the Japanese invasion that never came.

They used to shoot up trappers' cabins, just for the hell of it. They'd be on a route march or something and they'd pass a trapper's cabin and just start firing away. They had these ack-ack guns, and they'd use the eagles as targets, and that made a lot of people mad. On one man's farm they just wheeled in their ack-ack guns into his farm, his pasture, without permission of any kind and they started shooting at a target being pulled by a plane back and forth 2,000 feet over the river. His cows quit giving milk and his hens stopped laying, and life on that farm was anything but serene.

These soldiers just sort of took over, so that most civilians had little pity for them or for what they were supposedly doing. One guy made me laugh once. He said, "Those bastards were crawling all over the town. They were so fast with our women that before a girl could say she wasn't that kind of a girl, she was."

•◂▸• *We Called Them Cowards*

Now that I look back on it, it was funny. Here we were down at Steinbach, that's south of Winnipeg, all Mennonites through that part of the world, and of course, our religion forbids us to bear arms. To fight in wars.

Some they took away, the young fellows, and put them in what we called C.O. [conscientious objector] camps. I think there was one in Manitoba and another in British Columbia. Anyway, you never knew who would be taken, like it was almost like pulling names out of a hat. I had cousins taken, but none of my three brothers were. It was stupid, really, because we were good farmers and a good Mennonite boy on a tractor could do ten times more for the country than being a soldier, but that's the way they did things.

Now, there were these Zombies. Remember? They were fellows who were conscripted, called up, whatever, and wouldn't sign to fight overseas, and so they were considered pretty low. People were usually against them, like calling them Frenchies, because a lot were French Canadians. That sort of thing. We called them cowards, right in our own house, around the kitchen table. My father would say they should be shot, things like that.

And yet now, I think how ironic it all was. My own cousins, some of the Rempel boys, others we knew, they were in these conscientious objector camps because they wouldn't join up, and here we were calling the French Canadians a bunch of cowards because they wouldn't fight. Somehow, then, we couldn't see that our cousins and the Zombies were one and the same. Canada was sure a crazy country in those days.

•◄►• *A Form of Punishment*

In the winter of 1941 we got a bunch of Zombies in to train. Some French Canadians, but a lot of Ukrainians, and what-have-you from towns and places in Manitoba and Saskatchewan. This was in Brandon, and these guys were conscripted under the National Resources Mobilization Act. They didn't have to enlist for overseas service. Just to defend Canada.

Our C.O. at Brandon, he told us to run the asses off them if we wanted. I think we would have, if we'd known what the situation was going to be like in '44 when our regiments in Italy and Europe couldn't get men, and these guys were sitting on their butts in Canada.

There was one thing, though. We called it P.T., physical training, and the syllabus said it could come at the end of the day or the start. We decided these Zombies better start the day right. Most of them were cow milkers anyway, so 6 A.M., 6:30, what the hell, it shouldn't make any difference to them. It did to us, though, because we were the guys who had to get up ahead, roust them up, run them over to the cookhouse, the mess hall for some cocoa, and then get them going for 40 minutes. Except, Christ almighty, when I think of it, there was no gymnasium, no drill hangar, and here's these Zombies running through the streets of this town at 6:30 in the morning and it would often be 20 below. Hell, even colder. And in gymwear too! I think we froze them so silly they couldn't get going for the rest of the day, but anyway, they knew they were in the army, and they knew they were N.R.M.A. crud because the regular troops didn't get this treatment.

Sure, sure, oh sure, you're darned right it was a form of punishment. The C.O. sure meant it to be, and we did too. I always figured if they were in this man's army, whether they wanted to be or not, they would damn well act like soldiers. It toughened 'em up, anyway, although I'm not sure it got any of them to go active service.

•◄►• *The Assault on Kiska*

Well, naturally they didn't tell the troops where they were going, not from the time they loaded them on the troop carriers at Nanaimo and then up at Prince Rupert until we were off Kiska. There were American forces on the ships too. Our men were Zombies, mostly from French Canada. They wouldn't go overseas to fight, but Kiska is one of the Aleutian chain, south and west of Alaska there, and that's part of North America.

At Kiska the aerial reconnaissance showed a pebble beach where the Americans were to land. Pebble beach! My God, when they started ashore those pebbles were as big as staff cars. The Canadian troops were landing at a place called Green Beach and so the Americans swung over and in behind us. I don't know how many there were, maybe 2,000 Canadians and more than that many Americans, and we didn't know how many Japanese there were on Kiska.

You see, Kiska was occupied by the Japs. Nobody knew how many or what they were doing there, but it caused a terrific amount of commotion and worry for the Canadian and American governments as that meant the Japs were right on our front door. I guess it was the first time troops had ever gone into action against an enemy so close, and it was the Zombies in action.

Green Beach was at the mouth of a ravine and they started up and the Americans poured in behind them and hell, there was no way to retreat if they had to. The island is a mudhole, not very big, always foggy, and with the Americans behind there was only one thing to do, dig in or get up there, so they went charging up—and there was nobody there. They found two gun emplacements, two field machine guns, which if they had been manned could have wiped out an awful lot of our men.

They had quarters there, the stoves were still warm, there was coffee on the stoves. In other words, the Japs had just left in one hell of a hurry. Maybe 12 hours before, maybe a lot less. Who knows? With that fog, who knows.

We found pig pens. We called them that. Pens with those Japanese two-man submarines. The ordnance under a Colonel Sherman took those and I'm sure they helped a lot to show the Americans what they were up against in the Pacific where the big battles were going on.

There wasn't a shot fired. Nobody was killed. The Japs were all gone, just ahead of us. A few accidents, just like you'd have in a camp, around barracks. Some guys get careless, you know.

One thing, the French Canadians were good soldiers. They were well trained. Once they got out and into the field, and they went ashore in carriers, they proved out to be good men. The officers, the chaplains and everybody were really pleased with them. They just didn't want to fight overseas for somebody else, that's all.

•◄► • *A Very Canadian Mutiny*

All the goddamned ill feeling for years between who was going overseas to fight and who wasn't, wound up in the mutiny at Terrace in November, '44, with the Zombies sitting up on the hill with the 25-pounders trained on the C.M.R. trains, threatening to blow them off the tracks if anyone moved them. The trains were to take the Zombies east to ship them to Europe, where our troops needed them.

Ottawa ordered the air force in to bomb them with tear gas. But Pearkes [General Pearkes, commandant of the Sixth Division, Pacific Command] wouldn't go along with that. I guess in a way he and I helped to start the whole thing.

You see, Pearkes wasn't very happy that our Prime Minister and McNaughton [General Andrew McNaughton, Minister of Defence] wouldn't institute conscription which the people of Canada had voted for in a plebiscite.

So what started this thing, me being a bit of a barracks-room lawyer I told Pearkes that we had seven V.C.'s [Victoria Cross winners] in the command as various commandants, and he called a press conference and the V.C.'s made statements on the conscription question, saying that all these guys up in the bush should volunteer to go overseas to fight because our units over there were getting pretty damn low on manpower. The units needed men and lots of them, and these guys were sitting here in Canada.

The only way these V.C.'s could say these things was because there was some sort of a law which said that no V.C. would be discredited in the eyes of the public. Having made the statements, they couldn't be brought up on a charge. They hadn't violated security, they had only expressed an opinion, but only the V.C.'s could do that. And of course when this was printed, this got the Zombies riled up, mad as hell.

Most of the rough ones at Terrace were from French Canada because most of the rest of the country volunteered, but when they called them up for 30 days' training, once that was over they kept them in and said, "You're in the army, bub." They didn't like that. Some had been in for years. If they took off, they'd put them in jail.

Anyway, these remarks triggered the whole damn thing.

These Zombies had been properly trained, yeah, they were field artillery, and they moved up on to the hill with their 25-pounders and they knew how to choose firing positions and they had enough grub and they sent word down, "Okay, you move that train six inches and we'll blow it off the tracks."

And that's the way it went. That train didn't load any troops as far as I know. The troops were in full command. The officers just wandered around, I guess.

When the mutiny was over, it was because of a compromise. They had some conferences and no action was taken, and they were promised that they would be given 14-day furloughs at their homes and then they would return to their units and they would be part of the regular army and would be shipped overseas. And, surprisingly, most of them did that. Most of them reported.

There was no action taken. No court-martial. Nothing like that. The whole thing was just quietly hushed up because at that time, you know, for the morale and security of the country no paper would dare print that story.

Nobody was hurt—and you could say it could only have happened in Canada.

•◄►• *They Used Bullwhips*

I remember, we lived in Halifax and a neighbour who was a dock worker he said that some of the men who didn't want to get on the ships were prodded on by the military police with rifles. And they used bullwhips and forced them on. This was near the end of the war. I didn't like to hear about that, this forcing these men to go and fight. I don't think that man makes a good soldier, do you?

Oh, my brother saw it too. He said it was horrible. When these men went up the ramp some of them lay down, they cried, they'd run back, they wanted to jump in the water, but they put them back, they used bullwhips to put them men back on.

Yes, these were Zombies. Conscripts.

•◄►• *A View from the Front*

I'd just been shifted from the Princess Pats over to the Cape Breton Highlanders over on the Fiumicino, and settling in, I realized things were worse than I thought. Men were short, and worn out, and there wasn't enough reinforcements coming up. The reinforcement pool was just about empty, and I guess Northwest Europe was getting most of the new men. It was really a rough situation and I can tell you this—you don't expect too much from a man in battle at the start. It takes time, getting that experience.

What ground our asses down was these N.R.M.A.'s in Canada. I don't know how many. Many thousands. Certainly, thousands. Twenty or thirty thousand, the ones they called Zombies. Fight for Canada but not for democracy, if you want to put it that way. They wouldn't sign for overseas.

But listen to this. What we didn't know was that one stroke of the pen, one decision by Mackenzie King, and those troops would have been on their way. Maybe they'd have been marched at bayonet point up the gangplanks, but once we got them on the Fiumicino we'd have straightened them up. There, it was fight and work together or you don't survive. Twenty or thirty thousand men safe and sound in Canada and here we were yanking clerks out of orderly rooms and extra cooks out of mess halls and giving them a rifle and saying, "Remember your advanced training? This is a bullet and this is a magazine and the magazine goes on here and when you crank this, it puts this bullet up the spout and you fire it." We were hurting for men and losing heavily, far more men than we could afford, and there was Mackenzie King, fat like a little toad, sitting in Ottawa and thinking of his political skin, his goddamned worthless skin, just so he wouldn't offend the French, in Quebec, who gave him his balance of power in Parliament.

Sure, I know, I know. Later he did pass that order-in-council, but it was too late to get the Zombies over. A few made it over but damn few. Maybe a thousand or two. Maybe less.

I remember our colonel saying to us one day when we were discussing the manpower question because I believe they were talking about breaking up a couple of the weaker regiments and putting the men through the corps, in other regiments, and the colonel said, kind of wryly, I thought: "If this was wartime and Mackenzie King was doing what he is doing now, he'd be shot as a traitor."

That was the best chuckle we'd had all week.

•►• *A Passage to Vancouver*

This uncle of mine had a half-share in a seiner. He fished out of Prince Rupert and down the coast. I signed with him one season. My uncle had crew's rations for six but he always hired only three but drew for six and then he'd scout around Rupert. There was always somebody who knew somebody who was hiding out.

These were Zombies from the camp at Terrace who'd sneak down on the railroad and hide up in town. The place was roaring then, American Army, whores, Indians, contractors, a wild place. So he'd find a couple of guys who wanted to get to Vancouver, and there wasn't much chance of them getting down, past the law and everything, except by sea. Things were pretty tightly buttoned up in that country during the war. These guys he'd hire were deserters. Zombies. Guys who were conscripted and wouldn't sign to go overseas. The country was full of them.

My uncle would take them on, and as he was mostly delivering to a fish packer and taking on from the oil barges at sea and getting his rations the same way, they were pretty well prisoners. He worked the devil out of them by telling them he'd pay them off, maybe 50 dollars a month for three months and drop them by the ship's boat in Stanley Park in the dark before pulling into the fish wharf down by Main Street. So these guys, French Canadians, would work their asses off. Fishing's a tough life and I think seine fishing when the salmon are running is the toughest, and here's these Frenchies getting a quick course in fishing. Sometimes 18 hours a day. If you didn't learn a lot in three months . . . well, you just did. That's all.

This day we're coming home, season over, and I can't figure why my uncle pulls into Deep Bay on Bowen Island and drops the hook. He says he wants to clean up the old scow, but that's bullshit. Vancouver is only two hours away and he wants to get home as much as any of us, but then just at dusk he winds her up and we report to the signal station by Point Atkinson and get cleared through and he veers over towards Navvy Jack Point as we're coming up on the Narrows. I figure the old man's lost his marbles. There's artillery over on the other shore and they're jumpy and if we don't show up soon some idiot might yank a lanyard. Not likely at all because there are houses along the shore, but they'd done some dumb things.

The old man tells me to take the wheel and cut her back to about two knots, just making way, and then he takes a shotgun out of the locker and calls down to the two Frenchies. To come up on deck. They come up and they're staring right into the big eyes of that 12-gauge. It's what the hell this and goddamn it that, but the old man just tells them it's only 50 feet to shore and another 200 up to Marine Drive and so get going quick, over the side and start swimming. They've got no choice. Over they go, cursing all the way. He tells them to shut up or the cops will be along.

That's it. You see his game. Works these guys like slaves for three months and then dumps them over the side, and he's got them signed on under other names at full pay and shares, and the engineer and the cook and me split one guy's pay three ways and my uncle gets the other guy's share and the other owner gets bugger-all.

The Frenchies can't go to the cops because they are deserters, so it's a sweet deal. My uncle pulled it three times. A real character.

•◄►• *Pity for the Zombies*

Pity. Just plain pity. That was our attitude when they finally sent the Zombies to Europe and they came into our lines. Pity. First, resentment, of course, because of all the trouble they had caused over the years because they wouldn't fight.

But when we saw them go into action, then it was pity. They didn't know anything, hadn't been properly trained, and they didn't know enough even to keep their heads down. The whiz-bangs and H.E. was flying around and they'd poke their heads up and say, "What was that? Eh, what was that?" They goddamned soon knew what it was. They had a terrific casualty rate.

•◄►• *We Didn't Want Them*

No, we didn't want the Zombies when they started sending them over. I know we were all grousing about not getting enough replacements, but we didn't want them. Anyone who acted like them all through the war, who's going to say they'll make good soldiers in battle? It was just as well not to take a chance.

I know some outfits got a few, but there never were enough sent over to make any difference, to even say how they were. A few got killed. Just a few. Forty or fifty.

No, my outfit didn't want them, didn't ask for them, and as far as I know, we didn't get them. We just carried on with what we had.

•◀▶• *Darn Good Soldiers*

The Zombies I had under my command were darn good soldiers. They were obedient and they were intelligent and they were co-operative and they were good natured. I had no complaints about them at all.

You must remember, these chaps were French Canadians and they considered Canada's army an English army and they had heard from friends who had volunteered that they'd find themselves in an English-speaking unit, and that they were just being used to fill up the gaps in these English-speaking units. A lot of them had no access to a Catholic padre and a lot of them couldn't talk English.

If they had been intelligently handled and not pushed around like so much meat there would have been no problems with the French Canadian soldier whatsoever. I believe that. Everything was handled from the beginning to the end so damned stupidly.

When I was in Montreal once I met Ralston [Canadian Defence Minister] and I asked him to fix it so I could take the unit over to England, into action, as a unit, as a French Canadian unit and I assured him that I knew that at least 95 percent of those men would have volunteered for active service and that there would have been no trouble whatsoever. I said at least 95 percent of my men would come with me.

You do that, I told him, you treat them right, as individuals, and everything will go right, but keep them together. But he said there was no way they could do it. What utter nonsense. They just handled the whole situation completely wrong, in a stupid manner. I certainly had my belly full of that whole situation.

◆► *No Right to the Battle Medals*

We were in Euston Station, me and a sergeant from a rifle company of this famous Calgary regiment, and we were waiting for a train. The war was over. It had been for about six weeks and I was going to Glasgow to see relatives and he was along, going up there too.

All of a sudden we see this guy go by us, you know, smart as a goddamn whip, boots gleaming, bullet rings in the bottom of his pants, blancoed to the last degree and he had the patches of this sergeant's regiment. It might have been the Calgary High-landers. Anyway, the sergeant yelled, "Soldier!" and the guy turns around and comes back and he's got a funny look on his face. You can see he'd love to just take off, but after all, my friend is a sergeant.

Then Pow! And I do mean Pow! one right in the mush, and this soldier goes down and everybody's looking, and usually the stations were crawling with M.P.'s but there were none this time. The sergeant hauls the other guy to his feet and rips off his medals and throws them on the ground and spins him around and kicks him right up the keester with that size 11 he had and throws his haversack at him.

I don't ask questions then. We just head for our gate and away from trouble, but on the train he tells me. The guy came from his home town, down in southern Alberta and since about 1942 he'd been a reserve conscript. You know, a Zombie. The sergeant knew him since he was a kid and I guess his wife or parents had kept writing him letters, so he knew all about the district and he knew this guy was a Zombie. I'm not sure the guy actually recognized the sergeant at first, but when the sarge was yanking him to his feet, I heard him saying something to the fellow.

Remember, by late '44 we were so short of infantry that the rifle companies were about half strength. That would mean maybe 50 guys in a company. Should have been a hundred. So the government is forced to send some of these Zombies overseas and this guy with the sore ass is one of them. It's pure fluke, of course, that he wound up in a company of an outfit from his own district. Usually they just shoved them willy-nilly into the nearest outfit, or the one taking the heaviest casualties. I don't think many ever heard the bullets zing around.

What pissed the sergeant off, really off, was this guy had come up to join his outfit at the Rhine, just at the very ass end of the war. So, okay, he had a right to wear the shoulder flashes of the regiment, but he sure as hell had no right to wear the battle medals, the combat theatre medals the way he had them plastered over his chest.

Probably bought the goddamn things over at the Army and Navy by Victoria Station this very day. I remember the sergeant saying. "He ain't wearing them when I've still got breath in my body."

French and English

"Bon Jour!" . . . Enemies—Marcel and Bob . . . Those
Black Crows . . . Blame It All on the Politicians . . . Quebec
City Was the Worst . . . All Them Guys Speak English . . .
You Had to See Their Point . . . Deserters in the Basement

The war drove English Canada and French Canada apart. The
Zombie issue was the most obvious example of the breach. That
undoubtedly brought back bad memories of the conscription
troubles in the first world war to both sides, and the presence of
so many French-speaking Zombies in the West when the local
young men were being killed overseas did not help the situation
one bit. And, undoubtedly, stupid things happened; "Rocket"
Richard, the great Montreal Canadien, was booed every time he
stepped onto the ice at the Maple Leaf Gardens. The Toronto
crowd's simple-minded theory was that he was French, he was not
overseas in uniform, and therefore he was both a traitor and a
coward.

But it wasn't easy for a French-speaking Canadian in
uniform during the war. In the navy and the air force English was
the language and only English, and all the special language courses
and tender loving care couldn't quite make a French-Canadian feel
at home. This is what they have told me.

In the army it was different, for they had their own regi-
ments, some of the finest in the army, with long and glorious
traditions. It is also a fact that when the war broke out, these
regiments filled up with volunteers faster than any others. After
the debacle at Dieppe, recruiting officers throughout Quebec
noticed a fresh surge of volunteers, which did not occur in the rest
of the country.

I served with French Canadians, from Montreal, Quebec,
Hull, Three Rivers, the Gaspé, and until then I had never met a
Quebecker. We got along fine. I've always thought the French
Canadian deserved better than he received in the whole mess.

•◄►• *"Bon Jour!"*

Montreal was a wonderful city. I'll never forget a man friend taking me into a bar, my first bar, and all those bottles there and the
soft lights, and after stick-in-the-mud Vancouver, where you

couldn't even get a decent meal any time, I thought this was really living.

I worked with a woman who is dead now, so I won't mention her name. She was dumb, she was lazy and I couldn't stand her. We had two, me and her in our section, the English section, and there were six in the French section. Every morning the French people would come in, smile and say, "*Bon jour*," and I didn't know 50 words of French but I'd say, "*Bon jour*," and smile and say a few more words because I was trying to learn French. It is a beautiful language, I love it, and I love the French Canadians and I loved their culture and their buildings in Montreal and what they had done to make their city wonderful.

And this other woman with me, this bitch, every morning would say, "*Bon jour*," pronouncing it wrong and then say in English, "Whatever the hell that means." That was a wonderful way to keep good relations between the French and English, especially when there was that conscription thing all through the war which wasn't good, and caused a lot of problems. But the people we worked with were really nice.

•◆• *Enemies—Marcel and Bob*

I think it affected everyone, the conscription crisis, but especially if you were non-French in Montreal. Montreal was much more French than it is now and they didn't call you Anglo-Canadians or whatever. If they didn't like you they called you "m'ongee bloke," which I'm not sure even today what it is, but it means something like "rotten Englishman." We called them "Jean Baptistes" and "frogs" and "pea soupers."

We lived in Verdun and I'd dealt with this one garage around the corner for ten years and to me he was Marcel and I was Robert or Bob and his kids played with mine, so on and so forth. But when this conscription thing got to be a pretty hot affair and there was a lot of crap going on back and forth, fights between youth gangs downtown, and French Canadian soldiers getting beaten up in Halifax by the navy or even right on St. Catherine's Street, then it got pretty much. But Marcel and me, we were still good friends. He could always squeeze out a little extra gas for me when my coupons ran out, and little things like that. Hell, with rationing, that was a pretty big thing.

Then one day I pull in and he comes out looking pretty grim and he starts ki-yi-yi-ing at me in French. Now I don't understand French. Maybe I should but I don't, but I know the usual

French swear words so I think he's having fun with me, you see, so I give them back to him. But no, he isn't having fun. He's bloody serious. And this is Marcel, my drinking buddy sometimes at ye Old Canadian Legion. I ask what's the matter and he speaks back in French. French, and then more French.

So I get out of the goddamned car and I walk into the front part and I take out two Cokes, which were a nickel each then, and I hand him one and then I ask him, "What's this bullshit?"

He takes the Coke and he says he's sorry but there's a war on, don't I know, and I say for Christ sakes, yes, don't I know, I got a kid in the air force and another just itching to grow up so he can join up too. So he says, "Then we're enemies." He pronounced it en-eh-mees, with a hard pronunciation. It sure came out as an ugly sound. I said not to give me that crap, and we get talking and it comes out, he's only a lessee, understand, and the supervisor of the company has told him to go hard on the English. It doesn't matter, he says, if you're English or Greek or Jew, you're English and I said, "Marcel, you dumb bastard, I'm Canadian and so are you. Ain't it the same war for both of us?"

I'm making this up, you understand. What I mean is that this is the way it happened, but I'm sort of dramatizing it, making up the conversation. Anyway, old Marcel stands there with his greasy little company hat perched on his head and drinking my Coke and he says, "Sorry, Bob, but that's the way she's gotta be. The boss man says so."

Well, I've got a temper too and I slam out of there and even forget to pay, and he doesn't come running around after it, and next day I send over two bucks with my kid. I figure that's enough to cover the gas, and I got the coupons too. He never took them. It's the little things you remember. The upshot of it is, I started going to another station which wasn't so good, as they didn't know me there, and it wasn't until a couple of years after the war, when my kids were going steady to Marcel's station, that I went back and did business. But it never was the same. Something was always missing.

You couldn't blame Marcel, I guess. Blame that asshole of a supervisor who had the big chip on his shoulder. Maybe his kid got beat up by the navy.

But when you think back on it a little harder, it might not have been the supervisor so much as the goddamned politicians. There's nothing like a French Canadian politician, you believe me. Slimy, slippery as hell. Houde. Duplessis, the whole lot. And the Church too. From the cardinal right on down to the village priest, they were in it up to their necks. Make Canada more united and the politicians, the church, could see their power slipping away. The politicians and those thousands of black crows, walking around looking so holy, they were probably behind it all.

No, I never blamed Marcel. But things were just never the same again.

•—→—• *Those Black Crows*

Like I'm saying to you, there were a lot of guys worse than Mayor Houde who was saying you should not carry a gun for Queen Victoria. The priests. There were the priests. Those guys.

In those little towns, little villages back up there where some people the only words they knew in English were Ford and Chevrolet and Coca-Cola, before the war the priests they did everything. Those black crows. The ran everything, and in the council meetings the priest would be there and sitting near the Mr. Mayor and if he didn't like something, shake of the head. If it's okay, nod. It was like that.

They'd say to these poor dumb farmers not to let their kids go to fight the war. It is the Englishman's war, so let him fight it. If the cops come, you know where these kids hide? No, not in the bush, not in a haystack. In the priest's house sometimes, and the cops they go to the church, too, so they don't go in. My God, no, they don't go in.

You ask anybody, my friend, and he'll tell you. It's not like that today, but then in that war those priests they tell the boys not to go and fight, and they don't go. They hide, sometimes for years and the priests are happy. You see, this makes the church stronger. The church she was strong in those days.

Old Houde in Montreal he was really a nothing. Nobody knows now, I bet, if he is alive or dead. I think maybe dead.

•—→—• *Blame It All on the Politicians*

I can't remember much antagonism in Quebec. Of course I went overseas in July of '43 but until then, well, there didn't seem much. Certainly nothing like the past few years.

My father had a store in Three Rivers. We are English, but I spoke French. My father and mother spoke French. My class-mates at school mostly were French. In fact, I still speak French.

When I trained I wore the General Service badge, but a lot of the fellows didn't. I was young then, of course, but I can't remember any antagonism. I certainly had none. If they wanted to serve in Canada, to fight for Canada and Canada alone, all right, that was just fine. We were all in the army, weren't we? After all, the way the army was set up, there was the active force for overseas and the non-overseas force, who then were starting to be called Zombies. This was the way the army was set up. You volunteered and you went in the active force. Or you were called up and you had the choice. Active or not.

As I recall, the Mackenzie King government couldn't or didn't even try to live up to its promises to anybody. It was all politics, of course, the attitude of the politicians in Ottawa and in Quebec City and the monkey business that has always gone on between them. But you asked me about the attitude of the average bloke in the street. I don't think he had much of an attitude, when you really get down to it.

Mind you, he was told he had to have an attitude. Like old Houde [Camillien Houde, mayor of Montreal] who said fight conscription, don't go for it. That was an attitude, a leader telling them to lay off. So they throw him in detention camp in Pettawawa with a bunch of Nazis and Fascists and Italians. So some people get mad. The politicans in Quebec are jumping back and forth. Mackenzie King brings in Louis St. Laurent, a high-priced corporation lawyer, and makes him justice minister, and he says conscription is good for Canada. French Canada must do its share. And on and on and on.

But all this is politics. Strictly politics. Mackenzie King knows the Conservatives are going to get in if he loses the French vote, so he's jumping back and forth too.

You know one attitude, why a good friend of mine wouldn't volunteer to go overseas? I'll tell you. He's got three brothers. He's the fourth to go. One brother loses an eye in an explosion in England. Another is a wireless air gunner. A third guy is also in the army. Jacques is fourth, and his mother says she doesn't want him to go overseas. He's the last she's got, and the other three could get killed, so he says okay, "Okay Mom, I won't go." That's an attitude. But they made his life hell. The army, officers, sergeants, trying to get him to go active. They called him a coward, yellow streak down his back. The whole works. So he says, well, bugger you guys. I probably would have gone sometime, he tells me, but not after that. So, you see, that's another attitude.

You think families whose ancestors came to Canada when

Montreal was an Indian village, who'd been in the country for 400 years, you think they weren't patriotic to Canada? I said to Canada, not England. Canada, and not King George. If you don't think so, then you must be crazy. Of course they were patriotic. But the whole thing was so messed up by the politicians that there was no way of making it come out right after a while. Just a complete screw-up.

•—➤• *Quebec City Was the Worst*

For that kind of thing Quebec City was the worst, by far. It was all French, you see. Just one big French town. We were part of a group trying to combat the sinking of Allied shipping in the St. Lawrence and we thought we were doing a good job. As it turned out we did one hell of a job, but that didn't cut any ice with the Frenchies.

When we went ashore we'd go in a bunch. You never went with a buddy or by yourself because that way you could wind up in the gutter beaten up. Those guys were good at kicking you when you're down. There is a guy from our ship walking around today with a glass eye because some bastard kicked out his eye when he was down. He was drunk and didn't know what was happening and when he staggered back to the ship there was this eye all smashed and busted up. A god-awful mess.

In broad daylight, right in the city, people would make remarks at you. You couldn't understand them but you knew they were insulting, like why fight a war to pull England's fat out of the fire. The guys would spit on you. At your feet or on your clothes and when they did that they'd smile and say, *"Merci."* Nothing you could do about it. Not a damn thing. All you would be asking for was a beating.

We could never really figure how so many guys our age, guys up to say thirty or so, could stay out of uniform. They couldn't all have had pull. A lot, I guess, worked in the shipyards there which was classed essential. Some took to the woods, and I guess some just hid and only came out at night.

It never seemed fair that every time we pulled out up the river we were risking our lives, every hour. Now you see my point. Back in Quebec City there were hundreds, maybe thousands of guys my age who weren't in service, didn't intend to, and had the whole population backing them up. No wonder this country is in the mess it's in today.

•◄►• *All Them Guys Speak English*

There was this bad thing, you see. Some guys I know, they don't want to go into the army, but maybe they like the air force or maybe the navy better. Funny, some guys out along there at that time they been fishermen, but they say no, I don't want the navy, I want to fly. The air force. You get it?

So they go in to Montreal or Quebec City or maybe Three Rivers if they live close, and the guy, maybe the navy guy in the barracks, he'll say it is best for you to join the army because you don't speak English. Or maybe he says you don't speak English so good and how can we put you in a ship with all these English guys and the guys they're all talking English and what do you do? *Eh bien?* So they say, the air force, all them guys they speak English too, and what good is it for you to join them because you've got to learn. They maybe send you to school again. A guy of twenty-one like you, to school. How you like that, eh?

He smile and say, "What I'll do, I'll do this. I'll phone the army recruiting place and you wait here and in five minutes a station wagon it'll be outside, see, and off you go. By noon you're in the army."

Well, my friend, a lot of guys don't want that. They don't want that at all. They say, okay, that's the way she is, I'll go to Levis, go shipbuilding, Montreal, lots of work in the war factories, and I don't have to be in your goddamned army. Some guys, you know, they just don't think so fast as other guys and so they say, okay, I guess I got to go so they say, okay, phone for your station wagon. Then some of these guys they find out how bad the army is, how really bad it is, and they say to hell with it.

They run away. Maybe to the bush, you see, and work for Abitibi or Price Brothers or maybe some relatives this guy has, or maybe they take another name. Some go to Portland, Bangor, even Boston and down there at Lowell where they got Yanks for relatives and they work in war plants. Some guys, two I know, they just sleep in the attic, which is hidden, you know, and play cards. Then they get tired, you know, and the police find them and I don't remember it is jail for them. Just the army again and they say, oh for Christ sakes, we stay. What else is there to do?

•◄►• *You Had to See Their Point*

I don't think there were all that many French Canadians who were Zombies. I mean there were lots, but there were lots from the rest of Canada too. There were some damn good regiments from

Quebec, and a couple of those Maritime outfits were larded with French. They fought bloody well, battle honours by the score. The Royal Twenty-second. The Chaudières, for another. I could name quite a few, and they fought like hell.

You had to see their point too. After all, if Mackenzie King is going to play politics with the reservists and the active army and Quebec against Ontario and the rest of Canada—and remember this has been going on a hell of a long time—then you mix in the priests and the church and the Momma Dorval and Grandmother Boulanger and all these women who ran the French families, and have for generations, and they're saying that French Canada is getting screwed again, give your blood to save England, you can see the point. Some guys just got their dander up. They'd fight for Canada, on Canada's shores and to the last inch, but why fight for England?

"What has England ever done for us?" Sure, that's what they'd say. Hah! You should hear some of those guys talk. They had it all down in black and white and green and red. England, they'd say, hadn't done a bloody thing for French Canada and neither had R. B. Bennett, and Mackenzie King was a thieving little rat, and what had English Canada done for them? Eh, what had English Canada done for them?

When you walked away from one of those arguments—and you didn't have them unless you knew the guys, fellows in your platoon—you knew one hell of a lot more about Canada and the French than you did before. In fact, maybe you were wondering why Canada was fighting in England's wars. That's a fact. I know it.

I don't think anybody can say any of the French were yellow. That would be a stupid thing to say. Just plain stupid. I think they were brave, and I know they had guts because they stood up under that hammering for two or three years when other guys, and their officers, were doing everything but calling them yellow. They weren't cowards. Far from it. A long way.

A lot, I think, would have joined up, to go overseas, a long, long time ago but it was the way the English went about it, trying to force them into it, giving them all the shit that came along. Making life so miserable that finally their principles about only defending Canada on Canada's soil hardened. It was like a ball of clay in a hot fire. Soon they developed such a tough shell that nothing could break it open.

They were all kept together. We'd call it segregation. They were all together and they just said, "Okay, if you can't understand our feelings about this, and you want to break your

promises right and left, all right, then fuck you guys. All of you."
I think a lot of that was in it.

•◄►• *Deserters in the Basement*

There was one time when our basement she's filled with 16 guys
from the Régiment de Hull who were being grabbed by the police
to make them go overseas.

    Knock, knock, knock, on the door, she's way after mid-
night, and my old man would go with the flashlight and say,
"Who's there?" and it's some guy who says he's deserting, and that
they're trying to take him overseas. He's not going, he says, and
they say my old man can hide him. You got to be careful with
each guy, you know, because he might be a cop and then, my
God, the trouble. But it doesn't happen to us.

    We got to feed these guys, you see, and half the people on
the street know what the business is and they bring things,
potatoes and carrots, some oatmeal in a sack. And this goes on,
and soon one guy goes and then another and one night a truck
comes and they all go. About 10 then, and away they go down the
lane and that's the end of them. There was maybe 15 or 16 guys in
our house maybe three or four weeks, down in the basement.

Women

*It Was a Nice Coat . . . She Handled That Farm Like a Man
. . . Working for the Government . . . Women Found
Freedom . . . The Kitchener Toe . . . A Wonderful Two
Weeks . . . Halting D-day in Calgary . . . Jam for Britain . . .
Boots to Be Proud of . . . The Cockroaches' Lunch . . . One
Hell of an Old Gal . . . The Chicken Thief*

---

*Although the phrase had not been invented then, the war did
wonders for the cause of Women's Lib. Originally it was unladylike for a woman to work. Then during the Depression, when the
most ladylike women would have crawled on broken glass for even
the most unladylike job, there were no jobs. Then suddenly, war
production began and there were thousands of jobs going
a-begging, and it was the patriotic thing for a woman to do to
work in a war plant and "Put the Hun on the Run."*

*So they flowed into the factories in the thousands, into
the shipyards, the aircraft factories, the textile plants and the
foundries, they worked in lumber mills and in dairies and they ran
farms single-handed, until it was estimated that at the time of peak
production, half of the 1,100,000 Canadians "fighting Hitler at
home" were women. Significantly, too, they were finding that all
the jobs they tried, they were able to handle very well indeed. It
was, in every sense, a liberating experience.*

•◄►• *It Was a Nice Coat*

I remember, I was just a kid but we'd lost the farm to taxes long
ago and just stayed on because Dad could get a little work with
the government and he fiddled in an orchestra Saturday nights. I
think he got a dollar and a half a night for that.

In 1940 everything else seemed to be getting better in
Canada except on the farms in Saskatchewan, so Dad and Mom
took us to Regina and I went into school there and then Selma my
sister finished school and went to work in a packing plant. She was
up to her waist in guts half the time, she said. It was very hard
work.

You got paid by the month then and Selma figured her
pay cheque would be about 65 dollars or so and Mom was looking

forward to it. We were living in a little house darn near out on the prairie and it was no fun, but Mom figured she could brighten up things a bit with Selma's first pay. Yellow curtains and things.

Selma's late coming home that Saturday and when she comes, in she waltzes, full of beans, and she has this box and out of it comes a coat. A muskrat coat, which was pretty big stuff in those days. It was a nice coat.

Mother said, very quietly, "What's that?"

Selma said, "What's it look like? It's a muskrat coat, and it fits me just right. And here's the hat and gloves to go with it," and she takes out two bags and shows us. Brown gloves and a little hat with some stuff on top of it.

Mother said, "Where's your pay cheque?"

Selma said, "Spent. All spent. On this, and this, and my wonderful coat."

I'd say our family fell apart right at that moment. Mother picked up her wicker sewing basket and whanged Selma right across the face with it and cut loose. I think "You little bitch" was one of her kinder expressions. She's screaming, and Selma's yelling and holding the coat to her, and Mom is trying to grab it and it is just one awful mess. What's worse than a family fight?

It was easy to see Mom's side. Six years out on the Saskatchewan prairie, drought years, dry as a bone by June, and we ate free pork and whitefish, they gave it away by the ton, and potatoes and turnips until they're coming out our ears, and when she gets things turned around and seeming to go right, her daughter spends her first pay cheque. Puts it on her back, and at that Mom couldn't even afford a sweater. She was the Good Will's best customer.

Course, I could see Selma's point too. Girls that age are pretty damned unreasonable, but she must have waded through a lot of guts to earn that money. Figured every penny was hers.

It ended up with Mom getting hold of the coat, Selma storming out of the house and Mom taking the coat back to the tailor downtown on Monday. He told her she could have 40 dollars for it. After all, he says, it's a second-hand garment. Selma quits her job, goes to stay with a girlfriend and next week, after raising a bit of hell around town, she joins the army. The women's army corps. And, my friend, that was the last we saw of her.

Every year Mom would get a Christmas card. About every third year it would say there was a new kid, but that's all. She's out in Vancouver somewhere, married again, probably doing quite well. Mom's dead.

•←• *She Handled That Farm Like a Man*

Yes, I'd like to tell you about my niece Dorothy. She'd been born on a farm, raised on a farm but she'd gone to the city, Edmonton, and been a nurse and then she married Grant, who had farmed just down the road from her Dad's place, and he was a good man. He was a good farmer and his folks had been in the district for many years.

Early in 1940 Grant takes it into his head to enlist. I'm not sure he talked it over with Dorothy, but all of a sudden there he is in the army and she's at home with three kiddies from eight down to four and three quarters of a section. It's good land and he's got a good line of equipment, but when all is said and done, he's in the army and she's on the farm.

Dorothy is a big girl, a big strapping girl, and when Grant gets shipped to Winnipeg for training she decides to put in a crop. Grant's brother lives about five miles away and he comes over quite a bit and soon she's got the hang of it. As I remember, that first year it was half a section in and a quarter in summer fallow, so she's a farmer now and if Grant had wanted to get a deferment then, to go home and help, I'm sure he could've but he's got this stubborn streak—all his family has—and he says no, he's joined up and he's going to see it through.

My husband and I used to drive out and see her, after Grant was gone, and she'd often be up on the tractor, pounding, chugging the way tractors do, and we'd walk over the summer fallow and she'd stop and she'd have to wipe her face with an old rag so you could see it was a pretty girl, and in all those years, and this is without a word of a lie, I never heard her complain. Not once, and that is saying something.

She handled that farm like a man, and she drove that truck and tractor and one-way and combine like a man, and she even did a bit of custom farming around the district. I'll say this for Grant. He was progressive and he was one of the first to get a combine and it held out until the end of the war. If it had been horses I don't think she could have swung it. No, I don't think so. If something broke on some machinery her brother-in-law would probably come over but she could do most things. Replace teeth on the mower or clean out the carburetor on the tractor, things like that.

She was a first-class cook. She could have cooked in a lumber camp, and she and the kids kept that house clean as a whistle. It wasn't a big house but it was clean. You could eat off the floor, windows shiny, all that.

She curled in the winter and taught Sunday school in

town, and she'd go out on deer shoots with the men of the district and if you weren't close, in those rubber boots and overalls you'd think she was a man. We'd sometimes go out for Sunday dinner and in the fall she'd drive over to a lake, a pothole really, and bring back four or five mallards. She was a wonder, that woman.

I don't think she fooled around, either. I'm sure she could have. No trouble there, I'd say. She was a big girl and I think if she got interested in a man she could give him quite a time, but all that time I never heard one word about her. Like the wife in the Bible, you might say.

All this time Grant was overseas and what he was thinking, I don't know. I know what she was thinking, though. When he came home she gave him their bankbook and she said, and this is about what she said, "There's more money in there than we've ever had in our lives. Just don't go away again."

•◄►• *Working for the Government*

I'll never work for a government again. I worked for the Wartime Prices and Trade Board during the war and never worked so little and got so much money and remember, I was used to working 14 hours a day, and I never saw so much stupidity and prejudice and plain meanness and laziness than I saw in that one year.

We'd come to work about nine-thirty and at ten we'd go down to the canteen for coffee for an hour, and it was two hours for lunch and about three-thirty this woman, my boss, would say, "Oh, it's snowing out, so we'd better go home," or, "It's raining out," or "The sun is too hot," and so on. So the phones were hardly ever answered, but she was the boss so I had to do what she said and when one of the newspapers or radio stations would phone up asking about something, she'd just say, "Not for publication," or, "That's on the censored list," and bang down the phone. Most of the time she just didn't want to talk to them, and here we were, in the information office of the prices board in Canada's biggest city. It used to make me sick.

I remember we did one constructive thing in all that time. So many men were in uniform and the government figured a lot of precious cloth could be saved if their double-breasted suits, which they weren't using, could be tailored into smart women's suits. They could, and it was a good idea. So I got this idea. Frank Sinatra, he was just a kid then, he was coming to town, and we got him to donate one of his suits and some woman won it in a raffle or a draw and we got a lot of very good publicity on that. But that was the only thing we did that was of any use. Only that, and it was my idea, and then she took all the credit. I'm just not bitching about one person. This is the way the whole government worked. Or did not work.

•◄►• *Women Found Freedom*

My daughter is in Women's Liberation. When I was just about her age there was nothing like that. There had been a lot of talk about emancipation, you know, years before, but that was women getting the vote, wasn't it? But no Women's Liberation. Looking back on it, we had a pretty poor time of it.

That's what the war did, though. Got thousands, my goodness, tens of thousands of women and girls out of the home. In 1936, I came to Winnipeg from Dauphin. Just out of high school. There were three things you could do. You could work as a waitress and have some Chinese cook pawing you. I know, I tried that for two weeks. You could work at Eaton's Mail Order for 11 or 12 dollars a week and walk out of there half dead every night to a lonely room somewhere, and I had friends who did that, and that was enough of that. Or you could go to work for a family. Of course, you were cook, bottle-washer, ran errands and washed floors and were the baby-sitter, but back home in Dauphin that's what I did anyway. I got in through a friend of a friend with a nice family named Gilbert in a nice house and I had a room in the basement, a bathroom with shower and I got Thursday afternoons and Sunday afternoons off after the noon dinner. The pay was only 14 dollars a month but all in all, that wasn't bad. I was probably better off than those poor girls in Eaton's or some insurance office because my bed and food was paid for. That went on until 1940.

In 1940 there were war plants starting and I went to Toronto because there was an airman stationed at Trenton that I was ga-ga about, but that didn't work out. But it sure got me out of Winnipeg and I've never been back, except passing through. It was good to be there when I was there, but when my girlfriend and me landed in Toronto, you could say we were in a different world. Toronto was a big city and Winnipeg was a widening of the road on the prairies.

In the radio plant we both worked at, there were hundreds of women. All the bosses were men, but we expected that. Today they'd be demanding women bosses, but not then. Hundreds of women from all over Canada, and I've stood at the same bench working with women who actually had hired girls like me as domestics. You know, at 5 dollars a week, and now they were complaining that they couldn't get maids to work 14 hours a day

.

cooking and washing and doing their dirty work because they had all gone into war plants at 25 or 30 dollars a week for a nine-hour day. You'd have thought we were all traitors. I asked one why she was working in the plant and she said her husband was an officer in the air force overseas and she just didn't have much to do. So she was working in a plant, next to maids like me. Funny.

I guess you'd call me a stepper. That's a person who steps out. You never hear it now. Means a girl who likes a good time, likes to go out dancing and partying a lot, and not with one fellow but with lots of fellows. Well, I sure stepped out in Toronto. I learned what this old world was all about, and I had a good time during the war and I made good money and because I always had dates, I saved some money after I had spent for clothing and lipstick, and stockings when I could get them. And our pay kept getting better and better.

The war killed all this servant business, being a maid, and I think it did a lot to finish off the idea that a woman's place and her only place was in the home. My God, there were tens of thousands of us living a kind of life we'd never known before, money and good times and lots of men and, more than anything, I guess you could say freedom. Yes, I'll admit some just couldn't handle the freedom, but they were just a few.

Husbands and boyfriends came back from the war and found their wives and girlfriends just weren't prepared to start washing dishes again. It must have been quite a shock. But some women had ferried air force bombers to Britain, and others drove ambulances and worked in canteens serving the troops, or in war plants handling very expensive tools working on equipment, planes, instrument panels and things, and the companies found they could do better than men. It is no lie. And any girl, provided she wasn't two-headed, could walk into any store, dress goods shop, good restaurant anywhere, and get a job and no questions asked and find she was respected and well paid. And also, and don't you forget this, she found she enjoyed working, outside, with real, live people and not being cooped up in a home talking baby-talk to an eighteen-month-old and a three-year-old.

You could almost say that women fought a war the same as their men, the war against them just being women, household machines. And because of the circumstances I'd say they won it so easily that they didn't even realize they were fighting it. I know I didn't, but the war and working in the plants so changed me I became an entirely different person. I wish I'd kept a diary. It would have made a good book.

•◄►• *The Kitchener Toe*

Christ, as long as I live I'll never forget what I called The Great Kitchener Toe Controversy. It was a way of knitting socks for soldiers just so. The Kitchener Toe Method.

I've got these two old biddie aunts, and Uncle Bert, a coal miner. They'd knit, all three of them, Aunt Annie, Aunt Bessie and Uncle Bert, they'd knitted for years. Nobody could tell them about knitting, so when the wool and the instructions came from the Red Cross, they just ignored the details, just went ahead like they had for 50 years or so.

And then the shit hit the fan. I think Aunt Bessie had about 10 pairs sent back. No Kitchener Toe. Aunt Annie, maybe 10 pairs. With a little note, firm little note. Rip them out and do them over. Well, by God, war was declared.

And it went on and on. They wrote letters to the editor in the papers. They phoned their Member of Parliament. They roared, and there's mild old Uncle Bert roaring the hardest. Roar, roar, roar, what's this country coming to? That sort of thing. There were articles in the paper and people got talking about the Kitchener Toe.

It was quite a fight and went on and on, mutter, mutter, anger, and the Red Cross wouldn't budge an inch and finally after a few months it all died down because people got tired of such foolishness and the old biddies decided that if they were to win the war they'd better do it the right way. But for a time there it was sure hot and heavy, the fur flying, and all these old ladies insulted as hell at some little snippet of a Red Cross girl daring to reject their masterpieces. Yeah, war is hell, ain't it.

•◄►• *A Wonderful Two Weeks*

They asked 30 of us Junior Hostesses if we'd like to go for a vacation to Coal Harbor and entertain the air force guys and we jumped at it. It was for eleven days as I remember, and the government would put us up in the officers' quarters and feed us, and we paid our own way. I know that seems strange now, all of us going up to help the air force fellows and entertain them and the government making us pay our own way, but we jumped at the chance. Anyway, we all went. The west coast of Vancouver Island. It could have been on the moon.

The first night there was a big coffee party for everybody and we all got to meet everybody, and we were tired so we went to bed in the officers' quarters and it had these chutes from the second and third floors. Fire escapes, you know the kind. And all the girls were taking showers and the fire escapes were lined with air force fellows who had taken off their boots and socks and climbed up these slippery chutes to get a better look at us, and you looked out the windows and on every branch of a tree you could see another man's face. You know what women are like, they scream and yell but they loved it, this attention, even if they were capering around the shower room like kids.

Then we'd have breakfast with 30 of the fellows and lunch with another 30 and dinner with another 30 and so on, for about ten days and we got to know an awful lot of fellows. They'd slick down the tarmac at night and bring out music and we'd have dances out there until we were ready to drop. In the days we'd go swimming and walking through the woods.

Any one of us girls could have been bow-legged and cross-eyed and we'd still have had a ball. It was a wonderful two weeks.

•◄►• *Halting D-day in Calgary*

I used to work the summers for Canadian Press as stooge, joe boy, and after I graduated from the University of Manitoba they sent me out to Calgary to the bureau there. They got me a train berth and I spent all night reading the manual about how to operate the tape machine, the teletype, in the office.

The morning the invasion came was my first day, and when the first flashes and bulletins about D-day came through on the tape they couldn't send them from Winnipeg to Vancouver until the whole line was clear. Right through. They had to have my signal that the line was clear before they could go ahead with the invasion. All I had to do was punch out C-A-L and then a few spaces and then C-L-R and that meant "Calgary Clear" and so the whole line would be open from Winnipeg to Victoria and the war could go on.

In other words, three letters, a space and three letters, and I punched it out and my career as a bureau chief, in a one-woman bureau, had begun. But I was so excited or something that I must have punched something wrong and the carriage return shot back and the whole thing went wild, with bells ringing and everything happening. I couldn't think. I was absolutely shattered. I knew it was the biggest story of the war and there I was, lousing up my end of it. I started to faint and hung out the window in this little room no bigger than a closet and I tried to phone the phone company while I was hanging out the window and trying to get air, and on the wire everybody was signalling: "When are we going to get this war going in the West?" and stuff like that. Finally Don Miller up in Edmonton figured out what I was up to and realized I was in a panic, and since he was connected on the same circuit with me he just knocked out "Calgary Clear" and the war began again.

•◄►• *Jam for Britain*

One thing we did was Jam For Britain. I'd like to get all the women together who worked on Jam For Britain and have a few laughs.

Every year we'd have an objective and all the Red Cross chapters would work with the W.I. [Women's Institutes] and we'd collect all the berries and fruit in the valley that was donated and it would come in trucks, in wagons, sacks and boxes—mountains of fruit and berries of every kind—and Harry Beach who owned a jam factory at Mission, he'd supervise us. All the women would go out and work, in the factory, just like factory hands making jam. Oh, it was a messy business, but oh, it was a splendid undertaking. There you could really feel you were doing something for the Motherland, messing around in all that juice and pulp and with all that equipment.

The last year, 1945, I remember our quota was 60 tons of jam. Think of how much one ton of jam is. But we produced *68* tons. Now that is a lot of jam!

•◄►• *Boots to Be Proud of*

Just at the start of the war I worked for a company called Greb. This was in Kitchener and they made boots for the Canadian Army. They were good boots. I've worked in shoe plants since, in Montreal and Winnipeg, and I've never seen boots that were better made. Those were boots you could be proud of.

This girl who worked beside me as a checker, she and I figured it would be a lot of fun if we put our name and address on a little piece of paper and a couple of sentences about who we were, and then we'd put it in the shoe and hope some soldier would write us. It was a bit like putting a message in a bottle if you're on an island.

These boots, and this was about 1940, early in '40, these boots were sent to England, and the soldiers of the First Division were wearing them. Believe me, we got lots of replies to our notes. I think maybe I got a dozen or so, and Jennie got that many too. Mostly friendly thank-you notes.

I remember one chap from Winnipeg transferred to the air force and was sent back to Canada to train and we arranged to meet in Toronto for a date. Not that anything came of it, he just wasn't my type, but it was an interesting experience. Dinner and dancing, but that's all. He said Greb's boots were the best he'd ever worn, and that made me happy.

•━►• The Cockroaches' Lunch

The C.P.R. wanted people to work in their freight shed down on Logan. I was pregnant with Gerald so I couldn't work a full shift, 10 hours I think, but I got called in a lot, overtime, night time, time other people didn't want to work.

On weekdays, when there were others around, the cockroaches would stay hidden. But when I was alone on Sundays, alone in that big waybill room, they'd come out. I was scared deathless of them, so I would break my jam sandwiches for lunch in half and I'd put them out on the table that I worked on, and this little trick would stop them from running all over my work table. They'd stop and eat the jam instead.

The war wasn't a fun time for me in any way, shape or form. Oh God, but was I ever pregnant that time.

•━►• One Hell of an Old Gal

We went overseas in July, I think, of '42, just a bunch of air force guys in a troopship loaded with army guys. Anyway, on the dock there was a few women and they had baskets and they were passing out apples, little bags of things like hardrock candy, razor blades, maybe an orange, socks, all these kind of things. They were just ladies of the town Halifax, and somebody said they weren't really supposed to be there, but nobody actually turned them away. They'd say, "Good luck, soldier," or, "Cheerio, airman," and one old lady said to me, "Be sure and write your mother." I always remembered that because I wasn't much of a letter writer.

Okay, it's three years later. November, 1945, another troopship. We come off the gangplank and there is ambulances for some of the guys who need them, but mostly it's just us, thinner, maybe a bit wiser, and I'll be damned but if there isn't this same old lady and she says as we pass by, she says as she hands me an orange and the Halifax paper, she says, "Did you write your mother, son?" and I nearly dropped dead. I think, did she remember me? No, because I hear her say it to a guy about two back in line.

And you know what, that old biddy must have been doing that job, rain or shine, mostly rain, I'll bet, passing out little goodies and asking the guys if they would please write to their mothers. One hell of an old gal. Year after year after year. Somebody should have pinned a medal on those old gals. Maybe somebody did.

•◄►• *The Chicken Thief*

I was a Rosie the Rivetter. Working on the planes. This plant was right in the middle of a lot of farmers' fields, their barnyards. There were a couple of places where you could get under the fence so you could check in and then sneak out and go into the little town that was close, and then you'd sneak back in about an hour before the shift ended. Then you'd punch out like usual for a day's pay. That went on.

The farmers were complaining about losing a lot of things. Mostly chickens but garden stuff too. It was these people sneaking out through under the fence; they'd go chicken raiding and stealing. The plant decided they'd start frisking. The night they did, and we didn't know about it, of course, one girl had sneaked out and stolen a farmer's chicken and had put it in her big lunchbox and that kept it alive. But when we were going through the gate and saw the guards she said, "Oh, my god," and somebody told her to put this chicken down in her cover-alls. We wore cover-alls those days working on the planes.

So just as we're up to the gate, at the gate, this stupid chicken starts crashing around inside her pants and the matron reaches down in and hauls out a live chicken. And this girl, what a crazy nut, she says, "That's the best thrill I've had in months." You see, there was a man shortage and she said, "Leave it there, the best thrill I've had in a long time."

P.O.W.'s

*Hong Kong and After . . . Captor and Captive . . . Every-
body Was Kept Busy . . . The Swiss Escape Route . . .
Where Do You Hide the Dirt? . . . Eighty of Us Were
Trying to Bust Out . . . Next-of-kin Parcels . . . The Boy
Scouts . . . Fun and Games, Hell . . . The Escape Committee
. . . The End of the War . . . My Health Was Not Too Good
. . . The Woman at Home . . . I Shook Her Hand*

---

*One man who was in a German prisoner of war camp rather
blithely throws it off as being "three years in the slammer," while
another, a captive of the Japanese after the fall of Hong Kong, still
cannot talk about it for long without his eyes misting and his voice
beginning to break.*

*The Articles of the Geneva Convention of 1929 governed
the treatment of both men—but with a difference. The evidence
mainly shows the Germans lived up to the Articles as best they
could, while the Japanese acted as though they never existed.*

*Many of the prisoners held by the Japanese were officers
and men of the Winnipeg Grenadiers and the Royal Rifles of
Quebec who were captured after a gallant but futile battle at Hong
Kong in 1941. In military parlance, both units were "destroyed,"
and it is a tribute to their heroism in battle that the Canadian
government took steps to reconstitute them into the active army.
The Japanese put their prisoners into P.O.W. cages and used them
as slave labour. Many of them have since died, weakened by poor
treatment and lack of food during those long years behind barbed
wire.*

*Things went better for Canadians on the other side of the
world. They were behind the wire too, but they were treated more
fairly, and were allowed to keep in touch with the world outside
through the Red Cross.*

*The Red Cross contribution was staggering. By war's end,
16,500,000 parcels worth $48,000,000 had been sent through the
International Committee in Geneva—this vast outpouring to
prisoners of every nation was the direct contribution of the
Canadian civilian.*

*Canadian treatment of German and Italian prisoners in
camps in northern Ontario and southern Alberta was far more
humane than German treatment of Allied prisoners, and many
Germans and Italians returned to Canada later as immigrants.*

Hong Kong and After

We were in Hong Kong only three weeks when war broke out. How was the fighting? Pretty desperate. Pretty desperate. As you know, we had little equipment or ammunition, and towards the end we were using only our rifles and firing smoke bombs from our mortars. That is all we had left. That's all I remember.

We were intermixed, the British and us, and two regiments of Indians, one Punjabi. The British were the Royal Scots and the Middlesex. The Japs cut through the centre of the island the first night, and the Royal Scots and Middlesex were extremely good. Of course, they were seasoned soldiers. A lot of our boys had not even fired a rifle, but they gave a good account of themselves, a very good account of themselves. Hadn't fired a rifle at all. However, I guess they thought that when we got back from Jamaica we were going on guard duty in Hong Kong. Our intelligence must have been wrong, and we were unfortunate enough to be there. The other regiment, of course, was the Royal Rifles, from Quebec.

Anyway, we were captured, and before we went to Japan we helped build the airport in Hong Kong. The one that juts out into the water, you know the one. There was a mountain there, and we carried that out in baskets on our shoulders down to the sea and it is now the Hong Kong airport. We dumped most of that earth there.

The first two months were probably the worst because we only got one cup of rice, one cup of rice like soup, *a day,* and that's where we lost our weight. We got so weak that four of us would get together and we would take turns going for our ration so we could conserve our strength, but that was the worst, and then it picked up a little.

In Japan, I don't think we got any less than their own people did, to be quite honest. They were very short of food.

Captor and Captive

We got to know our guards. Oh yes, we had quite a strange relationship with them. Perhaps you'd better ask a psychologist about that. I mean, who was the prisoner and who was the guard? They were there, chained to us because we were the enemy, and vice-versa, but often we did not consider ourselves as such. As enemies. As guard and captive.

There was always the challenge, well, that we were supposed to escape and get back. And they understood, and we did, too, that if they caught us escaping, they would shoot us. But all in all, it was like a teeter-totter. Up and down, them and us, and the camp wouldn't work without all of us working together.

A lot of them spoke English. Some of us learned German. We exchanged notes. I remember one chap who was a lecturer in the classics in some university and his guard was a student of the classics, and that was one kind of a relationship. Or it could be that each had a son aged five and a daughter aged eight and they'd discuss things together. The German might tell the Canadian type what his son and daughter were doing, and from that the Canadian would have some idea of how his own children were growing up. But the basis of it all was that they were soldiers and we were soldiers, airmen, and there was a recognition of this between us.

Besides, there wasn't one hell of a lot of difference between captor and captive. They had the guns and the dogs and the barbed wire, of course, but we all were hungry. I have one photo of our guards rummaging around in our garbage disposal area, the place where we threw the tins and containers from Red Cross parcels. They were looking for anything we might have tossed out, hoping they could use it. Food. They were hungry too.

Do you know where that camera came from to take that picture? It came from a guard. He traded it through the wire to one of our guys for something he wanted from a Red Cross parcel. Maybe a sweater knit by some dear old lady in Owen Sound or a can of powdered milk. Maybe concentrated coffee. A slab of chocolate. Gum. They loved gum, and as I remember, life-savers. These were things they hadn't seen in years.

I just had no contact with German officers—or I should say, any contact was usually a bad one for me. They weren't the nicest guys in the world. But the average guard, yeah. He was okay. Often he'd been wounded or had a double hernia or was too old for the front or something. You rarely saw the real, tough Hitler Youth graduates and if you did, he was a no-no. A real no-no.

•◄►• *Everybody Was Kept Busy*

In any camp you're going to run across the complete cross-section of life. So you'd have actors or chaps who wanted to be actors, and directors and producers, script writers, set designers, set-makers, make-up artists, lighting men. Men who would build you a stage, and there were costume-makers and . . . well, you had every-thing to put on shows.

The point of the whole thing was, naturally, to keep everybody interested. Keep them moving, keep them busy. There was a whole list of things I could tell you about, from handicrafts to hi-jinks, but the theatre provided a lot of expended energy for guys who'd been behind the wire for two years, three years.

There is probably a tremendous amount of latent talent in each one of us. Well, in a prisoner of war camp all this came out. Take a man from the wilds of Manitoba, who probably would never have seen live theatre in his life unless he'd been nabbed at Dieppe or shot down over Essen. He suddenly finds himself making sets, making costumes, maybe acting. Maybe he'll be one of those pretty little geishas and he doesn't care about the fairy aspect of it, he's no more queer than you or I.

It was the same for the guys who raised vegetables or made radios that worked out of parts they begged, borrowed or stole, or spent their time digging tunnels or just bedevilling the guards—and that was important. In a prison camp you know you're behind the wire. You know it all the time, just like a prisoner in the penitentiary knows. There's the outer wire, the dogs, lights on at night. There's the food, which you can't ever forget. There's the inspections, the checks, the hunt all the time by the guards, because with 5,000 guys in a camp they know there is about 15 funny things going on all the time. They don't have to be told. They know it. They know all the tricks, so we'd have to just keep inventing new ones, or polishing up old ones. Ask any prisoner. The thing was to keep that old brain turning over.

You see, every camp was run by committees. Food Committee. Red Cross. Sick Committee. Special Events. Escape Committee. A lot like you'd run a city or a big town. That's what we were, essentially. Inside the wire, we pretty well ran our own affairs. So, an Entertainment Committee.

The work on a play would go on for two, three months. Just like on Broadway. Making sets—papier mâché, cardboard, Klim dried milk cans, tin of all kinds, old uniforms. Some of those sets were absolutely amazing. Fantastic costumes too, and music of course. Take 5,000 men and how many musicians have you got? Five hundred, of varying shades of competence, I guess. The Germans allowed the Red Cross to provide instruments—that's where the bagpipes came from. The scripts and music probably came from the Red Cross too.

Rehearsals, dress rehearsals, opening night and maybe a week's run. Everybody would go. Even the Germans. Why not? The only game in town.

Gilbert and Sullivan were very popular—*The Mikado,*

Gondoliers. Torrid things like *White Cargo.* There was one called *The Grouse in June;* that was an English period piece. Delderfield could have written it. Another called *Up the Pole.*

Everybody was kept busy. There was a job if you wanted it, and the thing was, keep working, keep in every possible way a routine which would make every man think that there was hope. Keep him achieving, even behind the wire. It was quite a job, but if you had a good committee setup—and you needed really top men in them—then it could work. I know, because it did work. I saw it work.

•◄►• *The Swiss Escape Route*

It was an unwritten rule between the Swiss, the escaping prisoners and the Huns, I guess, that if you could get across the border about 30 kilometres and could remain there for 48 hours then you were safe. The Swiss wouldn't hand you back to the Germans. Short of the 30 kilometres and less than 48 hours and they would. They didn't want, I guess—and this seems natural—they didn't want to jeopardize their relations with Germany over two or three escaped prisoners of war.

If you made it safely, then the Swiss would contact your consulate or a friendly consulate and eventually you would be moved out to Portugal. It was a system that worked fairly well.

But it was difficult to remain undetected for the required 48 hours. So the thing you did, the thing our escape committee told us to do, was to bring yourself to the attention of the authorities rather forcefully. That meant throwing a rock through the largest window in the main street of the village where you found yourself. You would be arrested, then you would be held in jail, and by the time your case was disposed of, the 48-hour period would have elapsed and you were safe. Freedom meant, in the long run, a rock through some innkeeper's window. I've often given it some thought, I should go back to Switzerland and pay that innkeeper or his family for that window I smashed. Glass was hard to get in those days.

•◄►• *Where Do You Hide the Dirt?*

One of the things most difficult to decide was how to get rid of the dirt when a tunnel was being built. Think about it now. You've got a tunnel, maybe 3 feet wide, 4 feet high and anywhere from 200 to 400 feet long. Those are my figures. They would vary, naturally, depending on the layout of the camp.

So, problem, big and hairy problem: What do you do with the dirt? That's hundreds of bags of dirt, and it comes out a pocketful at a time, a handkerchief full at a time, a sprinkling in the cuff of a pair of pants, rolled in a roll around the waist but not too thick. And that's about it. And be careful. Nobody could be caught. Not even once.

And what do you do to get rid of it? Making gardens, that was an old trick but remember, subsoil is often a different colour and grain than surface soil. Do you sprinkle it over the compound? Toss it in handfuls over the fence? Hide it under the floors of the huts, or in the rafters, or just what the hell did you do? Great minds were always at work and great schemes were thought up. But on the other side, Jerry was no slouch either. It was where we tried to escape and they tried to stop us, and in some ways it was like a game.

One commandant was so proud of the tunnel that we'd dug that he kept it in shape, didn't have it filled in, and he'd show it off to visiting officers to show them how smart and efficient his prisoners were. It was a masterpiece.

•◄►• *Eighty of Us Were Trying to Bust Out*

The whole exercise was to break out. The Germans expected it, and we had a better chance than their fellows did. All we had to do was get to Switzerland or get to Spain. I knew one fellow who crossed the Pyrenees in winter, deep snow and those mountain passes—he froze his feet but he made it. Not too many did. But the Germans in Britain, somehow they had to get across the Channel and that meant a boat. So they had a tougher time.

This camp I'm talking about was in Bavaria and we ran this tunnel from inside one of the huts, down and then along and under the perimeter wire. One of our fellows was an engineer in civil life so, using instruments he had made, he figured just how far it would be until we could break out again. Our plan was this. Imagine the tree line, pine trees. They were about 85 feet from the perimeter, the wire perimeter which guards patrolled at night. So this engineer said all we had to do was get up to this line of trees. Then we'd push up through the earth in one hour or so, just a couple of feet, and away we'd go. We'd be among the trees and we'd time it so that every time the searchlight went past us, another man would get up and get away.

That was fine, except for one thing. The engineer let us down because when we opened up the tunnel, we were not on the other side of the trees. Nope. We were just about three feet this side of the trees and, therefore, in full view of the patrolling guards.

But that wasn't disaster yet. We could still get up one at a time when the searchlight went past us. It just made it tougher, that's all.

Mistake number two. One of our fellows, an Australian, insisted on taking a pack with him. That was okay, but the fool insisted on wearing his pack while he crawled along the tunnel and then, when the time came for him to pop out of the hole, damn it all but he got stuck. Dragging his pack would have been easy. With his pack on his back he was just twice as big, and he and his pack got stuck in the escape hole. Stuck there, damn it all. By the time he heaved himself out, the searchlight had come back over him and a guard was right there.

So I guess the guard is thinking, "What the hell's a man doing out there?" and this Australian, for no reason that I can think of, he gives the guard a little wave. Just a little "hi" kind of a wave. And the guard waves back and marches on about seven or eight steps and then he does one of those movie double-takes and Christ, that did it! Bells ringing, shots being fired, everything.

About 80 of us were trying to bust out and I think 40 of us made it. I was one of the first three or four out and I heard the firing start up when I was about two kilometres away and I thought, "Well, that's it."

This other chap and I, we walked for two days through the forest, down foresters' trails and we never saw another person, but we were getting pretty hungry and suddenly we walked around a corner of a trail and bang, we're right in the middle of a tiny Bavarian village. Everybody saw us, of course, and so there was no point in trying to run or skirt around the village. We tried to pass ourselves off as French peasants. There was a lot of slave labour working in those forests but my French was ten times worse than my English, hah! It didn't work. We were picked up right away by the village police.

•◆• *Next-of-kin Parcels*

If your son was in a German prisoner camp you could send him parcels. I think it was one every three months. These parcels were great morale builders for the boys because they knew people at home, their families, were thinking of them. The families would buy food that would keep, and they'd send jams and jellies and hard candies too. There wasn't all that much you could send. Chipped beef. Tinned butter. And love. Lots of love. But, of course, not hack saws. The parcels, every parcel that went over was checked.

Then we [the Red Cross] would give them things they maybe couldn't obtain, couldn't buy to put in the parcels. We had priority. Little things but very important to a boy in that sort of a prison. Socks. Even pajamas. Think of it. Towels. Hankies. Lots of them. Then we could get chocolate and packages of Oxo so they could have a nourishing drink and tinned apples, tinned beans, peanut butter. Peanut butter as I remember was a great favorite. Salt. The little things that are important. Each parcel was like a Christmas stocking.

You must remember though that this was only for the boys in the hands of the Germans. It did not include the Japanese. The Japanese did not, would not even think of allowing those parcels in. They wouldn't even communicate, except very occasionally. They had a completely different attitude. A completely rotten attitude. Completely rotten. They'll never be forgiven for much of the things they did to our boys.

•◄►• *The Boy Scouts*

We always knew what was going on—from the B.B.C. We had a radio in our camp and the parts or the radio itself came from the guards.

You see, there was a lot of buying went on. The guards wanted things that were in our parcels and we wanted a radio to listen to the British Broadcasting Corporation. So, and I'm not sure of this, they got the parts, or maybe they got the radio complete.

It was hidden in a hollowed-out beam in a shack that the Boy Scouts had. Yes, Boy Scouts. They were a front, of course, for the radio. The camp commandant let these Boy Scouts have this shack, just eight by eight, something like that, and they put the radio in this shack, in a hollowed-out beam.

Yes, I said Boy Scouts. Sure, they were grown men. They were P.O.W.'s—English, Anzacs, Canadians. And they had these Boy Scout troops and they had Boy Scout uniforms. At least they cut off their pants short and had badges and things. There was always one troop in the shack or outside it. Whenever guards came looking, then the guys outside would give the warning and the guys inside would by tying knots, doing first aid, all the things Boy Scouts do. Flag signalling, all this stuff. Go for little hikes around the camp.

They played the game as long as they wanted and Jerry never found out. They never found the radio. In a camp as big as that one was, there were thousands of places where a set could have been hidden. They never found it because they never looked all that hard in the Boy Scout shack.

Then when the news came on, the Scouts would fan out through the camp and tell what was happening. In 15 minutes everyone would know.

•◄►• *Fun and Games, Hell*

There are P.O.W. associations in all countries, going after better pensions and medical help and just mutual protection, so why not do something about that bloody nonsense on television called "Hogan's Heroes?" You know, fun and games and jolly German guards in a P.O.W. camp. Fun and games, hell. Run the show off television. That's what I'd have done. Boycott the sponsor.

I'd like to know what's funny about short rations and cutting railroad ties in their forests in the coldest of winter and them holding up your mail and poking into your Red Cross parcels for smokes. And what's funny about sadistic guards clubbing a guy just because they didn't like the way he looked, or maybe the guard just happened to get up wrong side of the bed that morning? Holding up the mail? Stealing our rations and selling them in the towns around? Clubbing our guys with their rifle butts? I got a broken nose out of it, for one thing, a lot of guys worse.

When I first saw that comedy, I thought what in hell is the world coming to? What in hell is going on? Do people forget so easy, just so some television producers and actors and a company that sells motor oil or sanitary napkins can make some dough? Christ!

•◄►• *The Escape Committee*

In the camp I was in, in Bavaria—and by the way, this was quite near the camp which was the basis for the book and movie *The Great Escape*—the escape committee was set up by long-time prisoners, boys who knew the score, men who had been captured in France at the time of Dunkirk or in Greece, and they had expertise in forgery, in photography, map-making and so on. In this camp, Auflagen, about 5,000 men, there were 12 or 15 people on the committee, two or three air force, a couple of engineers for tunnel planning, two men from the King's Royal Rifles who were masters in the art of forgery and had served time, and then we had one pickpocket. Probably the best one in Britain.

The pickpocket, his job was obvious. German brass would visit us from time to time, and we had a time-serving English soldier who had a bugle and when the brass came, he would blow "A-hunting we will go"—no, I'm not kidding you, that was the signal—and two or three hundred men would mill around the main gate when the brass came in, often with some Swiss inspectors or Y.M.C.A. or Red Cross, and through their innate arrogance these Germans would be pleased they were getting such a royal welcome from the prisoners. Of course, with the milling around, it was simple for this professional pickpocket to dip their wallets, and they would be passed out quickly, inspected, money taken out and documents, passes, any documents which would be of use, all photographed—and with cameras which had been bought from a guard, by the way. And then the wallets were returned to the right officers. This alone took a tremendous amount of organization, skill, but it was done.

•◄►• *The End of the War*

We were working in a Japanese copper mine. We had a radio in the camp, and the day the emperor told his people that they had gone under, we immediately took over in the camp.

We ran ourselves. The head of our camp was an American officer, a Captain Ziegler from Wichita Falls, and he just took over. He told the Japanese, "You people just stay over there. The war's over, come and we'll show you [how we know]," and he took out a radio—I still have the ear phones—and this radio was put together out of odds and ends, bits and pieces, and it worked beautifully. I worked in the battery shop and it was rather danger-ous to bring out batteries for our radio. I once carried a small wet-cell battery under my hat, and I didn't dare stumble or anything because the acid would have been down my head. It was the only way we could get them into camp.

We became the conquerors and they became the prisoners, so to speak, even though we were still in the camp. In a couple of days planes off an aircraft carrier came and asked us to lay out a signal, what we needed, food, medical supplies, and they started dropping big boxes of stuff. We gained a lot of weight quickly, but because we weren't used to the food, a lot of people were sick.

The Americans came in a month after the signing, about the 19th of September, and they took us down and put us on a hospital ship and gave us a shower, a spray, and took all the new clothes they had dropped by plane and just shovelled them overboard and gave us new uniforms.

That was funny. We'd decided that when we marched out of that camp we'd wear our new uniforms so we wore our old clothes, the ones we'd been in for years, for that last month. Then when we got aboard the hospital ship they took away those uniforms, so here they were throwing away uniforms that had only been worn a few hours. After going four years without clothes, it was a shattering experience.

Funny thing happened in Guam, in the hospital. We were put in these Quonset huts, all made up neat with bunks and pajamas, and our boys all got in bed and they turned out the lights and then you'd hear "thump" and "thump" and "thump," and the lights went on, and the nurses and orderlies came in and we were all laying on the floor. Soft beds. We couldn't sleep in them, so after about three times they told us to sleep where we liked.

The next morning the Red Cross people came in, girls, tried to get us to talk to them, write letters home and so on. It took about a day to get used to it. We hadn't seen women for so long we couldn't talk to them, we didn't know how to act with them.

•◄►• *My Health Was Not Too Good*

Really, when we arrived home [from four years in a Japanese prison camp] the first information I had that my folks were even alive was when I got to Seattle and I phoned a cousin in Vancouver to find out if they were alive and he said yes, as far as he knew, and then I moved from there to Victoria and from there I phoned my home in Winnipeg, not knowing if they were still there or anything else. I can get a little worked up even today about it.

My father picked up the phone, they were living in an apartment, and he turned the phone over to my mother right away. That's the first they knew I actually was alive except for a letter they got from me in 1942, and I had mentioned as many names in it as I could [of the Winnipeg Grenadiers' survivors] and the Canadian government took this as a casualty list. It was in fact the first casualty list they got. This was eight, nine months after the fall of Hong Kong. The Japanese didn't release any casualty list, there was no known dead, no wounded, no anything else. The Winnipeg Free Press gave a big write-up to my letter. The regiment came from Winnipeg, you see.

And the only parcel I ever got, the only letter I ever got, I got two weeks after I arrived home. The Japanese didn't allow parcels or mail. None for any of us. It had been sent to Tokyo, brought back to Canada and delivered to me, at my parents' home.

My parents' reaction when I phoned? Well, about as upsetting as my own. It's rather difficult to talk about it. My father had had a stroke so he gave the phone to Mom, and I didn't talk to her long, but she was very calm, very elated. Then they told the rest of the family right away.

I had to stay two weeks, ten days in Victoria. My health was not too good, although I had spent a month in an American naval hospital in Guam and they had been fattening us up. When the Japanese surrendered I was 89 pounds. I had been about 150 when Hong Kong fell.

But all in all, during the trip across Canada from Vancouver to Winnipeg, I was in a very nervous condition. I was the only Hong Kong survivor on that particular train, and at every stop the Red Cross girls would come on because they heard there were Hong Kong men on the train, and they would ask, did I want to phone home, here's candy. It was just too much. Piles of attention, more than my share. It was very upsetting.

•◆• *The Woman at Home*

My husband was a German prisoner of war for four years. His plane was shot down in the North Sea about November of '41. They were laying mines and a Danish fishing boat picked them up, he and the tail gunner. He was a wireless air gunner then, a sergeant, and he was in several camps. They seemed to move them around quite a bit for no good reason that he could ever see, but he thought that every time they were planning an escape the Germans got wind of it and broke them up. I think he was in four camps altogether.

I was living in the upstairs of an old house on Furby Street and I suppose I should have gone back to my mother's place in Trail but I didn't. This place on Furby was where Kenny and I had come when we were married, and maybe I just felt that some day the door would open and it would be him standing there. Anyway, I stayed in Winnipeg.

I know it was a very hard time for him, but it was hard for

me too. I tried bringing in another girl to live with me, but it didn't work out, I guess it's because I was a loner. She was always wanting to bring her boyfriend up and that's why I told her it wouldn't work. She said, "Well, why don't you get yourself a boyfriend too?" and I just blew up. Maybe I should have at that. The Lord knows I could have. I was considered very attractive then. But I didn't.

You know who the most important man in my life was? The postie. Our old postman who knew my husband was a P.O.W., and when there was a letter or a card he'd call up the stairs to me. When he called, then I knew there was something for me. If he didn't, there was nothing. He was an old dear, Mr. Robertson. How the years go by. I haven't thought of him for a long time. Every month he used to give me $2.50. It was his present for Kenny, he'd say. You see, the cost of a Red Cross parcel was $2.50. He'd say he hoped Kenny would get the very parcel that his $2.50 provided, but naturally that was his little joke. He was a Scotsman and very generous.

The cards and letters couldn't say much. Just a few words. Feeling fine. Thanks for the socks, the parcel, the candy, the photograph. Things like that. You treasured them, I guess, they didn't actually mean that much. Only that he was alive. The words themselves didn't seem to mean too much. And then the censor would cut them, cutting out words and you never knew why. For instance, in one camp there was a censor who cut off the signature. Kenny would sign it "Kenny" and this censor would cut off everything but the "K." Oh, it was the little things like that that used to irritate me.

There were quite a few P.O.W. wives in Winnipeg and some of us used to work as Red Cross volunteers. It was the Red Cross who arranged for the parcels and they expected you to be a volunteer and if you didn't, they got quite snarky about it. So I worked for the Red Cross and I worked as a waitress down on Portage Avenue and I tried working at the Ford plant and didn't like it.

Kenny wrote and said he was studying French in the camp's classes and was working for his high school diploma and so I started learning French, too, and on Sundays I'd walk over to a store in St. Boniface and buy the French Sunday papers of the week before, the Montreal papers, and read them, but my heart wasn't in it and my life went on and I led a pretty generally useless life, all in all. It was four years lost out of my life. I guess at that age, twenty-two to twenty-six I should have been having babies but how could I?

Then the war ended and Kenny came home and he had all that back pay and all that extra pay, and we went on a trip to Vancouver to see his parents and then we came back, and by that time we both knew it wasn't going to work. He had been in a prison for four years but I had been in one, too, and we were entirely different people. So we decided to get a divorce. It wasn't easy and people who knew us criticized me and looking back now, maybe I should have made more effort, but then everything seemed dead and I had been faithful to him but I wanted to start a new life. I think he felt the same way. He married. A girl he'd gone to school with. I married when I was thirty and I guess things worked out for the best. I'm happy in my own way and I hope Kenny is, too.

•◄►• *I Shook Her Hand*

I don't know if everybody expected us to be only 85 pounds and be wearing rags, but when we came to Canada they treated us like we were in cotton batting. They meant well, and I guess it was right that we should be grateful. Think of it, not everybody had spent one-sixth of their life in a Japanese prison camp. I was twenty when Hong Kong was captured and I was twenty-four when we got home.

Everything was a blur. I mean that. We didn't eat much but potato soup with some fish in it, but we stole more than our share of rice, and the Americans who first had us looked after us pretty well, so when I got home, I was in pretty fair shape. Except I was very nervous and I would cry sometimes over little things, and I didn't know what was happening. Canada was a changed place. The people were different, it seemed.

I remember coming home on the train. I don't know if we were the first Grenadiers to come home but they treated us pretty good and some reporters and photographers got on our coach at Brandon and rode with us to Winnipeg and it was one long string of asking questions and taking pictures and I was afraid. I don't know why, but I didn't say anything. Then this photographer came back and he said he'd done something wrong with his camera and he'd like to take another picture and I broke down and started to cry. The photographer looked like a nice guy and it was smoothed over.

Then we got into Winnipeg, the station across from the Fort Garry. I used to play in the old fort in the park there when I was a kid. I'd joined up when I was nineteen. I think there were lots of people in the station. Maybe the mayor, for all I know.

What I should be telling you now, if I can, is that I had a wife too, but I didn't know what she looked like. I mean I wasn't sure. The Japs had taken away our wallets and things and when I got mine back, or maybe it was my paybook, her picture was gone. Her name was Mary. We'd had a few dates. I couldn't afford much. We'd go bowling, five pins, and then have a Denver sand-wich, and then I'd walk her to her boarding house and that would be it. Three weeks before I went to Hong Kong we got married, and I was afraid I wouldn't know what she looked like. I don't think my brain was working all that well.

I guess I should say that I didn't really know her. Hadn't heard from her, you see. We got no mail. A couple of guys did, but the Japs always seemed to lose mine.

I can't remember much about the station. Maybe there was a ceremony. There were a lot of people moving around and then, just like that, I hear this voice say, "Hello, Johnny." I turn around and there she is, and it's not the girl I thought it would be, because I honestly couldn't remember. It was all a blur.

You know what I did? I'm not kidding. I shook her hand. Like that, I shook her hand. She was a little thing.

I remember her saying, "C'mon, Johnny, we're going home. Have you got your bag?" and I had a little bag and I picked it up and walked out. It was October. The sun was shining. I remember that. About eleven in the morning. I could stretch this out and tell you other things, but all I remember is, I was crying and a taxi guy jumps out and opens the door and we get in. I couldn't remember if I'd been in a taxi in the past four or five years, but if I had I guess it was in Victoria or Vancouver. Wherever we landed. I can't, I don't think I can remember.

It was just a short trip, a few blocks. She just held my hand, and I must have just held hers and wiped my eyes with the other, with a hankie, and then we got out at the Garrick Hotel. I don't know if it is still there, but it was a funny little place. Little but tall, and we got out and she said, "Here's home for now, Johnny," and I got out and I remember when we were walking up the first flight of stairs the taxi driver comes charging up and he's got my bag. I'd left it. There was nothing in it anyway. I had nothing, just army stuff. Not even a gift. When he got to us he held out the bag to Mary and he squeezed my arm, right here where the muscle is, and he said, "Everything's gonna be fine. You wait and see." I'll always remember that guy.

We got to the room, just an ordinary hotel room in an

ordinary hotel, you might say. It wasn't even a good room. A 2-dollar room, I'd say. I did some dumb things, like going to the dusty window and making knots-and-crosses in the dust, playing a game with myself. I asked her how her dad was and she said fine. I think I wasn't crying any more. Hell, this was 30 years ago. How can I remember everything?

I sat down on the bed and she went to her bag and brought out a bottle of Johnny Walker Red Label. Never forget it. She held it up and said, "You're home, Johnny. Johnny's home," and I got up and hugged her. That was the first time. I think, honestly, that that was when she just started to get through to me. That she just wasn't some little girl who had picked me up in the station.

I said we weren't altogether right. We looked okay, 150 pounds, new haircut, new uniforms, the medals we'd earned, and I guess I had about 3,000 bucks back pay coming and enough for a start, but we weren't right. We weren't right emotionally. We weren't ready for our wives. Know that?

I poured myself a drink and one for Mary and another and another and in about an hour we had finished the bottle. I mean I had. She had a couple, maybe three. Then I took off my tunic and lay down on the bed and zonk, that was it. Out. Before I went under I saw Mary taking off her blouse and her little skirt and she lay down beside me and she held me.

That was the start of my coming back to the world. I can't put it any other way. It took a long time and I was terrified a lot, but that was the start and that was it. The start.

Nearing the End

This Animal Kind of Noise ... This Proud Army ... A
Vest-pocket Hitler ... Walking Corpses ... In Germany
... Berlin Souvenirs ... Slaves in the German Army ...
... Mercy Flights ... Returning P.O.W.'s and V.I.P.'s ...
The Halifax Riot ... Just Another Bomb ... A Little Wild
Riot in Sudbury ... A Toast to the War

The war was winding down. Everybody knew it. Men were still
dying on all fronts but as spring approached the optimism of
September of 1944 returned, and the world knew that the German
war machine had but a short distance to run.

Now the German planes that came up to meet the fleets of
bombers and their buzzing beehives of fighters were few in
number and the quality of the pilots was ragged. The German
Navy, such a threat in early days, was finished. Every U-boat that
ventured into the Atlantic was virtually on a suicide mission, so
deadly and methodical had the Allies' air cover and detection
methods become. And on land, German soil was being trampled
by enemy troops for the first time in living memory. Most of her
cities were now junk piles from bombing raids, and now the
smaller cities, the towns and villages were being smashed by artil-
lery and tank fire. This was the end, and even the Germans knew
that, apart from one madman in a concrete bunker in Berlin.

On the home front, every front page in Canada carried
headlines on new victories, and mothers and wives prayed: "One
more month, two more months, and please don't try and win a
medal." The men in battle heard those prayers only too well, and
did some praying of their own.

•◄►• This Animal Kind of Noise

Oh, at the end there, you could see the difference. Germany was
scraping the bottom and our armies were in first-class shape. Our
tanks and vehicles were in good condition, maintained like they
were Daimlers. We had plenty of ammunition, ammunition for
everything. The men got at least one hot meal a day, although it
might be late, and billeting was good. They shaved, and we had
orders that whenever it was possible, they'd have a laundry unit in.
They got their mail fast.

In short, they knew they were winning, and morale was good. They knew Germany was falling apart. We had the artillery, the tanks, the organization and we knew what we were doing. We kept moving forward, consolidating, moving ahead, and this army could have beaten the Russians. Easily.

But it was the Germans. Terrifying. I remember once about 1,000 surrendered to about four of our Bren gun carriers, and the boys told me they heard them before they came upon them. It was hilly country and they heard this animal kind of noise, and it was those Germans wailing, groaning, crying out, cursing, the wounded crying, muttering, and it made a noise you could hear a long way, they said. Imagine. Terrifying. More than 1,000 men, maybe 1,500, so demoralized, so shocked, so mad, I guess, that they were not humans. This is what they were, they were one large animal. Does that make sense? One large animal, lying on its side, wounded and crying.

No guns. No boots, Why did so many lose their boots, or have only one? I could never figure that one out. Some with no shirts. Dirty. Filthy, after a while they just seemed to live in dirt. They'd just look at you, and if you shot the two men on either side of them, the fellow still alive would just look at you. Like a dumb animal. It was terrifying.

•◂▸• *This Proud Army*

This was Holland, clean country, fairly open country to fight in and a lot of artillery, we used that, and small tank battles, and in a month the only enemy you would actually see was in the P.O.W. compound.

I could never understand it though. How the Germans— and of course they had Hungarians and Poles and Russians, and I think even a few French—how they could be so badly messed up?

Their officers were always smart as a whip, surrendering their side arms with a little ceremony and that kind of crap, but the men—how could they lose their boots, or their jackets? They'd surrender in bare feet, or with no pants on. Only the kids, and there were quite a few around fourteen or so, I'd reckon, the kids were clean-shaven, but the men looked like wild men of the mountains. Unshaven. Dirty. Some drunk. Oh, lots of times we took prisoners so drunk they were falling around in the dirt. We used to wonder, where is this proud army, just giving up that way?

⟨•⟩ *A Vest-pocket Hitler*

This was east of Cleve, and about the fourth day of our major assault and a tank comes back, sent back by the squadron commander, and it comes to our headquarters and there in the turret with a lieutenant is a German officer.

This was a bit of a prize, a patrol capturing a German officer like this. He was a lieutenant, from a regiment from Pomerania. But he wasn't saying anything, just his name, rank and regimental number, but he was willing to talk to anyone about anything else. Actually he appeared at first like a good stick in his own way, but then it became clear he was still pretty hopped up on Hitler and Nazism. He'd been a Hitler Youth and so on and knew nothing but Hitler. A perfect result of Goebbels' propaganda tactics. This chap was also helping to turn out other products because he'd been, so he said, attached to the psychological warfare unit of his regiment and probably wasn't a combat soldier at all. But he sure knew the lingo.

We asked him didn't he know Germany was finished and he said yes, the Russians had beaten them in the east, but in 15 or 20 years there would be a new Germany. Ready to go. Didn't give us much credit for kicking the daylights out of their best divisions in Normandy. He said he loved Hitler because he had given Germany the glory it deserved, and efficiency and strength and greatness, and so on and so on, and the more he talked the more he sounded like a vest-pocket Hitler. We were bored with it all and our major, a very, very hard man, had this grim look to him and finally he said, "Lieutenant, take two good men and walk this man to the edge of the trees and give him a running start. Five yards. He will be shot for attempting to escape."

He wasn't bluffing. This guy never bluffed. So I took our prisoner by the arm and as I led him out he said to our C.O., he said, "I expected more from an officer in the Canadian Army. We have always considered you fair and worthy opponents." Something like that.

So there I was, stuck. The fellow didn't deserve shooting and he shouldn't be. Not by the Rules of War. So I turned back and Old Fishface is giving me the eye and I said, "Sir, the Geneva Convention?" A question, you see. And he put down his pipe, very wearily I thought, and he said, "Yes, you're quite right. Then we'd be playing their game, wouldn't we," and he said, "Do whatever you do with people like this," and I did, handing him over to a Provost sergeant and told him to deliver him to the rear.

When he got in the jeep the German said, "Thank you, Lieutenant," and I said, you know, something like "Forget it, we've all got to make a living." Something inane. Then he said, "Would you consider, sir, that I was lucky?" and I said, "If you live to be a hundred and five years old, lieutenant, you'll never be so lucky again." Then he stuck out his hand and what the hell, what could I do? I shook it.

•◄►• *Walking Corpses*

There were times in the last month or so of the war when I'd be walking late at night through the streets of Brussels and I'd see a truck pull up at an intersection and the tail gate would clang down and men would get off and they would be like walking corpses. They might ask for a cigarette and they'd have death heads and skeletal hands and they smelled of something and I never quite could figure it out. They'd disperse, one going down this street, one going down another. They wouldn't say anything to each other except they might mutter a few words of farewell and then they'd sort of crab off down these streets, to their homes, I guessed.

These were survivors of German death camps. Belsen, Auschwitz, you name it. Others we've probably never heard about. And they were coming home to families they did not know still lived.

Terrible, lonely-looking figures in the dark of the night, going home. We had heard vaguely that the Germans had these slave labour and death camps where men and women were worked until they died. But when we saw the films of Belsen, the terrible, terrible scenes, then I put two and two together, the men getting out of those trucks looking like corpses and the corpses in that film, crawling around in their striped uniforms, crawling at the feet of the Americans who liberated them, too weak even to stand. That's what I remember.

•◄►• *In Germany*

After it was all over we had to go into these German towns and villages looking for S.S. types, checking documents, looking over food supplies, just nosing around. In the odd town you'd see a few houses or buildings banged up. Some crazy Canadian or Yank in a Sherman going hellbent down the main drag when they went through and letting slam with that 17-pounder pop gun. That would just take your ordinary house and open it up like a can of sardines. I don't think these towns put up any opposition because if they had, there wouldn't have been a town left. Have you ever seen, and I guess you haven't, what a squadron of Shermans and 15 minutes of artillery work can do to a town? Well, there just ain't no town left. Just wreckage, and try and find what you're looking for in the ruins and it would be a tough job. No, these towns we were checking had been good little towns. I guess you'd call them cooperative little towns.

They were dead, though, dead towns in another way. You never saw any men. Anybody over fourteen or so, any male, was gone, and everybody under sixty, any male, was gone. I think the German High Command literally scraped the bottom of the barrel. But what you did see was the women. All in black, in mourning. The older women, they would have lost their husbands during the first world war, the Kaiser's War. Shuffling along the street, trying to do some marketing in the morning when there wasn't anything to buy. The younger women, say eighteen to thirty-five or forty, they'd be dressed in black too, in mourning, and you'd just look down that street and everyone would be in black. You'd say to yourself, "For Christ sakes, did we kill every man who ever came from this town?" I said this once to the captain, the head of our group and he said, yes, we and the Russians had done this.

We never found any suspicious characters in those towns. It was like a holiday for us. It was just S.S., the Gestapo, we were looking for, and they had probably turned into meek and mild Austrians a couple of weeks before the war was over. One old woman came up, and she spoke quite good English and she said the same thing. I remember her saying, "You'll find none of the schwein here. Gone. They're gone. I'd give this if I could point out just one to you," and by this, she meant a medal she was wearing around her neck. It was the Iron Cross, a medal for bravery, much like our Military Cross, I'd say. She said the Iron Cross meant a great deal to her because her dead son had won it on the Russian front, but she'd give it up if she could turn over to us just one S.S. Those bastards must have been just as hard on their own people as they were on everybody else.

•◄►• *Berlin Souvenirs*

I got into Berlin with a whole bunch of confused Canadians after our convoy was held up for two hours by the obstreperous Russians, who put a great bloody pine tree across the road while some bandy-legged little bod from the Urals tootled off in the direction of Berlin to get an order they probably already had in their pockets anyway.

We weren't supposed to be there, or maybe we were, but the Russians held the city, so I suppose we weren't. But anyway they let us through.

This was after the city fell, of course. Three weeks or so, as I recall. But the blackened gas can and the blob were still on the ground outside of Hitler's bunker, where he and Eva were cremated. The bunker was stony cold, that I recall.

A couple of us mooched into the Reich Kanalei [the Chancellory] down a flight of stairs into a dark big basement with our flashlights. We were about to cut some bloody great oil paintings out of their frame, thereby ensuring riches for evermore, when half a city block away—the building was that big—another bandy-legged little Russian opened a door and a shaft of light hit us. We decided right then and there to go straight, for the logical reason that he was pointing a machine gun at us.

After a few sickly smiles and a lot of arm-waving we were allowed to amble out with our only booty, some tunics full of German medals and one of those eight-foot banners, complete with black swastika and gold wire embroideries that old movies will tell you used to hang on flagstaffs over the offices of Hitler, Goering and Goebbels and the rest. I think mine came from Goering's office. I've still got it, but I had to cut a chunk off it to get it shipped back to Canada.

•◀▶• *Slaves in the German Army*

We grabbed a dozen Germans once in a farmhouse and we wanted to know where the rest of them were. You just didn't have a dozen guys without more being around and we had this sergeant, Bronco, we called him. Bronco had been sergeant down to private and up again and down again, and he was tough. Our captain told Bronco to soften up one or two of these donkeys, so we could find out the score and so he went up and he had this .45 Luger automatic and he just slapped this one prisoner alongside the head, with the barrel. It doesn't leave any mark, but you don't forget it for a long time. Pistol-whipping. It made you wonder what Bronco did before the war. On the other side, slap and this P.O.W. sort of sags and says something in German. He's kind of crying when he says it.

What he's saying is that he is Russian. And Bronco speaks Russian. Bronco is a Russian from somewhere north of Edmonton. Well, they jabber back and forth, and Bronco is sort of rubbing this guy's head where he slapped him and they are buddies and it turns out, every one of these shitheads was a slave of some sort. Russian, Poles, everything but Italian. Apparently they didn't let Italians up to the front. Too unreliable.

So this guy and his buddies convince Bronco that they're alone and nobody else is with them nearby and they're hungry, so we toss some C-rations at them and they're sooooooo damned happy to be away from the Germans. It's dark by this time and we all use the house we found them in and they talk and Bronco does the translating, and what it's all about is this. The Germans have maybe millions of conscripts, slave labor. Deserters from the Russians. A lot of them. More than you'd think. Even Cossacks. And I guess through this combination of fear and promise—fear they're going to be killed if they don't act right, and promise they will get land when the war is over, they go along with the Germans and fight for them. To us, where you fight for your country, right or wrong, God Save the King and all that, this was quite an eye-opener. Not to these guys. Just life to them.

But the thing that got me was, here's Germany, with a population at 60 million, something like that, surrounded by its enemies at one time and yet on its way to winning the war—and they could have won it all if it weren't for the American ships and tanks and planes, and especially in Russia—and here's the damned Jerries making millions of guys work for them, in artillery regiments, transport and support units, some pretty tricky jobs, and keeping them in line for months, hell, for years. That Russian had been captured at Moscow and when was that, 1942? This was '44 I'm talking about. You had to hand it to them, all right.

•◄►• *Mercy Flights*

I got my ops in on Operation Manna. You know the biblical story about the starving Israelites being saved by food called manna coming down from the sky? Same thing with us. We flew food to the Dutch. There was no such thing as a flight engineer on those flights, or a mid upper gunner or even a bomb aimer. We'd just fly over these towns and villages and on the edges of cities and where they wanted us to drop, we all worked getting the food out. It wasn't gourmet food, but it was food. Compo rations, dried stuff, fish, blankets, medicine, Red Cross parcels. This was in May. We called it the Grocery Run. We did The Hague, Haarlem, Amsterdam, all around there. There was some sort of a deal made, probably under the table, that German ground troops wouldn't fire on us. I think some did, though, but not with us.

We'd practised how to drop the food. We used a system of panniers and we could be pretty accurate. Of course, it was all extremely low bombing, if that's the proper word. Naturally the stuff dropped free in bundles, but I don't think much of it was damaged. Some probably burst open, but the way the Dutch were, I imagine they didn't lose much of it anyway.

We dropped hundreds of tons of stuff, and they needed it because while I think they managed to survive fairly well during the war, under the Occupation, when the big battles were going on, civilians are the low people on the totem pole and it was this period which gave them a real rough time, so I hear.

Our units were on the ground, directing us, helping the Dutch who already had their underground committees and so on and so forth, but our ground units couldn't feed them. At that time I think they were having a hard time feeding themselves.

That's where we came in. I think we flew two missions a day for nine straight days, and other squadrons were going way into Germany and Poland and other countries and bringing back prisoners of war. British, Canadian, American, anybody but Russians and those in the Russian sphere. Mostly British, well, Commonwealth and American, and they were flown straight to camps in England. Mercy flights, that's what they were.

•←→• *Returning P.O.W.'s and V.I.P.'s*

What we did, in the days immediately after the war, we flew into fields in Holland, Belgium, and brought back prisoners of war, British, Canadians, Australians, Americans, and that was a very moving thing because they were in all stages of physical condition and wearing every old kind of rags, and some of them had been in captivity for years.

I'd fly low over the Channel, right up to and then over the cliffs of Dover, and you know how white they are and how much they mean to Englishmen, and these guys were crying and weeping and we'd send them up into the mid upper gun turret and to the astro hatch to see England, and I remember the guys were so excited they were running around inside and they were changing our trim. We weren't equipped to carry passengers. Not in Lancasters, no way. So they were all stashed around in the plane, about 25 at a time and because of the noise we couldn't communicate with them and they weren't on the inter-com and so these guys were running around, excited as hell.

I tell you, bringing those prisoners back, it was a very moving experience.

But we also took people from England back to the Continent, people from Holland and Belgium who had escaped to Britain. They'd be taken out to the airfield, with just a bag of clothes, and they were going home and they didn't know whether their loved ones were alive or dead. They were just as excited too. This is where I first heard the expression "V.I.P.," because a lot of these people had been with the Dutch and Belgian provisional governments or worked against the Germans from England, and they wanted nothing more than to get home.

I remember one time, a day or two after the war ended and this was all very emotional—the way everything was in the war, emotional—a group going back to their homeland took up a collection for our crew and I said, "Oh no, we couldn't take that." It wasn't much money at all, because they didn't have much money, really, and I thought, well, I was an officer and a gentleman and you couldn't take money, and these people were quite hurt because I wasn't gracious enough to accept it. It was their contribution to us. What I should have done was take it and take the crew out on the town.

But I was embarrassed. You know, it was one of those dumb little things that always stuck in my mind, that here they wanted to give us some money out of gratitude and I had turned it back to them. I had hurt these people's feelings and they were so grateful.

•⟷• *The Halifax Riot*

We were in Halifax when the war ended. I've read since that there was a lot of violence but I can't say I saw much of it. The Halifax paper said four million dollars, something like that, but you know how papers are.

The day after the armistice was the day of the official celebration, and the damn fools closed down the town. Restaurants, beer parlours, the whole works, and with about seven, eight, nine, ten thousand troops, army and navy around, what the hell, what was everybody to do? I think they had a street dance or two, but just how juvenile can you get? A lot of these guys were back from Europe and a lot more were tough navy guys off the ships, frigates, destroyers, escorts and these guys were tough eggs—and they close down the town and throw a street dance. There's a towering mind for you.

Somebody said they were going to open up the two liquor stores. Open up was the word I remember, and it wasn't long before hundreds of guys and gals, soldiers, civilians, were coming out with arms full of booze. Mickeys, rye, rum, gin, everything and I remember seeing one Army Service Corps truck backed up to a rear window and the guys and army girls were just pushing cases through a broken window and into the truck. There must have been at least a thousand dollars' worth of booze in that truck and where it went, well, I haven't the slightest idea.

As I remember, the police just kept off the streets. There was nothing they could do except start a real riot if they tried to arrest people—and it would have been some riot. The military police just tore off their armbands. What was the point? If they wanted to get tough, too, they wouldn't have lasted five minutes. I remember hearing the municipal council, they all left town.

You could see dozens of people going up Citadel Hill, a long line of them, with beer and booze. I had 13 mickeys of rye stashed around me, in my uniform. Even about four in my bloomers, in my jacket and shoulder purse. Thirteen, and wherever you looked on the hill there was people drinking. Two's, four's, eight's, big parties and let me say, more than the usual quota of screwing.

We weren't looking for violence, the guys I was with. Just a party.

We hid a lot in cemeteries, Scotch, rum, rye, what we got from the liquor store. There's cemeteries all over Halifax and I remember stashing a lot of bottles in one of them. People would just go up and dig them in. No, not open up graves, but you dug a hole in the dirt and laid in a few bottles and covered them over. I tried to remember some of their names a few days later. A guy named Powell was one, but I couldn't find that grave. Maybe somebody came along and saw the turned-over earth and found it. Beside the headstones.

The Halifax riot, to us girls in my quarters, was mostly about getting drunk. We were so young, eighteen, nineteen, or so. Probably the same way kids would act today. We were in the army and it was pure excitement all the way.

•◄►• *Just Another Bomb*

We were playing bridge in the officers' mess at Shilo, that's a training camp in Manitoba, and whoever was dummy got up to turn up the radio for the news and at the head of the news there was this announcement that the Americans had dropped a thing called an atomic bomb on Japan. A Japanese city.

We didn't know from hades what an atomic bomb was. Just another bomb, although if we had thought of it we should have known they wouldn't have all the blather about just another bomb. But we didn't. We'd been instructors, and at Shilo for two years in that godforsaken desert country, and I guess we were numb to everything.

The four of us were training our troops for the assault on Japan and then I guess we'd be going along with the regiment, and little did we know as we sat there bidding and laying down cards that the war was over for us.

Looking back, it was like somebody coming up and giving you a million bucks in an envelope, and you just stick it in your pocket without looking at it.

•◄►• *A Little Wild Old Riot in Sudbury*

We had quite a little wild old riot in Sudbury when the Japs surrendered, but I'm not so sure it was ever written up. The whole downtown was smashed up and they called out the reserve troops and half the buggers they couldn't get hold of because they were doing the rioting with us.

It wasn't exactly a riot but just the boys out of the mines taking over the liquor store and the wine store and having parties in the streets and lighting bonfires and kicking in some store windows. It was mostly the hard-rock miners and their women. A tough lot. You see, the miners were in what you'd call priority jobs and stuck in them until the war was over. No quitting and joining the army, no quitting and heading for Toronto. Just month after month underground, and this was their blow-out. Can't see as I blame them.

I read after that about 3,000 took a hand in it, and they got away with about 4,000 or 5,000 bottles of hooch. They also jumped the beer warehouse, too. Everybody was downtown and drinking right in the streets, right out of the neck. You never saw so many drunks in your life. Fucking going on right, left and centre, and guys walking around in duds they'd taken out of clothing stores and carrying on like crazy.

They started using tear gas and fire hoses on them after a while and got the place cleared up, but they never got back the hooch. About 20 or 30 stores were kicked in, and I think a bunch of guys were arrested but I forget what happened to them. Probably nothing. Those were pretty high and wild old days. Sudbury was a rough town. A hard-rock miners' town, tough.

It was something of a letdown. I think all of us felt it, and I've talked to English people about it and they agreed, that when it was all over we found something important and vital was missing from our lives.

I guess it was that the war was over from all our lives and we all had to go back to the ordinary business of living. The trouble is, or was, too, that so many of us had never had what I call "the ordinary business of living." Myself, for instance. I came out of a small village in Bruce County and I took a year of university and then I joined the air force. So all I knew was my father's dairy farm, high school, one year at McMaster and then the air force. The only people I knew after three years away from home, coastal command and then bombing Germany, all I knew were people in the air force and a few English people. I didn't know anybody in Canada and I didn't know what I wanted and I certainly didn't know how to earn a living.

Once we were sitting around the mess and yakking and there were a few English girls, officers in the W.D.'s. Awfully nice kids. There were some Aussies and a few New Zealanders and a couple of English and Scottish lads because we were kind of a polyglot squadron, and we were talking and one of the girls said, "One thing I miss, the sound of the engines. You fellows coming home in time for tea." We all laughed.

An Australian chap said, "I'm sorry it's all over. I'll never have so much fun again. Now it's back to the salt mines for me, bloody dull Melbourne."

I'd like to think we were all shocked, but we weren't. We'd had it pretty good to very good, although a lot of guys died. Anyway, there was a few seconds while everybody thought about it and guys were nodding their heads or saying "yeah" and "right, buddy" and then one of the girls lifted her glass and said, "A toast, to the war," and we all drank to it.

Coming Home

Comic Book for Killers ... A Spoonful of Canadian Dirt ... One Hell of a Send-off ... My Start in the Post-war World ... "How Many, Dad?" ... Coming Home ... "If They Only Knew" ... Three Days ... "She Beat Me to It" ... A Strange War in Ottawa ... "Want Your Old Job Back?" ... A Pink Milkshake ... "My Father, My Hero" ... "Welcome Home, Son"

And when it was all over they came home.

They came from camps across Canada, from Britain, northwest Europe, Italy, from places they never knew existed before they joined up. Others came from prison camps in Germany and then from Japan when the Imperial Empire collapsed—all as quickly as the government could do the job.

They came in six-tiered stinking troop ships and in sleek peacetime liners made grimy and cranky by so many years of war, and in jammed transport aircraft and packed into bombers and they often made the last miles in swaying colonist cars, trucks, buses—to the city, town, village, where somebody waited for them.

For once, after six years of war, all roads led back home.

•◄►• Comic Books for Killers

I went overseas when I was nineteen and was over there four years. I picked up one wound in Normandy and two more at the same time in Holland, and the worst of those two sent me home.

We got back to Canada and when we came off the ship here's the Red Cross or the Sally Ann, some girls, they give us a little bag and it has a couple of chocolate bars in it and a comic book.

Here, we had gone overseas not much more than children but we were coming back, sure, let's face it, as killers. And they were still treating us as children. Candy and comic books.

•◄►• A Spoonful of Canadian Dirt

Only about 1,200 Canadians were assigned to India, and this restaurant in Calcutta was only one of about a dozen that wasn't off bounds to us, or all Allied troops. We went in there one day when we'd had a few drinks, and we decided we would try eating snakes. They raised them domestically, and they tasted real chickeny but a little more oil, like a duck has. It was very, very good, but you couldn't get your mind off that you were eating snakes.

Some of the fellows ordered locusts, which were supposed to be a delicacy, but I wasn't drunk enough to do that. But what I did do was I vowed that if I ever got out of India alive and got home, I would eat a spoonful of Canadian dirt. A spoonful.

So when we arrived at Halifax all my buddies were primed for me and they were determined I was going to eat that dirt. And just by chance, there was a reporter there and so I had to go through the whole thing—and I'll tell you this, I may have taken a spoonful of that dirt, but I sort of pushed it in around my tongue and behind my gums and walked around for a while until I had a chance to get rid of it. But I still have the clipping today, about the Canadian who ate the spoonful of Canadian dirt.

•◄►• *One Hell of a Send-off*

Nobody will ever forget the send-off we got when our radar bunch left England. We were going home to Canada to refit there on some new radar equipment and then our radar gang and the two squadrons would proceed to China, to bomb Japan.

So we got to Liverpool. This would be about late June. Our troopship was the *Samaria* and after a week of loading up, you know, getting everything ready to go, a Royal Canadian Air Force band came to dockside to serenade us. I remember one of the tunes. "Going to Take a Sentimental Journey Home." It was a big hit that year, in '45.

And then, while the band was still playing, we saw the air full of bombers flying a few thousand feet up, and then one peeled off and dived straight down, dive-bombing us, and just a few hundred feet above the ship it zoomed up, and every other plane did it too. Remember, these were Lancasters, big four-engine bombers, and when you saw them coming straight at you, that was something to see.

Our radar bunch knew who it was, of course. It was the boys of 434 and 431 squadrons coming over to give us a personal goodbye. The captain and his officers were on the bridge absolutely livid with rage, shaking their fists, and everybody else had taken cover, and there we were out on the deck waving our arms madly, waving goodbye to these guys we'd been attached to for so long. It was one hell of a send-off.

I came back in early '45, January, as I remember. I had a D.F.C. A real big flyboy. As I remember I went into the mess one night and just inside the door was a basket filled with the things and it said, "Take one," so I took one and pinned it on. No, hell, that's a joke. To some guys the Distinguished Flying Cross meant something. Not to me.

But back in Hamilton they still meant something. I mean it made the old man proud and it worked with the girls. Hero and all that sort of thing. If you were good-looking and wore your cap at just that right go-to-hell angle you were in. Some guys used to practise that cap look in the mirror. If you had a gong like the D.F.C. then you were home free. Anyway, they were booting me out. Who wanted a broken-down pilot anyway, and I had a swaddle of gratuities or whatever they called them then. Must have been 1,600 dollars. It was my start in the post-war world.

I looked up the best girl in high school and yes, she was still around. She was doing something for the C.B.C. up in Toronto, had her own apartment, and you had to scratch pretty deep to find the same Frances you knew when you were both in that History or Latin or English class.

I phoned Frances, and I honestly can't remember her last name now, and I said, "Let's take off for New York," and I remember she laughed like a drain. I said I had about sixteen hundred or so, and when it was gone I'd put her on a bus for home and find my way home.

Christ almighty but we had fun, and everything from dinner at the Twenty-One Club to a night of singing and clowning around at the Pepsi-Cola Canteen in Times Square. Did everything, saw everything, screwed all the time, and I was treated like a bloody goddamned hero. "A Canadian! Don't see many of you around. Here, have a drink. Have two. Dinner's on me. Want to come out to the place this weekend?" And we'd go, and it would be 320 acres and a curving driveway half a mile bloody long and a house you couldn't explore in a week, and a wine cellar like some Franciscan monastery. I got my ideas of high living during that month, in a couple of those places out on Long Island.

It lasted a month and then Frances had to go back to work and I was pretty tired of it all. I still had 500 bucks left despite how hard I'd tried to spend it, and we took the train back and said goodbye at Union Station. She said she'd had a good time and I said so too, and apart from seeing her, Frances, at a few parties over the next few years, that was it. I eventually married a nice woman and have three kids, all grown up now, flown from the nest.

•◄►• "How Many, Dad?"

Coming home from the war is a pretty big event in any man's life but I managed to blow it, at least in the eyes of my son Kenny. He was only eleven then, and pretty bloodthirsty. Like any eleven-year-old I guess you could say, what with four years of absorbing through every pore the huge masses of propaganda they poured out. Newspapers, radio, movies, comic books. Hell, you could breathe the stuff out of the air.

My wife drove the car home from the station. I still had a wonky shoulder I'd stupidly buggered up in a jeep accident and didn't trust myself to drive yet, and there's Kenny looking at me like I was the king. I guess I was, in his world. Uniform, medals. Big hero.

So one of the first questions he asks me is how many Germans did I kill. How many, Dad? Well, I hadn't actually anticipated that kind of question and if I'd said, "Oh, a few," that probably would had done the trick. But I wanted to play the whole thing down so I said I didn't think I'd killed any. Well, that little face of his just fell. So I said that soldiers in action might do a lot of firing, but they never really knew if they hit anyone. And that's the truth. It never was face to face, or very rarely, and certainly not hand-to-hand combat like in his comic books.

I mean, this wasn't the truth. I remember once on a patrol we sneaked up on this house, far deeper behind the lines than Jerry ever thought a patrol would get, and there were about 15 or so soldiers in this house playing a card game, and making a lot of noise and I threw in four grenades one-two-three-four and the ones that were left we piled them up at the door with our Sten guns—but I'm not about to tell an eleven-year-old that.

Maybe I should have told him that, and that would have been the end of it. But to this day that son of mine, I'm sure that lad thinks I conducted my own kind of phony war over there, in Italy and then in Holland, and I guess he thinks less of me for it.

•◄►• Coming Home

I'd been in the army two years and I got as far as Britain and no further. I was a radio instructor and, as they say, my skills were more valuable in training and refresher courses than behind a Number Nine set somewhere in northern Germany. What I mean is, I never saw combat.

I was low on the point system. What did you need, 150 or something? My chances of getting out were low and maybe I was heading for the Pacific War, but then along came this university thing, and I whistled a letter off to my father and he fired back my high school credentials and in about two weeks I was heading for Canada. Leaving, of course, men who had far more points than I, but not the credentials for first year university. That's another story, naturally. Made a lot of fellows very bitter.

I was lucky to get on a flight, a transport back. Scotland to Greenland, to Gander to Toronto and then, almost zip, onto a train and I was in Winnipeg about two and a half days later. I didn't write my parents because the letter would have arrived after me, and maybe I didn't want to. Just walk in on them.

Fort Osborne Barracks, I got there at night and didn't phone home either, and next morning I'm out on the street by eleven. I'm given the quickest medical you ever saw, a pack of documents and money, gratuity pay, and told to sign here and here and here and a shake of the hand and there I am, duffel bag on my shoulder, and climbing aboard an Academy Road Street Car, transfer to Osborne car and half a mile walk and home.

On the Osborne Streetcar I was just another young soldier, going home. I remember thinking the people around me wouldn't know whether I had been in a P.O.W. camp or won a Victoria Cross or spent the war washing dishes in Dundurn, Saskatchewan. The war seemed awful far away that October day.

I had to walk about half a mile and then there was this small round park, really an amazing little park, so beautiful and peaceful. When you got through the park my home was only three houses down and it was early in October. The sun was warm and I knew my dog would be sunning himself on the front step. It would be warm and he was getting old, too old for playing at being dog any more. I'd had him for about twelve years.

I used to call him from anywhere by giving a high-pitched *Hi-yump! Hi-yump!* It meant nothing, not his name, but it was just the way I'd call him. You've got to remember he was getting pretty old and he hadn't heard that yell for nearly three years but I let it go—and in about three seconds this brown streak comes racing out of the yard and heads for me. I let it go again, just for the hell of it, and when old Jim is about ten yards from me he takes off into the air. He just takes off, and *whomp,* he hits me dead centre in the chest. I drop the bag and nearly fall back and he's licking my face and whimpering and I'm ruffing his neck like I used to, and I think I'm crying a little.

Now you've got to picture it. There's this beautiful day in October, warm and soft, and I'm coming home, back from the wars, in a manner of speaking, and I'm walking down the middle of the road with my duffel bag on my shoulder and on my chest, my arm wrapped around my little dog Jim, my wonderful little friend Jim, and I feel like a conquering army.

I know nothing can go wrong. It's a new world, a new life, everything bad is behind and everything ahead is going to be wonderful.

•◆• *"If They Only Knew"*

We landed in Montreal and they issued us summer khaki dress and paid us off, and for a couple of days I just wandered around Montreal with my eyes hanging out. Honestly, for those first hours in Montreal I had the horrible feeling that those people had not been in a war.

I can't be unique. I'm sure every soldier, sailor and airman had the same feeling when he got back home, and I don't care what country the guy came from.

Here was a city all lit up, and thousands of cars and traffic lights and store windows lit up at night, and windows piled full of stuff, candies, chocolates, clothes, everything anybody could ever want and far more than anybody could ever buy. Once when two other guys and myself drank a 40-ouncer, I felt like standing at the corner by Peel Street and yelling at everybody: "Goddamn it, don't you know that over there there are cities that will take years to build up again, and millions and millions of men and women and children dead, by bullets and grenades and bombs, and an awful lot of people over there are eating mud to keep from starving?" Well, something like that, and then I thought, well, they'll just look at me like I'm crazy and call a cop.

Because less than two weeks before, I had seen Manchester and the great piles of rubble and the empty spaces brought on by the bombs, and the port of Liverpool with broken wharves, shattered buildings, and that was just a tiny part of England. You should have seen London, and France, Germany. My God, you just wouldn't believe it, and I don't think I have the imagination to think what a lot of Russia was like.

I remember thinking, as drunk as I was was, "God, if these people only knew. If they only knew one percent of it."

•➤• *Three Days*

When I came back I didn't realize how silent I had been through those four years, and I became silent, or I continued silent. It was funny. Everything was strange. Ah, my father and mother hadn't changed one bit but my younger brothers had grown up but . . . well, let me put it this way. I came home and I sat in the parlour of our house, my home, for four weeks and I never talked to anybody.

One day my mother came home in a cab, a thing she never did, and the cabbie came to the door with her and he was carrying a case of beer and I went to the door and opened the door for my mother, the way I was brought up, and when we got into the parlour I said, "What's the beer for?" She said, "For yoooooahh," and she started to cry and I asked what the matter was and she said, "Do you know, since you've been home you've been sitting in the front room playing solitaire and this is four weeks now, and I asked your father what we should do and he said to buy you a case of beer and let you get drunk."

And believe it or not, I got tight. Sitting in the parlour with my father who didn't drink beer, and I didn't talk. Just drank. I got drunk.

The next night was the 24th of December and I went to midnight mass with my sister and she had a girl with her. Yes, the girl was for me. And I didn't come home for three days. I missed Christmas. I missed Boxing Day, which was my mother's birthday, and the third day I came home and I walked into the hall and the front room and my father was in the room and he put down his newspaper. He asked, "Was she pretty?" You see, the whole family was jumping in, trying to get me squared away again, so he knew about what my sister had done, and I said, "Yes." He said, "You shouldn't have forgotten her birthday." That's all he said. Nothing about Christmas. I said yes, I knew that.

And from that point on, everything just dropped into place. Yeah. It was just that. The guys I had gone to high school with, they weren't around. Big Itch was killed. Paul was killed. Others were killed. It seemed I was the only one left. Malloy dead. Freddie killed. My gang was just not there any more. And for those four weeks I must have been crying for them, and wondering.

And then those three days brought me back to life. Strange. Very strange. I went out and got a job next day, and here I am.

Here's a goodie. We had this fellow with us named Starbuck, on radar with me at our base, and he was what you'd call a ladies' man. Like Jesus, he loved 'em all. Then he got stuck on this little Land Army girl, really stuck, and like they say you used to take the pledge, he plighted his troth to her. Gonna get married.

We come home, as a unit. Everybody knows Starry wants no more of his Toronto wife and we land at Union Station and he meets his wife and they walk up to each other and I'm watching and they don't kiss, don't hug, they just say something and walk away.

That night I'm at my mother's place, she lived on Parliament Street, and it's Starry on the phone and he wants to come over. In fact, he wants a bunk and we're having a coming-home affair and I yell into the phone for him to come over. Half an hour, there's a knock and there is Corporal Starbuck, Royal Canadian Air Force, and drunk.

I ask the trouble once I get him a beer poured and he says, "The bitch. The goddamned bitch. She wants a divorce." This is his wife he's talking about, the one he met in the station. I say what the hell's the matter, isn't that what he was getting up guts all the way from England to do, ask the old lady for a divorce?

He says, "Yeah, right, but before I could say I wanted rid of her, she tells me she wants rid of me. Right there in the station. Goddamn her. I wanted to see the look on her dumb face when I told her I was bailing out and she beat me to it. Takes all the fun out of coming home."

Good old Starry. You wonder about guys like that— especially when he and his old lady didn't get no divorce and he didn't marry the little Limey gal.

A Strange War in Ottawa

I remember coming home and thinking that everyone on the home front, as they called it, seemed to have had a very good time. I'd seen plenty of action, Italy, Germany, Holland, but it didn't seem the thing to talk about, you know what I mean. After all, it was over and done with.

My wife had the upper half of a house in Hull because she'd moved there to be with her mother who had died when I was away, and so she stayed. I mean she didn't go back to Windsor and she had made a whole circle of friends, people I had never met, although she mentioned this one and that one in her letters, you understand. They were mostly desk material, back in Ottawa, in things like supply and the information end of it, protocol and pay corps and this and that and hardly my cup of tea, but all in all they were a decent bunch. But the thing I remember most was what a good time they seemed to have had in the war.

Joan and I would go to their parties, and bloody fine homes some of them had, and they'd talk about how they'd used the black market, and the extra books of gas coupons they got, and how so and so had a farm near Montreal and supplied them with a ton of maple sugar, and things like that. They seemed always to have unlimited supplies of whiskey, any kind of whiskey, and I noticed on the bar of one place that all the bottles of scotch had no excise stamp, no tax stamp on it, and that meant of course that it cost them maybe a dollar a bottle from some friend, smuggled in, of course.

There were times, you understand, when I wanted to get up on my hind legs and blast, literally blast, the whole supercilious lot. Give them both barrels right between the eyes, but I never did. More for Joan's sake than anything, because they were her friends and had been for two or three years. I was really an interloper, if you want to put it that way.

They would talk about how Dickie this would be a deputy of a major air force branch and Ronnie that would be just two or three steps from the top of the ladder, that sort of thing. Once to Joan on our way home I said, "I could tell them about when Ronnie, or whatever his name was, visited our front and saw his first dead men, dead in combat, and how he threw up all over his shiny Sam Browne belt," and that set her off and she told me not to be a goddamned hero. They were her friends, she said, and if I didn't like it I could lump it.

I've often thought, that must have been a very strange war they fought in Ottawa in '43, and '44, and I wonder how many of them cracked up when the last of the Chivas Regal ran out.

•➤• *"Want Your Old Job Back?"*

I joined up in '40 and I was making 15 dollars a week as a despatcher for this trucking company, Toronto, Hamilton, London, Windsor. I was living at home, figured I was doing pretty good, and I was. The last day on the job the girls in the office had a little party, and the two bosses came around and had a beer or two with us, and one said I had a job with the firm when I came back, whenever I wanted it. You know, I guess, that it was the law, anyway, that returning vets had to be given back their old job. That was the law.

I come back in '45. I'd married this little gal, my wife, in Scotland; she'd come home a month ahead of me and was staying with my folks, and when I get back I take a week off. To get acquainted with the world, I guess you'd say.

I go down to the company. Only a couple of the girls are left, but we chat and then I go in and see the boss. The big hello. "Welcome back, son. Want your old job back? When can you start? Monday? Good." You know, the conversation went something like that. I mention the wage. He leans back and says, "Well, you were making 15 dollars a week when you left here so I guess we can start you at 18 dollars. How's that? You can work your way up from that."

What I should have said is that he could work that 18 dollars right up his ass, but I didn't. I told him I had a wife, I was twenty-four and not twenty, and being a sergeant in the Canadian Army meant more than pushing a bunch of paper around a desk. I argued that I was worth at least 25 dollars.

There was no point in talking to a guy like that. He'd stuck to the law. He'd offered me my old job back, and I couldn't deny that. He'd offered me a raise. Three dollars. Three lousy stinking bucks. Finally, flat out, I accused him of not being fair, of taking advantage of a veteran. He said, and I'll remember this to my dying day, he said, "Look, boy, you're not on the public tit any more. When you left here it was a 15 dollar-a-week job and the kid that's doing it now is getting $17.50 a week, so as far as I'm concerned, I'm doing you a favour."

The public tit! Four years out of my life, through a lot of crap and corruption, and he calls it the public tit. I told him to kiss my Royal American. That was all.

A week later Jennie and I packed our bags, said goodbye, got on the rattler for British Columbia and when the train stopped at Vancouver that's where we stopped, and in the first half day I got three job offers. I took one at 35 dollars a week and we've been doing hunky-dory ever since.

•◄►• *A Pink Milkshake*

When we got off the boat in Montreal they marched us over to the Lachine Depot and got us squared away. Then I went downtown and my first impression was the lights and signs on St. Catherine's

Street and the lingerie and the coloured clothes in the store windows. It's hard to describe, but to eyes that had seen no signs or colour in store windows for more than three years it was overwhelming.

I remember walking into a drugstore and going up to the fountain, and I ordered up a pink milkshake. It was the colour, strawberry pink, that really got to me. The ice cream and the cream and the flavour.

•◄►• *My Father, My Hero*

Nobody told us our father was coming home, and when the milk truck dropped him off at the outer gate even my mother didn't know him. It was the same man, but four or five years—well, it does make a difference.

I was twelve and filled with the war and here was my father, my hero, back, and it was just like he'd come back from turning the horses into another pasture.

It was morning, you see, and my mother made him breakfast and my sisters and I sat around and watched him eat, and then he said, incredibly, at this distance of years later, "Well, Butch, they haven't moved the schoolhouse yet, have they?" and I was puzzled and said no, and he said then it was time to get moving. After five years, and he just wanted us out of the house. I was stunned. It was hard to take, let me say that.

After all, five years and no medals, nothing on his jacket. What had he been doing? My mother found about ten in his pack later that day. But I was pretty down, let me tell you. My Dad home, and nothing to boast about. And wanting us out of the house, not even the day off, a big party.

My Mom was filling the big honey pail with lunch and Dad said he'd walk around the place with me. I'd been doing the heavy work. Twelve, eleven, but I did it. The cutting bar on the old mower was rusty and he gave me a reprimand for that, and there was a loose bar on the cattle gate, and I got knocked for that too. Then we went to school, and my head was down between my legs. My hero, and some hero.

That was my dad coming home. England, Iceland, France, Holland, and Germany and two wounds, both in the legs, and he could have been coming in from moving the horses from one pasture to the one down by the coulee. I guess some men are that way.

•◄►• *"Welcome Home, Son"*

We landed at Halifax coming home and got on a troop train, one of those Colonist cars they used 50 years ago, and when we started going through Nova Scotia and New Brunswick there were people standing at every station cheering us. We honestly didn't know why.

The reason was we were the troops coming home and in all these little towns and cities the railroad operator, I guess you would say the telegrapher, was told a troop train was coming through. For five years they'd all been going the other way, *to* the war. Now it was coming west, taking the boys back home. The telegraphers, I guess they'd tip off the people in the towns.

It had been ten days since we left England. We'd slept in our uniforms, our buttons were tarnished with sea air, our hair frowsy. In fact, we looked like so much scruff, but we were the boys coming home. This meant the war really was over.

In Montreal we got a huge welcome, and in all the little towns in northern Ontario, and a band played on the platform in Winnipeg and people stood by the tracks in little towns in Saskatchewan and waved and cheered, and in Edmonton there was a great big reception there for the home-town boys who got off the train. And then came Vancouver. There was my mother and a few of her friends and there were a few relatives of others on the train, but no signs of any welcome home. It was zilch. Nothing, after all those years, we got nothing.

Oh, I forgot. My mother and I and her friends, we walked through the C.N. station and there were no taxis so we took the streetcar on Main Street. When we got on the streetcar the conductor took one look at me, my bag and ribbons and he said, "Welcome home, son," and he wouldn't let me pay my fare. I believe it was seven cents in those days. I guess I was feeling a bit upset about no welcome, even though I was so damn glad to be home. But no matter, after meeting that conductor I felt better and it made me realize that the Canadian people out west really cared. I guess that guy saying, "Welcome home, son," I guess that was about the nicest welcome home anyone ever received.

Looking Back

Why? ... The Heroes ... Still Taking Casualties ...
Nothing to Say ... "No Complaints" ... The Impact on
the University ... At the Service Club ... A War Bride ...
Some War ... Where I'd Been ... A Huge Crime Wave ...
Just a Goddamned Civilian ... Everything Worked Out
Pretty Well ... Remembrance Day

For Canada, the war had many obvious lasting effects. We know,
for example, that Canada emerged as a strong industrial nation,
and its graph of production and accomplishment has continued to
rise ever since. This growth has given us one of the highest
standards of living in the world, plus the advantage of being one of
the "in" nations of the world, not an "inner circle" nation, but
one that has never known hardship in recent decades.

But what of the people—those 2,170,000 who served in
uniform and in war work; and the other 9,000,000, men, women,
young and old who in their own way kept the country going from
1939 to 1945? What do they think, those who are still with us, of
Canada's war and what it did to them? Am I supposed to speak for
them? I cannot. It would be like putting rice, a grain at a time, into
an empty barrel, and trying to figure out what impact each grain
has upon the growing fullness of the barrel. It just can't be done.

The answer lies within each one of us—we must look
within to find it.

•◄►• Why?

When he was younger my son asked me once: "Daddy, why did
you fly those bombers with bombs over Germany if you knew you
were going to be killed?"

I sat talking with him for a while and said things like
patriotism and our country and that Germany was the aggressor,
that Germany stood for wrong and we stood for the right, and
when I'd gone around the whole circle I suddenly realized that I
couldn't answer him. Maybe to his satisfaction because I don't
think the little shaver cared all that much, but I sure couldn't
answer the question to my satisfaction.

Why did we?

•◆• *The Heroes*

If a woman sees her husband at breakfast and he's got a gut and his head is getting bald and all he's eaten for breakfast for five years is an egg and instant coffee and she's thinking, "Well, after all these years, this is what I wound up with," then let her listen to this. Or the guy on Skid Road, he may be a bum, chances are he is a bum and nobody treats him as human. Or the taxi driver. Now driving a cab is not quite the same as running the Bank of Montreal and he may bootleg or have a couple of girls on the side, but take a look at that man too.

Suppose the guy at breakfast, in what we call now the middle-executive bracket, he may have been in the army. His age is right. So is the bum—he could have been in the air force. The cabbie, the navy, and so it goes.

Well, what I'm trying to say and not doing too well is that today you look at them and at guys like me, fifty years old, still a mortgage, a wife so used to me I'm not even there half the time, a couple of kids I'm not sure I like or I don't like . . . aw, hell, you know what I mean.

We were never heroes. I always felt heroes made themselves, they set out to be heroes. But we just went over and we did our jobs and we had good times and bad times, some very bad times, and then we came back and got married, went back to school, took a job and maybe, like me, a job I didn't like and still don't. Who likes being chief checker in a hardware warehouse? But we came back, back to the wives, the women, the kids for some, and goddamn it, man, this may sound right around the bend, but I think we were the heroes and not the guy with fourteen gongs on his chest. Because we took our shit and, like they say, we paid our debt to society, which we didn't owe anyway, and we came back—and some in less than one piece, let me add that—and we helped build up this society and put it where it is today.

So don't look at the guy with the scuffed briefcase on the bus or the bum on lower Yonge street or the cab driver who might try and butter you up for a good tip. If they were in the war, if they did their time, then for Christ sakes give them that much.

•◆• *Still Taking Casualties*

We're still taking casualties, as the battle description goes. Five, no six of our boys died just last month [1974], and all of them were pretty well directly attributable to the treatment they got in the

Japanese prison camps, the slave labour camps after the fall of Hong Kong. They're still dropping off something terrible, because of vitaminosis, which the federal government is in the process of declaring an incurable or permanent disease, caused by long lack of vitamins. No decent food.

You see, we were in the hands of the Japanese from the end of 1941 to late in August of 1945. That's a long time to live on a diet of straw. Well, it might as well have been straw for the essential vitamins it gave us. It gave us none, no vitamins at all. This is what caused the beriberi, the swelling, the wet beriberi. Eating straw. Just about that.

A lot of our boys have gone blind, loss of teeth, just dropping out. Loss of motor co-ordination. The brain, to the extent that some committed suicide, and this has been linked to it. The heart, of course. Dropping all the time from heart.

And it can be proven that the incidence of death in our age group is much higher than in any other age group. That's right. They did a brother comparison. They took all the fellows who had brothers in other theatres of war and examined both of them and they came up with the finding that our condition was ten times worse than the other brothers.

•◄►• *Nothing to Say*

No, there's nothing to talk about. We had a job to do and we did it. It just took a Christ of a lot longer than we thought.

Or just that everybody back in Canada seemed to enjoy the war an awful lot. That's the impression I got. Like it was one big party where everybody got to know each other. Everybody seemed to have had a real good time. I know my wife did. It wasn't but two months after I got back that I threw her out of the house, for good and for ever. If she wanted to keep on with her party, then she could, but not in my house.

•◄►• *"No Complaints"*

For seven years I have watched my husband in such pain. From his back. He had to quit his job as an engineer on the railroad three years ago because he was finished, and all because of the war. He is a proud man and it is a terrible thing to see him there every day in such pain.

He was hurt in England. He was with the tank corps for five years, three overseas, and when they were preparing the tanks for the big fight, you know, the invasion, yes, D-day, one of the tracks flung out and hit him in the back. Those tank tracks are very heavy.

At the time of his discharge he said, "No complaints," because he was strong and healthy and he wanted to get out in a hurry, not be held up by a lot of tests, and some of his buddies, some had lost an arm, a leg, eh, and he said, "Well, what have I got to complain about? I've still got all of my faculties, you know." And those two words, "No complaints," have caused him more trouble than any two words should ever cause anyone trouble.

But then, what he didn't know was that he was to suffer for the rest of his life with disc trouble in his back, and because he said, "No complaints," to the man checking his discharge papers he hasn't been able to get a pension. The back is a very tricky thing, you know. I have been trying for seven years to get a pension for that man and all I get is the run-around, and I'm sure there must be hundreds like him, men from Canada who risked their lives and got hurt and didn't know they had been hurt so they said, "No complaints." And all I get is the run-around. From the government.

And when I think of all these young people, these welfare bums, the people who have never worked, never paid taxes, never paid unemployment insurance, never done a single blessed thing and sitting around drawing two and three hundred a month in welfare and my husband, who risked everything, five years out of his life, and he sits there in pain every day, every day of his life, and we can't get a pension to make our lives a little easier, I wonder if there is a God or what it, the war, was all about.

•◄►• *The Impact on the University*

Everything was for the veterans. It was handed to you on a platter. If you didn't have grade eleven, then go into a pressurized course and take it and then you could go to a trade school, special courses, or university. College.

This country is swarming with guys who are doing well, doctors, lawyers, businessmen, executives, who would still be walking around looking for jobs or shifting cases around in some warehouse or ploughing land if it wasn't for our D.V.A. That's Department of Veterans' Affairs.

Let's see. They paid tuition, and not just some hick college near your home town. If you lived in Regina and you wanted to go to the University of Toronto and could make the qualifications, then that's where you'd go. I believe there was some sort of built-in travel allowance too, and there was also living allowance. I was single and I got 65 dollars a month to start and I think it went up later. Now, 65 dollars seems like chickenfeed, but remember this was '46, '47, and so on and things were cheap. Sixty-five bucks would go a long way. It would give you board and room in the university dorm or downtown, pay carfare, beer and you got by. I never went short, what with the money I got from work in the summer vacations.

I decided I'd go to the University of Manitoba. It was the closest. Arts. It didn't do me much good, I'll admit that, but it was fun. Plenty of girls and all nice and young and I learned to play bridge pretty well. A lot of good times.

I don't think I've ever read anything about the impact on the university. Like in my case, I got home about two weeks after registration and didn't have a shred of civvie clothes. I'd filled out so much I wasn't the kid I was when I left. So for the first few weeks most of us attended classes in battle dress, uniform. Dyed dark brown, nut brown although there were a few horses' asses who still wore war stripes, wound marks, medals and all the other crap.

But it was the way we hit the halls. Take in '44, say the U. of M. had 3,000 students. That's my estimate. Then take 1945. Suddenly it has got 6,000 students, maybe 7,000, and more than half of them are veterans. They must have been warned we were coming, but I can't say they were prepared. No more than we were prepared.

I think we scared the shit out of them. I mean everybody. Like the administration and the faculty and, of course, the students who, for the most part, seemed like kiddies to us. Yeah, kids. Like your little brother. You're twenty-two and starting out first year and he's nineteen and is in second year. How do you treat him? Or better still, how does he treat you?

So you've got these halls and lecture theatres and seminars and they are jammed, and I mean jammed, with veterans. Guys who flew Lancs, 70 or 80 missions over Dusseldorf. See what I mean? Guys who went ashore on D-day and came out with three wounds. Stuff like that. Fellows who had been commanders of frigates, motor patrol boats. Or just ordinary sergeants or privates, leading seamen, aircraftsmen, but they'd been in Burma and Iceland and Egypt and jumped in Yugoslavia to help Tito or wiped out a sub in the North Atlantic with one stick of bombs. On and on.

You're all jammed in together and you've got some guy, some wee wisp of a guy with big glasses telling you what T. S. Eliot meant when he wrote about three white horses running across a dark field, or what it means in philosophy when Hitler mixed Hegel and Marx and a couple of other of the old boys together and came up with his philosophy, and all over the room you could hear guys saying, "Bullshit," or, "Get some hours in," and things like that. There was no such thing as educational anarchy because we knew as well as the next person that the little twerp spouting off, straight out of the textbook; we knew he could pass us or fail us, but most of us were going through the motions. We knew, just as the kids know today, that what we needed was that diploma and not the learning that went with it. We knew the score.

What was fun, once we stopped considering it as kid stuff, was the girls. I'm not saying there was all that much screwing, because after all, this was still '45 and '46, but there was some and anyway, there was a lot of fun. Dances, football games—guys who had never had a chance to sing or to act or debate or work on a newspaper, they could do all these things. It was like a city inside a city. But I think the main thing was the girls. We took them away from the chaps their age, just whip, and out would come the rug. I just had one hell of a lot of fun.

About the second year and from then on, the vets started taking over the student government too. President, sports council, student council and all these other duties. The newspaper. Drama. Glee club. It was inevitable. Most of the fellows had been trained as leaders of one sort or another and the courses were such duck soup, so easy, that you could go through most of them just making the motions like you were dog-paddling in a river. I never worked, never put any effort into my classes.

• ◄►• *At the Service Club*

I came back and I'd say this was in December of 1945. All the guys were dribbling back. A few were killed but most made it.

A service club, the Jaycees or the Optimists or one of those, the bright young up-and-coming businessmen of the town, they decided to give the returning servicemen a luncheon. The gimmick was, of course, to get us into their club.

Mr. Blair, the manager of the store, he says I'd better go. It was business and politics to him. I guess I thought of it only as a bore and a free lunch and I wasn't hanging around anyway. I already had a job lined up in Toronto in the new year but to please Blair I went to this lunch. The usual crap, I guess you'd call it. Everybody with a name tag and saying, "Hi, Bill," and, "Glad to meet ya, Joe," although there were a few I could have said, "How come you weren't lugging a rifle like I was, you jerk." I didn't though.

I remember, tables for eight. Four veterans to a table, four club members and the talk was the usual nothing. Then somebody said something about the war and this was when the Nuremberg Trials or the Kurt Meyer trial was going. The German general who ordered a bunch of Canadians shot. Remember those days of long ago? Somebody says something about these German atrocities and I laughed. I remember Charlie Harrington laughing too. He's at this table I'm at.

One of the other fellows, one who didn't go in the service, he asks what's so funny and I made some remark that Canadians always think it was just the Germans who were the bad guys. I said we did some of that shooting too.

They said, one of the fellows said he just couldn't believe that, and I told about one time when a patrol brought in four Germans, a sergeant and three privates. They'd jumped them. They'd been on patrol too. I said the lieutenant was questioning them and they were just standing there grinning and saying "nein" and acting dumb and acting smart-ass and finally the lieutenant turned to our sergeant and said, "Shoot these jerks." Just like that. The sergeant and a guy with a Sten pushed the four Jerries over towards a house door in this village we were in, and they went in and bang, bang, bang, bang. Weapons fired inside make a helluva noise, believe me. I think the most surprised guys of all were the Germans. I know I wasn't. It had happened before, but usually when we just didn't have anybody to spare, to escort them back to one of the cages. A few of the replacements were shocked, I think. But not too much. They were getting to get the hang of the whole business.

But at that table in the bloody hotel! Wow! You'd have thought we'd raped the Virgin Mary. One guy looked sick and another said he'd blackball me until he was blue in the face before he ever okayed me for membership. I remember me saying, "Why don't you smarten up, Buster?" and I got up and walked out. Charlie, Charlie Harrington came with me, and we went and had a beer.

I remember him wondering whether this Mr. Goody-goody was just playing games with us, not believing, and I said no, he just didn't have a clue.

•◄►• *A War Bride*

I was seventeen when the war started and twenty-one when I married my husband and I think we were only together not more than a total of 10 or 12 days because he was in France and Germany and then he was sent back to Canada as his regiment was going on to Japan to fight, so there I was at twenty-three years of age on a troopship sailing to Canada to meet a husband I didn't really know.

I was just a lassie from Inverness and to be honest, I didn't know much about anything and if you'd asked me where Alberta was I couldn't have put my finger on the Canadian map. Oh, I knew where the Rockies were and Banff. Everyone knows that, but a place called Lethbridge? It might have been the moon.

My husband had told me things would be hard. Dave didn't try and pull the wool over my eyes that way. He said we'd have to live with his father for a while and it was a farm many miles from Lethbridge and the nearest town was just what you'd call a hamlet—a store, a garage, a community hall and a few houses and some Indians. I guess he didn't think to tell me that the stove was for wood and the little house was out at the back and there were no neighbours for two or three miles and his dad was a cranky old rascal. I know one thing he didn't tell me. The weather. He didn't tell me it got down to 30 and 40 below, and I got a taste of it because it was 25 below the day I arrived on the train.

I honestly think I didn't know how tough I really was. I mean I was tougher than I thought I was, because I would not give in to the loneliness and the frustrations and I would never admit to being homesick. I settled myself into being a Canadian rancher's wife and took everything that was dished out to me and I know I'm a better person for it.

•◄►• *Some War*

Towards the end of the war I began to get worried. Manly and Betty thought their daddy was going to come marching home in a shiny uniform, medals on his chest, and he'd start in building a farm the like you never seen, taking us away from the boxcar we lived in. There was no reality in it at all, but I was scared because those kids were believing it now and talking about it all the time and telling the kids at school and all that. Once I tried to tell them that their dad, who they hardly remembered by this time as a person, like you could touch, I told them all the jobs he'd ever had after I married him. He was driving a weed killer along the roads for the municipality and working for farmers around the district, but it was no use.

I thought I'd meet Jake at the station if I could and tell him to stay away, go away and don't come back, but I was too late even for that, even if I'd of known when he was coming, because he came in one night at supper. He'd been drinking in the beer parlour all afternoon, that's how he talked the waiter into giving him a lift.

He was drunk when he came home and he stayed drunk for days, and he slobbered and yelled and swore and threw things and he hadn't been any big hero like the kids thought he had been. He hadn't been in the fighting even but cutting down trees for telephone poles in Scotland. That was his war.

After about two weeks of this baloney I just kicked him out one day. Just kicked him out. It didn't matter to the kids, because by this time their hearts were like stone to him, and they wouldn't have taken a big farm from him if he'd offered it to them on a silver platter. That was some war.

•➔• *Where I'd Been*

I came back, five years later, to Regina and I stayed in the Y.M.C.A. because it was the best I could get. And in the Y I had a roommate I never saw. All I knew about that roommate was that he wore terribly loud ties and he was a fruit nut and he also made model airplanes. They were scattered all over the place. I worked nights and he worked days and we never saw each other. My wife was in the hospital sick, and I went back to my old job.

You go through a war, five years, and in the last year, hell bent for leather, blasted towns, the conquerors, the fall of Berlin, meeting the Russians, being a hero of sorts—and then you come back to the Y.M.C.A. in Regina. It's hard, you know. Wife in hospital. Working in a job you didn't particularly like, at a wage hardly enough to keep body and soul together.

I didn't know many people in Regina and one day on the street I met this old man from the town I came from and he shook my hand—and remember I had gone away as a boy of nineteen and now I was a man of twenty-four—and this old codger shook my hand and asked me where I'd been. Where I'd been? For Christ sakes.

And for ten years after . . . no, let's make that five years after, to be more accurate, I was praying that someone would start another bloody war.

•◆• A Huge Crime Wave

I can't remember a huge crime wave after the war, although I could be wrong. A lot of people were predicting there would be one, men coming back with souvenir German weapons, Lugers, and taking the town apart, robbing banks, shooting people.

It just didn't happen. I saw men overseas do things I don't think I'm even going to tell you about, dreadful things, acts of cruelty, and if you were where the heavy stuff was flying all around you, for a week, two weeks at a time, you developed a disregard for human life. It was just natural.

And yet these men came home and took off their uniforms, hung them up in the closet, bought a new outfit or tried to get into the clothes they had when they volunteered, and went right out into life, getting up in the morning, going to work, coming home at night, some going to university, getting married, having fun, just as if there never had been a war on.

One of the toughest cookies I ever knew, absolutely the toughest and hardest nut of them all, a few months after the war I see him and his wife and their kid skating at the arena downtown on Sunday afternoon and he looked no different from fifty other guys skating around and I said to myself: "If Thompson can go through all he's been through and come back and just be a civilian again, then there isn't going to be any Gunfight at the OK Corral." Then I knew everything was going to be all right. Up until that time I was a bit worried.

•◆• Just a Goddamned Civilian

It's terrible to see what happens to men after a war. I only went to one reunion. About 1948. In Winnipeg. I was sort of deked into it but anyway I went. We had a real rapscallion of a fellow named Watson who was in our outfit, and he'd be a lance corporal one day and a corporal the next and a sergeant the next and then he'd be back down to private and this went on and on. But he was a magnificent soldier. Magnificent. He was always doing something hairy, you see.

So there's this reunion and I sit with Watson and a few others and this Watson was an admirable man in action but at this reunion, at about midnight, he looked at his watch and said he had to go home. His wife had said be home by such and such a time. Here was a man who had been reduced to a Milquetoast by two years of peace. Marriage, you see. And off he went. And I thought, "How sad this is."

Here was one of these men who would go up ahead into a field and dig a hole and fight off everything that came his way. He thrived on war, he enjoyed it. But when the clock strikes midnight and the little woman is waiting up, he packs his bags and leaves his comrades and away he goes home. Sad. No more juices. Just a goddamned civilian again.

•◄►• *Everything Worked Out Pretty Well*

Oh, the war brides. Oh yes, I remember them. They'd be landed off the boats in Montreal and the Red Cross Corps would take them to Toronto and then pass them on to Winnipeg, those who were left, and then to Calgary or Edmonton where we'd meet them and bring them to Vancouver.

Some were terrified. They were a jolly bunch and laughing, and they'd been through a lot, a lot of adversity, rationing, bombing, years of war, but as they got closer to Vancouver some would come up to me and say, "Do you think I'll know him?" and I'd say sure, you'll know him and she'd say, "But I only knew him for a week or six weeks, and then he came home wounded and that's the last I've seen of him. Do you think he'll be in uniform so I'll know him?" I'd have to say no, he probably wouldn't be in uniform, but he'd know her. That used to cheer them up. And, you know, when we arrived there always was somebody to meet them and they'd all find their husbands.

But the night before. Oh, the excitement! Some of them had babies, little children, and there was always one nurse with them, an R.N., and two of us Red Cross Corps for every three cars of girls and they'd be asking us hundreds of questions, and the night before we got to Vancouver the porters would bring in big tubs of hot water and everybody would bathe. They'd do each other's hair. They'd laugh and joke and sing, but you could see they were terrified, a lot of them. Some were very nervous. There wasn't too much sleeping done that night, I can tell you.

And some were led on, very badly, you know. Soldiers telling the girls their parents were wealthy and when they'd tell me where they were going, showing me the addresses, my heart used to sink. Down on East Hastings, down in there, on the Skid Road, and I used to think how terrible the shock was going to be.

Some would be disillusioned before they even got off the train. The country terrified them. It was so big, the ride was so long. I'd tell them that once they left the prairies it was like going into another country, a beautiful country, and the mountains and the great rivers, the Thompson and the Fraser, those rivers absolutely fascinated them.

Some, of course, got quickly disillusioned once they got with their husbands too. There would be no big ranch but just a shack in the hills somewhere. Things like that. These lads often led the girls on terribly. But they came through it, most of them. Some of them went home, of course. But I never saw one girl, I don't think, who on the train wasn't prepared to be a good wife and to give her husband a good life. It's just that for some it didn't work out. But by and large I think everything worked out pretty well.

•◀▶• *Remembrance Day*

I've never paid much, if any, attention to Armistice Day, Remembrance Day as they call it now. Maybe if I'm switching the TV I might watch, but there's the lieutenant governor putting down a wreath or the mayor doing something and an honour guard and a few people. It means nothing to me. For one thing it's in a city far away and, besides, the war is far away. It's all gone, like you know, it's all in the past.

And then I saw this Armistice Day service in this small town. It was south of Calgary, just a little place, one street, a big school, three or four elevators and some cattle pens and that just about did it. Maybe 1,000 people altogether, wouldn't you say? Just an Alberta cow town.

We'd stopped there overnight because the wife had an aunt there and nothing would do but we stop in and see Aunt Maggie. And next morning just as we're loading the car I hear band music and damn it all, I walk over a block to the main drag. This is about 10:45 and we want to make Kamloops that night, but I walk over anyway.

It was one of these lousy November days. You know the type. There's this parade from the church to the Cenotaph and I looked at that Cenotaph later and the only inscription on it was "Our Children," just like in France you see the same ones, in the same place in the town, village and they'll read, "Nos enfants." Our children.

There was a strong wind and dirt at the edge of the pavement was swirling up and you could smell snow in the air. You know how a westerner can smell snow and everybody wonders how, and pretty soon, along comes the first snow of winter. That kind of a day. Grey and snow coming.

The colours came first and then the school band, blowing away at something. Probably off key. Aren't them kind of bands supposed to be off key? Then the minister, padre, chaplain, whatever he was, and two of the town Mounties and then the vets. And what a lot. After all those years they could still keep step, even to that music. The first world war guys, why, I'll bet some of them had trouble getting from their easy chair in the parlour to the can, but there they were, keeping up, heads back, arms swinging, medals in one and two rows on their chest, and in among them, the younger ones. I mean the older ones were in the seventies and eighties from the first world war, and the young ones, well, say from the very youngest of forty-five up to sixty, seventy. Swinging along.

Nobody on the street. All snug in their beds or watching TV nursing hang-overs or gone to town visiting. Just a few people looking out the windows at these old bastards swinging along, but there were about 15 or 20 at the Cenotaph, standing around looking cold, and a kid with a big camera and I figured he was from the local paper.

There was the short service and I looked at those guys standing at attention, and during the Last Post, the laying of the wreaths and the Two Minutes' Silence I thought of the guys from the west I'd known in my outfit. It was a coast regiment, but there were a lot of Alberta guys from this part of the country in it. They were different, you know. It was as if they came from a different country. Oh, I know they did. Ranching country. There were the foothills there and over to the west you could see the Rockies even on a lousy day, and I guess that did something to the people. These guys in the parade were mostly, I'd judge, ranching people, owners, sons, hired hands, townspeople who served them. Maybe a couple of railroad men in there, and, of course, the old retired guys were too. Retired ranchers, cowboys.

In the army they seemed to be themselves. What they wanted to be, they were. Like with officers. They treated an officer as if he was just an ordinary person and often, if they liked them, an ordinary soldier as if he was an important person. But you never quite got to know them. Somebody in a novel once said they got those eyes they have from looking at faraway spaces all the time. They were smart and strong and intelligent and they made the best officers I ever saw. They had this moral code too. A lady, even if she was an old whore, well, somehow they made her feel a little more like a lady.

They could be the best friends a man ever had and they were damned good fighters. They were doggone good soldiers, and if any joined the navy or air force, then they would have been good at that too. I liked them. They weren't romantic people though. Not like in books. They were ordinary guys in some ways and very unordinary guys in other ways. You could go a long way with them.

This is what I was thinking when I stood at the Cenotaph watching, and then I slipped over and stood in the ranks with them, just for those last few minutes and one old geezer winked at me and said, "Welcome, mate," and I felt right at home. Doggone, but I liked these kind of men.

When the "Parade, dismiss!" came, we all started over to the Legion and the old chap came up and linked his arm into mine, and he didn't know me from Adam's off ox and he didn't make any big thing of it but he said, "Come on, join us in a brew," and I said I would. Now, I wasn't planning to go, we had a long way to drive that day but somehow I just joined up with them.

Inside, just a small place, with a bar, a piano for dancing, the honour roll and about 20 tables, and the old man led me over and we sat down with about six or so other guys. A couple were old, but most my age and I introduced myself. Bruce James, Vancouver, just passing through, joined your service, hope you don't mind, glad to meet you, glad to meet you, nice meeting you, sir. That kind of thing.

They didn't talk about Vimy Ridge or Normandy. None of that. A couple of words about some of the old-timers who'd passed on, but mostly about cattle, the weather, the government, taxes and I enjoyed myself and thought what a wonderful bunch they were, and by the time I looked at my watch it was one o'clock and my wife would be steaming, just black-eyed because she wanted to get to Kamloops that night, and so I said goodbye all around, and they're all my friends now, Jack and Harry and so on. I didn't want to go.

As I was leaving, one of these busybody women, you know the kind, always head of the women's auxiliary, she gets up on the stage with the piano and says there's going to be a little sing-song and thump, thump, bang, crash and she's pounding out "Roll Out the Barrel," and I stand at the door and sing a couple of choruses with them before I go out and I thought, damn it all, you can say all you want about the old vets and Legions and that sort of thing, but it gets to you, it reaches you and takes you back 30 years and to the good days, standing around a piano in an English pub and yelling "Roll Out the Barrel." It gave me a great feeling.